ANTHROPOLOGY THROUGH LITERATURE

EDITED BY

JAMES P. SPRADLEY, MACALESTER COLLEGE

GEORGE E. McDONOUGH, HAMLINE UNIVERSITY

ANTHROPOLOGY
THROUGH
LITERATURE

CROSS-CULTURAL PERSPECTIVES

LITTLE, BROWN AND COMPANY BOSTON

LIBRARY OF CONGRESS CATALOG CARD NO. 72-13633

FIRST PRINTING

Published simultaneously in Canada
by Little, Brown & Company (Canada) Limited

PRINTED IN THE UNITED STATES OF AMERICA

Cover: THE STATUE OF OUR LADY OF THE KWAKIUTL, CARVED
BY DON "LELOOSKA" SMITH, STANDS IN THE CHAPEL OF ST.
AUGUSTINE'S CENTER FOR AMERICAN INDIANS, CHICAGO.
PHOTOGRAPH IS THE WORK OF ORLANDO CABANAN AND IS USED
WITH THE PERMISSION OF REV. PETER J. POWELL, D.D., SPIRI-
TUAL DIRECTOR OF THE CENTER.

To Barbara Spradley and Roxy Elizabeth McDonough

ACKNOWLEDGMENTS

We wish to express our appreciation to Patricia K. Gill for her assistance. She participated in the preparation of the manuscript from its conception to its completion. She tracked down numerous literary sources, evaluated many selections, and provided valuable editorial help. Throughout the project she was a constant source of inspiration. Without her work this book would not have been possible.

CONTENTS

PART FOUR

POLITICS, GOVERNMENT, AND LAW

PART FIVE

RELIGION AND WORLD VIEW

As we come into touch with other beings, we discover ourselves. . . . As I experience the presence of a tree or a field or a stream or another person or a tremor that runs through me with a force of its own, I know myself through that experience. If I turn my glance always inward, I will look into the dark. The dark is real and rich, and it is surely there. But I will know nothing about it by looking into it, for I will see nothing. I will see into the dark only if I look at you. Then the dark will stir, will be stirred by our friction; a light will float like a feather in that dark and my whole being will shake in the creation that happens.

M. C. Richards
Centering in Pottery, Poetry, and the Person

INTRODUCTION

Anthropology through Literature: Cross-Cultural Perspectives is an invitation to self-discovery. It is an opportunity to encounter other human beings across the boundaries of culture. In the selections you will have the possibility of touching persons who are living out their lives in ways that are very different from your own. We believe that these selections offer two fundamental kinds of insight: understanding other cultures and discovering ourselves.

In many ways this book is the result of our own experience in crossing the boundaries of our respective academic cultures. It was more than twelve years ago that our friendship began, when our offices were across the hall from one another in a small college in the Pacific Northwest. Over cups of coffee in the student union, on hikes in the Olympic Rain Forest, in front of the fireplaces of our own homes, on lakes in northern Wisconsin we learned from each other. Intermittently for more than a decade we talked about our backgrounds, the settings in which we were born and reared, our parents, our children, our education, the coming of war, our religious and philosophical pilgrimages, our own search for meaningful life-work—these and all the other thoughts that preoccupy men like ourselves. And we seasoned our observations with illustrations, examples, and parables from the large reservoir of characters who peopled our own histories as well as those we knew from literature and anthropology.

Within the compass of each other's consciousness, we found a growing richness for ourselves. One of us was the spokesman for the methodology of science, the other stressed the point that truth has to be felt in a personal epiphany if people are to be lifted into new areas of insight, decision, and behavior. One talked of cross-cousin marriage, potlatches, and the Kwakiutl Indians; the other pointed to the literary incision of Lawrence Durrell in rendering an Englishman's buying a house on Cyprus really comprehensible, or the contemporary relevance of Aristotle's *Poetics*. One humanized the tramp who panhandled on Seattle streets; the other tested the capacity of rhetoric to convey ideas and experience. Over this long period our encounters were open-ended, with a delightful mutuality of teaching and learning. Across our disciplinary boundaries we recognized our common interests: the enduring features of human nature; the origin and destiny of man; the means by which people subsist in various parts of the world; the varieties of politics, government, and law; the intricacies of human language and communication; the manner in which people everywhere change and how they resist change; the way in which each culture shapes human feelings, emotions, and values. All the arts and sciences were windows to let in the light. All offered us unique angles of vision.

Over a year ago we began to think more concretely about how literature could serve as a vehicle for the insights of anthropology. Our discussion moved to the works of contemporary authors that provided us not only with anthropological insight, but also with a sensitivity that was often missing in conventional anthropological writing. These works were a pleasure to read. They possessed style, that mysterious merging of substance and form which makes us want to endorse them, recommend them to others, and return to them ourselves. We knew of some anthropologists and discovered others who had written short stories, novels, and research reports in a style that blended the best of our two disciplines, such as Oscar Lewis's *Five Families*, Chad Oliver's *The Edge of Forever*, Victor Barnouw's *Dream of the Blue Heron*, and Colin Turnbull's *The Lonely African*. We began to search systematically for other selections. We engaged in what the poet John Ciardi called the "self-delighting" pains of culling what we considered the best selections from an immense body of international writing as well as soliciting the recommendations of more than sixty anthropologists across the United States. This distillation process yielded the present collection.

We became increasingly aware of the many connections between anthropology and literature and the variety of purposes that could be served by their marriage. Our aim in this book is quite specific: to *help readers understand the concepts and data of anthropology through the medium of literature*. This aim might be accomplished in several ways.

Anthropology is a broad study of mankind. The goal of anthropologists is to describe and explain social behavior. In the pursuit of this goal they go to the far corners of the earth to observe the many ways people have devised of being human. This task is called "ethnographic fieldwork," and it means that the investigator is inevitably caught up in the flow of events and activities that occur in the alien society. In the midst of life he learns existentially from the perspective of cultural traditions other than his own, and in doing so he always learns about himself. Months, perhaps years later, his fieldwork experience will be analyzed, digested, summarized, and finally written down in scholarly form to be published in a professional journal or as an ethnographic monograph. This communication is in a highly specialized language and is intended to be a scholarly description of some aspect of a culture or an analysis of cross-cultural regularities and variations.

A strange thing happens to cultural events and behavior on the way to an ethnographic monograph. The wholeness and vividness of life, the immediate experience the anthropologist knew in the field—the people, their environment, their needs, and their everyday problems—all these are often lost, and in their place we find abstract categories and the relationships among them. But this is strange only to outsiders, because the goal of anthropology is to describe and explain cultural behavior—and that requires abstraction. As Kenneth Read emphasized:

> Why, then, is so much anthropological writing so anti-septic, so devoid of anything that brings a people to life? There they are, pinned like butterflies in a glass case, with the difference, however, that we often cannot tell what color these specimens are; and we are never shown them in flight, never see them soar or die except in generalities. The reason for this lies in the aims of anthropology, whose concern with the particular is incidental to an understanding of the general.[1]

Scientific generalizations are tested by repeated observations of specific instances. But attention is most often given at the level of generalities, not particulars. Between these levels is the process of abstraction, which is always part of cultural description.

The concept of culture is itself an abstraction, which means that no anthropologist ever saw or experienced a cul-

---

[1] Kenneth E. Read, *The High Valley* (New York: Scribner's, 1965), p. ix.

ture pattern. It is an abstraction the scholar creates to make sense out of the behavior he observes. Consider, for example, the Tlingit who live on the Northwest coast of America. Anthropologists have reported the existence of the *avunculate relationship* among these Indians. But such an abstract category is based upon hundreds of specific observations: boys living with their fathers and mothers until age six or seven when they move into their uncles' houses; frequent visits to nephews from their uncles during the first six or seven years of life; discussion between a sister and her brother about her son's development; boys inheriting wealth and position from their mother's brother; nephews contributing to their uncles' potlatches. The concept of avunculate relationship is a shorthand way of summarizing how mothers' brothers and sisters' sons relate to each other. Although such abstract categories enable the anthropologist to make cross-cultural comparisons, they often hide the vividness of everyday life.

Abstract culture patterns also obscure the way in which different aspects of life are woven together, interlaced into a wholeness. For example, each anthropological concept— wealth, kinship, inheritance, and socialization—could be a separate chapter in an ethnographic monograph on the Kwakiutl Indians of British Columbia. In the continuing events of life it is difficult to separate the experiences that anthropologists fit into these categories. The following recollection of James Sewid, a contemporary Kwakiutl Indian, underscores this fact:

> There was a big potlatch going on given by Spruce Martin, my uncle. He was Mungo Martin's older brother. It was the way of the Indians that if someone wanted to use a certain kind of dance they couldn't just go and use it because it belongs to someone. My grandfather owned a special dance that Spruce Martin wanted to use in this big do that he was putting on. He went in to see my grandmother to see if he could use me and told them, "He is the right boy, I want to use him because he is my nephew." Of course my grandmother said to him, "Sure you can use him." I was only five years old then but I can remember that morning before the dance. It was early in the morning before daylight and I was to go and practice that dance with Toby Willey's mother. She was up in the woods chanting the songs that were to be used that night. It was near the same place where I was born behind that barn, and I was so cold that she just tucked me into her arms under the blanket that she had around her, singing away early in that morning and all the dancers were gathered that morning getting ready to go into the big community house that

night. I remember that they had a big dance that night and when I walked into that big house and danced as a little boy everybody was saying something to me.[2]

Anthropologists may say that Kwakiutl children are socialized into the value of nonmaterial wealth, inheritance patterns, and kinship rights, but for those who have not learned to appreciate the specialized language of anthropology, reports of immediate experiences like James Sewid's are far more meaningful. The selections in this book have been chosen to help the reader experience other cultural situations. They are meant to provide vicariously the kinds of events and experiences the anthropologist has in another society.

But *Anthropology through Literature* is not only a device for making anthropology more interesting. More important, the selections in this book will enable the student to discover culture patterns and to abstract and generalize in the way anthropologists in the field must. Although the ethnographer has learned a set of categories for understanding behavior, his cultural description is built from the concrete events of everyday life. The selections that follow—some from the autobiographies of natives, some from anthropologists, and some from literary writers—have one thing in common: they portray the details and events of daily life. They do not interrupt the stream of behavior to build a dam of analytic concepts. The reader is left with the same task faced by every ethnographer: to analyze the implicit categories and cultural rules that people in the stories are using to organize their behavior.

These selections have another important characteristic. Unlike most ethnographic monographs that use the perspective of an outside observer, these stories take you to the inner world of the actors. In this sense, they are far more like the field notes of the anthropologist than his final publications. One of the cornerstones of cultural anthropology is that understanding of another culture must occur *from the inside out*. No detached observer will discover the inner meaning of life in another society. This means participation as well as observation. It means learning a language and paying attention to the subtle nonverbal cues to which people are responding. It means a kind of incarnation in another cultural world. It also means standing back from events and pondering them as an outsider, with all the accompanying pain of culture shock. We think that this is indispensable to the anthropological perspective and is often missing in the abstractions of anthropological writing.

[2] James P. Spradley, ed., *Guests Never Leave Hungry: The Autobiography of James Sewid, a Kwakiutl Indian* (New Haven: Yale University Press, 1969), pp. 43–44.

From our mutual perspectives each selection had to meet at least the following criteria:

1. It had to have anthropological relevance and yield anthropological insight. But it also had to make us aware that we were doing more than just studying *them*—we were studying ourselves as well.

2. It had to give us a sense of presence by making persons, places, and things come alive to us. We wanted to be *there*, wherever there was; we wanted to be with *them*, whoever they were.

3. It had to be written in the language of experience rather than that of classification and abstraction. The author had to make us believe that he "knew" his subject; that is, that he let whatever he was depicting come through his own individuality without conscious or unconscious deceit. The literary result had to have a "rightness" about it.

4. It had to let the author "in." As Yeats wrote:

> O body swayed to music, o quickening glance,
> How shall I tell the dancer from the dance?[3]

No human artifact comes into being without an artificer. There is no performance without a performer, no writing without a writer, no science without a scientist. The anthropologist is as much a part of anthropology as are his data. None of our selections were created or chosen by a disembodied eye. We do not believe in the cult of objectivity. In everything we ever read, we encounter the author, no matter how unaware we are of the fact.

5. It had to have unity, to leave us with a sense of completeness. Completeness, as we are using the word in this context, does not necessarily signify resolution or insensitivity to overtones, paradox, and conflict. Quite the contrary, it means that the ambiguities of life have been vividly mediated to us by an author, as in Chaim Potok's *The Promise*, and we recognize and accept them.

6. It had to have a tone that was free from ethnocentrism; the author had to have an attitude toward human social behavior that evoked something akin to this response in us: "What a revelation to find other human beings, like us, and yet not at all like us, living out their days in this way. That is important for us to realize in our growing perception of a complex world."

7. It had to have clarity.

8. It had to seem worth reading and rereading. Both of us had to enjoy it.

[3] *Collected Poems of W. B. Yeats* (New York: Macmillan, 1946), p. 251.

Our criteria for selection guided the choices of what to include; they did not help to establish a framework in which to organize the selections. Almost none of the chapters used here fits neatly into the analytic categories of anthropology, for social life is never divided into a time for kinship, a time to speak language, a time for government or religion. There would have been some merit in presenting thirty-nine chapters, randomly arranged, under the subtitle of this book. It would have been possible to organize selections geographically into regions, such as Africa, North America, the Arctic, India, China, and Europe. Neither alternative seemed appropriate. Instead, we have arranged the selections under seven major headings that reflect the fundamental interests of anthropology and the general functions of culture.

Part I, "Human Nature and Culture," includes selections that call attention to what it is that makes us human and the significance of cultural meaning systems.

Parts II through VI are based on the fact that the fundamental requirements of human existence are the same everywhere. As a species, mankind shows greater variation in behavior than any other animal. The range of exotic cultures and strange customs that confront the student who is introduced to anthropology can overshadow a much more important fact: each human culture, no matter how different from the others, has the same job to do. If a culture fails to satisfy a limited number of basic requirements for human existence, a society and its members become extinct.

In some ways human existence is a precarious adventure. Our body temperatures must be maintained within a very limited range or death occurs. Food and moisture in the proper amounts must be constantly supplied. Emotional stability within definite limits is required or individuals will destroy themselves or others. Without meaningful answers to the ultimate questions he asks, man will become apathetic, and anomie and social disorganization often result. These are only a few basic requirements.

Anthropology is the study of cultural differences, but it is also a search for the *function* of different aspects of each culture. Parts II through VI are organized on the basis of the most important general functions that every culture fulfills to maintain human existence.

Part II, "Subsistence and Economic Exchange," illustrates how the material requirements for survival are met. Part III, "Social Organization—Kinship and Groups," demonstrates the fact that man is a social animal and that his survival depends on a social existence. In every society kinship is the fundamental way in which social relationships are organized although it is not always the most important. These chapters do not merely describe human social organizations; they take the reader inside the dynamics of families, villages, and even into a department of anthropology.

Part IV, "Politics, Government, and Law," is composed of stories and autobiographical selections related to the requirement every society has of controlling the range of individual behavior. What men *can* do as individuals and what they *must* do if they are to live in a society are often at odds. Every society develops institutions of social control to maintain a modicum of internal order.

The selections in Part V, "Religion and World View," show how different cultures deal with the subject of death, contact with the supernatural, the meaning of life, and other such ultimate matters. Part VI, "Language and Communication," includes chapters that highlight the most distinctive feature of human life and one of our most important requirements for survival—the ability to communicate. The absence of speech, or even the confusion of tongues, as portrayed in the ancient story of the Tower of Babel, can be a sufficient cause for the disintegration of society.

Interaction across cultural boundaries is illustrated in Part VII, "Culture Contact and Change." Of course, the major theme that unequivocally runs through nearly every chapter in this book is the importance of culture contact and the ways in which people deal with culture change. But because it is such an important phenomenon we have included a separate section dealing with the processes.

Each selection could have been placed under any of the topics we have used. The events of human existence are many-faceted and our abstract pigeonholes can distort as well as enlighten. For this reason, we urge the reader to observe the full range of culture patterns that are exemplified in each selection. Although social organization, subsistence, or language may predominate, each always has minor themes and overtones reflecting other areas of social life.

Our hope is that we have been judicious and discriminating and that professor and student alike will find it worthwhile to discover what lies between these covers.

ANTHROPOLOGY THROUGH LITERATURE

PART ONE

HUMAN NATURE AND CULTURE

Cultural anthropology is itself an expression of human nature; it involves men and women searching for man's past, examining his present, and wondering about his future. Though this kind of intellectual activity goes on in every human society, no other animal has systematically studied its own nature or the universe in which it lives. Others feed themselves, defend themselves, prepare for the winter, construct nests, and even groom themselves; only man seeks to understand himself.

Man is unquestionably an animal. We share many features of biological structure with other species. We acquire and utilize energy by the process of metabolism. Our cells and organs are regulated and controlled by nervous and hormonal systems. Like other animals we reproduce our kind and each new member of the human family participates in the cycle from conception to death. People inherit physical behavioral characteristics from their parents through genetic processes like other animals. And like other animals, man adapts to his environment and slowly changes in the process of evolution. But for all the similarities, certain features make us unique creatures in the animal kingdom.

Man is an unspecialized animal. We are not fashioned for swift running across open plains like the horse. We cannot live in the water of the earth's oceans like the largest of all mammals, the whale. We have no biological capacity to adapt to cold winters by hibernation; we cannot adapt to forest or glen because nature has given us colors that blend with the environment. In place of the biological specialization that matches animal and ecological niches, evolution has conferred upon us a specially constructed brain with a greatly enlarged cortical region. This is the basis for our unique kind of specialization, *cultural adaptation*. Where biology enables some animals to adapt to extreme cold, man uses his culture to build fires, sew warm clothing, and construct shelters from ice and snow. Where biology enables some mammals to survive in the sea, man builds boats and learns to navigate by observing the stars or by listening to the direction of waves slapping against his canoe.

Man is an animal with culture, an animal most of whose patterns of behavior are learned from others. Culture is a social inheritance. We have a greater capacity to learn than any other animal and a longer period of dependency to go along with it. From infancy until maturity, and for many years thereafter, each human being acquires a culture for organizing his behavior. Although other animals are born with ready-made ways of interpreting the world and responding to it, man alone must learn about socially constructed reality and how to behave in it.

The possession of culture means that values and meaning have taken their place at the center of human existence. Our animal drives are satisfied, channeled, and controlled by what men consider desirable, and these cultural value systems are often at odds with these animal desires. Although what is good differs from one society to another, the sense that some things are good and others bad, some valuable and others undesirable, is a universal feature of human social life. Human society is more than a social order; at the core it is a moral order. And every culture provides its members with the meaning of life; and life itself thrusts upon us the quest to expand that sense of meaning and purpose.

Human nature and culture are difficult to study because we have no contrasting examples of human beings without a human nature and culture. If we could locate a world of large-brained, bipedal, upright creatures who live in social groups *without culture*, we could learn more about the fundamental characteristics of this unique human possession. Because we lack that, comparisons with other primates and with individuals and groups living under conditions of extreme deprivation give us important insights about mankind. The selections that follow are intended to raise the large questions about human nature and culture in this way. They do not provide answers; they are intended to open up our sense of wonder about this creature which is man.

TRANSFUSION

The machine stopped.

There was no sound at all now, and the green light on the control panel blinked like a mocking eye. With the easy precision born of long routine, Ben Hazard did what had to be done. He did it automatically, without real interest, for there was no longer any hope.

He punched a figure into the recorder: 377.

He computed the year, using the Gottwald-Hazard Correlation, and added that to the record: 254,000 B.C.

He completed the form with the name of the site: Choukoutien.

Then, with a lack of anticipation that eloquently reminded him that this was the three hundred seventy-seventh check instead of the first, Ben Hazard took a long preliminary look through the viewer. He saw nothing that interested him.

Careful as always before leaving the Bucket, he punched in the usual datum: Viewer Scan Negative.

He unlocked the hatch at the top of the Bucket and climbed out of the metallic gray sphere. It was not raining, for a change, and the sun was warm and golden in a clean blue sky.

Ben Hazard stretched his tired muscles and rested his eyes on the fresh green of the tangled plants that grew along the banks of the lazy stream to his right. The grass in the little meadow looked cool and inviting, and there were birds singing in the trees. He was impressed as always by how little this corner of the world had changed in fifty years. It was very much as it had been a thousand years ago, or two thousand, or three. . . .

It was just a small corner of nowhere, lost in the mists of time, waiting for the gray sheets of ice to come again.

It was just a little stream, bubbling along and minding its own business, and a lonely limestone hill scarred with the dark staring eyes of rock shelters and cave entrances.

There was nothing different about it.

It took Man to change things in a hurry, and Man wasn't home.

That was the problem.

Ben took the six wide-angle photographs of the terrain that he always took. There were no animals within camera range this trip. He clambered through the thick brown brush at the base of the limestone hill and climbed up the rough rocks to the cave entrance. It was still open, and he knew its location by heart.

He well remembered the thrill he had felt the first time he had entered this cave. His heart had hammered in his chest and his throat had been so dry that he couldn't swallow. His mind had been ablaze with memories and hopes and fears, and it had been the most exciting moment of his life.

Now, only the fear remained—and it was a new kind of fear, the fear of what he *wouldn't* find.

His light blazed ahead of him as he picked his way along the winding passage of the cave. He disturbed a cloud of indignant bats, but there was no other sign of life. He reached the central cavern, dark and hushed and hidden under the earth, and flashed his light around carefully.

There was nothing new.

He recognized the familiar bones of wolf, bear, tiger, and camel. He photographed them again, and did manage to find the remains of an ostrich that he had not seen before. He took two pictures of that.

He spent half an hour poking around in the cavern, checking all of the meticulously recorded sites, and then made his way back to the sunlit entrance.

The despair welled up in him, greater than before. Bad news, even when it is expected, is hard to take when it is confirmed. And there was no longer any real doubt.

Man wasn't home.

Ben Hazard wasn't puzzled any longer. He was scared and worried. He couldn't pass the buck to anyone else this time. He had come back to see for himself, and he had seen.

Imagine a man who built a superb computer, a computer that could finally answer the toughest problems in his field. Suppose the ultimate in computers, and the ultimate in coded tapes; a machine—however hypothetical—that was never wrong. Just for kicks, suppose that the man feeds in an easy one: *What is two plus three?*

If the computer answers *six*, then the man is in trouble. Of course, the machine might be multiplying rather than adding—

But if the computer answers *zero* or *insufficient data*, what then?

Ben Hazard slowly walked back to the Bucket, climbed inside, and locked the hatch.

He filed his films under the proper code number.

He pushed in the familiar datum: Field Reconnaissance Negative.

He sat down before the control board and got ready.

He was completely alone in the small metallic sphere; he could see every inch of it. He *knew* that he was alone. And yet, as he had before, he had the odd impression that there was someone with him, someone looking over his shoulder. . . .

Ben Hazard had never been one to vault into the saddle and gallop off in all directions. He was a trained scientist, schooled to patience. He did not understand the soundless voice that kept whispering in his mind: *Hurry, hurry, hurry*—

"Boy," he said aloud, "you've been in solitary too long."

He pulled himself together and reached for the controls. He was determined to run out the string—twenty-three checks to go now—but he already knew the answer.

Man wasn't home.

When Ben Hazard returned to his original year of departure, which was 1982, he stepped out of the Bucket at New Mexico Station—for the machine, of necessity, moved in space as well as time. As a matter of fact, the spatial movement of the Bucket was one of the things that made it tough to do an intensive periodic survey of any single spot on the Earth's surface; it was hard to hold the Bucket on target.

According to his own reckoning, and in terms of physiological time, he had spent some forty days in his check of Choukoutien in the Middle Pleistocene. Viewed from the other end at New Mexico Station, he had been gone only five days.

The first man he saw was the big M.P. corporal.

"I'll need your prints and papers, sir," the M.P. said.

"Dammit, Ames." Ben handed over the papers and stuck his thumbs in the scanner. "Don't you know me by now?"

"Orders, sir."

Ben managed a tired smile. After all, the military implications of time travel were staggering, and care was essential. If you could move back in time only a few years and see what the other side had done, then you could counter their plans in the present. Since the old tribal squabbles were still going full blast, Gottwald had had to pull a million strings in order to get his hands on some of the available Buckets.

"Sorry, Ames. You look pretty good to me after a month or so of old camel bones."

"Nice to have you back, Dr. Hazard," the M.P. said neutrally.

After he had been duly identified as Benjamin Wright Hazard, Professor of Anthropology at Harvard and Senior Scientist on the Joint Smithsonian-Harvard-Berkeley Temporal Research Project, he was allowed to proceed. Ben crossed the crowded floor of the room they called Grand Central Station and paused a moment to see how the chimps were getting along.

There were two of them, Charles Darwin and Cleopatra, in separate cages. The apes had been the first time travelers, and were still used occasionally in testing new Buckets. Cleopatra scratched herself and hooted what might have been a greeting, but Charles Darwin was busy with a problem. He was trying to fit two sticks together so he could knock down a banana that was hanging just out of reach. He was obviously irritated, but he was no quitter.

"I know just how you feel, Charles," Ben said.

Charles Darwin pursed his mobile lips and redoubled his efforts.

What they won't do for one lousy banana.

Ben looked around for Nate York, who was working with the chimps, and spotted him talking to a technician and keeping track of his experiment out of the corner of his eye. Ben waved and went on to the elevator.

He rode up to the fourth floor and walked into Ed Stone's office. Ed was seated at his desk and he looked very industrious as he studied the dry white skull in front of him. The skull, however, was just a paper weight; Ed had used it for years.

He stood up, grinned, and stuck out his hand. "Sure glad you're back, Ben. Any luck?"

Ben shook hands and straddled a chair. He pulled out his pipe, filled it from a battered red can, and lit it gratefully. It felt good to be back with Ed. A man doesn't find too many other men he can really talk to in his lifetime, and Ed was definitely Number One. Since they were old friends, they spoke a private language.

"He was out to lunch," Ben said.

"For twenty thousand years?"

"Sinanthropus has always been famous for his dietary eccentricities."

Ed nodded to show that he caught the rather specialized joke—Sinanthropus had been a cannibal—and then leaned forward, his elbows on the desk. "You satisfied now?"

"Absolutely."

"No margin for error?" Ed insisted.

"None. I didn't really doubt Thompson's report, but I wanted to make certain. Sinanthropus isn't there. Period."

"That tears it then. We're up the creek for sure."

"Without a paddle."

"Without even a canoe." Ben puffed on his pipe. "Blast it, Ed, where *are* they?"

"You tell me. Since you left, Gottwald and I have gotten exactly nowhere. The way it looks right now, man hasn't got any ancestors—and that's crazy."

It's more than crazy, Ben thought. It's frightening. When you stop to think about it, man is a lot more than just an individual. Through his children, he extends on into the future. Through his ancestors, he stretches back far into the past. It is immortality of a sort. And when you chop off one end—

"I'm scared," he said. "I don't mind admitting it. There's an answer somewhere, and we've got to find it."

"I know how you feel, Ben. If this thing means what it seems to mean, then all science is just so much hot air. There's no cause and effect, no evidence, no reason. Man isn't what he thinks he is at all. We're just frightened animals sitting in a cave gaping at the darkness outside. Don't think I don't feel it, too. But what are we going to *do?*"

Ben stood up and knocked out his pipe. "Right now, I'm going home and hit the sack; I'm dead. Then the three of us—you and I and Gottwald—are going to sit down and hash this thing out. Then we'll at least know where we are."

"Will we?"

"We'd better."

He walked to the elevator and rode down to the ground floor of New Mexico Station. He had to identify himself twice more before he finally emerged into the glare of the desert sunlight. The situation struck him as the height of irony: here they were worried about spies and fancy feuds, when all the time—

What?

He climbed into his car and started for home. The summer day was bright and hot, but he felt as though he were driving down an endless tunnel of darkness, an infinite black cave to nowhere.

The voice whispered in his brain: *Hurry, hurry—*

His home was a lonely one, lonely with a special kind of emptiness. All his homes seemed deserted now that Anne was gone, but he liked this one better than most.

It was built of adobe with heavy exposed roof beams, cool in the summer and warm in winter. The Mexican tile floor was artfully broken up by lovely Navaho rugs—the rare Two Gray Hills kind in subdued and intricate grays and blacks and whites. He had brought many of his books with him from Boston and their familiar jackets lined the walls.

Ben was used to loneliness, but memories died hard. The plane crash that had taken Anne from him had left an emptiness in his heart. Sometimes, late in the evening, he thought he heard her footsteps in the kitchen. Often, when the telephone rang, he waited for her to answer it.

Fifteen years of marriage are hard to forget.

Ben took a hot shower, shaved, and cooked himself a steak from the freezer. Then he poured a healthy jolt of Scotch over two ice cubes and sat down in the big armchair, propping his feet on the padded bench. He was still tired, but he felt more like a human being.

His eyes wandered to his books. There was usually something relaxing about old books and long-read titles, something reassuring. It had always been that way for him, but not any longer.

The titles jeered at him: *Mankind So Far, Up from the Ape, History of the Primates, Fossil Men, The Story of Man, Human Origins, The Fossil Evidence for Human Evolution, History of the Vertebrates . . .*

Little man, what now?

"We seem to have made a slight mistake, as the chemist remarked when his lab blew up," Ben said aloud.

Yes, but where could they have gone wrong?

Take Sinanthropus, for example. The remains of forty different Sinanthropus individuals had been excavated from the site of Choukoutien in

China by Black and Weidenreich, two excellent men. There was plenty of material and it had been thoroughly studied. Scientists knew when Sinanthropus had lived in the Middle Pleistocene, where he lived, and how he lived. They even had the hearths where he cooked his food, the tools he used, the animals he killed. They knew what he looked like. They knew how he was related to his cousin, Pithecanthropus Erectus, and to modern men. There was a cast of his skull in every anthropology museum in the world, a picture of him in every textbook.

There was nothing mysterious about Sam Sinanthropus. He was one of the regulars.

Ben and Gottwald had nailed the date to the wall at 250,000 B.C. After Thompson's incredible report, Ben himself had gone back in time to search for Sinanthropus. Just to make certain, he had checked through twenty thousand years.

Nobody home.

Sinanthropus wasn't there.

That was bad enough.

But *all* the early human and pre-human fossils were missing.

There *were* no men back in the Pleistocene.

No Australopithecus, no Pithecanthropus, no Neanderthal, no nothing. It was impossible.

At first, Ben had figured that there must be an error somewhere in the dating of the fossils. After all, a geologist's casual "Middle Pleistocene" isn't much of a target, and radiocarbon dating was no good that far back. But the Gottwald-Hazard Correlation had removed that possibility.

The fossil men simply were not there.

They had disappeared. Or they had never been there. Or—

Ben got up and poured himself another drink. He needed it.

When the Winfield-Homans equations had cracked the time barrier and Ben had been invited by old Franz Gottwald to take part in the Temporal Research Project, Ben had leaped at the opportunity. It was a scientist's dream come true.

He could actually go back and *see* the long-vanished ancestors of the human species. He could listen to them talk, watch their kids, see them make their tools, hear their songs. No more sweating with a few broken bones. No more puzzling over flint artifacts. No more digging in ancient firepits.

He had felt like a man about to sit down to a Gargantuan feast.

Unhappily, it had been the cook's night out. There was nothing to eat.

Every scientist knows in his heart that his best theories are only educated guesses. There is a special Hall of Fame reserved for thundering blunders: the flat Earth, the medical humors, the unicorn.

Yes, and don't forget Piltdown Man.

Every scientist expects to revise his theories in the light of new knowledge. That's what science means. But he doesn't expect to find out that it's *all* wrong. He doesn't expect his Manhattan Project to show conclusively that uranium doesn't actually exist.

Ben finished his drink. He leaned back and closed his eyes. There had to be an answer somewhere—or somewhen. *Had* to be. A world of total ignorance is a world of terror; anything can happen.

Where was Man?

And why?

He went to bed and dreamed of darkness and ancient fears. He dreamed that he lived in a strange and alien world, a world of fire and blackness and living shadows—

When he woke up the next morning, he wasn't at all sure that he had been dreaming.

Among them, an impartial observer would have agreed, the three men in the conference room at New Mexico Station knew just about all there was to know concerning early forms of man. At the moment, in Ben's opinion, they might as well have been the supreme experts on the Ptolemaic theory of epicycles.

They were three very different men.

Ben Hazard was tall and lean and craggy-featured, as though the winds of life had weathered him down to the tough, naked rock that would yield no further. His blue eyes had an ageless quality about them, the agelessness of deep seas and high mountains, but they retained an alert and restless curiosity that had changed little from the eyes of an Ohio farm boy who had long ago wondered at the magic of the rain and filled his father's old cigar boxes with strange stones that carried the imprints of plants and shells from the dawn of time.

Ed Stone looked like part of what he was: a Texan, burned by the sun, his narrow gray eyes quiet and steady. He was not a big man, and his soft speech and deliberate movements gave him a deceptive air of lassitude. Ed was an easy man to underestimate; he wasted no time on frills or pretense, but there was a razor-sharp brain in his skull. He was younger than Ben, not yet forty, but Ben trusted his judgment more than he did his own.

Franz Gottwald, old only in years, was more than a man now; he was an institution. They called him the dean of American anthropology, but not to his white-bearded face; Franz had small respect for deans. They stood when he walked into meetings, and Franz took it as his due—he had earned it, but it concerned him no more than the make of the car he drove. Ben and Ed had both studied under Franz, and they still deferred to him, but the relationship was a warm one. Franz had been born in Germany—he never spoke about his life before he had come to the United States at the age of thirty—and his voice was still flavored by a slight accent that generations of graduate students had tried to mimic without success. He was the Grand Old Man.

"Well?" asked Dr. Gottwald when Ben had finished his report. "What is the next step, gentlemen?"

Ed Stone tapped on the polished table with a yellow pencil that showed distinct traces of gnawing. "We've got to accept the facts and go on from there. We know what the situation is, and we think that we haven't made any whopping mistakes. In a nutshell, man has vanished from his own past. What we need is an explanation, and the way to get it is to find some relatively sane hypothesis that we can *test*, not just kick around. Agreed?"

"Very scientific, Edward," Gottwald said, stroking his neat white beard.

"O.K.," Ben said. "Let's work from what we know. Those skeletons *were* in place in Africa, in China, in Europe, in Java—they had to be there because that's where they were originally dug up. The bones are real, I've held them in my hands, and they're still in place in the museums. No amount of twaddle about alternate time-tracks and congruent universes is going to change that. Furthermore, unless Franz and I are the prize dopes of all time, the dating of those fossils is accurate in terms of geology and the associated flora and fauna and whatnot. The Buckets work; there's no question about that. So why can't we find the men who left the skeletons, or even the bones themselves in their original sites?"

"That's a question with only one possible answer," Ed said.

"Check. Paradoxes aside—and there are no paradoxes if you have enough accurate information—the facts have to speak for themselves. *We don't find them because they are not there.* Next question: Where the devil are they?"

Ed leaned forward, chewing on his pencil. "If we forget about their geological context, none of those fossils are more than a few hundred years old. I mean, that's when they were found. Even Neanderthal only goes back to around 1856 or thereabouts. Science itself is an amazingly recent phenomenon. So—"

"You mean Piltdown?" Gottwald suggested, smiling.

"Maybe."

Ben filled his pipe and lit it. "I've thought about that, too. I guess all of us have. If one fossil man was a fake, why not all of them? But it won't hold water, and you know it. For one thing, it would have required a world-wide conspiracy, which is nonsense. For another—sheer manpower aside—the knowledge that would have been required to fake all those fossils simply did not exist at the time they were discovered. Piltdown wouldn't have lasted five minutes with fluorine dating and decent X-rays, and no one can sell me on the idea that men like Weidenreich and Von Koenigswald and Dart were fakers. Anyhow, that idea would leave us with a problem tougher than the one we're trying to solve—where did man come from if he had no past, no ancestors? I vote we exorcise that particular ghost."

"Keep going," Gottwald said.

Ed took it up. "Facts, Ben. Leave the theories for later. If neither the bones nor the men were present back in the Pleistocene where they belong, but the bones were present to be discovered later, then they *have* to appear somewhere in between. Our problem right now is *when*."

Ben took his pipe out of his mouth and gestured with it, excited now. "We can handle that one. Dammit, *all* of our data can't be haywire. Look: for most of his presumed existence, close to a million years, man was a rare animal—all the bones of all the fossil men ever discovered wouldn't fill up this room we're sitting in; all the crucial ones would fit in a broom closet. O.K.? But by Neolithic times, with agricultural villages, there were men everywhere, even here in the New World. That record is clear. So those fossils *had* to be in place by around eight thousand years ago. All we have to do—"

"Is to work back the other way," Ed finished, standing up. "By God, that's it! We can send teams back through history, checking at short intervals, until we *see* how it started. As long as the bones are where they should be, fine. When they disappear—and they have to disappear, because we know they're not there earlier—we'll reverse our field and check it hour by hour if necessary. Then we'll know what happened. After that, we can kick the theories around until we're green in the face."

"It'll work," Ben said, feeling like a man walking out of a heavy fog. "It won't be easy, but it can be done. Only—"

"Only what?" Gottwald asked.

"Only I wonder what we'll find. I'm a little afraid of what we're going to see."

"One thing sure," Ed said.

"Yes?"

"This old world of ours will never be the same. Too bad—I kind of liked it the way it was."

Gottwald nodded, stroking his beard.

For months, Ben Hazard virtually lived within the whitewashed walls of New Mexico Station. He felt oddly like a man fighting a rattlesnake with his fists at some busy intersection, while all about him people hurried by without a glance, intent on their own affairs.

What went on in New Mexico Station was, of course, classified information. In Ben's opinion, this meant that there had been a ludicrous reversion to the techniques of magic. Facts were stamped with the sacred symbol of *CLASSIFIED*, thereby presumably robbing them of their power. Nevertheless, the world outside didn't know what the score was, and probably didn't care, while inside the Station—

History flickered by, a wonderful and terrible film.

Man was its hero and its villain—but for how long?

The teams went back, careful to do nothing and to touch nothing. The teams left Grand Central, and pushed back, probing, searching. . . .

Back past the Roman legions and the temples of Athens, back beyond the pyramids of Egypt and the marvels of Ur, back through the sun-baked villages of the first farmers, back into the dark shadows of prehistory—

And the teams found nothing.

At every site they could reach without revealing their presence, the bones of the early men were right where they should have been, waiting patiently to be unearthed.

Back past 8,000 B.C.

Back past 10,000.

Back past 15,000—

And then, when the teams reached 25,000 B.C., it happened. Quite suddenly, in regions as far removed from one another as France and Java, the bones disappeared.

And not just the bones.

Man himself was gone.

The world, in some ways, was as it had been—or was to be. The gray waves still tossed on the mighty seas, the forests were cool and green under clean blue skies, the sparkling sheets of snow and ice still gleamed beneath a golden sun.

The Earth was the same, but it was a strangely empty world without men. A desolate and somehow fearful world, hushed by long silences and stroked coldly by the restless winds. . . .

"That's it," Ben said. "Whatever it was, we know when it happened—somewhere between 23,000 and 25,000 at the end of the Upper Paleolithic. I'm going back there."

"*We're* going back there," Ed corrected him. "If I sit this one out I'll be ready for the giggle factory."

Ben smiled, not trying to hide his relief. "I think I could use some company this trip."

"It's a funny feeling, Ben."

"Yes." Ben Hazard glanced toward the waiting Buckets. "I've seen a lot of things in my life, but I never thought I'd see the Beginning."

The machine stopped and the green light winked.

Ed checked the viewer while Ben punched data into the recorder.

"Nothing yet," Ed said. "It's raining."

"Swell." Ben unlocked the hatch and the two men climbed out. The sky above them was cold and gray. An icy rain was pouring down from heavy, low-hanging clouds. There was no thunder. Apart from the steady hiss of the rain, France in the year 24,571 B.C. was as silent as a tomb. "Let's get this thing covered up."

They hauled out the plastic cover, camouflaged to blend with the landscape, and draped it over the metallic gray sphere. They had been checking for eighteen days without results, but they were taking no chances.

They crossed the narrow valley through sheets of rain, their boots sinking into the soaked ground with every step. They climbed up the rocks to the gaping black hole of the cave entrance and worked their way in under the rock ledge, out of the rain. They switched on their lights, got down on their hands and knees, and went over every inch of the dry area just back of the rock overhang.

Human Nature and Culture

Nothing.

The gray rain pelted the hillside and became a torrent of water that splashed out over the cave entrance in a hissing silver waterfall. It was a little warmer in the cave, but dark and singularly uninviting.

"Here we go again," Ed muttered. "I know this blasted cave better than my own backyard."

"I'd like to see that backyard of yours about now. We could smoke up some chickens in the barbecue pit and sample some of Betty's tequila sours."

"Right now I'd just settle for the tequila. If we can't figure this thing out any other way we might just as well start looking in the old bottle."

"Heigh-ho," Ben sighed, staring at the waiting cave. "Enter one dwarf and one gnome, while thousands cheer."

"I don't hear a thing."

Ed took the lead and they picked and crawled their way back through the narrow passages of the cave, their lights throwing grotesque black shadows that danced eerily on the spires and pillars of ancient, dripping stone. Ben sensed the weight of the great rocks above him and his chest felt constricted. It was hard to breathe, hard to keep going.

"Whatever I am in my next incarnation," he said, "I hope it isn't a mole."

"You won't even make the mammals," Ed assured him.

They came out into a long, twisted vault. It was deep in the cave, far from the hidden skies and insulated from the pounding of the rain. They flashed their lights over the walls, across the dry gray ceiling, into the ageless silence.

Nothing.

No cave paintings.

It was as though man had never been, and never was to be.

"I'm beginning to wonder whether *I'm* real," Ed said.

"Wait a minute." Ben turned back toward the cave entrance, his body rigid. "Did you hear something?"

Ed held his breath and listened. "Yeah. There it is again."

It was faint and remote as it came to them in the subterranean vault, but there was no mistaking it.

A sound of thunder, powerful beyond belief.

Steady, now.

Coming closer.

And there had been no thunder in that cold, hissing rain. . . .

"Come on." Ben ran across the cavern and got down on his hands and knees to crawl back through the twisting passage that led to the world outside. "There's something out there."

"What is it?"

Ben didn't stop. He clawed at the rocks until his hands were bloody. "I think the lunch hour's over," he panted. "I think Man's coming home."

Like two frightened savages, they crouched in the cave entrance and looked out across the rain-swept valley. The solid stone vibrated under their feet and the cold gray sky was shattered by blasting roars.

One thing was certain: that was no natural thunder.

"We've got to get out of here," Ben yelled. "We've got to hide before—"

"Where? The Bucket?"

"That's the best bet. It's almost invisible in this rain, and we can see through the viewer."

"Right. Run for it!"

They scrambled down among the slick rocks and ran across the wet grass and mud of the valley floor. It was cold and the rain pelted their faces in icy gray sheets. The deafening roar grew even louder, falling down from the leaden sky.

Fumbling in their haste, they jerked up a corner of the plastic cover so that the viewer could operate. Then they squirmed and wriggled under the plastic, dropped through the hatch, and sealed the lock. They dripped all over the sphere but there was no time to bother about it. Even inside the Bucket they could feel the ocean of sound around them.

Ben cut in the recorder. "Start the cameras."

"Done."

"Hang on—"

The shattering roar reached an ear-splitting crescendo. Suddenly, there was something to see.

Light.

Searing white flame stabbing down from the gray skies.

They saw it: Gargantuan, lovely, huge beyond reason.

Before their eyes, like a vast metal fish from an unknown and terrible sea, the spaceship landed in the rain-soaked valley of Paleolithic France.

The long silence came again.

Fists clenched, Ben Hazard watched the Creation.

The great ship towered in the rain, so enormous that it was hard to imagine that it had ever moved. It might have been there always, but it was totally alien, out of place in its setting of hills and earth and sodden grasses.

Circular ports opened in the vast ship like half a hundred awakening eyes. Bright warm yellow light splashed out through the rain. Men— strangely dressed in dark, close-fitting tunics—floated out of the ship and down to the ground on columns of the yellow light.

The men were human, no different physically from Ben or Ed.

Equipment of some sort drifted down the shafts of light: strange spider-legged machines, self-propelled crates that gleamed in the light, shielded stands that might have been for maps or charts, metallic robots that were twice the size of a man.

The yellow light deflected the rain—Ben could see water dripping down the yellow columns as though solid tubes had been punched through the air—and the rain was also diverted from the men and their equipment.

Human Nature and Culture

The men from the ship moved quickly. They fanned out and went to work with the precision of trained specialists who knew exactly what they were doing.

Incredible as it was, Ben thought that he knew what they were doing too.

The spider-legged machines stayed on the valley floor, pulsing. Most of the men, together with three of the robots and the bulk of the self-propelled crates, made their way up to the cave Ben and Ed had just left and vanished inside.

"Want to bet on what's in those crates?" Ben whispered.

"Haven't the faintest idea, but two-bits says you spell it b-o-n-e-s."

The great ship waited, the streams of yellow light still spilling out into the rain. Five men pored over the shielded stands, looking for all the world like engineers surveying a site. Others worked over the spider-legged machines, setting up tubes of the yellow light that ran from the machines to the rocky hills. Two of the robots, as far as Ben could see, were simply stacking rocks into piles.

After three hours, when it was already growing dark, the men came back out of the cave. The robots and the crates were reloaded through the ship's ports and the uniformed men boarded the ship again.

Night fell. Ben stretched to ease his cramped muscles, but he didn't take his eyes from the viewer for a second.

The rain died down to a gentle patter and then stopped entirely. The overcast lifted and slender white clouds sailed through the wind-swept sky. The moon rose, fat and silver, its radiance dimming the burning stars.

The impossible ship, towering so complacently beneath the moon of Earth, was a skyscraper of light. It literally hummed with activity. Ben would have given a lot to know what was going on inside that ship, but there was no way to find out.

The pulsing spider-legged machines clicked and buzzed in the cold of the valley night. Rocks were conveyed along tubes of the yellow light to the machines, which were stamping something out by the hundreds of thousands. Something. . . .

Artifacts?

The long, uncanny night ended. Ben and Ed watched in utter fascination, their fears almost forgotten, sleep never even considered.

Dawn streaked the eastern sky, touching the clouds with fingers of rose and gold. A light breeze rustled the wet, heavy grasses. Water still dripped from the rocks.

The uniformed men came back out of the ship, riding the columns of yellow light. The robots gathered up some immense logs and stacked them near the mouth of the cave. They treated the wood with some substance to dry it, then ignited a blazing fire.

Squads of men moved over the valley floor, erasing all traces of their presence. One of them got quite close to the Bucket and Ben felt a sudden numbing chill. What would happen if they were seen? He was no longer worried about himself. But what about all the men who were to live on the Earth? Or—

The squad moved away.

Just as the red sun lifted behind the hills, while the log fire still blazed by the cave, the ship landed the last of its strange cargo.

Human beings.

Ben felt the sweat grow clammy in the palms of his hands.

They floated down the shafts of yellow light, shepherded by the uniformed men. There were one hundred of them by actual count, fifty men and fifty women. There were no children. They were a tall, robust people, dressed in animal skins. They shivered in the cold and seemed dazed and uncomprehending. They had to be led by the hand, and several had to be carried by the robots.

The uniformed men took them across the wet valley, a safe distance away from the ship. They huddled together like sheep, clasping one another in sexless innocence. Their eyes turned from the fire to the ship, understanding neither.

It was a scene beyond age; it had always been. There were the rows of uniformed men, standing rigidly at attention. And there were the clustered people in animal skins, waiting without hope, without regret.

An officer—Ben thought of him that way, though his uniform was no different from the others—stepped forward and made what seemed to be a speech. At any rate, he talked for a long time—nearly an hour. It was clear that the dazed people did not understand a word of what he was saying, and that, too, was older than time.

It's a ceremony, Ben thought. *It must be some kind of ritual. I hadn't expected that.*

When it was over, the officer stood for a long minute looking at the huddle of people. Ben tried to read his expression in the viewer, but it was impossible. It might have been regret. It might have been hope. It might have been only curiosity.

Then, at a signal, the uniformed men turned and abandoned the others. They walked back to their waiting ship and the columns of yellow light took them inside. The ports closed.

Ten minutes later, the ship came to life.

White flame flared beneath its jets and the earth trembled. The terrible roar came again. The people who had been left behind fell to the ground, covering their ears with their hands. The great ship lifted slowly into the blue sky, then faster and faster—

It was gone, and only the sound remained.

In time, that, too, was gone.

Ben watched his own ancestors with an almost hypnotic fascination. They did not move.

Get up, get up—

The skin-clad people stood up shakily after what seemed to be hours.

They stared blankly at one another. As though driven by some vague instinct that spoke through their shock, they turned and looked at the blazing fire that burned by the mouth of the cave.

Slowly, one by one, they pulled themselves over the rocks to the fire. They stood before it, seeking a warmth they could not understand.

The sun climbed higher, flooding the rain-clean world with golden light.

The people stood for a long time watching the fire burn down. They did nothing and said nothing.

Hurry, hurry. The voice spoke again in Ben's brain. He shook his head. Was he thinking about those dazed people out there, or was someone thinking about *him?*

Gradually, some of them seemed to recover their senses. They began to move about purposefully—still slowly, still uncertainly. One man picked up a fresh log and threw it on the fire. Another crouched down and fingered a chipped piece of flint he found on a rock. Two women stepped behind the fire and started into the dark cave.

Ben turned away from the viewer, his unshaven face haggard. "Meet Cro-Magnon," he said, waving his hand.

Ed lit a cigarette, his first in eighteen hours. His hand was shaking. "Meet everybody, you mean. Those jokers planted the other boys— Neanderthal and whatnot—back in the cave before they landed the living ones."

"We came out of that ship too, Ed."

"I know—but where did the *ship* come from? And why?"

Ben took a last long look at the people huddled around the fire. He didn't feel like talking. He was too tired to think. None of it made any sense.

What kind of people could *do* a thing like that?

"Let's go home," Ed said quietly.

They went out and removed the plastic cover, and then set the controls for New Mexico Station in a world that was no longer their own.

Old Franz Gottwald sat behind his desk. His white suit was freshly pressed and his hair was neatly combed. He stroked his beard in the old familiar gesture, and only the gleam in his eyes revealed the excitement within him.

"It has always been my belief, gentlemen, that there is no substitute for solid thinking based on verified facts. There is a time for action and there is a time for thought. I need hardly remind you that action without thought is pointless; it is the act of an animal, the contraction of an earthworm. We have the facts we need. You have been back for three days, but the thinking is yet to be done."

"We've been beating our brains out," Ben protested.

"That may be, Ben, but a man can beat his brains out with a club. It is not thinking."

"*You* try thinking," Ed said, grinding out a cigarette.

Gottwald smiled. "You are too old to have your thinking done for you, Edward. I have given you all I can give. It is your turn now."

Ben sat back in his chair and lit his pipe. He took his time doing it, trying to clear his mind. He had to forget those frightened people huddled around a fire, had to forget the emotions he had felt when the great ship had left them behind. Gottwald was right, as always.

The time had come for thought.

"O.K.," he said. "We all know the facts. Where do we go from here?"

"I would suggest to you, gentlemen, that we will get no answers until we begin to ask the right questions. That is elementary, if I may borrow from Mr. Holmes."

"You want questions?" Ed laughed shortly. "Here's one, and it's a dilly. There's a hole in all this big enough to drive the American Anthropological Association through in a fleet of trucks. What about the apes?"

Ben nodded. "You quoted Conan Doyle, Franz, so I'll borrow a line from another Englishman—Darwin's pal Huxley, 'Bone for bone, organ for organ, man's body is repeated in the body of the ape.' Hell, we all know that. There are differences, sure, but the apes are closer to men than they are to monkeys. If man didn't evolve on Earth—"

"You've answered your own question, Ben."

"Of course!" Ed fished out another cigarette. "If man didn't evolve on Earth, then neither did the apes. That ship—or some ship—brought them both. But that's impossible."

"Impossible?" Franz asked.

"Maybe not," Ben said slowly. "After all, there are only four living genera of apes—two in Africa and two in Asia. We could even leave out the gibbon; he's a pretty primitive customer. It *could* have been done."

"Not for all the primates," Ed insisted. "Not for all the monkeys and lemurs and tarsiers, not for all the fossil primate bones. It would have made Noah's ark look like a rowboat."

"I would venture the suggestion that your image is not very apt," Gottwald said. "That ship *was* big enough to make any of our ships look like rowboats."

"Never mind," Ben said, determined not to get sidetracked. "It doesn't matter. Let's assume that the apes were seeded, just as the men were. The other primates could have evolved here without outside interference, just as the other animals did. That isn't the real problem."

"I wonder," Ed said. "Could that ship have come out of *time* as well as space? After all, if we have time travel they must have it. They could do anything—"

"Bunk," Gottwald snorted. "Don't let yourself get carried away, Edward. Anything is *not* possible. A scientific law is a scientific law, no matter who is working with it, or where, or when. We know from the Winfield-Homans Equations that it is impossible to go back into time and alter it in any way, just as it is impossible to go into the future which does not yet exist. There are no paradoxes in time travel. Let's not make this thing harder than it is by charging off into all the blind alleys we can think of. Ben was on the right track. What is the real problem here?"

Ben sighed. He saw the problem all too clearly. "It boils down to this, I think. *Why* did they plant those fossils—and probably the apes too? I can think of fifty reasons why they might have seeded men like themselves on a barren planet—population pressure and so forth—but why go to all the trouble of planting a false evolutionary picture for them to dig up later?"

"Maybe it isn't false," Ed said slowly.

Franz Gottwald smiled. "Now you're *thinking*, Edward."

"Sorry, Ed. I don't follow you. You saw them plant those bones. If that isn't a prime example of salting a site, then what the devil is it?"

"Don't shoot, pal. I was trying to say that the fossils could have been planted and *still* tell a true story. Maybe I'm just an old codger set in his ways, but I can't believe that human evolution is a myth. And there's a clincher, Ben: Why bother with the apes if there is no relationship?"

"I still don't see—"

"He means," Gottwald said patiently, "that the fossil sequence is a true one—*some place else.*"

Ed nodded. "Exactly. The evolutionary series is the genuine article, but man developed on their world rather than on ours. When they seeded men on Earth, they also provided them with a kind of history book—if they could read it."

Ben chewed on his pipe. It made sense, to the extent that anything made sense any more. "I'll buy that. But where does it leave us?"

"Still up that well-known creek. Every answer we get just leads back to the same old question. *Why* did they leave us a history book?"

"Answer that one," Gottwald said, "and you win the gold cigar."

Ben got to his feet. His head felt as though it were stuffed with dusty cotton.

"Where are you going?"

"I'm going fishing. As long as I'm up the creek I might as well do something useful. I'll see you later."

"I hope you catch something," Ed said.

"So do I," Ben Hazard said grimly.

The car hummed sleepily across the monotonous flatlands of New Mexico, passed through the gently rolling country that rested the eye, and climbed into the cool mountains where the pines grew tall and the grass was a thick dark green in the meadows.

Ben loved the mountains. The happiest times of his life had been spent up next to the sky, where the air was crisp and the streams ran clear. He needed the mountains, and he always returned to them when the pressure was too much to bear.

He turned off the main road and jolted over a gravel trail; paved roads and good fishing were mutually exclusive, like cities and sanity. He noted with approval that the clouds were draping the mountain peaks, shadowing the land below. When the sun was too bright the fish could see a man coming.

He took a deep breath, savoring the tonic of the air.

Relax, that's the ticket.

He checked to see that no interloper had discovered his favorite stretch of water, then parked his car by the side of Mill Creek, a gliding stream of crystal-clean water that tumbled icily out of the mountains and snaked its lazy way through the long green valley. He grinned like a kid with his first cane pole.

Ben pulled on his waders, assembled his rod with practiced skill, and tied on his two pet flies—a Gray Hackle Yellow and a Royal Coachman. He hung his net over one shoulder and his trout basket over the other, lit his pipe, and waded out into the cold water of Mill Creek.

He felt wonderful. He hooked a nice brook trout within five minutes. He felt the knots and the tensions flow out of him like melting snow, and that was the first step.

He *had* to relax. There was no other way.

Consider the plight of a baseball player in a bad slump. He gives it all he has, tries twice as hard as usual, but everything he does backfires. His hits don't fall in, he misses the easy grounders. He lies awake at night and worries.

"Relax, Mac," his manager tells him. "All you gotta do is *relax*. Take it easy."

Sure, but how?

It was the same with a tough scientific problem. Ben had long ago discovered that persistent and orderly logic could take him only so far. There came a time when no amount of forced thinking would get the job done.

The fresh insights and the new slants seldom came to him when he went after them, no matter how hard he tried. In fact, the more he sweated over a problem the more stubbornly recalcitrant his mind became. The big ideas, and the good ones, came to him in a flash of almost intuitive understanding. The trick was to let the conscious mind get out of the way, let the message get through—

In Ben's case, go fishing.

It took him two hours, seven trout, and part of a banana to get the answer he sought.

He had taken a long, cool drink from the stream, cleaned his fish, and was sitting down on a rock to eat the lunch he had packed when the idea came.

He had peeled a banana and taken one bite of it when his mind was triggered by a single, innocuous word:

Banana.

Not just any old banana, of course. A specific one, used for a specific purpose.

Remember?

Charles Darwin and Cleopatra, two chimpanzees in their cages. Charles Darwin pushing his ape brain to the limit to fit two sticks together. Why?

To get a banana.

One lousy banana.

That was well enough, but there was more. Darwin might get his banana, and that was all he cared about. But who had placed the sticks in the cage, who had supplied the banana?

And why?

That was an easy one. It was so simple a child could have figured it out. Someone had given Charles Darwin two sticks and a banana for just one reason: to see whether or not he could solve the problem.

In a nutshell, a scientific experiment.

Now, consider another Charles Darwin, another problem.

Or consider Ben Hazard.

What is the toughest problem a man can tackle? Howells pointed it out many years ago. Of all the animals, man is the only one who wonders where he has come from and where he is going. All the other questions are petty compared to that one. It pushes the human brain to the limit . . . .

Ben stood up, his lunch forgotten.

It was all so obvious.

Men had been seeded on the Earth, and a problem had been planted with them—a real problem, one capable of yielding to a true solution. A dazed huddle of human beings had been abandoned by a fire in the mouth of a cave, lost in the morning of a strange new world. Then they had been left strictly alone; there was no evidence that they had been helped in any way since that time.

Why?

To see what they could do.

To see how long it would take them to solve the problem.

In a nutshell, a scientific experiment.

Ben picked up his rod and started back toward the car.

There was one more thing, one more inevitable characteristic of a scientific experiment. No scientist merely sets up his experiment and then goes off and forgets about it, even if he is the absolute ultimate in absent-minded professors.

No.

He has to stick around to see how it all comes out. He has to observe, take notes.

It was monstrous.

The whole history of man on Earth. . . .

Ben climbed into his car, started the engine.

There's more. Face up to it.

Suppose that you had set up a fantastic planetary experiment with human beings. Suppose that you—or one of your descendants, for human generations are slow—came back to check on your experiment. What would you do, what would you be?

A garage mechanic?

A shoe salesman?

A pool room shark?

Hardly. You'd have to be in a position to know what was going on. You'd have to work in a field where you could find out the score.

In a word, you'd be an anthropologist.

There's still more. Take it to the end of the line.

Now, suppose that man on Earth cracked the time barrier. Suppose a Temporal Research Project was set up. Wouldn't you be in on it, right at the top?

Sure.

You wouldn't miss it for anything.

Well, who fit the description? It couldn't be Ed; Ben had known him most of his life, known his folks and his wife and his kids, visited the Texas town that had been his home.

It wasn't Ben.

That left Franz Gottwald.

Franz, who had come from Germany and never talked about his past. Franz, with the strangely alien accent. Franz, who had no family. Franz, who had contributed nothing to the project but shrewd, prodding questions. . . .

Franz.

The Grand Old Man.

Ben drove with his hands clenched on the wheel and his lips pressed into a thin, hard line. Night had fallen by the time he got out of the mountains, and he drove across an enchanted desert beneath the magic of the stars. The headlights of his car lanced into the night, stabbing, stabbing—

He passed the great New Mexico rocket base, from which men had hurled their missiles to the moon and beyond. There had been talk of a manned shot to Mars. . . .

How far would the experimenters let them go?

Ben lit a cigarette, not wanting to fool with his pipe in the car. He was filled with a cold anger he had never known before.

He had solved the problem.

Very well.

It was time to collect his banana.

It was after midnight when Ben got home.

He stuck his fish in the freezer, took a shower, and sat down in his comfortable armchair to collect his thoughts. He promptly discovered yet another fundamental truth about human beings: when they get tired enough, they sleep.

He woke up with a start and looked at his watch. It was five o'clock in the morning.

Ben shaved and was surprised to find that he was hungry. He cooked himself some bacon and scrambled eggs, drank three cups of instant coffee, and felt ready for anything.

Even Franz.

He got into his car and drove through the still-sleeping town to Gottwald's house. It looked safe and familiar in the pale morning light. As a matter of fact, it looked a lot like his own house, since both had been supplied by the government.

That, he thought, was a laugh.

The government had given *Gottwald* a house to live in.

He got out of his car, walked up to the door, and rang the bell. Franz never got to the office before nine, and his car was still in the garage.

His ring was greeted by total silence.

He tried again, holding his finger on the bell. He rang it long enough to wake the dead.

No answer.

Ben tried the door. It was unlocked. He took a deep breath and stepped inside. The house was neat and clean. The familiar books were on the shelves in the living room. It was like stepping into his own home.

"Franz! It's me, Ben."

No answer.

Ben strode over to the bedroom, opened the door, and looked inside. The bed was tidily made, and Franz wasn't in it. Ben walked through the whole house, even peering inside the closets, before he was satisfied.

Franz wasn't home.

Fine. A scientist keeps records, doesn't he?

Ben proceeded to ransack the house. He looked in dresser drawers, on closet shelves, even in the refrigerator. He found nothing unusual. Then he tried the obvious.

He opened Gottwald's desk and looked inside.

The first thing he saw was a letter addressed to himself. There it was, a white envelope with his name typed on it: *Dr. Benjamin Wright Hazard.*

Not to be opened until Christmas?

Ben took the letter, ripped it open, and took out a single sheet of paper. He started to read it, then groped for a chair and sat down.

The letter was neatly typed. It said:

My Dear Ben: I have always believed that a scientist must be capable of making predictions. This is not always an easy matter when you are dealing with human beings, but I have known you for a long, long time.

Obviously, you are searching my home, or you would not be reading this note. Obviously, if you are searching my home, you know part of the truth.

If you would like to know the rest of the story, the procedure is simple. Look behind the picture of the sand-painting in my bedroom. You will find a button there. Press the button for exactly five seconds. Then walk out into my patio and stand directly in front of the barbecue pit.

Trust me, Ben. I am not a cannibal.

The letter was signed with Gottwald's scrawled signature.

Ben got up and walked into the bedroom. He looked behind the picture that was hanging over the dresser. There was a small red button.

Press the button for exactly five seconds.

And then—what?

Ben replaced the picture. The whole thing was a trifle too reminiscent of a feeble-minded practical joke. Press the button and get a shock. Press the button and get squirted with water. Press the button and blow up the house—

No. That was absurd.

Wasn't it?

He hesitated. He could call Ed, but then Ed would insist on coming over right away—and Ed had a wife and kids. He could call the police, but the story he had to tell would have sounded absolutely balmy. He had no proof.

He went back to Gottwald's desk, found some paper, and typed a letter. He outlined the theory he had formed and wrote down exactly what he was going to do. He put the letter into an envelope, addressed the envelope to Ed, stamped it, and went outside and dropped it in the mailbox on the corner.

He went back into the house.

This time he did not hesitate—not for a second.

He punched the button behind the picture for exactly five seconds. Nothing happened. He went out into the patio and stood directly in front of the barbecue pit.

The wall around the patio hid the outside world, but the blue sky overhead was the same as ever. He saw nothing, heard nothing.

"Snipe hunt," he said aloud.

Then, with breathtaking suddenness, something *did* happen.

There was an abrupt stillness in the air, a total cessation of sound. It was as though invisible glass walls had slipped silently into place and sealed off the world around him.

There was no perceptible transition. One moment the cone of yellow light was not there, and the next it was. It surrounded him: taut, living, seething with an energy that prickled his skin.

He knew that yellow light.

He had seen it once before, in the dawn of time. . . .

Ben held his breath; he couldn't help it. He felt strangely weightless, buoyant, a cork in a nameless sea—

His feet left the ground.

"Good God," Ben said.

He was lifted into the yellow light, absorbed in it. He could see perfectly, and it didn't help his stomach any. He could see the town below him—there was Gottwald's patio, the barbecue pit, the adobe house. He began to regret the bacon and eggs he had eaten.

He forced himself to breathe again. The air was warm and tasteless. He rose into the sky, fighting down panic.

Think of it as an elevator. It's just a way of getting from one place to another. I can see out, but of course nothing is visible from the outside.

But then how did I see the yellow light before?

This must be different. They couldn't risk being seen—

Relax!

But he kept going higher, and faster.

The Earth was far away.

It was an uncanny feeling—not exactly unpleasant, but he didn't care for the view. It was like falling through the sky. It was impossible to avoid the idea that he was falling, that he was going to hit something. . . .

The blue of the sky faded into black, and he saw the stars.

Where am I going, where are they taking me?

There!

Look up, look up—

There it was, at the end of the tunnel of yellow light.

It blotted out the stars.

It was huge even against the immense backdrop of space itself. It stunned his mind with its size, but he recognized it.

It was the same ship that had landed the first men on Earth.

Dark now, dark and vast and lonely—but the same ship.

The shaft of yellow light pulled him inside; there was no air lock. As suddenly as it had come, the light was gone.

Ben stumbled and almost fell. The gravity seemed normal, but the light had supported him for so long that it took his legs a moment to adjust themselves.

He stood in a cool green room. It was utterly silent.

Ben swallowed hard.

He crossed the room to a metal door. The door opened before he reached it. There was only blackness beyond, blackness and the total silence of the dead.

Ben Hazard tried to fight down the numbing conviction that the ship was empty.

There is an almost palpable air of desolation about long deserted things, about empty houses and derelict ships and crumbling ruins. There is a special kind of silence about a place that has once known life and knows it no longer. There is a type of death that hovers over things that have not been *used* for a long, long time.

That was the way the ship felt.

Ben could see only the small green room in which he stood and the corridor of darkness outside the door. It could have been only a tiny fraction of the great ship, only one room in the vast city in the sky. But he *knew* that the men who had once lived in the ship were gone. He knew it with a certainty that his mind could not question.

It was a ghost ship.

He knew it was.

That was why his heart almost stopped when he heard the footsteps moving toward him through the silence.

Heavy steps.

Metallic steps.

Ben backed away from the door. He tried to close it but it would not shut. He saw a white light coming at him through the dark tunnel. The light was higher than a man—

Metallic steps?

Ben got a grip on himself and waited. *You fool, you knew they had robots. You saw them. Robots don't die, do they?*

Do they kill?

He saw it now, saw its outline behind the light. Twice the size of a man, its metal body gleaming.

It had no face.

The robot filled the doorway and stopped. Ben could hear it now: a soft whirring noise that somehow reminded him of distant winds. He told himself that it was just a machine, just an animated hunk of metal, and his mind accepted the analysis. But it is one thing to know what a robot is, and it is quite another to find yourself in the same room with one.

"Well?" Ben said. He had to say something.

The robot was evidently under no such compulsion. It said nothing and did nothing. It simply stood there.

After a long, uncomfortable minute, the robot turned around and walked into the dark corridor, its light flashing ahead of it. It took four steps, stopped, and looked back over its shoulder.

There was just one thing to do, and one way to go.

Ben nodded and stepped through the doorway after the robot.

He followed the giant metallic figure along what seemed to be miles of featureless passageways. Ben heard no voices, saw no lights, met no living things.

He felt no fear now; he was beyond that. He knew that he was in a state of shock where nothing could get through to him, nothing could hurt him. He felt only a kind of sadness, the sadness a man knows when he walks through the tunnels of a pyramid or passes a graveyard on a lonely night.

The ship that men had built was so vast, so silent, so empty.

A door opened ahead of them.

Light spilled out into the corridor.

Ben followed the robot into a large, comfortable room. The room was old, old and worn, but it was alive. It was warm and vital and human because there were two people in it. Ben had never before been quite so glad to see anyone.

One of the persons was an elderly woman he had never met before.

The other was Franz Gottwald.

"Hello, Ben," he said, smiling. "I don't believe you know my wife."

Ben wasn't sure whether he was coming into a nightmare or coming out of one, but his manners were automatic.

Human Nature and Culture

"I'm very pleased to meet you," he said, and meant it.

The room had a subtle strangeness about it that once more reminded Ben of a dream. It was not merely the expected strangeness of design of a new kind of room, a room lost in the lonely miles of a silent spaceship; it was an out-of-phase oddness that at first he could not identify.

Then he caught it. There were alien things in the room: furniture that was planned for human beings but produced by a totally different culture pattern, carvings that were grotesque to his eyes, rugs that glowed in curiously wrong figures. But there were also familiar, everyday items from the world he knew: a prosaic reading lamp, a coffee pot bubbling on a table, some potted plants, a framed painting by Covarrubias. The mixture was a trifle jarring, but it did have a reassuring air of homeliness.

How strange the mind is. At a time like this, it concentrates on a room.

"Sit down, sit down," Franz said. "Coffee?"

"Thank you." Ben tried a chair and found it comfortable.

The woman he persisted in thinking of as Mrs. Gottwald—though that was certainly not her actual name—poured out a cup and handed it to him. Her lined, delicate face seemed radiant with happiness, but there were tears in her eyes.

"I speak the language too a little," she said hesitantly. "We are so proud of you, so happy—"

Ben took a sip of the coffee to cover his embarrassment. He didn't know what he had expected, but certainly not *this*.

"Don't say anything more, Arnin," Franz said sharply. "We must be very careful."

"That robot of yours," Ben said. "Couldn't you send him out for oiling or something?"

Franz nodded. "I forgot how weird he must seem to you. Please forgive me. I would have greeted you myself, but I am growing old and it is a long walk." He spoke to the robot in a language Ben had never heard, and the robot left the room.

Ben relaxed a little. "You two up here all alone?"

An inane question. But what can I do, what can I say?

Old Franz seated himself next to Ben. He still wore his white suit. He seemed tired, more tired than Ben had ever seen him, but there was a kind of hope in his eyes, a hope that was almost a prayer.

"Ben," he said slowly, "it is hard for me to talk to you—now. I can imagine how you must feel after what you have been through. But you must trust me a little longer. Just forget where you are, Ben—a spaceship is just a ship. Imagine that we are back at the Station, imagine that we are talking as we have talked so many times before. You must think clearly. This is important, my boy, more important than you can know. I want you to tell me what you have discovered—I want to know what led you here. Omit nothing, and choose your words with care. Be as specific and precise as you can. Will you do this one last thing for me? When you have finished, I think I will be able to answer all your questions."

Ben had to smile. *"Be as specific and precise as you can."* How many times had he heard Franz use that very phrase on examinations?

He reached for his pipe. For a moment he had a wild, irrational fear that he had forgotten it—that would have been the last straw, somehow—but it was there. He filled it and lit it gratefully.

"It's your party, Franz. I'll tell you what I know."

"Proceed, Ben—and be careful."

Mrs. Gottwald—Arnin?—sat very still, waiting.

The ship was terribly silent around them.

Ben took his time and told Franz what he knew and what he believed. He left nothing out and made no attempt to soften his words.

When he was finished, Gottwald's wife was crying openly.

Franz, amazingly, looked like a man who had suddenly been relieved of a sentence of death.

"Well?" Ben asked.

Gottwald stood up and stroked his white beard. "You must think I am some kind of a monster," he said, smiling.

Ben shrugged. "I don't know."

Mrs. Gottwald dried her eyes. "Tell him," she said. "You can tell him now."

Gottwald nodded. "I am proud of you, Ben, very proud."

"I was right?"

"You were right in the only thing that matters. The fossils *were* a test, and you have passed that test with flying colors. Of course, you had some help from Edward—"

"I'll give him part of the banana."

Gottwald's smile vanished. "Yes. Yes, I daresay you will. But I am vain enough to want to clear up one slight error in your reconstruction. I do not care for the role of monster, and mad scientists have always seemed rather dull to me."

"The truth is the truth."

"A redundancy, Ben. But never mind. I must tell you that what has happened on Earth was *not* a mere scientific experiment. I must also tell you that I am not only a scientist who has come back, as you put it, to see how the chimpanzees are doing. In fact, I didn't come back at all. We—my people—never left. I was born right here in this ship, in orbit around the Earth. It has always been here."

"For twenty-five thousand years?"

"For twenty-five thousand years."

"But what have you been doing?"

"We've been waiting for you, Ben. You almost did not get here in time. My wife and I are the only ones left."

"Waiting for *me?* But—"

Gottwald held up his hand. "No, not this way. I can show you better than I can tell you. If my people had lived—my other people, I should say, for I have lived on the Earth most of my life—there would have been an impressive ceremony. That can never be now. But I can show you the history lesson we prepared. Will you come with me? It is not far."

The old man turned and walked toward the door, his wife leaning on his arm.

"So long," she whispered. "We have waited so long."

Ben got up and followed them into the corridor.

In a large assembly room filled with empty seats, somewhere in the great deserted ship, Ben saw the history of Man.

It was more than a film, although a screen was used. Ben lived the history, felt it, was a part of it.

It was not a story of what King Glotz did to King Goop; the proud names of conventional history fade into insignificance when the perspective is broad enough. It was a story of Man, of all men.

It was Gottwald's story—and Ben's.

Ben lived it.

Millions of years ago, on a world that circled a sun so far away that the astronomers of Earth had no name for it and not even a number, a new animal called Man appeared. His evolution had been a freakish thing, a million-to-one shot, and it was not likely to be repeated.

Man, the first animal to substitute cultural growth for physical change, was an immediate success. His tools and his weapons grew ever more efficient. On his home world, Man was a patient animal—but he was Man.

He was restless, curious. One world could not hold him. He built his first primitive spaceships and set out to explore the great dark sea around him. He established colonies and bases on a few of the worlds of his star system. He looked outward, out along the infinite corridors of the universe, and it was not in him to stop.

He tinkered and worked and experimented.

He found the faster-than-light drive.

He pushed on through the terrible emptiness of interstellar space. He touched strange worlds and stranger suns—

And he found that Man was not alone.

There were ships greater than his, and Beings—

Man discovered the Enemy.

It was not a case of misunderstanding, not a failure of diplomacy, not an accident born of fear or greed or stupidity. Man was a civilized animal. He was careful, reasonable, prepared to do whatever was ethically right.

He had no chance.

The Enemy—pounced. That was the only word for it. They were hunters, destroyers, killers. They were motivated by a savage hunger for destruction that Man had never known. They took many shapes, many forms.

Ben saw them.

He saw them rip ships apart, gut them with an utter ferocity that was beyond understanding. He saw them tear human beings to shreds, and eat them, and worse—

The Beings were more different from Man than the fish that swim in the sea, and yet. . . .

Ben recognized them. He knew them.

They were there, all of them.

Literally, the Beings of nightmares.

The monsters that had troubled the dark sleeps of Earth, the things that crawled through myths, the Enemy who lived on the black side of the mind. The dragons, the serpents, the faces carved on masks, the Beings shaped in stones dug up in rotting jungles—

The Enemy.

We on Earth have not completely forgotten. We remember, despite the shocks that cleansed our minds. We remember, we remember. We have seen them in the darkness that lives always beyond the fires, we have heard them in the thunder that booms in the long, long night.

We remember.

It was not a war. A war, after all, is a specific kind of contest with rules of a sort. There were no rules. It was not a drive for conquest, not an attempt at exploitation. It was something new, something totally alien.

It was destruction.

It was extermination.

It was a fight between two different kinds of life, as senseless as a bolt of lightning that forked into the massive body of a screaming dinosaur.

Man wasn't ready.

He fell back, fighting where he could.

The Enemy followed.

Whether he liked it or not, Man was in a fight to the finish.

He fought for his life. He pushed himself to the utmost, tried everything he could think of, fought with everything he had. He exhausted his ingenuity. The Enemy countered his every move.

There was a limit.

Man could not go on.

Ben leaned forward, his fists clenched on his chair. He was a product of his culture. He read the books, saw the tri-di plays. He expected a happy ending.

There wasn't one.

Man lost.

He was utterly routed.

He had time for one last throw of the dice, one last desperate try for survival. He did his best.

He worked out the Plan.

It wasn't enough to run away, to find a remote planet and hide. It wasn't enough just to gain time.

Man faced the facts. He had met the Enemy and he had lost. He had tried everything he knew, and it hadn't been good enough. One day, no matter how far he ran, he would meet the Enemy again.

What could he do?

Man lives by his culture, his way of life. The potential for any culture is great, but it is not limitless. Culture has a way of putting blinders on its bearers; it leads them down certain paths and ignores others. Technological complexity is fine, but it is impotent without the one necessary ingredient:

Ideas.

Man needed new ideas, radically new concepts.

He needed a whole new way of thinking.

Transplanting the existing culture would not do the job. It would simply go on producing variants of the ideas that had already been tried.

Man didn't need transplanting.

He needed a transfusion, a transfusion of ideas.

He needed a brand new culture with fresh solutions to old problems.

There is only one way to get a really different culture pattern: grow it from scratch.

Sow the seeds and get out.

Man put the Plan into effect.

With the last of his resources, he outfitted four fugitive ships and sent them out into the wastes of the seas between the stars.

"We don't know what happened to the other three ships," Franz Gottwald said quietly when the projection was over. "No ship knew the destination of any other ship. They went in different directions, each searching for remote, hidden worlds that might become new homes for men. There is no way of knowing what became of the others; I think it highly unlikely that any of them survived."

"Then Earth is all there is?"

"That is what we believe, Ben—we have to go ahead on that assumption. You know most of the rest of the story. This ship slipped through the Enemy and found Earth. We landed human beings who were so conditioned that they could remember little or nothing, for they had to begin all over again. We planted the fossils and the apes as a test, just as you supposed."

"But why? There was no need for such a stunt—"

Gottwald smiled. "It wasn't a stunt, my boy. It was the key to everything. You see, we had to warn the men of Earth about what they had to face. More than that, once their cultures had developed along their own lines, we had to share what we had with them. I need hardly remind you that this ship is technologically many thousands of years ahead of anything the Earth has produced. But we couldn't turn the ship over to them until we were *certain* they were ready. You don't give atomic bombs to babies. The men of Earth had to *prove* that they could handle the toughest problem we could dream up. You solved it, Ben."

"I didn't do it alone."

"No, of course not. I can tell you now that my people—my other people—never did invent time travel. That was a totally unexpected means of tackling the problem; we never could have done it. It is the most hopeful thing that has happened."

"But what became of the men and women who stayed here on the ship?"

Franz shook his head. "Twenty-five thousand years is a long, long time, Ben. We were a defeated people. We worked hard; we were not idle. For one thing, we prepared dictionaries for every major language on Earth so that all the data in our libraries will be available to you. But man does not live well inside a ship. Each generation we became fewer; children were very scarce."

"It's like the old enigma of the cities, isn't it?"

"Exactly. No city in human history has ever reproduced its population. Urban births are always lower than rural ones. All cities have always drawn their personnel from the surrounding countryside. The ship was sealed up; we had no rural areas. It was only a matter of time before we were all gone. My wife and I were the last ones, Ben—and we had no children."

"We were so afraid," Mrs. Gottwald said. "So afraid that you would not come before it was too late."

"What would you have done?"

Franz shrugged wearily. "That is one decision I was spared. I did cheat a little, my boy. I was careful to give you no help, but I did plant some projectors near you that kept you stirred up. They broadcast frequencies that . . . ah . . . stimulate the mind, keep it in a state of urgency. Perhaps you noticed them?"

Ben nodded. He remembered the voice that spoke in his skull:

Hurry, hurry—

"Franz, what will happen now?"

Gottwald stroked his beard, his eyes very tired. "I can't tell you that. I don't know the answer. I have studied the men of Earth for most of my life, and I still don't know. You are a tough people, Ben, tougher than we ever were. You have fought many battles, and your history is a proud one. But I cannot read the future. I have done my best, and the rest is up to you."

"It's a terrible responsibility."

"Yes, for you and for others like you it will be a crushing burden. But it will be a long fight; we will not live to see more than the beginning of it. It will take centuries for the men of Earth to learn all that is in this ship. It's an odd thing, Ben—I have never seen the Enemy face to face. You will probably never see them. But what we do now will determine whether mankind lives or dies."

"It's too much for one man."

"Yes." Gottwald smiled, remembering. "It is."

"I don't know where to begin."

"We will wait for Edward—he will be here tomorrow, unless I don't know him at all—and then the three of us will sit down together for one last time. We will think it out. I am very tired, Ben; my wife and I have lived past our time. It is hard to be old, and to have no children. I always thought of you and Edward as my sons; I hope you do not find this too maudlin."

Ben searched for words and couldn't find any.

Franz put his arm around his wife. "Sometimes, when the job was too big for me, when I felt myself giving up, I would walk up into the old control room of this ship. My wife and I have stood there many times. Would you like to see it?"

"I need it, Franz."

"Yes. So do I. Come along."

They walked for what seemed to be miles through the dark passages of the empty ship, then rode a series of elevators up to the control room.

Franz switched on the lights.

"The ship is not dead, you know," he said. "It is only the people who are gone. The computers still maintain the ship's orbit, and the defensive screens still make it invulnerable to detection—you wouldn't have seen it if you had not been coming up the light tube, and there is no way the ship can be tracked from Earth. What do you think of the control room?"

Ben stared at it. It was a large chamber, acres in extent, but it was strangely empty. There were panels of switches and a few small machines, but the control room was mostly empty space.

"It's not what I expected," he said, hiding his disappointment.

Franz smiled. "When machinery is efficient you don't need a lot of it. There is no need for flashing lights and sparks of electricity. What you see here gets the job done."

Ben felt a sudden depression. He had badly needed a lift, and he didn't see it here. "If you'll forgive me for saying so, Franz, it isn't very inspiring. I suppose it is different for you—"

Gottwald answered him by throwing a switch.

Two immense screens flared into life, covering the whole front of the control room.

Ben caught his breath.

One of the screens showed the globe of the Earth far below, blue and green and necklaced with silver clouds.

The other showed the stars.

The stars were alive, so close he could almost touch them with his hand. They burned like radiant beacons in the cold sea of space. They whispered to him, called to him—

Ben knew then that the men of Earth had remembered something more than monsters and nightmares, something more than the fears and terrors that crept through the great dark night.

Not all the dreams had been nightmares.

Through all the years and all the sorrows, Man had never forgotten.

I remember. I remember.

I have seen you through all the centuries of nights. I have looked up to see you, I have lifted my head to pray, I have known wonder—

I remember.

Ben looked again at the sleeping Earth.

He sensed that Old Franz and his wife had drawn back into the shadows. He stood up straight, squaring his shoulders.

Then Ben Hazard turned once more and looked out into the blazing heritage of the stars.

I remember, I remember—

It has been long, but you, too, have not forgotten.

Wait for us.

We'll be back.

CHAPTER 2   JANE VAN LAWICK-GOODALL

IN THE SHADOW OF MAN

For about a month I spent most of each day either on the Peak or overlooking Mlinda Valley where the chimps, before or after stuffing themselves with figs, ate large quantities of small purple fruits that tasted, like so many of their foods, as bitter and astringent as sloes or crab apples. Piece by piece, I began to form my first somewhat crude picture of chimpanzee life.

The impression that I had gained when I watched the chimps at the msulula tree of temporary, constantly changing associations of individuals within the community was substantiated. Most often I saw small groups of four to eight moving about together. Sometimes I saw one or two chimpanzees leave such a group and wander off on their own or join up with a

From *In the Shadow of Man* Copyright © 1971 by Hugo and Jane Van Lawick-Goodall. Reprinted by permission of the publisher Houghton Mifflin Company and Collins & Publishers, London.

Human Nature and Culture

different association. On other occasions I watched two or three small groups joining to form a larger one.

Often, as one group crossed the grassy ridge separating the Kasekela Valley from the fig trees in the home valley, the male chimpanzee, or chimpanzees, of the party would break into a run, sometimes moving in an upright position, sometimes dragging a fallen branch, sometimes stamping or slapping the hard earth. These charging displays were always accompanied by loud pant-hoots and afterward the chimpanzee frequently would swing up into a tree overlooking the valley he was about to enter and sit quietly, peering down and obviously listening for a response from below. If there were chimps feeding in the fig trees they nearly always hooted back, as though in answer. Then the new arrivals would hurry down the steep slope and, with more calling and screaming, the two groups would meet in the fig trees. When groups of females and youngsters with no males present joined other feeding chimpanzees, usually there was none of this excitement; the newcomers merely climbed up into the trees, greeted some of those already there, and began to stuff themselves with figs.

While many details of their social behavior were hidden from me by the foliage, I did get occasional fascinating glimpses. I saw one female, newly arrived in a group, hurry up to a big male and hold her hand toward him. Almost regally he reached out, clasped her hand in his, drew it toward him, and kissed it with his lips. I saw two adult males embrace each other in greeting. I saw youngsters having wild games through the treetops, chasing around after each other or jumping again and again, one after the other, from a branch to a springy bough below. I watched small infants dangling happily by themselves for minutes on end, patting at their toes with one hand, rotating gently from side to side. Once two tiny infants pulled on opposite ends of a twig in a gentle tug-of-war. Often, during the heat of midday or after a long spell of feeding, I saw two or more adults grooming each other, carefully looking through the hair of their companions.

At that time of year the chimps usually went to bed late, making their nests when it was too dark to see properly through binoculars, but sometimes they nested earlier and I could watch them from the Peak. I found that every individual, except for infants who slept with their mothers, made his own nest each night. Generally this took about three minutes: the chimp chose a firm foundation such as an upright fork or crotch, or two horizontal branches. Then he reached out and bent over smaller branches onto this foundation, keeping each one in place with his feet. Finally he tucked in the small leafy twigs growing around the rim of his nest and lay down. Quite often a chimp sat up after a few minutes and picked a handful of leafy twigs, which he put under his head or some other part of his body before settling down again for the night. One young female I watched went on and on bending down branches until she had constructed a huge mound of greenery on which she finally curled up.

I climbed up into some of the nests after the chimpanzees had left them.

Most of them were built in trees that for me were almost impossible to climb. I found that there was quite complicated interweaving of the branches in some of them. I found, too, that the nests were never fouled with dung; and later, when I was able to get closer to the chimps, I saw how they were always careful to defecate and urinate over the edge of their nests, even in the middle of the night.

During that month I really came to know the country well, for I often went on expeditions from the Peak, sometimes to examine nests, more frequently to collect specimens of the chimpanzees' food plants, which Bernard Verd-court had kindly offered to identify for me. Soon I could find my way around the sheer ravines and up and down the steep slopes of three valleys—the home valley, the Pocket, and Mlinda Valley—as well as a taxi driver finds his way about in the main streets and byways of London. It is a period I remember vividly, not only because I was beginning to accomplish something at last, but also because of the delight I felt in being completely by myself. For those who love to be alone with nature I need add nothing further; for those who do not, no words of mine could ever convey, even in part, the almost mystical awareness of beauty and eternity that accompanies certain treasured moments. And, though the beauty was always there, those moments came upon me unaware: when I was watching the pale flush preceding dawn; or looking up through the rustling leaves of some giant forest tree into the greens and browns and black shadows that occasionally ensnared a bright fleck of the blue sky; or when I stood, as darkness fell, with one hand on the still-warm trunk of a tree and looked at the sparkling of an early moon on the never still, sighing water of the lake.

One day, when I was sitting by the trickle of water in Buffalo Wood, pausing for a moment in the coolness before returning from a scramble in Mlinda Valley, I saw a female bushbuck moving slowly along the nearly dry streambed. Occasionally she paused to pick off some plant and crunch it. I kept absolutely still, and she was not aware of my presence until she was little more than ten yards away. Suddenly she tensed and stood staring at me, one small forefoot raised. Because I did not move, she did not know what I was—only that my outline was somehow strange. I saw her velvet nostrils dilate as she sniffed the air, but I was downwind and her nose gave her no answer. Slowly she came closer, and closer—one step at a time, her neck craned forward—always poised for instant flight. I can still scarcely believe that her nose actually touched my knee; yet if I close my eyes I can feel again, in imagination, the warmth of her breath and the silken impact of her skin. Unexpectedly I blinked and she was gone in a flash, bounding away with loud barks of alarm until the vegetation hid her completely from my view.

It was rather different when, as I was sitting on the Peak, I saw a leopard coming toward me, his tail held up straight. He was at a slightly lower level than I, and obviously had no idea I was there. Ever since arrival in Africa I had had an ingrained, illogical fear of leopards. Already, while working at the Gombe, I had several times nearly turned back when, crawling through some thick undergrowth, I had suddenly smelled the rank smell of cat. I had forced myself on, telling myself that my fear was foolish, that only wounded leopards charged humans with savage ferocity.

On this occasion, though, the leopard went out of sight as it started to climb up the hill—the hill on the peak of which I sat. I quickly hastened to climb a tree, but halfway there I realized that leopards can climb trees. So I uttered a sort of halfhearted squawk. The leopard, my logical mind told me, would be just as frightened of me if he knew I was there. Sure enough, there was a thudding of startled feet and then silence. I returned to the Peak, but the feeling of unseen eyes watching me was too much. I decided to watch for the chimps in Mlinda Valley. And, when I returned to the Peak several hours later, there, on the very rock which had been my seat, was a neat pile of leopard dung. He must have watched me go and then, very carefully, examined the place where such a frightening creature had been and tried to exterminate my alien scent with his own.

As the weeks went by the chimpanzees became less and less afraid. Quite often when I was on one of my food-collecting expeditions I came across chimpanzees unexpectedly, and after a time I found that some of them would tolerate my presence provided they were in fairly thick forest and I sat still and did not try to move closer than sixty to eighty yards. And so, during my second month of watching from the Peak, when I saw a group settle down to feed I sometimes moved closer and was thus able to make more detailed observations.

It was at this time that I began to recognize a number of different individuals. As soon as I was sure of knowing a chimpanzee if I saw it again, I named it. Some scientists feel that animals should be labeled by numbers—that to name them is anthropomorphic—but I have always been interested in the *differences* between individuals, and a name is not only more individual than a number but also far easier to remember. Most names were simply those which, for some reason or other, seemed to suit the individuals to whom I attached them. A few chimps were named because some facial expression or mannerism reminded me of human acquaintances.

The easiest individual to recognize was old Mr. McGregor. The crown of his head, his neck, and his shoulders were almost entirely devoid of hair, but a slight frill remained around his head rather like a monk's tonsure. He was an old male—perhaps between thirty and forty years of age (the longevity record for a captive chimp is forty-seven years). During the early months of my acquaintance with him, Mr. McGregor was somewhat belligerent. If I accidentally came across him at close quarters he would threaten me with an upward and backward jerk of his head and a shaking of branches before climbing down and vanishing from my sight. He reminded me, for some reason, of Beatrix Potter's old gardener in *The Tale of Peter Rabbit*.

Ancient Flo with her deformed, bulbous nose and ragged ears was equally easy to recognize. Her youngest offspring at that time were two-year-old Fifi, who still rode everywhere on her mother's back, and her juvenile son, Figan, who was always to be seen wandering around with his mother and little sister. He was then about six years old; it was approximately a year before he would attain puberty. Flo often traveled with another old mother, Olly. Olly's long face was also distinctive; the fluff of hair on the back of her head—though no other feature—reminded me of my aunt, Olwen. Olly, like Flo, was accompanied by two children, a daughter younger than Fifi, and an adolescent son about a year older than Figan.

Then there was William, who, I am certain, must have been Olly's blood brother. I never saw any special signs of friendship between them, but their faces were amazingly alike. They both had long upper lips that wobbled when they suddenly turned their heads. William had the added distinction of several thin, deeply etched scar marks running down his upper lip from his nose.

Two of the other chimpanzees I knew well by sight at that time were David Graybeard and Goliath. Like David and Goliath in the Bible, these two individuals were closely associated in my mind because they were very often together. Goliath, even in those days of his prime, was not a giant, but he had a splendid physique and the springy movements of an athlete. He probably weighed about one hundred pounds. David Graybeard was less afraid of me from the start than were any of the other chimps. I was always pleased when I picked out his handsome face and well-marked silvery beard in a chimpanzee group, for with David to calm the others, I had a better chance of approaching to observe them more closely.

Before the end of my trial period in the field I made two really exciting discoveries—discoveries that made the previous months of frustration well worth while. And for both of them I had David Graybeard to thank.

One day I arrived on the Peak and found a small group of chimps just below me in the upper branches of a thick tree. As I watched I saw that one of them was holding a pink-looking object from which he was from time to time pulling pieces with his teeth. There was a female and a youngster and they were both reaching out toward the male, their hands actually touching his mouth. Presently the female picked up a piece of the pink thing and put it to her mouth: it was at this moment that I realized the chimps were eating meat.

After each bite of meat the male picked off some leaves with his lips and chewed them with the flesh. Often, when he had chewed for several minutes on this leafy wad, he spat out the remains into the waiting hands of the female. Suddenly he dropped a small piece of meat, and like a flash the youngster swung after it to the ground. Even as he reached to pick it up the undergrowth exploded and an adult bushpig ·charged toward him. Screaming, the juvenile leaped back into the tree. The pig remained in the open, snorting and moving backward and forward. Soon I made out the shapes of three small striped piglets. Obviously the chimps were eating a baby pig. The size was right and later, when I realized that the male was David Graybeard, I moved closer and saw that he was indeed eating piglet.

Human Nature and Culture

For three hours I watched the chimps feeding. David occasionally let the female bite pieces from the carcass and once he actually detached a small piece of flesh and placed it in her outstretched hand. When he finally climbed down there was still meat left on the carcass; he carried it away in one hand, followed by the others.

Of course I was not sure, then, that David Graybeard had caught the pig for himself, but even so, it was tremendously exciting to know that these chimpanzees actually ate meat. Previously scientists had believed that although these apes might occasionally supplement their diet with a few insects or small rodents and the like they were primarily vegetarians and fruit eaters. No one had suspected that they might hunt larger mammals.

It was within two weeks of this observation that I saw something that excited me even more. By then it was October and the short rains had begun. The blackened slopes were softened by feathery new grass shoots and in some places the ground was carpeted by a variety of flowers. The Chimpanzees' Spring, I called it. I had had a frustrating morning, tramping up and down three valleys with never a sign or sound of a chimpanzee. Hauling myself up the steep slope of Mlinda Valley I headed for the Peak, not only weary but soaking wet from crawling through dense undergrowth. Suddenly I stopped, for I saw a slight movement in the long grass about sixty yards away. Quickly focusing my binoculars I saw that it was a single chimpanzee, and just then he turned in my direction. I recognized David Graybeard.

Cautiously I moved around so that I could see what he was doing. He was squatting beside the red earth mound of a termite nest, and as I watched I saw him carefully push a long grass stem down into a hole in the mound. After a moment he withdrew it and picked something from the end with his mouth. I was too far away to make out what he was eating, but it was obvious that he was actually using a grass stem as a tool.

I knew that on two occasions casual observers in West Africa had seen chimpanzees using objects as tools: one had broken open palm-nut kernels by using a rock as a hammer, and a group of chimps had been observed pushing sticks into an underground bees' nest and licking off the honey. Somehow I had never dreamed of seeing anything so exciting myself.

For an hour David feasted at the termite mound and then he wandered slowly away. When I was sure he had gone I went over to examine the mound. I found a few crushed insects strewn about, and a swarm of worker termites sealing the entrances of the nest passages into which David had obviously been poking his stems. I picked up one of his discarded tools and carefully pushed it into a hole myself. Immediately I felt the pull of several termites as they seized the grass, and when I pulled it out there were a number of worker termites and a few soldiers, with big red heads, clinging on with their mandibles. There they remained, sticking out at right angles to the stem with their legs waving in the air.

Before I left I trampled down some of the tall dry grass and constructed a rough hide—just a few palm fronds leaned up against the low branch of a tree and tied together at the top. I planned to wait there the next day. But it was another week before I was able to watch a chimpanzee "fishing" for termites again. Twice chimps arrived, but each time they saw me and moved off immediately. Once a swarm of fertile winged termites—the princes and princesses, as they are called—flew off on their nuptial flight, their huge white wings fluttering frantically as they carried the insects higher and higher. Later I realized that it is at this time of year, during the short rains, when the worker termites extend the passages of the nest to the surface, preparing for these emigrations. Several such swarms emerge between October and January. It is principally during these months that the chimpanzees feed on termites.

On the eighth day of my watch David Graybeard arrived again, together with Goliath, and the pair worked there for two hours. I could see much better: I observed how they scratched open the sealed-over passage entrances with a thumb or forefinger. I watched how they bit the ends off their tools when they became bent, or used the other end, or discarded them in favor of new ones. Goliath once moved at least fifteen yards from the heap to select a firm-looking piece of vine, and both males often picked three or four stems while they were collecting tools, and put the spares beside them on the ground until they wanted them.

Most exciting of all, on several occasions they picked small leafy twigs and prepared them for use by stripping off the leaves. This was the first recorded example of a wild animal not merely *using* an object as a tool, but actually modifying an object and thus showing the crude beginnings of tool*making*.

Previously man had been regarded as the only tool-making animal. Indeed, one of the clauses commonly accepted in the definition of man was that he was a creature who "made tools to a regular and set pattern." The chimpanzees, obviously, had not made tools to any set pattern. Nevertheless, my early observations of their primitive tool-making abilities convinced a number of scientists that it was necessary to redefine man in a more complex manner than before. Or else, as Louis Leakey put it, we should by definition have to accept the chimpanzee as Man.

WOLF CHILD AND HUMAN CHILD

Kamala was to be her name; but for reasons passing strange, she did not come by her name until she was eight years old. We do not know what her mother called her.

India teems with life, with fathers, mothers, infants, domestic animals, wild beasts and jungles. Some even believe that India was the motherland of the human race and that from India also sprang the aboriginal wolf, progenitor of the European dog. No land is richer in folk lore which blends mankind and animal kind. Nowhere do animals and men live in closer association, both friendly and full of dread. Into this land Kamala was born.

India teems with villages; for not even the meanest farmer or goatherd wishes to live a solitary life. One of these villages is Godamuri, some seventy miles south and west of Calcutta in that luxuriant belt which stretches westward along the latitude of Bombay. In one of the mud and thatched huts of Godamuri a dark-skinned Hindoo mother, perhaps from the primitive tribe of Kora, gave birth to a daughter. An ancient midwife, we may suppose, gave attendance and comfort. Not much comfort was needed. Childbirth was an old story in this household. Perhaps there was expression of regret that this babe was a mere girl, when the father came home at evening with his white bullock dragging the plowshare which had turned the spring soil.

The manger of the bullock was near by. Man and beast lived in intimate association in this villager's hut. So thoroughly domesticated is the ox in India that he is reputed to have an almost human mien! If the ox did not hush his voice on seeing the newborn infant, he may yet have "bent trewe eyes of pitty ore the mow."

The very walls of this hut were covered with ox dung, applied as a kind of plaster which hardened in the Indian heat. And it was the dung of the ox which was burned in this hut when the chill air needed warming. The time would come when the sooty brown baby would need neither clothes nor fire to warm her even in the bleakest wintry weather.

She cried lustily enough for so young a child. But at a distance her cry sounded like a bleating not certainly distinguishable from the intermittent bleat of the kids stamping in the yard. In time, as we shall discover, that bleat was to transform into an unexampled high-pitched wail which, being of feral origin, was to sound unearthly to human ears.

From *Wolf Child and Human Child* by Arnold Gesell, pp. 9–13, 17–24, 27–33, 37–42, 47–53, and 62–63. Copyright 1940, 1941 by Arnold Gesell. Reprinted by permission of Harper and Row, Publishers, Inc.

Now the cry was addressed to the mother who gave heed and the child suckled. With a weaving, seeking movement of the head time and again by day and by night the baby sought the breast, found it without fail. And the child waxed and grew.

Most of the day as well as night the baby kept her eyes closed; but not because she feared the light. One evening at dusk, while she was basking in her corner in the folds of a villager's-wrapper, she caught sight of a lighted taper which the mother was carrying across the room quite slowly lest it blow out. The baby's eyes followed the flame across the void. This movement of the eyes was a significant expedition into the outer world. For weeks the infant had lain with head persistently averted to one side, but soon she was able to shift her head back and forth with increased freedom, exploring the universe which was more and more making its vast presence felt. Her arms likewise became emancipated, she flung them outward and then with infantile effort she brought her hands toward the midline as though she were intent to enfold this universe. And one day she succeeded in measure, for when she was about six months old, her dark-eyed brother dangled a rattling gourd before her: she seized it.

By such timely tokens it was evident that the baby was growing in mental as well as physical stature. She was becoming accustomed to surroundings; she was even building up expectations of what was about to happen. She turned her head responsively to the human voice; she gurgled and laughed on occasion.

She experienced the deepest satisfaction when she felt the snug pressure of adult hands, which held her in secure grasp and which rubbed her smooth swarthy skin with sweet-smelling ointment. In later years, but under strangely altered circumstances, she was again to feel hour upon hour the soothing massage of ministering hands. There was to be a dim reawakening and repetition of these profound tactile experiences of her infancy.

But in her own birthright she was already an active infant bent on creating experience rather than passively receiving it. She almost demanded to be propped up in a sitting position, so that she might survey the universe at eye level, for did not Nature intend that someday she was to stand erect and walk upright?

However, she also took an obvious delight in being placed on her stomach. She would momentarily erect her head with the alertness of a rabbit in the grass; but she could not sustain this head station long. Her head sank to the ground and then it would bob up again. She would rear her shoulders, too, and her back, and frog her legs as though to swim. Perhaps someday she would creep. Now, scarcely six months of age, even the tortoise could outstrip her. She could only sprawl. Yet wait. Someday she will indeed creep!

It was just at this time on a sunny afternoon late in autumn, and late in the day that her mother went out to the fields. Having other business (or this very business!) in mind, she laid her daughter prone in the stubble. The sky reddened; dusk crept over the fields, and in the distance out of a great white ant mound, stalked a wolf. Or was it the shadow of a wolf against the irradiated horizon?

It was a lone wolf, a she-wolf. She sniffed the air searchingly. She had smelled the comprehensive odor of the village, but in that complex there was a new specific trace of a fresh growing animal. Toward this molecular trace she pointed her nose. Her superb olfactory direction-finder sent immediate messages to her legs, and she hastened her steps to the exciting source. With extraordinary precision she arrived at the Baby-in-the-stubble.

It was a mother wolf; her teats were gorged; her eyes were preternaturally mild. She sniffed to test; she inspected; she sniffed in confirmation. She opened her jaws to an astounding, but not a threatening width. For with great gentleness she closed them softly and amply like prehensile forceps about the nape of the infant's neck.

And forceps they were. A wolf has no arms in which to carry a child. But a she-wolf whose whole being is warmed by the chemistry of maternal hormones can be as deft and gentle as a woman.

Slowly she ambled back to the great white mound from which she had emerged. It was now dark, but she knew her way unerringly. Gently she deposited her new-found cub among her other cubs.

·   ·   ·

There now were five cubs in the den if we count the man's cub. There were two or three adult wolves. Seven tunnels which led into the den allowed stray shafts of light to find a way to the dark interior. The white ants who had built this huge mound over ten feet high were no longer in possession. The low vaulted roof, the walls, the floor were earth. Furniture there was none. None was needed. These simple arrangements sufficed to make a home. They furnished a shelter to the foster infant for seven years.

Wolves are social animals. They keep in touch with each other through varied forms of communication. Their young can grow up only by looking and listening. Kamala also looked and listened. She began to troop along when at night the big wolves went on short expeditions. She imitated when she could. She "learned" to have her bowel movements outside the den and she even rubbed her haunches over the ground for cleanliness. She growled and bared her teeth defensively when she was molested while eating. She took the offensive with the wolves when they chased the vultures from coveted carrion.

She had no fear of the dark. If anything, she came to fear brightness and fire, for on occasion she noticed how her elders avoided them. Moreover, her eyes were not adapted to sunlight vision. Did she perhaps have a peculiar satisfaction in the vast redness of sunset, because this so often ushered in the pleasures of foray and food? She must have enjoyed many so-called animal satisfactions, of bodily activity, of gamboling, of hunger appeased, of muscles exercised and rested. And the night was better than the day.

During the day she dozed and idled in the den. The excitements came at night, and perhaps also a deep and mysterious sense of community with the pack.

This sense was yet more strangely stirred when Kamala was about seven years old. For then, of all unpredictable wonders, what should happen? Kamala's wolf mother adopted another human cub. And again it was a girl—Kamala's foster sister who was someday to be called Amala. Amala, too, was a tiny baby; but old enough to seek and secure sustenance as Kamala had done. And old enough to listen to sounds that had significance for the common life of the den and of the pack.

At three rather regular intervals throughout the night, at ten o'clock in the evening, and at one and three in the morning, the wolves would howl as though to announce their whereabouts to each other and to distant packs—a language cry, not an expression of rage or fear. Kamala and Amala both joined in this eerie cry.

It was a lesson they learned well; for later when they had been restored to a human abode in the Orphanage of Midnapore, they would howl as of yore. Three times in the dead of night, at ten, at one, and at three. Kamala's cry was a peculiar one, "neither human nor animal." It began with a hoarse voice and ended with a thrilling, shrilling wail—loud, continuous and piercing. It was one of her first and most important utterances: a generalized call not to her foster mother but to the whole pack. It was her vocabulary.

•   •   •

It was through an inspiration I was impelled to preach the Gospel to these people, in addition to the cares of the Midnapore parish.

Thus wrote the Reverend J. A. L. Singh in the Introduction to his notable *Diary of the Wolf Children of Midnapore.* And thus the pastor and his small party came upon a village named Godamuri bordering on Mourvanj.

We took shelter in a man's cowshed in the village. The man's name was Chunarem and he was Kora by race (one of the aboriginal tribes in India). At night he came to us and reported in great fear about a Man-Ghost in the jungle close by. The Manush-Bagha (Man-Ghost) was like a man in his limbs with a hideous head of a ghost. On inquiry, he told me that it could be seen at dusk. The spot he cited was about seven miles from the village. He and his wife begged me to rid the place of it as they were mortally frightened of it.

The same Saturday, October 9, 1920, evening, long before dusk, at about 4:30 or 5:00 p.m., we stealthily boarded the Machan *(a high platform from which to shoot wild animals) and anxiously waited for an hour or so. When all of a sudden, a grown-up wolf came out from one of the holes, which was very smooth on account of their constant egress and ingress. This animal was followed by another one of the same size and kind. The second one was followed by a third, closely followed by two cubs, one after the other. The holes did not permit two together.*

Close after the cubs came the ghost—a hideous-looking being—hand, foot, and body like a human being but the head was a big ball of something covering the shoulders and the upper portion of the bust, leaving only a sharp contour of the face visible, and it was human. Close at its heels came another awful creature exactly like the first, but smaller in size. Their eyes were bright and piercing, unlike human eyes. I at once came to the conclusion that these were human beings.

The first "ghost" appeared on the ground up to its bust, and placing its elbows on the edge of the hole, looked this side and that side, jumped out. It looked all round the place from the mouth of the hole before it leaped out to follow the cubs. It was followed by another tiny "ghost" of the same kind, behaving in the same manner.

These two "ghosts" were Kamala and Amala; though as yet they were not called by Christian names; nor were they obedient to the human voice.

•   •   •

On a Sunday morning several days later arrangements were made to dig into the den. Two grown wolves emerged and fled for their lives. The third—it was the mother wolf, stood her ground, gnashed her teeth with ferocity. In the confusion (for it had not been so planned) "the men pierced her through with arrows and she fell dead."

Kamala and Amala were now orphans indeed; and it was meet that they should be brought within the mercy of a missionary orphanage.

The new environment into which Kamala was thrust was extremely complicated when compared with the accustomed den, now demolished quite beyond recall. We must not overlook the difficulties of the novel surroundings, even though these were moderated at every turn by the humane spirit which pervaded the orphanage of Midnapore. Here Kamala would live the nine remaining years of her bewildering life.

It was a commodious, airy, sunlit establishment, with a cluster of closely related buildings, including a dormitory, dining room, laundry and school-room, a courtyard, many nooks and corners, pavements, paths, windows, doors, punkahs, cupboards, a well, a swing, and surrounding all a compound of over three acres. Of course there were books, rugs, carpets, dishes, toys, beds, big chairs, small chairs, middle-sized chairs, and an infinite variety of utensils and gadgets, so conspicuously lacking in Kamala's previous abode. There was a hen house for the chickens, a shed for the cow, shelter for puppies, goats, kids, and cats; a cage for the hyena cub. The grove of mango trees, the garden, the hayfield, the stream and the thick clump of lantana bushes—these must have seemed most "natural" of all to Kamala, particularly at night.

There were a score of children, most of whom walked upright, and made queer sounds with organs of speech, who laughed and scampered; and wore garments over their skins—these curious creatures in raiment must have seemed strange creatures to Kamala's untutored senses; in so far as there was any seeming at all.

There was a clock which guided and signaled the events of the day: the rising, the morning prayers, the bath and massage, the meals, lessons, the play hour, the stroll hours, church service, teatime, and bedtime. These events impinged upon Kamala, day in, day out, in recurrent routine and endless variation. To much she was at first indifferent, unaware or actually resistant. To all she was unattuned.

The food she understood best. But there was one occasion each day which in the end made the most profound penetration into her bewildered being. This was the morning massage. Every morning at four o'clock with rare devotion Mrs. Singh gave Kamala the benefit of her expert ministration. Bishop H. Pankenham-Walsh gives us the picture: "This massage was skillfully and tenderly done with many endearments from the top of the body down to the bottom, very special attention being given to those parts—the arms, hands, fingers, legs, feet, toes, etc., whose normal human development had been interfered with by the mode of life of the wolves. Mrs. Singh was a skilled masseuse and always stopped the massage of any part when Kamala seemed to be tired of it. The massage had a wonderful effect in strengthening and loosening Kamala's muscles for human use and in drawing her to trust in and love her tender foster-mother."

There is nothing more fundamental in the relationship between child and culture than a child's feeling of security. At first this feeling depends upon tactile-motor impressions, and on organic sensations of comfort. Especially during the first years of life, a child's sense of security is determined by the physical treatment he receives from day to day. He is psychologically so dependent that he cannot muster a sense of security out of his own being.

The sense of security is not a mysterious intuition, but an organic disposition built up cumulatively by daily experience. It is the patterned product of repeated, consistent satisfactions of organic needs. These needs include hunger and thirst, snugness and bodily safety; and later they include cravings for social attention and affection. Of all these needs the nutritional are the most profound and most insistent, and for these reasons the feeding experiences and the massage experiences of Kamala were fundamental to her rehabilitation.

Wolf ways Kamala retained, but she was also weaned from them. And in the long weaning process nothing proved more influential than the systematic massage—a truly therapeutic laying on of hands.

•   •   •

Kamala had adopted the ways of the wolf. How could she have done otherwise? And how could she be expected to shed these ways at once, even under the benign humanizing influences of her new-found home?

So wolf ways persisted. She ate her food by lapping it up; she slept and dozed by day or "mused" for long periods, sitting almost motionless with face directed toward the wall. She prowled about at night, and thrice in the night she howled in an unearthly manner which first startled the workers on the staff of the orphanage. But they soon became accustomed, from sheer repetition. For some time the weird nocturne remained in the ingrained behavior both of Kamala and Amala.

Night and day, reasoned the pastor, are by God's approving sanction, differently apportioned between man and animals. "As the day is for man, so the night is for animals. The whole creation is thus divided to suit both mankind and animal."

There is no doubt that the two wolf children were better suited for a nocturnal life. They had almost a photophobia. When the sun was shining they opened their eyes only narrowly and kept blinking. They could see well in shadow. In darkness a glow is said to have emanated from their eyes. From long habit, and perhaps metabolically, the children were well adapted to dark vision. Their movements took on freedom and courage at night. They roamed about the compound. Once they made an escape and ranged fearlessly about the fields, successfully playing hide-and-seek with their pursuers, from 11:00 P.M. to 2:00 A.M.!

Wolf ways persisted most strongly in Kamala's postural behavior. The basic framework of the action-system of all vertebrates is posture. Even in man the finer and subtler patterns of behavior are grafted on postural sets and postural attitudes. Kamala had basic ways of squatting, reclining, inspecting, sniffing, listening and of locomotion acquired in the wolf era of her developmental career. These motor sets constituted the core of her action-system and affected the organization of her personality.

She had two modes of prone progression: (1) on hands and knees; (2) on hands and feet. Accordingly she had three pairs of huge callosities: on the heels of her hands, on her knees, and soles. Human infants do not acquire such callosities for the prone stages of locomotion are transient. In the case of Kamala these modes of locomotion became all but fixed, and they would have continued had she lived with the wolves throughout childhood and adolescence. She used the hands-and-knees method for ordinary leisurely moving about in the den; she used the all-fours method for rapid transit outside the den and in pursuit of food. Even after several years of sojourn with upright human beings, quadrupedal locomotion was resorted to whenever speed was necessary. On two feet she never learned to run at all; on four feet she ran so fast it was hard to overtake her.

Nevertheless, it is recorded that on February 27, 1922, a year and a half after she was brought to the orphanage, Kamala *stood on her knees* whenever she chose to reach for something high. This was distinctly a developmental advance toward the mastery of standing. As a behavior pattern it was the counterpart of the spontaneous, independent standing observed in ordinary children soon after their first birthday. Kamala was at this time in her tenth year.

Three days later she walked forward on her knees. This is a most interesting observation. It means that in spite of a decade of quadrupedal locomotion the hereditary determiners for bipedal locomotion were available for a revised line of growth. Just as a normal infant who has gained the standing stance soon begins to walk on two feet, so Kamala had now arrived at a bi-patellar form of locomotion. The subsequent delay and difficulties in bipedal walking were due to orthopedic limitations rather than defective neural growth. The quadrupedal method of locomotion had modified the gross relationships of bones, muscles, and sinews.

The social behavior of Kamala bore the impress of wolverine ways and prejudices. The younger children tried to allure and entice her to play, but to no avail. She would sit aloof in a corner for hours at a stretch, her back to the children, her face to the wall, bestowing only forced or furtive glances on her well-meaning, would-be companions.

Toward Amala alone she showed a semblance of companionship; toward others, a mixture of shyness and aggressiveness. If approached she assumed a fierce expression and even showed her teeth.

But among the infants in the orphanage there was one named Benjamin who crawled about on the floor. For awhile it looked as though his quadrupedal status would have a socializing effect. Here was a chance for a palship; but on December 31, 1920, before the new year could begin, Kamala (and Amala too) scratched and bit Benjamin so severely that he never would approach them again. A month later they bit one of the orphan girls, and then escaped into the compound where it took much beating about in the bush to find them.

Kamala brought no table manners to the orphanage. She had never known a table. Hers were ground manners, and these she persisted in for at least two years. She brought her mouth to things, rather than things to her mouth. And since the orphanage had to adapt to Kamala (no less than Kamala had to adapt to the orphanage), food was habitually placed on the floor or ground rather than on a table. But in August, 1922, when Kamala was feeling the urge to stand upright, it was discovered that with a support to lean on she could stand on her knees at the edge of a table and use both hands to bring a plate of rice to her mouth.

Here was nothing less than an upward step toward true table manners. It was a fundamental step away from wolf manners. Noting this new behavior pattern, the Singhs stopped putting the food on the floor. They made nineteen small tables, thirty inches high, for Kamala and the younger babies, all of whom now began to take their food from the tables, kneeling.

Amenity came slowly. Kamala ate ravenously, rolled her eyes and made harsh sounds when any one approached while she was eating. Unprotected food, especially meat, she would steal without provocation. On the sixth of March, 1922, she found a dead chicken lying in the courtyard. She seized it in her jaws, ran on all fours into the bushes, and emerged with a telltale feather and particles of raw meat on lips and cheek. Questioned, she nodded a yes, possibly with a trace of contrition. She did much sniffing trying to locate food both inside and outside the house. As late as September, 1922 (two years after entering the orphanage), she was caught red-handed eating the entrails of a fowl which she had tracked down some eighty yards from the dormitory.

In varied directions wolf ways persisted even after human ways had been adopted. Before new habits became firmly fixed, rival old habits asserted their force. This did not, however, signify a split of personality. Even in the wolf den her mental organization must have remained integrated in spite of the enormously distorted realization of her potentialities. Her apparent reversions must not be weighted too heavily. She had much to shed as well as much to learn.

In the realm of feeding the learning came slowly. It was a triumph in the year 1922 to rise, if only on knees, to an upright posture to partake of food. It was an ascent from plantigrade posture. But it was not until five years later that meat could be left upon the table without Kamala's stealing it. However, by that time she had so far transcended wolf ways that she came regularly to the morning religious service, where she knelt in line with her fellow orphans who no longer called her "heathen."

Amala was an important factor in the weaning of Kamala. Poor Amala! If she had only lived she would have hastened and eased the transitions which it took Kamala years to achieve, for Amala was only a year and a half old when taken from the wolf den and she survived for less than a year more. Her wolf ways were much less firmly inwrought. Amala had been in the orphanage only two months when she said *bhoo* (water) to indicate thirst. Kamala, however, would only lick her dry lips. By reason of her tender age Amala gave promise of assimilating much more rapidly the human culture of the orphanage.

In all the social contacts with animals and with humans, Amala would take the lead and give the cue to Kamala. While Amala lived she was a support and a refuge for Kamala. Around Amala clustered a host of associations, tracing back to the ruined den, now so sorely missed. The windowless den with all its snugness and cosiness was gone forever. But there was Amala, a living familiar of the den—another wolf child with whom she had literally rubbed shoulders, day after day in the huddled companionship of waking and drowsing hours, and in the more intimate huddle of sleep. This was the tangible and visible Amala; there was also a reassuring olfactory aura about Amala. With Amala she had trooped at night. At Amala's side she had gorged many a meal. Perhaps she was even more attached to Amala than to the mother wolf who on that fateful morning died, pierced with arrows.

The drastic separation from den and foster mother, Amala and Kamala had suffered together. The death of Amala, Kamala suffered alone. For her departed sister Kamala shed her first recorded tears, one from each eye!

This second desolation coming within a year after the first was almost too much for the wolf girl to bear. There are no more pathetic lines in the diary than those which describe the grief and confusion of Kamala after the death of her human companion of the den.

Kamala clung with doglike tenacity to the spot where Amala lay dead. For two days she would neither eat nor drink. Water had to be forced upon her. For six days she sat in a corner all by herself. Ten days later (October 8) she was found smelling all the places where Amala had been. She no longer pursued the fowls in the courtyard as she had done. With panting tongue she remained outside in the heat. She moaned and roamed about in a dazed manner.

Kamala's confidence in the human species grew slowly but steadily. She looked with increasing intentness upon the activities of her orphanage mates. Early every morning at about five o'clock, Mrs. Singh instituted a greeting and short play period, for the benefit of all the children, but especially for Kamala. At first Kamala had regarded all this with indifference, but gradually she began to show interest. She also began to manifest interest in novelties like the new swing in the courtyard; a timid but positive curiosity displaced the former defiance. She grew softer in her ways and more amenable. She was more anxious to learn. When this learning attitude became habitual, another important stage in the weaning process had been reached; for with this fundamental change of attitude, wolf ways were increasingly shed for human ways.

In 1922 Kamala said *Ma* for Mrs. Singh, and later *bhoo bhoo* when hungry or thirsty. She learned to pull the punkah. One day she sat beside the large cloth frame and of her own accord seized the rope and began to pull it rhythmically. This became a favorite occupation. She liked to sit for hours at her self-appointed task which she performed so well that the official punkah-puller was greatly relieved.

She had become so socialized that she voluntarily went for strolls with the Singhs and the babies, though at these times she was animal enough still to run on all fours. She also cooperated in driving the crows away from the chicken feed. She had given up her previous ways so completely as to be afraid if left alone outside in the dark. She even howled on the old note when left thus alone.

In 1924 no marked advances in motor behavior were made. Language, however, increased rapidly. By February, 1924, she had six words, and under-

Human Nature and Culture

stood questions addressed to her, making verbal replies. She combined two words. By the end of the year it is noted that her vocabulary increased "by leaps and bounds, with small sentences." In this year she could name one color. During this year she exhibited even more fear of the dark than formerly, keeping close to the others when out at night for a walk. She showed a very human lonesomeness and peevishness when Mrs. Singh went away for a visit, and exhibited great pleasure when Mrs. Singh returned.

The change from wolf ways to human ways is succinctly shown in the behavior changes of daily routine which took place between 1921 and 1926. In 1921 Kamala lived like an animal, in the dark. Except when she was passively receiving attention from Mrs. Singh, she either roamed around outdoors, in the night, or sat quietly in a dark corner, facing the wall. She shunned sunlight and human company. Her chief vocalizations were wolf howls. Though she preferred to remain in the dark she slept little, perhaps four hours out of the twenty-four, at noon and midnight. She spent no time in spontaneous social relations with people and was awake and alone for approximately seventeen hours a day.

By 1926 Kamala was leading an essentially human existence. Her "behavior day" was comparable to that of other children in the orphanage. She now preferred daylight to darkness; human beings to animals. She spent the night in sleep in the dormitory as did the other children; she not only did not choose to roam around outside but was afraid if left alone outdoors. Of her own accord she spent most of her waking hours in the company of Mrs. Singh or of the other children, taking part in their activities. In contrast to her earlier solitary behavior, she now spent about twelve hours a day in sociable contact with others, and not more than three waking hours alone.

It is not without significance that after the year 1927 the entries of the diary are very meager. They make no mention of retrogressions. It appears that Kamala was now sufficiently normal to be taken for granted. Her behavior had become conventional and apparently she made consistent progress in speech for it is explicitly recorded that in her last illness she clearly distinguished by name between the two strange doctors who attended her. Although she became very weak and suffered long, she talked, and talked a great deal; and she talked "with the full sense of the words used."

But her life course had been run. In the quaint phrase of the diary, "Kamala, the wolf child, thus lingered in her last illness and gave up the ghost on the 14th morning at 4 A.M. in the month of November, 1929." The very word *ghost* startles memories of that earlier incarnation of the year 1920, when the terrified villagers of Godamuri reported the hideous *Manush-Bagha* (man-ghost) that emerged at dusk from the great white ant mound.

MAN'S SEARCH FOR MEANING

We waited in a shed which seemed to be the anteroom to the disinfecting chamber. SS men appeared and spread out blankets into which we had to throw all our possessions, all our watches and jewelry. There were still naïve prisoners among us who asked, to the amusement of the more seasoned ones who were there as helpers, if they could not keep a wedding ring, a medal or a good-luck piece. No one could yet grasp the fact that everything would be taken away.

I tried to take one of the old prisoners into my confidence. Approaching him furtively, I pointed to the roll of paper in the inner pocket of my coat and said, "Look, this is the manuscript of a scientific book. I know what you will say; that I should be grateful to escape with my life, that that should be all I can expect of fate. But I cannot help myself. I must keep this manuscript at all costs; it contains my life's work. Do your understand that?"

Yes, he was beginning to understand. A grin spread slowly over his face, first piteous, then more amused, mocking, insulting, until he bellowed one word at me in answer to my question, a word that was ever present in the vocabulary of the camp inmates: "Shit!" At that moment I saw the plain truth and did what marked the culminating point of the first phase of my psychological reaction: I struck out my whole former life.

Suddenly there was a stir among my fellow travelers, who had been standing about with pale, frightened faces, helplessly debating. Again we heard the hoarsely shouted commands. We were driven with blows into the immediate anteroom of the bath. There we assembled around an SS man who waited until we had all arrived. Then he said, "I will give you two minutes, and I shall time you by my watch. In these two minutes you will get fully undressed and drop everything on the floor where you are standing. You will take nothing with you except your shoes, your belt or suspenders, and possibly a truss. I am starting to count—now!"

With unthinkable haste, people tore off their clothes. As the time grew shorter, they became increasingly nervous and pulled clumsily at their underwear, belts and shoelaces. Then we heard the first sounds of whipping; leather straps beating down on naked bodies.

Next we were herded into another room to be shaved: not only our heads were shorn, but not a hair was left on our entire bodies. Then on to the showers, where we lined up again. We hardly recognized each other; but with great relief some people noted that real water dripped from the sprays.

While we were waiting for the shower, our nakedness was brought home to us: we really had nothing now except our bare bodies—even minus hair; all we possessed, literally, was our naked existence. What else remained for us as a material link with our former lives? For me there were my glasses and my belt; the latter I had to exchange later on for a piece of bread. There was an extra bit of excitement in store for the owners of trusses. In the evening the senior prisoner in charge of our hut welcomed us with a speech in which he gave us his word of honor that he would hang, personally, "from that beam"—he pointed to it—any person who had sewn money or precious stones into his truss. Proudly he explained that as a senior inhabitant the camp laws entitled him to do so.

Where our shoes were concerned, matters were not so simple. Although we were supposed to keep them, those who had fairly decent pairs had to give them up after all and were given in exchange shoes that did not fit. In for real trouble were those prisoners who had followed the apparently well-meant advice (given in the anteroom) of the senior prisoners and had shortened their jackboots by cutting the tops off, then smearing soap on the cut edges to hide the sabotage. The SS men seemed to have waited for just that. All suspected of this crime had to go into a small adjoining room. After a time we again heard the lashings of the strap, and the screams of tortured men. This time it lasted for quite a while.

Thus the illusions some of us still held were destroyed one by one, and then, quite unexpectedly, most of us were overcome by a grim sense of humor. We knew that we had nothing to lose except our so ridiculously naked lives. When the showers started to run, we all tried very hard to make fun, both about ourselves and about each other. After all, real water did flow from the sprays!

Apart from that strange kind of humor, another sensation seized us: curiosity. I have experienced this kind of curiosity before, as a fundamental reaction toward certain strange circumstances. When my life was once endangered by a climbing accident, I felt only one sensation at the critical moment: curiosity, curiosity as to whether I should come out of it alive or with a fractured skull or some other injuries.

Cold curiosity predominated even in Auschwitz, somehow detaching the mind from its surroundings, which came to be regarded with a kind of objectivity. At that time one cultivated this state of mind as a means of protection. We were anxious to know what would happen next; and what would be the consequence, for example, of our standing in the open air, in the chill of late autumn, stark naked, and still wet from the showers. In the next few days our curiosity evolved into surprise; surprise that we did not catch cold.

There were many similar surprises in store for new arrivals. The medical men among us learned first of all: "Textbooks tell lies!" Somewhere it is said that man cannot exist without sleep for more than a stated number of hours. Quite wrong! I had been convinced that there were certain things I just could not do: I could not sleep without this or I could not live with that or the other. The first night in Auschwitz we slept in beds which were constructed in tiers. On each tier (measuring about six-and-a-half to eight feet) slept nine men, directly on the boards. Two blankets were shared by each nine men. We could, of course, lie only on our sides, crowded and huddled against each other, which had some advantages because of the bitter cold. Though it was forbidden to take shoes up to the bunks, some people did use them secretly as pillows in spite of the fact that they were caked with mud. Otherwise one's head had to rest on the crook of an almost dislocated arm. And yet sleep came and brought oblivion and relief from pain for a few hours.

I would like to mention a few similar surprises on how much we could endure: we were unable to clean our teeth, and yet, in spite of that and a severe vitamin deficiency, we had healthier gums than ever before. We had to wear the same shirts for half a year, until they had lost all appearance of being shirts. For days we were unable to wash, even partially, because of frozen water pipes, and yet the sores and abrasions on hands which were dirty from work in the soil did not suppurate (that is, unless there was frostbite). Or for instance, a light sleeper, who used to be disturbed by the slightest noise in the next room, now found himself lying pressed against a comrade who snored loudly a few inches from his ear and yet slept quite soundly through the noise.

If someone now asked of us the truth of Dostoevski's statement that flatly defines man as a being who can get used to anything, we would reply, "Yes, a man can get used to anything, but do not ask us how." But our psychological investigations have not taken us that far yet; neither had we prisoners reached that point. We were still in the first phase of our psychological reactions.

The thought of suicide was entertained by nearly everyone, if only for a brief time. It was born of the hopelessness of the situation, the constant danger of death looming over us daily and hourly, and the closeness of the deaths suffered by many of the others. From personal convictions which will be mentioned later, I made myself a firm promise, on my first evening in camp, that I would not "run into the wire." This was a phrase used in camp to describe the most popular method of suicide—touching the electrically charged barbed-wire fence. It was not entirely difficult for me to make this decision. There was little point in committing suicide, since, for the average inmate, life expectation, calculating objectively and counting all likely chances, was very poor. He could not with any assurance expect to be among the small percentage of men who survived all the selections. The prisoner of Auschwitz, in the first phase of shock, did not fear death. Even the gas chambers lost their horrors for him after the first few days—after all, they spared him the act of committing suicide.

It was Lessing who once said, "There are things which must cause you

Human Nature and Culture

to lose your reason or you have none to lose." An abnormal reaction to an abnormal situation is normal behavior. Even we psychiatrists expect the reactions of a man to an abnormal situation, such as being committed to an asylum, to be abnormal in proportion to the degree of his normality. The reaction of a man to his admission to a concentration camp also represents an abnormal state of mind, but judged objectively it is a normal and, as will be shown later, typical reaction to the given circumstances. These reactions, as I have described them, began to change in a few days. The prisoner passed from the first to the second phase: the phase of relative apathy, in which he achieved a kind of emotional death.

Apart from the already described reactions, the newly arrived prisoner experienced the tortures of other most painful emotions, all of which he tried to deaden. First of all, there was his boundless longing for his home and his family. This often could become so acute that he felt himself consumed by longing. Then there was disgust; disgust with all the ugliness which surrounded him, even in its mere external forms.

Most of the prisoners were given a uniform of rags which would have made a scarecrow elegant by comparison. Between the huts in the camp lay pure filth, and the more one worked to clear it away, the more one had to come in contact with it. It was a favorite practice to detail a new arrival to a work group whose job was to clean the latrines and remove the sewage. If, as usually happened, some of the excrement splashed into his face during its transport over bumpy fields, any sign of disgust by the prisoner or any attempt to wipe off the filth would only be punished with a blow from a Capo. And thus the mortification of normal reactions was hastened.

At first the prisoner looked away if he saw the punishment parades of another group; he could not bear to see fellow prisoners march up and down for hours in the mire, their movements directed by blows. Days or weeks later things changed. Early in the morning, when it was still dark, the prisoner stood in front of the gate with his detachment, ready to march. He heard a scream and saw how a comrade was knocked down, pulled to his feet again, and knocked down once more—and why? He was feverish but had reported to sick-bay at an improper time. He was being punished for this irregular attempt to be relieved of his duties.

But the prisoner who had passed into the second stage of his psychological reactions did not avert his eyes any more. By then his feelings were blunted, and he watched unmoved. Another example: he found himself waiting at sick-bay, hoping to be granted two days of light work inside the camp because of injuries or perhaps edema or fever. He stood unmoved while a twelve-year-old boy was carried in who had been forced to stand at attention for hours in the snow or to work outside with bare feet because there were no shoes for him in the camp. His toes had become frostbitten, and the doctor on duty picked off the black gangrenous stumps with tweezers, one by one. Disgust, horror and pity are emotions that our spectator could not really feel any more. The sufferers, the dying and the dead, became such commonplace sights to him after a few weeks of camp life that they could not move him any more.

I spent some time in a hut for typhus patients who ran very high temperatures and were often delirious, many of them moribund. After one of them had just died, I watched without any emotional upset the scene that followed, which was repeated over and over again with each death. One by one the prisoners approached the still warm body. One grabbed the remains of a messy meal of potatoes; another decided that the corpse's wooden shoes were an improvement on his own, and exchanged them. A third man did the same with the dead man's coat, and another was glad to be able to secure some—just imagine!—genuine string.

All this I watched with unconcern. Eventually I asked the "nurse" to remove the body. When he decided to do so, he took the corpse by its legs, allowing it to drop into the small corridor between the two rows of boards which were the beds for the fifty typhus patients, and dragged it across the bumpy earthen floor toward the door. The two steps which led up into the open air always constituted a problem for us, since we were exhausted from a chronic lack of food. After a few months' stay in the camp we could not walk up those steps, which were each about six inches high, without putting our hands on the door jambs to pull ourselves up.

The man with the corpse approached the steps. Wearily he dragged himself up. Then the body: first the feet, then the trunk, and finally—with an uncanny rattling noise—the head of the corpse bumped up the two steps.

My place was on the opposite side of the hut, next to the small, sole window, which was built near the floor. While my cold hands clasped a bowl of hot soup from which I sipped greedily, I happened to look out the window. The corpse which had just been removed stared in at me with glazed eyes. Two hours before I had spoken to that man. Now I continued sipping my soup.

If my lack of emotion had not surprised me from the standpoint of professional interest, I would not remember this incident now, because there was so little feeling involved in it.

Apathy, the blunting of the emotions and the feeling that one could not care any more, were the symptoms arising during the second stage of the prisoner's psychological reactions, and which eventually made him insensitive to daily and hourly beatings. By means of this insensibility the prisoner soon surrounded himself with a very necessary protective shell.

Beatings occurred on the slightest provocation, sometimes for no reason at all. For example, bread was rationed out at our work site and we had to line up for it. Once, the man behind me stood off a little to one side and that lack of symmetry displeased the SS guard. I did not know what was going on in the line behind me, nor in the mind of the SS guard, but suddenly I received two sharp blows on my head. Only then did I spot the guard at my side who was using his stick. At such a moment it is not the physical pain which hurts the most (and this applies to adults as much as to punished children); it is the mental agony caused by the injustice, the unreasonableness of it all.

Strangely enough, a blow which does not even find its mark can, under certain circumstances, hurt more than one that finds its mark. Once I was standing on a railway track in a snowstorm. In spite of the weather our party had to keep on working. I worked quite hard at mending the track with gravel, since that was the only way to keep warm. For only one moment I paused to get my breath and to lean on my shovel. Unfortunately the guard turned around just then and thought I was loafing. The pain he caused me was not from the insults or the blows. That guard did not think it worth his while to say anything, not even a swear word, to the ragged, emaciated figure standing before him, which probably reminded him only vaguely of a human form. Instead, he playfully picked up a stone and threw it at me. That, to me, seemed the way to attract the attention of a beast, to call a domestic animal back to its job, a creature with which you have so little in common that you do not even punish it.

The most painful part of beatings is the insult which they imply. At one time we had to carry some long, heavy girders over icy tracks. If one man slipped, he endangered not only himself but all the others who carried the same girder. An old friend of mine had a congenitally dislocated hip. He was glad to be capable of working in spite of it, since the physically disabled were almost certainly sent to death when a selection took place. He limped over the track with an especially heavy girder, and seemed about to fall and drag the others with him. As yet, I was not carrying a girder so I jumped to his assistance without stopping to think. I was immediately hit on the back, rudely reprimanded and ordered to return to my place. A few minutes previously the same guard who struck me had told us deprecatingly that we "pigs" lacked the spirit of comradeship.

Another time, in a forest, with the temperature at $2°F$, we began to dig up the topsoil, which was frozen hard, in order to lay water pipes. By then I had grown rather weak physically. Along came a foreman with chubby rosy cheeks. His face definitely reminded me of a pig's head. I noticed that he wore lovely warm gloves in that bitter cold. For a time he watched me silently. I felt that trouble was brewing, for in front of me lay the mound of earth which showed exactly how much I had dug.

Then he began: "You pig, I have been watching you the whole time! I'll teach you to work, yet! Wait till you dig dirt with your teeth—you'll die like an animal! In two days I'll finish you off! You've never done a stroke of work in your life. What were you, swine? A businessman?"

I was past caring. But I had to take his threat of killing me seriously, so I straightened up and looked him directly in the eye. "I was a doctor—a specialist."

"What? A doctor? I bet you got a lot of money out of people."

"As it happens, I did most of my work for no money at all, in clinics for the poor." But, now, I had said too much. He threw himself on me and knocked me down, shouting like a madman. I can no longer remember what he shouted.

I want to show with this apparently trivial story that there are moments when indignation can rouse even a seemingly hardened prisoner—indignation not about cruelty or pain, but about the insult connected with it.

I shall never forget how I was roused one night by the groans of a fellow prisoner, who threw himself about in his sleep, obviously having a horrible nightmare. Since I had always been especially sorry for people who suffered from fearful dreams or deliria, I wanted to wake the poor man. Suddenly I drew back the hand which was ready to shake him, frightened at the thing I was about to do. At that moment I became intensely conscious of the fact that no dream, no matter how horrible, could be as bad as the reality of the camp which surrounded us, and to which I was about to recall him.

Because of the high degree of undernourishment which the prisoners suffered, it was natural that the desire for food was the major primitive instinct around which mental life centered. Let us observe the majority of prisoners when they happened to work near each other and were, for once, not closely watched. They would immediately start discussing food. One fellow would ask another working next to him in the ditch what his favorite dishes were. Then they would exchange recipes and plan the menu for the day when they would have a reunion—the day in a distant future when they would be liberated and returned home. They would go on and on, picturing it all in detail, until suddenly a warning was passed down the trench, usually in the form of a special password or number: "The guard is coming."

I always regarded the discussions about food as dangerous. Is it not wrong to provoke the organism with such detailed and affective pictures of delicacies when it has somehow managed to adapt itself to extremely small rations and low calories? Though it may afford momentary psychological relief, it is an illusion which physiologically, surely, must not be without danger.

During the latter part of our imprisonment, the daily ration consisted of very watery soup given out once daily, and the usual small bread ration. In addition to that, there was the so-called "extra allowance," consisting of three-fourths of an ounce of margarine, or of a slice of poor quality sausage, or of a little piece of cheese, or a bit of synthetic honey, or a spoonful of watery jam, varying daily. In calories, this diet was absolutely inadequate, especially taking into consideration our heavy manual work and our constant exposure to the cold in inadequate clothing. The sick who were "under special care"—that is, those who were allowed to lie in the huts instead of leaving the camp for work—were even worse off.

When the last layers of subcutaneous fat had vanished, and we looked like skeletons disguised with skin and rags, we could watch our bodies beginning to devour themselves. The organism digested its own protein, and the muscles disappeared. Then the body had no powers of resistance left. One after another the members of the little community in our hut died. Each

Human Nature and Culture

of us could calculate with fair accuracy whose turn would be next, and when his own would come. After many observations we knew the symptoms well, which made the correctness of our prognoses quite certain. "He won't last long," or, "This is the next one," we whispered to each other, and when, during our daily search for lice, we saw our own naked bodies in the evening, we thought alike: This body here, my body, is really a corpse already. What has become of me? I am but a small portion of a great mass of human flesh . . . of a mass behind barbed wire, crowded into a few earthen huts; a mass of which daily a certain portion begins to rot because it has become lifeless.

I mentioned above how unavoidable were the thoughts about food and favorite dishes which forced themselves into the consciousness of the prisoner, whenever he had a moment to spare. Perhaps it can be understood, then, that even the strongest of us was longing for the time when he would have fairly good food again, not for the sake of good food itself, but for the sake of knowing that the subhuman existence, which had made us unable to think of anything other than food, would at last cease.

Those who have not gone through a similar experience can hardly conceive of the soul-destroying mental conflict and clashes of will power which a famished man experiences. They can hardly grasp what it means to stand digging in a trench, listening only for the siren to announce 9:30 or 10:00 A.M.—the half-hour lunch interval—when bread would be rationed out (as long as it was still available); repeatedly asking the foreman—if he wasn't a disagreeable fellow—what the time was; and tenderly touching a piece of bread in one's coat pocket, first stroking it with frozen gloveless fingers, then breaking off a crumb and putting it in one's mouth and finally, with the last bit of will power, pocketing it again, having promised oneself that morning to hold out till afternoon.

I mentioned earlier how everything that was not connected with the immediate task of keeping oneself and one's closest friends alive lost its value. Everything was sacrificed to this end. A man's character became involved to the point that he was caught in a mental turmoil which threatened all the values he held and threw them into doubt. Under the influence of a world which no longer recognized the value of human life and human dignity, which had robbed man of his will and had made him an object to be exterminated (having planned, however, to make full use of him first—to the last ounce of his physical resources)—under this influence the personal ego finally suffered a loss of values. If the man in the concentration camp did not struggle against this in a last effort to save his self-respect, he lost the feeling of being an individual, a being with a mind, with inner freedom and personal value. He thought of himself then as only a part of an enormous mass of people; his existence descended to the level of animal life. The men were herded—sometimes to one place then to another; sometimes driven together, then apart—like a flock of sheep without a thought or a will of their own. A small but dangerous pack watched them from all sides, well versed in methods of torture and sadism. They drove the herd incessantly, backwards and forwards, with shouts, kicks and blows. And we, the sheep, thought of two things only—how to evade the bad dogs and how to get a little food.

Just like sheep that crowd timidly into the center of a herd, each of us tried to get into the middle of our formations. That gave one a better chance of avoiding the blows of the guards who were marching on either side and to the front and rear of our column. The central position had the added advantage of affording protection against the bitter winds. It was, therefore, in an attempt to save one's own skin that one literally tried to submerge into the crowd. This was done automatically in the formations. But at other times it was a very conscious effort on our part—in conformity with one of the camp's most imperative laws of self-preservation: Do not be conspicuous. We tried at all times to avoid attracting the attention of the SS.

There were times, of course, when it was possible, and even necessary, to keep away from the crowd. It is well known that an enforced community life, in which attention is paid to everything one does at all times, may result in an irresistible urge to get away, at least for a short while. The prisoner craved to be alone with himself and his thoughts. He yearned for privacy and for solitude. After my transportation to a so-called "rest camp," I had the rare fortune to find solitude for about five minutes at a time. Behind the earthen hut where I worked and in which were crowded about fifty delirious patients, there was a quiet spot in a corner of the double fence of barbed wire surrounding the camp. A tent had been improvised there with a few poles and branches of trees in order to shelter a half-dozen corpses (the daily death rate in the camp). There was also a shaft leading to the water pipes. I squatted on the wooden lid of this shaft whenever my services were not needed. I just sat and looked out at the green flowering slopes and the distant blue hills of the Bavarian landscape, framed by the meshes of barbed wire. I dreamed longingly, and my thoughts wandered north and northeast, in the direction of my home, but I could only see clouds.

PART TWO

SUBSISTENCE AND ECONOMIC EXCHANGE

All animals face the common challenge of biological survival. At least three conditions influence the maintenance of life: the material requirements of the organism, environmental conditions, and the characteristics and behavior of the organism. In contrast to man, one-celled animals require relatively little to maintain metabolism. Their temperatures may vary over a wide range, they can survive outside of a social existence, and each organism can supply its own food and moisture. For most animals the task of dealing with the environment to meet their material requirements is taken care of by unlearned, instinctual behavior. But man must learn the ways that will effectively meet his physical needs.

It is the function of every culture to provide the plans or blueprints for the production and distribution of goods and services necessary for physical survival. Numerous combinations can be worked into a cultural blueprint for producing food and clothing. Hunting and gathering generally provide a meager economic base unless a society has an unusually rich environment like the Northwest coast of America. There, such groups as the Tlingit, Tsimshian, and Kwakiutl were able to harvest enough salmon from rivers and streams to support a large population. The agricultural revolution has changed the nature of human societies, and for thousands of years man has produced his food by domesticating animals and plants. Producing goods by means of factories and industrialization has brought about another revolutionary change. Although some societies still depend upon one kind of subsistence activity, most use several strategies for meeting human needs.

In every culture, activities for producing goods to meet the basic physical requirements of man are allocated to different people. Every society has a division of labor. In hunting, gathering, and horticultural societies, men almost always hunt the larger game, and women may care for gardens, fish, or tend pigs. Agricultural and industrial societies have developed a much greater specialization of occupational roles. Because one person can rarely produce all the goods and services he requires, economic exchange occurs in every society, increasing with the specialization of economic roles.

There are at least three major principles of economic exchange: reciprocity, redistribution, and market exchange.

Reciprocity often resembles an exchange of gifts in which one person freely gives food or other goods to another. Implicit in this gift is the expectation that the recipient will return a gift from his own resources. Reciprocity operates between members of a group that share a minimum of trust and good will. Redistribution depends upon a powerful authority who receives goods from those under his power and redistributes them. Our own government collects taxes, which are then redistributed to various sectors of society in the form of highway funds, welfare payments, and farm subsidies. Market exchange is based on a competitive principle of supply and demand. Goods and services are often converted into monetary values for this kind of exchange.

The values that underlie subsistence and economic exchange differ from one society to another. More important, economic values in small societies are intertwined with kinship, religion, and political behavior. In the following selections people engage in behavior that meets their basic physical requirements, but often this behavior is bound up with activities that serve other ends. Subsistence and economic exchange always occur within a cultural context and have far more meaning to the individual than mere physical survival.

THE WHITE DAWN: AN ESKIMO SAGA

In the morning I awoke before dawn and heard people hacking and coughing. Men and women from the camp were stirring in the darkness of the tents, crawling from beneath the two big boats. Outside, the black rocks were slick with ice, but the wind was down, and the cold sea heaved smoothly with a long gray swell as though some monstrous beast lay beneath the surface, gasping, sighing, slowly expanding and contracting its great rib cage, causing the sea to ebb and flow endlessly against the long black arm of rock.

Men and women carried the hunting gear out quietly and laid it down beside the upturned kayaks. Out in the darkness of the heaving sea the low smooth rock lay wrapped in mist, hidden from us, waiting for our arrival. Dawn came slowly, gently unfolding its pale wings across the eastern sky. At first light men lifted their thin-skinned kayaks over their heads, carefully carried them down through the rocks and placed them cautiously in the water. I saw Poota and Sowniapik slip quickly into their long slim craft and push out into the powerful swell that bounded dangerously back from the rock face. Then Kangiak and the four others pushed away from the land and formed together like a loose wedge of geese. The women and children stood silently in front of the tents, watching the kayakmen stroke their way out steadily toward the rock.

With one hand the men arranged their gear around them. Each hunter placed his harpoon in the ivory rest on the right side of the slender deck and his killing spear on the left, and neatly coiled the harpoon line in the shallow drum that rested in the center of the narrow skin deck. Behind each kayakman on the back deck lay an airtight sealskin float, which was half inflated and attached by a long line to the harpoon.

As the others moved out, I followed behind them in the old widow's kayak. I could feel my throat go dry and my shoulders hunch as the strength ran tingling down through my arms. With the long, narrow double-bladed paddle I forced the slim craft forward until I reached the center of the wedge of kayaks and heard the soft slap of water on their sides.

When I looked back at the tents, I saw Sarkak's figure standing motionless and alone, down at the very edge of the water. On the highest boulder halfway between the women and the sea, I saw the three foreigners standing together. They must only now have become aware that a hunt was taking place, aware that something important was about to happen to us all.

The breeze shifted slightly, gaining strength with the coming of morning, and the smell of the walrus came to me again. It was overpowering this time, laden with the heavy night smell of rut and excrement. A light gust of wind opened the fog, and for a brief moment I could see the rock. It was covered with a solid living mass of walrus. All the kayakmen moved forward into the wind, confident that the weak-eyed animals could not see or smell them. Perhaps none of these sea beasts had ever seen a man before, yet we and the killer whales that ranged beyond the ice were their only true enemies. I felt my heart pounding as I saw the big muscular brown bodies humping forward in a rhythmic flow as they pressed tightly one against the other to allow more and more walrus to leave the sea and crowd up onto the smooth black rock, their breaths steaming white in the morning stillness.

As we paddled forward, I could feel the silence. Then suddenly the air filled with a strange wild tenseness. The whole herd had become aware of us. Suddenly the walrus stopped their endless swaying and became motionless. They became like an island of carved brown stones. Every head turned in our direction, the thin-tusked females listening, the big bulls holding their heads high, their heavy white tusks curving down dangerously like knives as they peered, weak-eyed and wary, into the fog.

Then we heard the first challenge, a deep-throated, grunting roar. Four times it rumbled up to us from the belly of a huge bull walrus weighing twenty times more than one of the men who hunted him. This big bull proclaimed himself the leader, the fighter, the strongest on the rock. He could smell us now and see us. He roared again, and shouldering the younger males and females aside, he violently heaved his great bulk down off the rock with a series of powerful thrusts on his short wide-webbed flippers. Out of the water he was battle-scarred and clumsy, but when he slipped his huge brown bulk into the sea, he seemed as sleek and graceful as a salmon disappearing smoothly beneath the surface. All of us eased our harpoons from their ivory rests and waited.

Our eight kayaks were strung out in a long curved line, waiting to see what would happen. Suddenly this great walrus rose out of the water, roaring, thrashing, red eyes rolling, warning us away from his females. He caught sight of Nowya's kayak first and lunged toward it. Nowya snatched up his harpoon. He swung his right arm smoothly backward and then darted it forward. The harpoon slipped through the air, flat above the water, the line whipping after it, uncoiling like a living entrail. Its sleek point drove deep into the thick leather that protected the bull walrus' neck. The whole harpoon head was buried, and the harpoon's heavy driftwood shaft collapsed, as it should, into three pieces loosely tied together. If it had remained stiff, it would have torn loose when the big beast thrashed in the sea.

The bull walrus dove, and Nowya swept his hand across the back deck of his kayak, knocking free the air-filled sealskin float. It flipped upright, danced on the water, then disappeared beneath the surface as the great bull lunged into the depths of the sea. In doing this the walrus snapped the sharpened harpoon head sideways, and it cut into the thick layer of blubber that lay beneath the tough brown leather of his skin. The point was now embedded forever. It would not come free until some human cut it from him with a knife. But this battle had only begun.

I was near Nowya and saw him as he turned his head sideways and gestured to us, so wild was he with the excitement of the hunt. He had been the first to set the point of his harpoon into this great prize. But he should not have turned his head or taken his thoughts from that enormous sea beast. As I watched him, I saw his body and then his whole kayak thrust violently upward out of the water. It seemed to pause for a moment, balanced on top of the great thrashing walrus head. Then the long thin kayak bent and skidded in the air as it turned over. I heard the sealskin tearing and the ribs breaking. Nowya was upside down. He was only half out of his broken kayak when he struck the freezing water. I saw his head snap back sickeningly as he disappeared and as the walrus' bulk seemed to crash down on top of him. The sea turned pink in a tangle of wreckage amid coils of skin line and a float that danced like a living thing. The empty broken kayak filled with water and began to sink beneath the surface. All we ever saw of Nowya was one black boot as it raised above the water, twitched and sank as he slipped away from us forever.

The big bull sulked beneath the surface of the sea until his lungs were almost bursting. Once more he flung himself boldly upward into our midst, gasping for air. Two harpoons flew out and struck him before he could draw his second breath, and we shouted at him in our anguish and hit the water with the flat sides of our double-bladed paddles. His instincts caused him to duck beneath the surface again, this time without enough air. We watched the three floats and drew near the place where he would have to surface again.

From the corner of my eye I could see and hear the whole herd on the rock, swaying with excitement, roaring in fear and confusion, bellowing their defiance as they started to lunge into the safety of the sea.

Suddenly this killer of Nowya reappeared among us, head flung back, red-eyed and roaring, lungs heaving, white tusks deadly. I do not think he even saw us. Sowniapik drove his paddle into the water with force, making his kayak slip forward and swing to the left, and instantly he snatched up his killing spear and drove it in and out of the bull's throat three times. Then, with his paddle in his left hand, he quickly drew back out of danger. The big bull coughed deeply, and pink blood came frothing up from his lungs. When he next rolled to dive, the water turned red, then almost black, as his heart pumped dark rich blood into the coldness of the sea. We turned away from him, for we knew that he was dying now and that all his meat was ours, safely held with three harpoons and floats.

With Kangiak beside me we turned our kayaks and went toward the rock. It was almost clear of walrus now, save one young bull who waited there, nervously holding back, roaring fiercely at some frightened females just below him in the water. All memory of Nowya's drowning faded from my mind as I thought of the huge abundance of meat swimming live before me, grunting and blowing and surging through the deep clear water.

I followed the young bull, who jealously herded a dozen females ahead of him, roaring and threatening them with his tusks when they panicked and tried to break away from him. I pressed in upon him, and he turned and lunged toward me across the surface of the water. My harpoon struck him in the fold of the neck, and as he dove, I used his great rolling body like a rock to shove my thin-skinned kayak away from him. As I waited for him to surface again, I peered nervously down into the water, not only for the young bull, but because the sea around me was full of frightened females scattered from the herd and swimming for their lives. When they rose for air or to search for the herd, they could easily turn over a kayak. Many men have drowned in this way.

Every kayakman seemed to have a walrus harpooned and fighting hard against a float. Their killing spears darted in their hands. My heart sang, and my hands trembled with joy, and gas thundered out of me and drummed against the boat bottom as I saw this great weight of meat around me. For in these few moments our whole camp had been allowed to push death away and return to life. I was shaking so in my excitement that it took several thrusts with the killing spear before the young bull ceased his thrashing and floated peacefully beside me. He left a shining trail of oil on the surface of the freezing water, reflecting like a rainbow of light as the new dawn filled the sky.

Far away on the long arm of rocky land I heard the faint screaming of the women, birdlike in their chorus of delight, and then for the first time that day I saw the umiak. Standing up in the bow was the big Portagee, and rowing hard behind him stood Kakuktak and Pilee. In the stern of the boat on the heavy gunwale sat Sarkak, short and squat in his bulky dog-skin parka, his hood flung back, his long hair blowing out in the wind, as he worked the stern oar with all the cleverness that he possessed.

I caught the harpoon line attached to my upturned floating walrus and pulled my kayak to him. Carefully I cut a hole in his thick upper lip beside his tusks and passed a strong line through it. Then, like the others, I started to paddle against the tide that was starting to run out with increasing force. I used all the strength of my arms, and yet I scarcely moved the kayak or the walrus, so great was the dead weight of that dear sea beast.

When I rested, I looked up and saw the big clumsy umiak approaching me, moving fast through the water. It was rowed by Kakuktak, Pilee and three of the strongest boys. They stood up facing the bow, pushing on the heavy oars. Sarkak sat high on the rear thwart, steering with the heavy stern sweep. In the bow stood Portagee, rigid as a stone carving. Everything about him seemed familiar to me, for was this not exactly as he had stood in the pantomime of the whaling boat up on the hill behind the camp?

He held the harpoon in a strange manner. His right hand cupped the butt and held it stiffly above his head; his left arm, straight before him, aimed the point at the water dead ahead of him. He stared down into the sea and waited.

A bull walrus rose before him, and I saw the oarsmen working desperately to close the gap. It dove, but when it rose again, Portagee was close enough. He swayed back stiffly and then smoothly sprung his whole body forward as he released the harpoon. I saw the point drive deeply into the swimming animal's back. A shout went up from Sarkak and the oarsmen in the boat.

Portagee should have flung the big sealskin float out of the thin-skinned boat, but instead he snubbed the skin line around the front thwart as he had done in their pantomime. The big bull walrus plunged deep into the sea, and I saw with horror that the line went tight, stretching like wet gut. Just before the taut line could tip the boat, the big brown foreigner paid out the line, a little at a time, grudgingly, as he desperately held onto this immense prize of food. I saw the old umiak stop and shudder, with its bow forced down almost to the water line. The stern, where Sarkak sat, rose up and trembled in the air. I was amazed at the strength of the new sealskin line. Imagine this crazy man trying to hold a full-grown male walrus tied to a thin-skinned boat. It was all madness, and I believed they would die together in the freezing water.

As the bull turned in his mad attempt to escape under the water, the boat stern slammed down into the waves, and the clumsy umiak jerked forward once more and raced through the water, pulled by this hidden force. I could not believe that Portagee would ignore Sarkak's angry shouting at him, that he would not throw the big sealskin float into the water. But that is exactly what he did. Kakuktak and Pilee were holding the sides of the boat, shouting with laughter as the old skin boat swayed and skidded across the reddened sea.

Portagee had no time to laugh. He worked like a wild man, head down, back humped, his muscles straining as he skillfully drew the line in, snubbed it, waited, then shortened it again, slowly closing the gap between the walrus and the boat. When the line was dangerously short, the walrus suddenly dove again, and the boat lunged crazily sideways. I started to paddle hard toward them, wondering if I could save one of them from the freezing sea. The line snapped downward, and the boat shuddered. Portagee still held fast, scarcely paying out an arm's length of line. The strain on the boat was immense as the beast fought to gain depth beneath the sea.

But slowly his muscles and his huge lungs failed him, and I could see that we had won. The walrus, mouth open, fighting for air, rose almost beneath the bow, and Portagee lanced him with the sharp point of the killing spear. Three times I saw him dart it into the big bull's throat between the great tusks. He did this neatly and swiftly, in a way I had never seen before. The walrus surfaced again, spinning crazily in the water, something that usually happens when the spirit is flying out of a sea beast. Then it was over, and the great weight of the walrus rolled belly up and floated peacefully just beneath the surface, with only the tusks rising above the red water, pointing upward like the curved white horns of some demon from beneath the sea.

The three *kalunait* roared, and Portagee slapped his own buttocks loudly. I was shocked to hear such laughing and shouting from a boat with a newly dead sea beast attached, and surprised that our young boys were so quick to call out and laugh in shameless imitation of the foreigners. Sarkak sat alone, an old man, gaunt and silent in the stern, for he, the great hunter and planner for us all, had acted only like a servant to these strange men.

Now Portagee flung the sealskin float out of the boat to mark the dead walrus, and they pursued two female walrus, managing to harpoon one of these in almost the same manner. They also lanced one young walrus with the killing spear alone and hauled it up bodily into the boat.

Portagee, not Sarkak, took command and gave the order to return to land. I watched them begin rowing, still shouting irreverently as they towed their great burden of meat back to the long black point of land. There the hungry women stood screaming with delight, and the babies wailed in terror. Each kayakman also paddled toward the camp, not caring about the walrus that swam quickly past, moving out and disappearing with the great ebbing tide. We stroked hard toward the women on the shore, each boat drawing a great floating prize.

Portagee and Kakuktak and Pilee now forced the big oars through the water, and as they did so they sang out some song that exactly matched the rhythm of their strokes. I wished I could have understood the words of their song, even though it was wrong of them to sing out there on the sea right after such a great killing. We knew that the waters must have been swarming with the souls of dead walrus, and at this time it was important that we show them respect, not triumph. For had they not come to us from some distant place and given their flesh to us so that we might live? Still, even with the foreigners rudely singing, we managed to reach the shore without another mishap, which made me think again that these three round-eyed people lived by other rules and perhaps would not be hurt by disobeying our taboos.

Subsistence and Economic Exchange

MAKING IT IN THE CITY

I lived in the Coq d'Or quarter for about a year and a half. One day, in summer, I found that I had just four hundred and fifty francs left, and beyond this nothing but thirty-six francs a week, which I earned by giving English lessons. Hitherto I had not thought about the future, but I now realised that I must do something at once. I decided to start looking for a job, and—very luckily, as it turned out—I took the precaution of paying two hundred francs for a month's rent in advance. With the other two hundred and fifty francs, besides the English lessons, I could live a month, and in a month I should probably find work. I aimed at becoming a guide to one of the tourist companies, or perhaps an interpreter. However, a piece of bad luck prevented this.

One day there turned up at the hotel a young Italian who called himself a compositor. He was rather an ambiguous person, for he wore side whiskers, which are the mark either of an apache or an intellectual, and nobody was quite certain in which class to put him. Madame F. did not like the look of him, and made him pay a week's rent in advance. The Italian paid the rent and stayed six nights at the hotel. During this time he managed to prepare some duplicate keys, and on the last night he robbed a dozen rooms, including mine. Luckily, he did not find the money that was in my pockets, so I was not left penniless. I was left with just forty-seven francs—that is, seven and tenpence.

This put an end to my plans of looking for work. I had now got to live at the rate of about six francs a day, and from the start it was too difficult to leave much thought for anything else. It was now that my experiences of poverty began—for six francs a day, if not actual poverty, is on the fringe of it. Six francs is a shilling, and you can live on a shilling a day in Paris if you know how. But it is a complicated business.

It is altogether curious, your first contact with poverty. You have thought so much about poverty—it is the thing you have feared all your life, the thing you knew would happen to you sooner or later; and it is all so utterly and prosaically different. You thought it would be quite simple; it is extraordinarily complicated. You thought it would be terrible; it is merely squalid and boring. It is the peculiar *lowness* of poverty that you discover first; the shifts that it puts you to, the complicated meanness, the crust-wiping.

You discover, for instance, the secrecy attaching to poverty. At a sudden stroke you have been reduced to an income of six francs a day. But of course you dare not admit it—you have got to pretend that you are living quite as usual. From the start it tangles you in a net of lies, and even with the lies you can hardly manage it. You stop sending clothes to the laundry, and the laundress catches you in the street and asks you why; you mumble something, and she, thinking you are sending the clothes elsewhere, is your enemy for life. The tobacconist keeps asking why you have cut down your smoking. There are letters you want to answer, and cannot, because stamps are too expensive. And then there are your meals—meals are the worst difficulty of all. Every day at meal-times you go out, ostensibly to a restaurant, and loaf an hour in the Luxembourg Gardens, watching the pigeons. Afterwards you smuggle your food home in your pockets. Your food is bread and margarine, or bread and wine, and even the nature of the food is governed by lies. You have to buy rye bread instead of household bread, because the rye loaves though dearer, are round and can be smuggled in your pockets. This wastes you a franc a day. Sometimes, to keep up appearances, you have to spend sixty centimes on a drink, and go correspondingly short of food. Your linen gets filthy, and you run out of soap and razor-blades. Your hair wants cutting, and you try to cut it yourself, with such fearful results that you have to go to the barber after all, and spend the equivalent of a day's food. All day you are telling lies, and expensive lies.

You discover the extreme precariousness of your six francs a day. Mean disasters happen and rob you of food. You have spent your last eighty centimes on half a litre of milk, and are boiling it over the spirit lamp. While it boils a bug runs down your forearm; you give the bug a flick with your nail, and it falls, plop! straight into the milk. There is nothing for it but to throw the milk away and go foodless.

You go to the baker's to buy a pound of bread, and you wait while the girl cuts a pound for another customer. She is clumsy, and cuts more than a pound. *"Pardon, monsieur,"* she says, "I suppose you don't mind paying two sous extra?" Bread is a franc a pound, and you have exactly a franc. When you think that you too might be asked to pay two sous extra, and would have to confess that you could not, you bolt in panic. It is hours before you dare venture into a baker's shop again.

You go to the greengrocer's to spend a franc on a kilogram of potatoes. But one of the pieces that make up the franc is a Belgium piece, and the shopman refuses it. You slink out of the shop, and can never go there again.

You have strayed into a respectable quarter, and you see a prosperous friend coming. To avoid him you dodge into the nearest cafe. Once in the cafe you must buy something, so you spend your last fifty centimes on a glass of black coffee with a dead fly in it. One could multiply these disasters by the hundred. They are part of the process of being hard up.

Subsistence and Economic Exchange

You discover what it is like to be hungry. With bread and margarine in your belly, you go out and look into the shop windows. Everywhere there is food insulting you in huge, wasteful piles; whole dead pigs, baskets of hot loaves, great yellow blocks of butter, strings of sausages, mountains of potatoes, vast Gruyère cheese like grindstones. A snivelling self-pity comes over you at the sight of so much food. You plan to grab a loaf and run, swallowing it before they catch you; and you refrain, from pure funk.

You discover the boredom which is inseparable from poverty; the times when you have nothing to do and, being underfed, can interest yourself in nothing. For half a day at a time you lie on your bed, feeling like the *jeune squelette* in Baudelaire's poem. Only food could rouse you. You discover that a man who has gone even a week on bread and margarine is not a man any longer, only a belly with a few accessory organs.

This—one could describe it further, but it is all in the same style—is life on six francs a day. Thousands of people in Paris live it—struggling artists and students, prostitutes when their luck is out, out-of-work people of all kinds. It is the suburbs, as it were, of poverty.

I continued in this style for about three weeks. The forty-seven francs were soon gone, and I had to do what I could on thirty-six francs a week from the English lessons. Being inexperienced, I handled the money badly, and sometimes I was a day without food. When this happened I used to sell a few of my clothes, smuggling them out of the hotel in small packets and taking them to a second-hand shop in the Rue de la Montagne St. Geneviève. The shopman was a red-haired Jew, an extraordinary disagreeable man, who used to fall into furious rages at the sight of a client. From his manner one would have supposed that we had done him some injury by coming to him. "*Merde!*" he used to shout, "*You* here again? What do you think this is? A soup kitchen?" And he paid incredibly low prices. For a hat which I had bought for twenty-five shillings and scarcely wore he gave five francs; for a good pair of shoes, five francs; for shirts, a franc each. He always preferred to exchange rather than buy, and he had a trick of thrusting some useless article into one's hand and then pretending that one had accepted it. Once I saw him take a good overcoat from an old woman, put two white billiard-balls into her hand, and then push her rapidly out of the shop before she could protest. It would have been a pleasure to flatten the Jew's nose, if only one could have afforded it.

These three weeks were squalid and uncomfortable, and evidently there was worse coming, for my rent would be due before long. Nevertheless, things were not a quarter as bad as I had expected. For, when you are approaching poverty, you make one discovery which outweighs some of the others. You discover boredom and mean complications and the beginnings of hunger, but you also discover the great redeeming feature of poverty: the fact that it annihilates the future. Within certain limits, it is actually true that the less money you have, the less you worry. When you have a hundred francs in the world you are liable to the most craven panics. When you have only three francs you are quite indifferent; for three francs will feed you till tomorrow, and you cannot think further than that. You are bored, but you are not afraid. You think vaguely, "I shall be starving in a day or two—shocking, isn't it?" And then the mind wanders to other topics. A bread and margarine diet does, to some extent, provide its own anodyne.

And there is another feeling that is a great consolation in poverty. I believe everyone who has been hard up has experienced it. It is a feeling of relief, almost of pleasure, at knowing yourself at last genuinely down and out. You have talked so often of going to the dogs—and well, here are the dogs, and you have reached them, and you can stand it. It takes off a lot of anxiety.

One day my English lessons ceased abruptly. The weather was getting hot and one of my pupils, feeling too lazy to go on with his lessons, dismissed me. The other disappeared from his lodgings without notice, owing me twelve francs. I was left with only thirty centimes and no tobacco. For a day and a half I had nothing to eat or smoke, and then, too hungry to put it off any longer, I packed my remaining clothes into my suitcase and took them to the pawnshop. This put an end to all pretence of being in funds, for I could not take my clothes out of the hotel without asking Madame F.'s leave. I remember, however, how surprised she was at my asking her instead of removing the clothes on the sly, shooting the moon being a common trick in our quarter.

It was the first time that I had been in a French pawnshop. One went through grandiose stone portals (marked, of course, *"Liberté, Égalité, Fraternité"*—they write that even over the police stations in France) into a large, bare room like a school classroom, with a counter and rows of benches. Forty or fifty people were waiting. One handed one's pledge over the counter and sat down. Presently, when the clerk had assessed its value he would call out, *"Numéro* such and such, will you take fifty francs?" Sometimes it was only fifteen francs, or ten, or five—whatever it was, the whole room knew it. As I came in the clerk called with an air of offence, *"Numéro* 83—here!" and gave a little whistle and a beckon, as though calling a dog. *Numéro* 83 stepped to the counter; he was an old bearded man, with an overcoat buttoned up at the neck and frayed trouser-ends. Without a word the clerk shot the bundle across the counter—evidently it was worth nothing. It fell to the ground and came open, displaying four pairs of men's woollen pants. No one could help laughing. Poor *Numéro* 83 gathered up his pants and shambled out, muttering to himself.

The clothes I was pawning, together with the suitcase, had cost over twenty pounds, and were in good condition. I thought they must be worth ten pounds, and a quarter of this (one expects quarter value at a pawnshop) was two hundred and fifty or three hundred francs. I waited without anxiety, expecting two hundred francs at the worst.

At last the clerk called my number: *"Numéro* 97!"

"Yes," I said, standing up.

"Seventy francs?"

Seventy francs for ten pounds' worth of clothes! But it was no use arguing; I had seen someone else attempt to argue, and the clerk had instantly refused the pledge. I took the money and the pawnticket and walked out. I had now no clothes except what I stood up in—the coat badly out at the elbow—an overcoat, moderately pawnable, and one spare shirt. Afterwards, when it was too late, I learned that it was wiser to go to a pawnshop in the afternoon. The clerks are French, and, like most French people, are in a bad temper till they have eaten their lunch.

When I got home, Madame F. was sweeping the *bistro* floor. She came up the steps to meet me. I could see in her eye that she was uneasy about my rent.

"Well," she said, "what did you get for your clothes? Not much, eh?"

"Two hundred francs," I said promptly.

"*Tiens!*" she said, surprised; "well, *that's* not bad. How expensive those English clothes must be!"

The lie saved a lot of trouble, and, strangely enough, it came true. A few days later I did receive exactly two hundred francs due to me for a newspaper article, and, though it hurt to do it, I at once paid every penny of it in rent. So, though I came near to starving in the following weeks, I was hardly ever without a roof.

My money oozed away—to eight francs, to four francs, to one franc, to twenty-five centimes; and twenty-five centimes is useless, for it will buy nothing except a newspaper. We went several days on dry bread, and then I was two and a half days with nothing to eat whatever. This was an ugly experience. There are people who do fasting cures of three weeks or more, and they say that fasting is quite pleasant after the fourth day; I do not know, never having gone beyond the third day. Probably it seems different when one is doing it voluntarily and is not underfed at the start.

The first day, too inert to look for work, I borrowed a rod and went fishing in the Seine, baiting with bluebottles. I hoped to catch enough for a meal, but of course I did not. The Seine is full of dace, but they grew cunning during the seige of Paris, and none of them has been caught since, except in nets. On the second day I thought of pawning my overcoat, but it seemed too far to walk to the pawnshop, and I spent the day in bed, reading the *Memoirs of Sherlock Holmes*. It was all that I felt equal to, without food. Hunger reduces one to an utterly spineless, brainless condition, more like the aftereffects of influenza than anything else. It is as though one had been turned into a jellyfish, or as though all one's blood had been pumped out and luke-warm water substituted. Complete inertia is my chief memory of hunger; that, and being obliged to spit very frequently, and the spittle being curiously white and flocculent, like cuckoo-spit. I do not know the reason for this, but everyone who has gone hungry several days has noticed it.

LEARNING TO WORK WAS LIKE PLAY

I was my grandfather's favorite. As soon as I was old enough to take advice, he taught me that it was a great disgrace to be called *kahopi* (not Hopi, not peaceable). He said, "My grandson, old people are important. They know a lot and don't lie. Listen to them, obey your parents, work hard, treat everyone right. Then people will say, 'That boy Chuka is a good child. Let's be kind to him.' If you do these things, you will live to be an old man yourself and pass away in sleep without pain. This is the trail that every good Hopi follows. Children who ignore these teachings don't live long."

He told me that I was a boy after his own heart and that he could look into my life and see that I would become an important man, perhaps a leader of the people. I wanted to be a medicine man as he was, but he told me that I could not be a very good healer because I was not a member of the Badger Clan, nor even of the Snake Clan. They made the best doctors, but he thought I might become a Special Officer in the ceremonies. He advised me to keep bad thoughts out of my mind, to face the east, look to the bright side of life, and learn to show a shining face, even when unhappy. While I was still sleeping with him he taught me to get up before sunrise, bathe and exercise my body, and look around for useful work to do. He said, "Work means life. No one loves a lazybones."

Learning to work was like play. We children tagged around with our elders and copied what they did. We followed our fathers to the fields and helped plant and weed. The old men took us for walks and taught us the use of plants and how to collect them. We joined the women in gathering rabbit-weed for baskets, and went with them to dig clay for pots. We would taste this clay as the women did to test it. We watched the fields to drive out the birds and rodents, helped pick peaches to dry in the sun, and gather melons to lug up the mesa. We rode the burros to harvest corn, gather fuel, or herd sheep. In housebuilding we helped a little by bringing up dirt to cover the roofs. In this way we grew up doing things. All the old people said that it was a disgrace to be idle and that a lazy boy should be whipped.

The importance of food was a lesson I learned early. My mother taught me never to waste it or play with it carelessly. Corn seemed to be the most important. A common saying was, "Corn is life, and piki is the perfect food." My mother-corn ears, which had been placed by my side at birth and used in my naming ceremony, were regarded as sacred and were kept a long time, but finally they were ground into meal and used for food before bugs got into them. Every family tried to keep a full year's supply of corn on hand and used it sparingly. There was always a pile of it in our house, neatly stacked in rows. A small supply of corn in a dry season was viewed with alarm, for to be without corn was a calamity. Whenever we shelled it we were careful to pick up every grain.

While the old people sat around shelling corn or spinning, they talked about the terrible famines that had come upon the people. It was sad to hear them. They said that on account of somebody's careless conduct the Six-Point-Cloud-People—our departed ancestors who live north, east, south, west, above, and below—refused to send rain and permitted droughts and famines. When the corn gave out the people prowled about the village looking for seeds and roots and scratched into trash piles for anything they could get. They scattered out over the desert digging for roots and wild potatoes. Some of them fell exhausted and died on their way up the mesa. Many people starved. Some stole food that others had stored, even digging tunnels under walls into neighbors' corn bins. A man might wake up in his own house and find all his corn gone but the first row. Some fled to the Santo Domingo Indians and traded their children for food.

I have heard that when a man and his wife sat down to eat they would look at each other like wildcats ready to spring, and hold the hands of their children to keep them from eating. Think of that! Some children were kidnapped and eaten. Their bones and skulls were found later in the foundations of some of the old houses. I saw them. The old people said that we youngsters could never know what awful misfortunes had come upon our people. They were handing these warnings down to us so that we could some day pass them on to our children.

The last big famine came when my father was a little boy. He told me how his grandfather was fairly well off and had much food stored which kept his family from starving. I saw how important it was to have food on hand. We ate the old Hopi foods such as corn, beans, squash, chilis, spinach, and many wild plants. We never tired of them. Occasionally we ate the food of the white people such as flat flour bread and drank a little coffee. Only the rich Hopis had this white bread as often as twice a week. We were frequently reminded that the old Hopi food was best and that our gods preferred that we eat it.

In the spring the older boys went out with soft eagle feathers fastened on their heads to collect wild spinach, which they gave to their girl friends in exchange for other foods. Our parents took us smaller children out to watch the procession and to exchange our own foods. Ceremonial officers guided the boys and girls in this work and advised them that it was important in order to have good crops and plenty to eat. After the collection of wild spinach we always had a Katcina dance. By these ceremonies I learned to know that the gods had given us certain wild plants as special food.

We were taught that whenever anyone came to our house we should sweep a clean place on the floor, set out the food, and invite him to eat. It was only after the company had eaten that my father ever asked, "What can I do for you?" My grandfather said that we must always observe this rule and feed visitors first, even when we were hungry or unhappy. I noticed that my mother and father stopped quarreling whenever company came. At mealtime we children were permitted to eat all that we wanted, but were told to behave and not to be greedy. It was no disgrace to break wind at mealtime or to laugh when someone else did. Whenever we went to a neighbor's house, we were told that we should eat their food to make them happy. It was proper to eat a little even when we were already full up to the neck. On a dance day we often ate ten or fifteen times.

As far back as I can remember, I noticed that my father, mother, and grandfather would take a little food before eating and put it aside. They said that it was to feed the Sun and other gods who protected us. Sometimes I heard them speak to these gods, inviting them to eat. They were especially careful to do this on dance days. Whenever my father asked the gods for anything, he fed them first. Sometimes he would take a bit of food, step outside and throw it to the Sun, then ask for something. We were told that there was no need to speak out loud in thanking our gods at the three daily meals. We could pray in our hearts: "Now this meal is prepared for me. I will put it into my body to make myself strong for work. May my Spirit Guide protect me."

Food was left on the graves, even the graves of very small babies who were buried among the rocks on the south and the northwest sides of the village. We children were not permitted to see a dead person or to go near the graves, but we could see our fathers taking food there in clay bowls.

I learned that it was important always to eat at mealtime. Once when my parents had scolded me, I sulked and refused to eat. After they had finished and gone out, I looked for the food that I expected them to leave for me, but there was nothing. I had tried to hurt their feelings, but I was starving myself. I ate at regular mealtime after that.

It was hard to learn what plants we could eat. Some of them were good for food and others for medicine, but still others were good for nothing save to make people sick or crazy. The locoweed would make even a horse crazy. I tried to remember the use of all the plants under my grandfather's instruction.

Food seemed most important on dance days. Our mothers fed the Katcinas and everybody had good things to eat. It was then, too, that the Katcinas presented their gifts such as watermelons, popcorn, hominy, mush, and piki. Those were happy days when children could be carefree and everyone was expected to be cheerful. At the end of the day the Father of the Katcinas sprinkled them with corn meal, made a farewell speech, and sent them to their homes in the San Francisco Peaks. He would ask them to send rain for our crops, and add, "Then our children, the little ones, will eat and surely be happy. Then all the people will live happily. Then our lives, reaching old age among our children, will be happily fulfilled." All this made it plain that food was necessary for life and happiness.

While I was learning the importance of food and trying to recognize the different things that were fit to eat, I kept going to my mother for milk and was still nursing at six. Whenever we boys set out to hunt kangaroo rats or other small game, I ran first to my mother, placed my bow and arrows on the floor, sat beside her, and drank from her breasts. The other fellows would say, "Come Chuka, come, or we will be late." "Wait, wait," I replied between draughts. But on account of their teasing, I finally gave up the breast in embarrassment. My mother did not wean me; I just decided to let her alone.

I also learned that water is as precious as food. Everybody appeared happy after a rain. We small boys rolled about naked in the mud puddles, doused each other with water, and built little irrigated gardens. In this way we used too much of the water from the little pond on the west side of the village where the women went to wash their clothes and the men to water their stock. Our parents scolded us for wasting water and once my mother spanked me on account of my dirty shirt.

During droughts we had strict rules for the use of water. Even small children were taught to be careful, and I saw mothers bathe their babies by spitting a little water upon them. By watching the old people I learned to wash my face with a mouthful of water—it is the safest way to wash without waste.

Sometimes water gave out. Then the men went with their burros to distant springs while the women stayed up all night taking turns to catch a little trickle that came from the Oraibi spring. My grandfather told me about the cistern that he had chiseled out of the solid rock to catch the rain that fell on the mesa shelf. He said that he had done this hard work when he married my grandmother in order that his children and his grandchildren might not suffer from thirst. My mother went daily to this well to fetch water. In winter she cut out chunks of ice from the rock ledges and brought them in on her back.

Whenever it rained, we were told to take our little pots and go out on the ledges, scoop up puddles, and fill the cisterns. There were about one hundred of these hewn out of the solid rock by our ancestors. The people pointed out that water is essential to life and taught us what to do out in the desert whenever we became so dry and thirsty that we could neither spit nor swallow. Then one should cut twigs off a cottonwood tree and chew them, eat the inner bark of the cedar, or hold dried peaches in his mouth.

The importance of water was impressed upon us by the way the old men prayed for rain and planted pahos in the springs to please the water serpents and to persuade them to send larger streams to quench our thirst. We were reminded that all the dances and ceremonies were for rain, not for pleasure. They were held in order to persuade the Six-Point-Cloud-People to send moisture for our crops. Whenever we had a good rain, we were told to show our happy faces and consider ourselves in favor with the gods. We made it a point never to praise the weather on fair, dry days. Whenever it rained during or just after a dance, the people praised highly those who had taken part in the performance. If a strong wind followed the dance, it was a sign that the people who had invited the Katcinas to come and dance had a bad heart or had done some evil.

We were told that there is health-giving power in water, and that it is a good practice to bathe in cold water, to wash our hands and faces in snow, and to rub it upon our bodies to make them tough. The old people said that warm water made wrinkles and shortened life. I saw them setting bowls of water outside to become ice-cold before using it for a bath. Some old men would go out naked and rub snow all over their bodies. My grandfathers, my aunts' husbands, often took me outside and rolled me in the snow on winter mornings. Talasemptewa did it many times. At first I thought he disliked me, but my mother explained that it showed he loved me and wanted me to grow up strong, healthy, and brave. I could see there was healing power in water, too, for my grandfather often had people drink warm water in order to vomit and clear out their systems. Sometimes he prescribed a person's own fresh warm urine for stomach trouble. Water then, like food, meant life and health and was a special gift from the gods to us in the desert. The gods could withhold rain when they were displeased, or they could pour it on us when they wanted to.

Most of my time was spent in play. We shot arrows at targets, played old Hopi checkers, and pushed feather-edged sticks into corncobs and threw them at rolling hoops of cornhusks. We wrestled, ran races, played tag, kickball, stick throwing, and shinny. We spun tops with whips and made string figures on our fingers. I was poor at races but good at string figures. Another game I liked was making Hopi firecrackers. I mixed burro and horse dung, burned a lump of it into a red glow, placed the coal on a flat rock, and hit it with a cow horn dipped in urine. It went "bang" like a gun.

We hunted rabbits, kangaroo rats, and mice to feed to hawks and eagles. We also waged little wars with children of unfriendly families who were most opposed to the Whites. They criticized us for accepting gifts from white people and we called them Hostiles. Their children would upset our traps for turtledoves and try to torment us in every way. We had many fights with them, and my brother and I fought a great deal, even throwing stones at each other.

Sometimes we got into mischief in our play. One day when I was out with a gang of boys, I decided to play a trick. I defecated in the path. Now one could make water almost any place except in bed and against the house walls where it washed away the adobe, but a boy had to be careful where he defecated. During the day a woman stepped in the feces with her bare feet. Learning from some children that I was the guilty person, she came to our house complaining. My grandfather was quite angry and said that this had to be stopped. He had never licked me, but I was scared. He got a willow switch about three feet long, took me by the hand, and struck me four blows below my shirt. He ordered me never to repeat the act, and raised his arm to strike again, when I promised. He stuck the switch up in the ceiling near the arrow and my dried placenta cord. Later I tried to get it down. In about a week I received a second thrashing of eight stripes for the same offense. Then I learned to defecate in the proper places.

In winter we played in the kivas and listened to the long stories which the men told while they worked at spinning, weaving, and other jobs. They often picked out a boy to take messages and trade for them from kiva to kiva, and frequently I was chosen. The men would collect the things that they wished to exchange—wool, yarn, pieces of calico, leggings, and perhaps a sheep. Since a trader boy naturally could not carry a large animal, the owner would tie some wool from a sheep, or the hair of a horse or burro, on a stick to represent the animal. I would go from kiva to kiva showing the objects of trade. If a man wanted to purchase an animal or other large objects represented by a stick, he would make the trade and take the stick as proof of payment. Of course I had to remember the value of these objects and know exactly what the owner would take in exchange. It was great fun, and it also taught me to measure and to count.

I learned to count up to twenty with my fingers and toes. That was as high as we went. If, for example, we wanted to indicate forty-four, we would say "two twenties and four." Four was a lucky number, but we had no unlucky numbers. In measurement we said "one finger wide" for about one inch, "from the reach of the thumb to the middle finger" for about six inches, and "one foot" for the length from heel to toe. For long distances we counted in steps. I did not learn much about the weight of things at this time. Morning and afternoon were determined by the direction of the shadows, and we told time at night by the position of the moon and stars. Promises to pay at a future date were expressed in number of days, the state of the moon, or the number of moons.

As soon as I was old enough to wander about the village my grandfather suggested that I go out to the Antelope shrine and look for my deer people who were invisible to ordinary human beings. Sometimes I thought I could see antelopes who changed into people. Whenever I dreamed of antelopes in the village, my parents would say, "That is to be expected, for you are an antelope child." Then when I was perhaps five I would wander off a mile or two from the village to a place where sunflowers grew and where it was known that the spirits of deer and antelope gathered to give birth to their young and to feed on the sunflowers. It was a miracle that I could see these deer while others could not. I would return home with a bunch of sunflowers and with the juice of the sunflowers spread around my mouth. My grandfather or parents would remark that I had been feasting with my relatives and would probably use my special power soon to heal some poor person who was sick and unable to urinate.

My grandfather had already taught me how to heal such diseases and people had begun sending for me whenever this trouble came upon them.

The first thing I did when working on a sick person was to put out my left hand with the palm up and pray, "Now my mother of the Antelope People, this sick person is in bad condition; come and cure his disease before I put my hands upon him; join with me and save his life."

After praying, I would rub him or her around the private parts and especially between the navel and the pubis. I would take piki, chew it, and feed it to the sick person from my fingers. My uncle, Talasquaptewa, said that a twin like myself was in an unfortunate position because sometimes such sufferers die in spite of all treatment, and then the person who had tried to help them feels responsible. But I seemed to be able to tell whether a patient would get well or die. Whenever I saw someone beyond help, I simply walked away, refusing to treat him. The old people praised my power to heal, but predicted that it would probably disappear as I grew into manhood. They warned me never to let the Whites know about it, because they would not be able to understand. . . .

By the time I was six, therefore, I had learned to find my way about the mesa and to avoid graves, shrines, and harmful plants, to size up people, and to watch out for witches. I was above average height and in good health. My hair was clipped just above my eyes, but left long in back and tied in a knot at the nape of my neck. I had almost lost one eye. I wore silver earrings, a missionary shirt or one made of a flour sack, and was always bare-legged, except for a blanket in cold weather. When no Whites were present, I went naked. I slept out on the housetop in summer and sometimes in the kiva with other boys in winter. I could help plant and weed, went out herding with my father, and was a kiva trader. I owned a dog and a cat, a small bow made by my father, and a few good arrows. Sometimes I carried stolen matches tucked in the hem of my shirt collar. I could ride a tame burro, kill a kangaroo rat, and catch small birds, but I could not make fire with a drill and I was not a good runner like the other fellows. At the races people teased me and said that my feet turned out so far that I pinched my anus as I ran. But I had made a name for myself by healing people; and I had almost stopped running after my mother for her milk.

THE SILKWORM FACTORY

I looked with indifference at the handful of tiny silkworms Rosina brought up from the town. I had seen silkworms before, in fact I had reared half a dozen on lettuce in my schooldays.

Rosina took them upstairs into a room which stood empty. A large tray was placed ready to receive them, and she put the little crawly things on to a sheet of perforated paper about a foot square. The tray itself was very large, about ten feet by four feet, and the bottom was made of reeds put close together. Four stout poles were fixed from floor to ceiling, and along one side of each pole a number of pegs projected. A stick was laid across two pegs at either end, and the tray was supported on this stick. It could be lowered or raised at will by shifting the stick on to lower or higher pegs.

Rosina was on her knees at the open fireplace, trying to light a fire, but it would not blaze and the room filled with smoke.

"You will kill them with all this smoke," I said, retreating towards the door, half choked.

But she thought that cold, more than smoke, would harm the cavalleri, as she called the silkworms. It was not a warm day, and the temperature of the room had to be kept between 66° and 72°F. if the silkworms were to thrive.

"This chimney never draws," she said, puffing at the wood.

"Where did you get the cavalleri?" I asked, "are they sold by the ounce or the gross?"

"They cost nothing, signora," answered Rosina, still on her knees, "they are given us by the society—but on condition that we sell them the cocoons. It is true they pay us a little less than other people, but then they send up an instructor to advise and help us. Pu! this smoke is cattivo!"

The silkworms survived the smoke. They had a good dose of it the first few days, but afterwards the weather turned warmer. In this part of Italy it was never warm enough for silkworms to be reared out of doors.

The lady instructor came up regularly every other day. She brought a large placard and pinned it on the wall. In a space for the purpose she noted down the dates when the worms shed their skins. This should take place on the 6th, 10th, 15th, and 23rd day after hatching. Badly fed silkworms are a day or so later. After inspecting the trays upstairs, the instructress went on to the village, where she had many houses to visit. Nearly every one had cavalleri.

From *Among Italian Peasants* by Tony Cyriax, 1922. Reprinted by permission of Collins Publishers, London.

It was an occupation which depended largely on the women, and was superintended by them. The men always assisted, but they were subordinates and did as they were told. For the time being the housewife reigned supreme and the men did not have much of a time, as you will see.

During the first two weeks Rosina cut the mulberry leaves into strips about a quarter of an inch wide, and gave them to the cavalleri like that, busying herself with them for a short time. But when they had grown bigger she gave them whole leaves and twigs.

Riccardo climbed the mulberry trees and picked the leaves, dropping them into a sack with a hoop at its mouth which he hooked to a branch. He would entirely strip a tree of its leaves, which were still small and immature. In a very short time, however, fresh leaves developed, and a tree that had been quite naked was soon clothed in green and presently stripped again.

In a short time the cavalleri spread over the large tray, and a second was brought upstairs for them. What had seemed but a handful turned out to be tens of thousands. They grew and flourished and every day they ate more, rearing up their heads and looking round for more leaves when the twigs were bare. Rosina was always giving them fresh leaves. Riccardo could not pick them fast enough, Paolino had to help him.

The perforated papers which the society provided were changed once a day, and together with the refuse were thrown on to the floor, and swept on to the balcony. They fell and fluttered down, close to the kitchen door. Bortolo did not trouble to carry them away. He was still busy in the fields, but found time to pick leaves every day. Riccardo had to help Rosina upstairs now, it was more than she could do single-handed. More and more trays were carried up, and the cavalleri grew bigger and bigger. They were in prime condition. I used to stand and listen to them gnawing at the leaves, they were so many they made a distinct noise. Rosina would pick them off the twigs with her fingers and put them on to fresh leaves. It was a tedious job; she was nearly always upstairs now.

The work told on her temper. She was very tired and very cross. She shouted at every one. Not before ten o'clock did she get to bed, and at midnight the alarm woke her and she had to get up and feed her ravenous charges again. At four o'clock the same relentless alarm tinkled. There was no shirking. Badly fed cavalleri spin small cocoons and the society buys by weight.

By means of continuous scolding and shouting, Rosina managed to be always supplied with leaves. She would come out on to the balcony and abuse Bortolo and the boys, singly or collectively. From three different trees, in three different directions, they would raise their voices in protest. She didn't care what she said.

As for the house, it was in an awful state. Rosina neither swept nor dusted for days and days. The kitchen floor was a disgrace. There was no water in the buckets when I came to do my cooking, no one had been to the spring. There was no fire-wood in the box. Dirty dishes and plates stood about. Bortolo, who vainly tried to keep things tidy, put everything in its wrong place. . . . Even the copper pots and brass candlesticks were not polished. Rosina never neglected those cherished articles when things were normal. Now she hadn't time for anything. She made a laudable effort to wash her face and hands before dinner, but often failed. She had no time to comb her own hair, nor Pina's either. She had no time for washing clothes nor for cooking. Bortolo made the polenta, and they practically lived on that alone. Meals were at unstated intervals. Rosina had no time to sit down at table, she snatched a chunk of polenta whenever she was hungry, and ate it amongst the silkworms. For supper she made a hasty sort of minestra—but it was not nice.

Neither Bortolo nor the boys complained. They had been through it before, and knew what to expect. Besides, who would dare complain when Rosina was on the warpath?

In spite of the fact that her family was neglected and her house uncared for, Rosina could always spare a few moments to serve customers with wine. She was never too busy for a little illicit trade, and she always had an ingratiating smile for the tourist.

I sometimes visited Rosina up in the silkworm room, which was by now her permanent abode, but she was in such a state of tension that I feared to tire her by talking. She ruled the house from the balcony or from within the room, from where she shouted her wants and instructions. Riccardo got his fair share of abuse every morning when he came up late from the town, as usual. He had to bring up the perforated papers from the society, and woe betide him if he forgot them.

By this time Bortolo had finished his work in the fields and was able to help Rosina all day and at night as well, and, of course, all three children were hard at work. It was a race between the ravenous cavalleri and the people feeding them.

Rosina was quite hoarse and the flesh round her mouth looked used and tired. She had grown very much thinner. How she longed for a night's rest—she was so tired.

We all suffered.

. . .

I spent a good deal of my time away from the house, but I had to walk far to get outside the radius of Rosina's voice.

"Riccardo, Riccardo—far prest, crettino—bastardo—mostro!" Such words could be heard beyond the fontana.

In the village I was amongst silkworms again. Anetta and her married daughter had some small trays of cavalleri in the kitchen, Lucia had cavalleri in her kitchen, Francesco's wife had cavalleri in an empty house, and the whole family of five grown-up people were busily employed. The Biscotti's also had cavalleri. It was a relief to find Nino's house free of them. Teresina was peacefully knitting socks. I asked for an egg and a roll, and afterwards for some lemonade, and sat in the little kitchen with her and Bigi, and another man.

When I had finished eating I asked Teresina what I owed her.

"There is nothing to pay," she said.

"Of course I must pay," I answered.

"No, signora." She looked determined.

I knew what she was driving at. She was thinking of Nino's fine, and this was her way of paying it back.

"Teresina," I said, "if you don't let me pay I shall be very angry. Besides—why shouldn't I—I ordered the food."

"Signora, I could not take a palanca for it, surely you can accept something . . . you have given Nino so much . . . so much tobacco."

She did not wish to mention the fine then before the others. But I wouldn't give in. It was hateful to give with one hand, and take back with the other.

"Teresina," I exclaimed, "the tobacco I have given Nino he has justly earned, and if you don't let me pay," I went on hotly, "I can never come and order anything here again."

"If it is a case of getting angry," said Teresina, "then I will accept the money . . . the cost is four palanche."

In other words, twopence.

"Eight palanche," I said, "would not be too much."

"The bread is one palanca, the butter one palanca, and the egg two palanche. Ecco four."

"But that is hardly cost price," I said, suddenly recollecting that Rosina was charging me four palanche for an egg—"they are never cheaper," she had said—"and how about the lemonade?"

"It is thrown in."

"And the cloth?"

"You have not soiled it, and I can use it again."

"And your trouble?"

"It has been no trouble."

It ended by my paying her twopence. She took it unwillingly, and I felt that after all she had got the better of me.

It was the first of several encounters I had with her. Usually I took the precaution of paying when I ordered a thing. Once, when·I forgot, she obstinately refused the money.

"Very well," I said, and remained quiet. Presently I called to little Battisti. "Here, Battisti—I have something for you."

Battisti didn't come a step nearer.

Teresina came to the kitchen door, defiant.

"Signora—you must not give him the palanche. I have told him that if he takes them I will thrash him!"

What foresight she had!

She was one too many for me, but I had to give her a parting shot.

"Next time Nino sits for me, Teresina, I shall give him two whole bottles of beer."

"Ah—signora," and she shook her finger at me.

• • •

On my way home I went to the house of Bertoldi Toni, and walking down the long passage gave the usual call of approach.

"Permesso?"

"Avanti, avanti," answered Lucia from the kitchen. She and the four girls were busy with the cavalleri.

The trays were very large and took up about one-third of the space, and excluded most of the light. The table had been carried into the passage, where they took their meals. Close to it was the door to the stairway, which led to the unsavory courtyard, and a number of plants in pots stood on the parapet.

I felt sorry for Toni, more sorry than I felt for poor Bortolo. Bortolo at least could get into the kitchen, and it didn't smell of silkworms, nor was the cooking done in a dark place. On the other hand, Lucia was not irritable. She was always soothing, managing Toni with a few words and a little tact. Rosina's method with the peace-loving Bortolo, was to treat him to a war of words, which left him exasperated but speechless.

I must not forget to mention that Lucia was the sister of the priest, which accounted for the fact that there was a small party in the village who wanted him to stay. Moreover, there were a few who wished him gone, but daren't do anything active for fear of falling out with Toni and his wife.

Every Sunday whilst the others were at Mass, Lucia would go down into the vaulted rooms under the church where the priest lived. A stairway led up into the vestry.

The church was built on the cliff-side, and the windows of the priest's rooms looked down between thick walls on to a precipice. The garden was two narrow terraces, with a parapet and flowering bushes and roses and a large cactus in a pot. Chickens and a young turkey pecked about, running right into the kitchen.

Lucia took upon herself to make the polenta, which was always ready the moment her brother came down from mass. I once accompanied her. The priest came down exhausted and perspiring. Whatever he may have been in private life, he conducted the church services with energy and fervour, perhaps atoning for his sins in that way. His housekeeper came down after him. She was a thin, hard, elderly female, who, it is said, drank as much as the priest did, or perhaps more. She, too, managed very cleverly to obtain wine without paying for it, and Nino's face was a study whenever she came into the inn. He daren't refuse her.

The polenta was ready, and Lucia sat on the hearthstone whilst they ate, and I too, for the priest was hospitable. But he sickened me with unpleasant jokes of double meaning. He found me very dense. After the meal he offered me a cigar.

But to return.

Lucia and the girls were changing the cavalleri on to fresh leaves, and the floor was littered with paper and refuse, faded leaves, and bare twigs. Little Emilio was toddling about trying to help, but squashing the cavalleri with his little fingers. Quite a number were in the part set aside for sick and wounded silkworms.

If the floor was untidy the inhabitants were worse. None of the children had brushed or combed her hair. All of them had dirty feet, and Emilio had a sore toe. Lucia's coiffure was from last Sunday, and would probably go on until next. They were an untidy crew, but made up for it by charm and temperament. I think it must have been Lucia who brought this untidy element into the family, as all the other Bertoldis were neat and clean. They formed the nucleus of the upper ten of the village, together with the Castellis and the Di Marchesis. They were worthy upholders of its best traditions.

Bertoldi Toni himself liked things to be spick and span, and he was very sensitive about his own appearance. He was ashamed of the patches on his trousers and of his ragged shirt. On a week-day he would slink out of the back door if he heard me coming; but when dressed in his Sunday clothes he would come and talk to me. He was ashamed, too, of his limp, and tried to hide it from me as much as possible. If we were together, he would walk a little behind me, and he could never bear to come towards me on the road. He would stand still and wait until I had passed by.

Above all things he cherished an old piano which was kept in a bedroom upstairs. He could play any tune on it, but was quite unable to read a note of music. I loved to hear him play. There was something about it which made up for lack of technique. He loved music and played from his heart. Many happy hours we spent in the room upstairs.

"La vegne sö—la vegne sö," he would say to me on a Sunday afternoon, "si'ora, la vegne sö," which means "signora, come upstairs."

We would go up and play by turns. The piano was miserable and out of tune, but we did not heed that. Sometimes we would go to the church and play the organ.

But Toni was not at home now. Probably he was only too pleased to escape from the cavalleri and climb a tree to pick mulberry leaves, or perhaps he was up on the Ridge of Chestnuts with his son, Vittorio, carting stones to the limekiln.

I sat down in the kitchen and discussed the cavalleri. They were much bigger than Rosina's, but then, they were a different sort. Lucia said they were Chinese.

There was a good deal of competition amongst the cavalleri rearers. I was always questioned about Rosina's worms, and when they had shed their skins, and how big they were compared with some one else's. Rosina always expected me to bring her detailed accounts of all the cavelleri I had seen in the village.

As usual, Lucia and I did most of the talking, the girls listened. Ghita once told me that listening to my conversation was the only means she had of improving her mind—which was somewhat embarrassing for me! We got on very well together; she was an interesting girl. In little things she was untruthful, but the lies were prompted by tact, and were so palpable that there was no deception.

I taught her to read music. She could pick out tunes in the way her father did, and she was very anxious to learn more. She mastered the principles of written music in a remarkably short time, and then it needed only practice. She was soon able to play easy exercises. Sometimes Toni would come upstairs and ask me to play them through from the book, in order to hear if Ghita had been practising them correctly.

"You are not like an Italian, signora," Ghita would say, "they never teach us anything—on the contrary, they jealously guard what they know from us. You are molta buona."

Ghita was seventeen, a fine girl in perfect health, dark skinned, with a blush on her cheeks. The girls all had beautiful dark eyes except Carolina, who had hazel eyes, drooping lids, and a pasty face. She had none of the capability and natural tact which distinguished Vittorio and Ghita. She had been ill for many years, and after the doctors had given her up she was cured by a quack from across the lake. She looked older than Ghita, but was a year younger. Paolino worshipped Carolina from a distance. "Signora," he had said to me in a burst of confidence, "Signora, that girl is far too beautiful!"

In a short time I went back to San Lorenzo. Half-way down I met Giacomi and his wife, and a donkey laden with sacks.

"Mulberry leaves," said the beautiful Francesca, following my glance, "mulberry leaves for the cavalleri."

"Have you no trees?" I asked in surprise.

"Yes," answered Giacomi, "I have several mulberry trees, but the cavalleri have eaten all the leaves up. So now we have to buy them."

"How is that done?" I asked.

"You hire the tree and pick the leaves as you want them. These are from the town."

"As far off as that?"

"Signora, that is nothing. Some years it is impossible to get leaves, and we have to send a much greater distance. . . ."

They passed on.

San Lorenzo looked very desolate.

Bortolo was making a grand mess carrying brushwood upstairs into the attic. It was for the cavalleri. The time had come for them to make the cocoons, and as soon as they showed signs of spinning, they were carried up and put on the brushwood. The whole attic was taken up with these bushes, which Bortolo carefully set up.

Besides the work of feeding the cavalleri, they now had to be closely watched. Those ready to spin had to be taken upstairs at once, before a cocoon was started, and all the trays had continually to be looked over. Even then many evaded Rosina's vigilance, and climbing up the pole to the ceiling, were spinning in the corners of the room.

The cavalleri were put on a large tin tray which Riccardo carried up into the attic, where he distributed them carefully on the bushes, for if they got too close together double cocoons are spun. I never realised the number of cavalleri Rosina had until I saw the thousands and thousands of golden cocoons amongst the brushwood. In the uncertain light of the attic they looked like myriads of Chinese lanterns. I do not know how many there were, but if the little handful Rosina had shown me weighed not more than one ounce, there must have been nearly thirty-five thousand cavalleri. It takes quite a ton of leaves to rear as many as that.

Of course they weren't all ready to spin on the same day, a few precocious ones began and the others followed, and more and more—they were carried up to the attic day and night.

It took only a few days for the cocoons to be finished. Then they had to be carefully picked off and put into baskets. A certain number had to be freed from floss, and the pupae kept for breeding purposes. The remaining cocoons were delivered as they were. The society announced the date for delivery, and the whole family were harder at work than ever getting all ready to time.

Rosina drooped. She was hoarse, and lacked the energy to shout, but it didn't matter, as every one was in the room with her. It was most tedious to free the pupae from floss. They were put on a board with an iron rod across it, and one of the boys turned the handle. The cocoons were tipped up against the rod and the threads caught on it, and yard after yard gradually wound off. The boys turned the handle all day, even Pina had to help. Bortolo kept running up to the attic to pick the cocoons off the brushwood. Then he came down and made the polenta, and they all ate chunks of it upstairs.

•   •   •

At last it was over and fresh flowers stood before the little image of St. Antonio on the landing.

Rosina, strengthened by a night's rest, was polishing copper pots in the kitchen. She was dismally thinking of her work that was so behindhand. There was so much washing she would have to ask Ghita to help her with it; there was mending to be done, there was sewing, there was Selina to whom she hadn't written for weeks. The whole house needed a clean up, and next week the weary work of bottle-washing must be begun. She hadn't been to mass for weeks. Madre mia, what slavery! She would never look at a silkworm if it wasn't for the money . . . one had to have money . . . and there were debts. How they weighed on her; not so Bortolo, he was always tranquillo,

nothing ever disturbed *him* . . . it was she—she who had to think of everything. . . .

And the cavalleri? The work, from start to finish, had covered forty days,
and Rosina's cocoons had weighed fifty-six kilograms. The society paid four
lire the kilo—so Rosina had earned exactly 224 lire, which is all but £9.

CHAPTER 9   LAWRENCE DURRELL

MAY INTRIGUE BE YOUR LOT—
HOW TO BUY A HOUSE IN CYPRUS

> *Last of all came the Greeks and inquired of the*
> *Lord for their gift.*
> *"What gift would you like?" said the Lord.*
> *"We would like the gift of Power," said the*
> *Greeks.*
> *The Lord replied: "Ah, my poor Greeks, you have*
> *come too late. All the gifts have been distributed.*
> *There is practically nothing left. The gift of Power has*
> *been given to the Turks, the Bulgarians the gift of*
> *Labour; the Jews of Calculation, the French of Trickery*
> *and the English of Foolishness."*
> *The Greeks waxed very angry at this and shouted,*
> *"By what intrigue have we been overlooked?"*
> *"Very well," said the Lord. "Since you insist, you*
> *too shall have a present and not remain empty-*
> *handed—may Intrigue be your lot," said the Lord.*
>
> *(Bulgarian Folk-tale)*

Sabri Tahir's office in the Turkish quarter of Kyrenia bore a sun-blistered legend describing him as a valuer and estate agent, but his activities had proliferated since the board was painted and he was clearly many things besides. The centre of the cobweb was a dark cool godown perched strategically upon a junction of streets, facing the little Turkish shrine of some saint or warrior whose identity had vanished from the record, but whose stone tomb was still an object of veneration and pilgrimage for the faithful. It stood under a dusty and desiccated pepper tree, and one could always find an *ex voto* or two hanging beside it.

Beyond was a featureless empty field of nettles in which stood a couple of shacks full of disembodied pieces of machinery and huge heaps of uncut carob and olive, mingled with old railway sleepers and the carcasses of buses which always turned up here at the end of the trail, as if to some Elephants' Graveyard, to be turned into fuel. Sabri's Empire was still in an embryonic stage, though it was quite clear that he was speculating wisely. A circular saw moaned and gnashed all day in one of the shacks under the ministrations of two handsome Turkish youths with green headbands and dilapidated clothes; a machine for making cement blocks performed its slow but punctual evacuations, accompanied by a seductive crunch.

Sabri could watch all these diverse activities from the darkness of his shop where he sat for the greater part of the day before a Turkish coffee, unmoved, unmoving, but watchful. His desk was in the far corner against the wall, and to reach it one traversed a *terrain vague* which resembled the basement of Maple's, so crowded was it with armchairs, desks, prams, cooking-stoves, heaters, and all the impedimenta of gracious living.

The man himself was perhaps forty years of age, sturdily built, and with a fine head on his shoulders. He had the sleepy good looks—a rare smile with perfect teeth, thoughtful brown eyes—which one sees sometimes in Turkish travel posters. But what was truly Turkish about him was the physical repose with which he confronted the world. No Greek can sit still without fidgeting, tapping a foot or a pencil, jerking a knee, or making popping noises with his tongue. The Turk has a monolithic poise, an air of reptilian concentration and silence. It is with just such an air that a chameleon can sit, hour after hour, upon a shrub, staring unwinkingly at the world, living apparently in that state of suspended judgement which is summed up by the Arabic word *kayf*. I have seen Sabri loading logs, shouting at peasants, even running down a street; but never has he conveyed the slightest feeling of energy being expended. His actions and words had the smoothness of inevitability; they flowed from him like honey from a spoon.

On that first morning when I stepped into the shadows of his shop, the headquarters of the empire, he was sitting dreamily at his desk mending a faulty cigarette-lighter. His good-morning was civil, though preoccupied and indifferent; but as I approached he paused for one instant to snap finger and thumb and a chair materialized from the shadows behind him. I sat down. He abandoned his task and sat silent and unwinking before me. "Mr. Sabri," I said, "I need your help. I have been making inquiries in Kyrenia and on all sides I am told that you are the most untrustworthy man of business in the place—in fact, the biggest rogue."

He did not find the idea offensive so much as merely interesting. His shrewd eye sharpened a trifle, however, and he lowered his head to scan me more gravely. I went on. "Now knowing the Levant as I do, I know that a reputation for being a rogue means one thing and one thing only. It means that one is *cleverer* than other people." I accompanied this with the appropriate gesture—for cleverness in the hand-language is indicated by placing the forefinger of the right hand slowly and portentously upon the temple: tapping slightly, as one might tap a breakfast-egg. (Incidentally, one has to be careful, as if one turns the finger in the manner of turning a bolt in a thread, the significance is quite different: it means to be "soft in the head" or to "have a screw loose.") I tapped my skull softly. "*Cleverer* than other people," I repeated. "So clever that the stupid are envious of one."

He did not assent or dissent from the proposition. He simply sat and considered me as one might a piece of machinery if one were uncertain of its use. But the expression in his eyes shifted slightly in a manner suggesting the faintest, most tenuous admiration. "I am here," I went on, convinced by this time that his English was good, for he had followed me unerringly so far, to judge by his face, "I am here as a comparatively poor man to ask you a favour, not to make you a business proposition. There is no money to be made out of me. But I want you to let me use your brains and experience. I'm trying to find a cheap village house in which to settle for a year or two— perhaps forever if I like it enough here. I can see now that I was not wrong; far from being a rogue you are obviously a Turkish gentleman, and I feel I can confide myself entirely to your care—if you will accept such a thing. I have nothing to offer except gratitude and friendship. I ask you as a Turkish gentleman to assist me."

Sabri's colour had changed slowly throughout this harangue and when I ended he was blushing warmly. I could see that I had scored a diplomatic stroke in throwing myself completely upon the iron law of hospitality which underpins all relations in the Levant. More than this, I think the magic word "gentleman" turned the trick in my favour for it accorded him an unaccustomed place in the consideration of strangers which he certainly merited, and which he thenceforward lived up to in his dealings with me. By a single tactful speech I had made a true friend.

He leaned forward at his desk, smiling now, and patted my hand gently, confidingly: "But of course, my dear," he said, "of course."

Then he suddenly threw up his chin and barked an order. A barefoot youth materialized from the shadows bearing Coca-Cola on a tray, apparently ordered by some invisible gesture a while before. "Drink," he said quietly, "and tell me what house you want."

"A village house, not a modern villa."

"How far away?"

"Not far. Among these hills."

"Old houses need doing up."

"If I can buy one cheaply I shall do it up."

"How much can you spend?"

"Four hundred pounds."

He looked grave at this and this was understandable, for the price of land had been soaring since the war, and indeed continued to soar until the time of my departure from the island when building plots in the centre of Nicosia cost roughly the same as those in Washington. "My dear," he said thoughtfully, and stroked his moustache. "My dear." Outside the darkness of his shop the spring sunshine glistened on trees loaded with cold tangerines; a cold wind touched the fronds of the palm-trees, quick with the taste of snow from the Taurus mountains across the water. "My dear," repeated Sabri thoughtfully. "Of course if you lived very far away it would be quite easy, but do you wish to be within reach of the capital?" I nodded. "If I run out of money then I shall have to work, and there is nothing to be found out of Nicosia." He nodded. "Somewhere not too far from Kyrenia you want an arty old house." That summed it up perfectly. Sabri took a thoughtful turn or two among the shadows and stubbed out his cigarette on the box. "Honestly, my dear," he said, "it will be a matter of luck. I do hear of things, but it is a matter of luck. And it is very difficult to find one person to deal with. You are at once in a bloody family, my dear." I did not then know what he meant. I was soon to learn.

"Do not be disappointed if you hear nothing from me for a while. What you ask is not easy, but I think I can do it. I will be working on it even if I am silent. Do you understand, my dear?" His handshake was warm.

I had hardly reached the main street on my way back to Panos' house when Renos the boot-black came out of a side street and took my arm. He was a tiny little wisp of a man with the sort of eyes one finds sewn on to rag dolls. "My friend," he said, "you have been to see Sabri." This is the favourite Mediterranean game, a tireless spying upon the movements of friends and acquaintances, and is common to all communities which do not read, whose whole life is built up by oral tradition and common gossip. "Yes," I said.

"Phew." He went through a pantomime in the hand language, burning his fingers on hot coals and blowing upon them. This meant "You will be stung." I shrugged my shoulders. "What to do?" I said cheerfully. "Aie aie," said Renos, laying one hand to his cheek and rocking his head commiseratingly as if he had toothache. But he said no more.

By the time I got home Panos himself had been informed of my visit— doubtless by bush telegraph. "You have been to see Sabri," he said as I crossed the brilliant courtyard of the church and joined him on his balcony over the bewitching blueness of the spring sea. "About a house?" I nodded. "You have done well," he said. "Indeed I was going to suggest it."

"Clito says he is a rogue."

"Nonsense. His dealings with me have been perfectly honourable. He is a pretty sharp business man, of course, which is not usual among Turks who are always half asleep. But he is no more of a rogue than anyone else. In fact, Clito himself is a rogue, if it comes to that. He overcharged me for this bottle of Commanderia. Incidentally did you tell Sabri how much money you have?"

"No, I told him less than I actually had."

Panos chuckled admiringly. "I see you understand business in these parts. Everything gets gossiped about, so that whatever price you would be prepared to pay would soon be known to everyone. You did right to put it low."

I accepted a glass of sweet Commanderia and a pickled pimento from the coloured china plate; the two children were doing a puzzle in the sunshine. The beadle crashed at the church bell in a sudden desultory burst of mania and then left the silence to echo round us in wing-beats of aftersound.

"I hear," said Panos when the vibrations had died away, "that your brother was killed at Thermopylae during the war."

"To be absolutely honest with you," I said, "I made the whole thing up in order to . . ."

"Tease Frangos!"

"Yes. I was afraid there would be a fight."

"Excellent. Capital." Panos was delighted by the subtlety of my imagination. He struck his knee delightedly as he laughed. "Capital," he repeated. "It is clear that as rogues go you are as bad as any of us." It was a compliment to be thus included in the rogues' gallery of Kyrenia.

That evening it was I who recited the geography lesson while Panos stood behind me, nodding approvingly as I picked out the salient points of the Kyrenia range with a forefinger, travelling gently over the blue spines of the hills from the point where Myrtou lay invisible among its hazy farms and vineyards to where Akanthou (equally invisible) drowsed among its fields of yellow-green barley. In truth, by now I had memorized the lesson so well that the very names of the places I had yet to visit communicated a sharp visual image of them. I could see the lemon-groves of Lapithos and feel the dense cool air of its orchards: hear the sullen thunder of the headspring as it gushed into the valley from the mountain's summit. The great double-combed crown of Hilarion stood almost directly behind us with its castle taking the last lion-gold rays of the evening upon its tawny flanks. Over the saddle below it ran the main road to Nicosia, piercing the range at its lowest point. East of us loomed other peaks whose sulky magnificence echoed each other, mingling like the notes of a musical chord: Buffavento, seat of the winds, with the silent and graceful Gothic abbey of Bellapaix below it in the foothills; Pendedactyl whose five-fingered peak recalled the fingerprints of the hero Dighenis; fading all of them, and inclining slowly eastward into the mist like the proud sails of some Venetian argosy, to where Cape Andreas drowsed in spindrift at the end of the long stone handle of the Karpass. The place names chimed as one spoke them like a carillon, Greek Babylas and

Myrtou, Turkish Kasaphani, Crusader Templos. . . . The mixture was a heady one.

"Very good," said Panos at last, with a sigh of real pleasure. "You really do know it. But now you must visit it." I had intended to ere this, but my preoccupations about a house had quite consumed me, while problems of correspondence and the transport of luggage, money, etc. had made my mind too turbid for use. I had left it all lying there, so to speak, multiplying itself in my imagination, until I should be ready to go out and meet it. Apart from a few short excursions around Kyrenia in search of spring flowers and mushrooms I had been nowhere; indeed had done nothing except bathe and write letters. Life in an island, however rich, is circumscribed, and one does well to portion out one's experiences, for sooner or later one arrives at a point where all is known and staled by repetition. Taken leisurely, with all one's time at one's disposal Cyprus could, I calculate, afford one a minimum of two years reckoned in terms of novelty; hoarded as I intended to hoard it, it might last anything up to a decade.

That is why I wished to experience it through its people rather than its landscape, to enjoy the sensation of sharing a common life with the humble villagers of the place; and later to expand my field of investigation to its history—the lamp which illumines national character—in order to offer my live subjects a frame against which to set themselves. Alas! I was not to have time.

The month or so of spring weather with its promise of summer to follow proved fraudulent. One day we woke to a sky covered in ugly festoons of black cloud and saw drift upon drift of silver needles like arrows falling upon the ramparts of Kyrenia castle. Thunder clamoured and rolled, and the grape-blue semi-darkness of the sea was bitten out in magnesium flashes as the lightning clawed at us from Turkey like a family of dragons. The stone floors turned damp and cold, the gutters brimmed and mumbled all day as they poured a cascade of rain into the street. Below us the sea dashed huge waves across the front where not a week ago we had been sitting in shorts and sandals, drinking coffee and *ouzo,* and making plans for the summer. It was a thrilling change, for one could feel the luxuriant grass fattening under the olives, and the spring flowers unwrapping their delicate petals on the anemone-starred slopes below Clepini.

It was hardly a propitious moment for Sabri to arrive, but arrive he did one black afternoon, wearing as his only protection a spotted handkerchief over his head against the elements. He burst through Panos' front door between thunder-flashes like an apparition from the underworld, gasping: "My dear." His suit was liberally streaked with rain. "I have something for you to see—but *please*" (in anguish almost) "don't blame me if it is not suitable. I haven't seen it myself yet. But it *may* be . . ." He accepted a glass of wine in chilled fingers. "It is in the village of Bellapaix, but too far from the road. Anyway, will you come? I have a taxi. The owner is a rogue of course. I can guarantee *nothing*."

I could see that he was most anxious that I should not judge his professional skill by what might turn out to be a mistake. Together we galloped across the rain-echoing courtyard and down the long flight of stairs by the church to where Jamal and his ancient taxi waited. The handles were off all the doors and there ensued a brief knockabout scene from a Turkish shadow-play among the three of us which finally resulted in our breaking into the vehicle at a weak point in its defenses. (Jamal had to crawl through the boot, and half-way through the back seat, in order to unlatch for us.) Then we were off through a landscape blurred with rain and the total absence of windscreen wipers. Jamal drove with his head out of the window for the sake of safety. Outside, the rain-blackened span of mountains glittered fitfully in the lightning-flashes.

Just outside Kyrenia a road turned to the right and led away across a verdant strip of olive and carob land towards the foothills where Bellapaix stood in rain and mist. "Nevertheless," said Sabri thoughtfully, "it is a good day, for nobody will be out of doors. The café will be empty. We won't cause the gossips, my dear." He meant, I suppose, that in any argument over prices the influence of the village wiseacres would seriously affect the owner's views. A sale needed privacy; if the village coffee shop undertook a general debate on a transaction there was no knowing what might happen.

I was prepared for something beautiful, and I already knew that the ruined monastery of Bellapaix was one of the loveliest Gothic survivals in the Levant, but I was not prepared for the breath-taking congruence of the little village which surrounded and cradled it against the side of the mountain. Fronting the last rise, the road begins to wind through a landscape dense with orange and lemon trees, and noisy with running water. Almond and peach-blossom graze the road, as improbably precise as the décor to a Japanese play. The village comes down to the road for the last hundred yards or so with its grey old-fashioned houses with arched vaults and carved doors set in old-fashioned mouldings. Then abruptly one turns through an arc of 150 degrees under the Tree of Idleness and comes to a stop in the main square under the shadow of the Abbey itself. Young cypresses bent back against the sky as they took the wind; the broad flower beds were full of magnificent roses among the almond trees. Yet it all lay deserted in the rain.

The owner of the house was waiting for us in a doorway with a sack over his head. He was a rather dejected-looking man whom I had already noticed maundering about the streets of Kyrenia. He was a cobbler by trade. He did not seem very exuberant—perhaps it was the weather—but almost without a word spoken led us up the boulder-strewn main street, slipping and stumbling amongst the wet stones. Irrigation channels everywhere had burst their banks and Sabri, still clad in his handkerchief, gazed gloomily about him as he picked his way among the compost heaps where the chickens browsed.

"It's no good, my dear," he said after we had covered about a hundred yards without arriving at the house. "You could never get up here." But still the guide led on, and curiosity made us follow him. The road had now become very steep indeed and resembled the bed of a torrent; down the centre poured a cascade of water. "My God," groaned Sabri, "it is a trout-stream, my dear." It certainly seemed like one. The three of us crept upwards, walking wherever possible on the facing-stones of the irrigation channel. "I am terribly sorry," said Sabri. "You will have a cold and blame me."

The atmosphere of the village was quite enthralling; its architecture was in the purest peasant tradition—domed Turkish privies in courtyards fanning out from great arched doors with peasant mouldings still bearing the faint traces of a Venetian influence; old Turkish screen-windows for ventilation. It had the purity and authenticity of a Cretan hamlet. And everywhere grew roses, and the pale clouds of almond and peach blossom; on the balconies grew herbs in window-boxes made from old petrol tins; and crowning every courtyard like a messenger from my Indian childhood spread the luxuriant green fan of banana-leaves, rattling like parchment in the wind. From behind the closed door of the tavern came the mournful whining of a mandolin.

At the top of the slope where the village vanished and gave place to the scrubby outworks of the mountain behind, stood an old irrigation tank, and here our guide disappeared round a corner, drawing from his breast an iron key the size of a man's forearm. We scrambled after him and came upon the house, a large box-like house in the Turkish-Cypriot mode, with huge carved doors made for some forgotten race of giants and their oxen. "Very arty, my dear," said Sabri, noting the fine old windows with their carved screens, "but what a place"; and then he kicked the wall in an expert way so that the plaster fell off and revealed the mysteries of its construction to his practised eye. "Mud brick with straw." It was obviously most unsatisfactory. "Never mind," I said, stirred by a vague interior premonition which I could not put exactly into words. "Never mind. Let's look now we're here."

The owner swung himself almost off the ground in an effort to turn the great key in the lock which was one of the old pistol-spring type such as one sees sometimes in medieval English houses. We hung on to his shoulders and added our strength to his until it turned screeching in the lock and the great door fell open. We entered, while the owner shot the great bolts which held the other half of the door in position and propped both open with a faggot. Here his interest died, for he stayed religiously by the door, still shrouded in his sack, showing no apparent interest in our reactions. The hall was gloomy and silent—but remarkably dry considering the day. I stood for a while listening to my own heart beating and gazing about me. The four tall double doors were splendid with their old-fashioned panels and the two windows which gave internally on to the hall were fretted with wooden slats of a faintly Turkish design. The whole proportion and disposition of things here was of a thrilling promise; even Sabri glowed at the woodwork which was indeed of splendid make and in good condition.

The floor, which was of earth, was as dry as if tiled. Obviously the walls of the house offered good insulation—but then earth brick usually does if it is laid thickly enough. The wind moaned in the clump of banana trees, and at intervals I could still hear the whimper of the mandolin.

Sabri, who had by now recovered his breath, began to take a more detailed view of things, while I, still obscured by premonitions of a familiarity which I could not articulate, walked to the end of the hall to watch the rain rattling among the pomegranates. The garden was hardly larger than twenty square yards, but crammed with trees standing shoulder to shoulder at such close quarters that their greenery formed an almost unbroken roof. There were too many—some would have to go: I caught myself up with a start. It was early for me to begin behaving like the house's owner. Abstractedly I counted them again: six tangerines, four bitter lemons, two pomegranates, two mulberry trees and a tall leaning walnut. Though there were houses on both sides they were completely hidden by greenery. This part of the village with its steep slope was built up in tiers, balcony upon balcony, with the trees climbing up between. Here and there through the green one caught a glint of the sea, or a corner of the Abbey silhouetted against it.

My reverie was interrupted by a moan and I feared for a moment that Sabri had immolated himself in one of the rooms upon the discovery of some dreadful fact about the woodwork. But no. A heifer was the cause of the noise. It stood, plaintively chewing something in the front room, tethered to a ring in the wall. Sabri clicked his tongue disapprovingly and shut the door. "A bloody cow, my dear," he smiled with all the townsman's indulgence towards the peasant's quirks. "Inside of the house." There were two other rather fine rooms with a connecting door of old workmanship, and a couple of carved cupboards. Then came a landslide. "Don't open it!" shouted the owner and flew to the help of the gallant Sabri who was wrestling with a door behind which apparently struggled some huge animal—a camel perhaps or an elephant? "I forgot to tell you," panted the owner as we all three set our shoulders to the panels. The room was stacked breast-high with grain which had poured out upon Sabri as he opened the door. Together we got it shut but not before the observant Sabri had noticed how dry the grain was in its store. "This is dry," he panted grudgingly. "So much I can say."

But this was not all; we were about to leave when the owner suddenly recollected that there was more to see and pointed a quavering finger at the ceiling in the manner of Saint John in the icons. "One more room," he said, and we now took a narrow outside staircase where the rain still drizzled, and climbed out upon a balcony where we both stood speechless. The view was indescribable. Below us, the village curved away in diminishing perspective to the green headland upon which the Abbey stood, its fretted head silhouetted against the Taurus range. Through the great arches gleamed the grey-gold fields of cherries and oranges and the delicate spine of Kasaphani's mosque. From this high point we were actually looking down upon Bellapaix, and beyond it, five miles away, upon Kyrenia whose castle looked absurdly like a toy. Even Sabri was somewhat awed by the view. Immediately behind, the mountain climbed into blue space, topped by the ragged outcrop and mouldering turrets of Buffavento. "My God," I said feebly. "What a position."

The balcony itself was simply a flat platform of earth with no balustrade. Up here in one corner of it was a rather lofty and elegant room, built on a bias, and empty of everything save a pair of shoes and a pile of tangerines. We returned to the balcony with its terrific panorama. The storm had begun to lift now and sun was struggling feebly to get out; the whole eastern prospect was suffused with the light which hovers over El Greco's Toledo.

"But the balcony itself," said Sabri with genuine regret, "my dear, it will need concrete." "Why?" He smiled at me. "I must tell you how the peasant house is built—the roof. Come down." We descended the narrow outside stair together, while he produced a notebook and pencil. "First the beams are laid," he said indicating the long series of magnificent beams, and at the same time scribbling in his book. "Then some reed mats. Then packets of osiers to fill the airspace, or perhaps dried seaweed. Then Carmi earth, then gravel. Finally it all leaks and you spend the whole winter trying to stop the leaks."

"But this house doesn't," I said.

"Some do sooner than others."

I pointed to the mason's signature upon the graven iron plaque which adorned the main door. It bore the conventional Orthodox cross embossed on it with the letters IE XR N (Jesus Christ Conquers) and the date 1897. Underneath, on the lower half of the plate, in the space reserved to record subsequent building or alteration was written only one date (9th September 1940), when presumably some restoration work had been undertaken. "Yes, I know, my dear," said Sabri patiently. "But if you buy this house you will have to rebuild the balcony. You are my friend, and so I shall insist for your own good."

We debated this in low tones on the way down the hill. Though the rain had slackened the village street was empty save for the little corner shop, a grocery store, where a thickset young man sat alone, amid sacks of potatoes and dry packets of spaghetti, playing patience on a table. He shouted good afternoon.

In the main square Jamal sat uneasily under the Tree of Idleness beneath an open umbrella, drinking coffee. I was about to engage the owner of the house in discussion as to the sort of price he had in mind for such a fine old relic when Sabri motioned me to silence. The coffee-house was gradually filling up with people and faces were turning curiously towards us. "You will need time to think," he said. "And I have told him you don't want to buy it at all, at any price. This will make the necessary despondence, my dear."

"But I'd like to have an idea of the price."

"My dear, he has no idea *himself*. Perhaps five hundred pounds, perhaps twenty pounds, perhaps ten shillings. He is completely vacant of ideas.

In the bargaining everything will get cleared. But we must take time. In Cyprus time is everything."

I rode regretfully down the green winding ways to Kyrenia thinking deeply about the house which seemed more desirable in retrospect than it had in actual fact. Meanwhile, Sabri talked to me in knowledgeable fashion about the drawbacks to buying out there. "You simply have not considered such problems," he said, "as water, for example. Have you?"

I had not, and I felt deeply ashamed of the fact. "Give me two days," said Sabri, "and I will find out about the land and water-rights of the property. Then we will ask the man and his wife for the big price-conversation at my office. By God, you will see how tricky we are in Cyprus. And if you buy the house I will send you to a friend of mine to do the rebuilding. He is a rogue, of course, but just the man. I only ask, give me time."

That night when I told Panos that I had seen what might prove to be a suitable house for me at Bellapaix he was delighted, for he had lived there for several years, teaching at the local school. "They are the laziest people in the world," he said, "and the best-natured in Cyprus. And you have honey, and also in the valley behind the house nightingales, my friend."

He did not mention silk, almonds and apricots: oranges, pomegranates, quince. . . . Perhaps he did not wish to influence me too deeply.

Sabri meanwhile retired into silence and contemplation for nearly a week after this; I imagined him sharpening himself for the coming contest of wills by long silent fasts—broken perhaps by a glass of sherbet—or perhaps even prayer for long stretches. The skies turned blue and hard again, and the orange-trees in the Bishopric put out their gleaming suns. The season was lengthening once more into summer, one felt; was stretching itself, the days beginning to unfold more slowly, the twilights to linger. Once more the little harbour filled up with its crowds of chaffering fishermen darning their nets, and of yachtsmen dawdling over caulked seams and a final coat of paint.

Then at last the summons came; I was to present myself at Sabri's office the next morning at eight. Panos brought me the message, smiling at my obvious anxiety, and telling me that Sabri was rather despondent because it now appeared that the house was owned not by the cobbler but by his wife. It had been her dowry, and she herself was going to conduct the sale. "With women," said my friend, "it is always a Calvary to argue. A Golgotha." Nevertheless Sabri had decided to go forward with the business. The intervening space of time had been valuable, however, because he had come into possession of a piece of vital information about the water supply. Water is so scarce in Cyprus that it is sold in parcels. You buy an hour here and an hour there from the owner of a spring—needless to say no quantity measure exists. The trouble lies here: that water-rights form part of property-titles of citizens and are divided up on the death of the owner among his dependants. This is true also of land and indeed of trees. Families being what they are, it is common for a single spring to be owned by upwards of thirty people, or a single tree to be shared out among a dozen members of a family. The whole problem, then, is one of obtaining common consent—usually one has to pay for the signatures of thirty people in order to achieve any agreement which is binding. Otherwise one dissident nephew and niece can veto the whole transaction. In the case of some trees, for example, one man may own the produce of the tree, another the ground on which it stands, a third the actual timber. As may be imagined the most elementary litigation assumes gigantic proportions—which explains why there are so many lawyers in Cyprus.

Now Sabri had got wind of the fact that the Government was planning to install the piped water supply to the village which had been promised for so long; moreover that the plans were already being drawn up. The architect of the Public Works happened to be a friend of his so he casually dropped into his office and asked to see where the various water-points were to be placed. It was a stroke of genius, for he saw with delight that there was to be a public water-point outside the very front door of the old house. This more than offset the gloomy intelligence that the only water the cobbler owned was about an hour a month from the main spring—perhaps sixty gallons: whereas the average water consumption of an ordinary family is about forty gallons a *day*. This was a trump card, for the cobbler's water belonged in equal part to the rest of his wife's family—all eighteen of them, including the idiot boy Pipi whose signature was always difficult to obtain on a legal document. . . .

I found my friend, freshly shaven and spruce, seated in the gloom of his office, surrounded by prams, and absolutely motionless. Before him on the blotter lay the great key of the house, which he poked from time to time in a reproachful way. He put his finger to his lips with a conspiratorial air and motioned me to a chair. "They are all here, my dear," he hissed, "getting ready." He pointed to the café across the road where the cobbler had gathered his family. They looked more like seconds. They sat on a semicircle of chairs, sipping coffee and arguing in low voices; a number of beards waggled, a number of heads nodded. They looked like a rugger scrum in an American film receiving last-minute instructions from their captain. Soon they would fall upon us like a ton of bricks and gouge us. I began to feel rather alarmed. "Now, whatever happens," said Sabri in a low voice, tremulous with emotion, "do not surprise. You must never surprise. And you don't want the house at all, see?"

I repeated the words like a catechism. "I don't want the house. I absolutely don't want the house." Yet in my mind's eye I could see those great doors ("God," Sabri had said, "this is fine wood. From Anatolia. In the old days they floated the great timbers over the water behind boats. This is Anatolian timber, it will last for ever"). Yes, I could see those doors under a glossy coat of blue paint. . . . "I don't want the house," I repeated under my breath, feverishly trying to put myself into the appropriate frame of mind.

"Tell them we are ready," said Sabri to the shadows and a barefooted youth flitted across the road to where our adversaries had gathered. They hummed like bees, and the cobbler's wife detached herself from the circle—or tried to, for many a hand clutched at her frock, detaining her for a last-minute consideration which was hissed at her secretively by the family elders. At last she wrenched herself free and walked boldly across the road, entering Sabri's shrine with a loud "Good morning" spoken very confidently.

She was a formidable old faggot, with a handsome self-indulgent face, and a big erratic body. She wore the white headdress and dark skirt of the village woman, and her breasts were gathered into the traditional baggy bodice with a drawstring at the waist, which made it look like a loosely furled sail. She stood before us looking very composed as she gave us good morning. Sabri cleared his throat, and picking up the great key very delicately between finger and thumb—as if it were of the utmost fragility—put it down again on the edge of the desk nearest her with the air of a conjurer making his opening dispositions. "We are speaking about your house," he said softly, in a voice ever so faintly curdled with menace. "Do you know that all the wood is . . ." he suddenly shouted the last word with such force that I nearly fell off my chair, "rotten!" And picking up the key he banged it down to emphasize the point.

The woman threw up her head with contempt and taking up the key also banged it down in her turn exclaiming: "It is not."

"It *is*." Sabri banged the key.

"It is *not*." She banged it back.

"It *is*." A bang.

"It is *not*." A counter-bang.

All this was not on a very high intellectual level, and made me rather ill at ease. I also feared that the key itself would be banged out of shape so that finally none of us would be able to get into the house. But these were the opening chords, so to speak, the preliminary statement of theme.

The woman now took the key and held it up as if she were swearing by it. "The house is a good house," she cried. Then she put it back on the desk. Sabri took it up thoughtfully, blew into the end of it as if it were a six-shooter, aimed it and peered along it as if along a barrel. Then he put it down and fell into an abstraction. "And suppose we wanted the house," he said, "which we don't, what would you ask for it?"

"Eight hundred pounds."

Sabri gave a long and stagy laugh, wiping away imaginary tears and repeating "Eight hundred pounds" as if it were the best joke in the world. He laughed at me and I laughed at him, a dreadful false laugh. He slapped his knee. I rolled about in my chair as if on the verge of acute gastritis. We laughed until we were exhausted. Then he grew serious again. Sabri was still fresh as a daisy, I could see that. He had put himself into the patient contemplative state of mind of a chess player.

"Take the key and go," he snapped suddenly, and handing it to her, swirled round in his swivel chair to present her with his back; then as suddenly he completed the circuit and swivelled round again. "What!" he said with surprise. "You haven't gone." In truth there had hardly been time for the woman to go. But she was somewhat slow-witted, though obstinate as a mule: that was clear. "Right," she now said in a ringing tone, and picking up the key put it into her bosom and turned about. She walked off stage in a somewhat lingering fashion. "Take no notice," whispered Sabri and busied himself with his papers.

The woman stopped irresolutely outside the shop, and was here joined by her husband who began to talk to her in a low cringing voice, pleading with her. He took her by the sleeve and led her unwillingly back into the shop where we sat pointedly reading letters. "Ah! It's you," said Sabri with well-simulated surprise. "She wishes to discuss some more," explained the cobbler in a weak conciliatory voice. Sabri sighed.

"What is there to speak of? She takes me for a fool." Then he suddenly turned to her and bellowed, "Two hundred pounds and not a piastre more."

It was her turn to have a paroxysm of false laughter, but this was rather spoiled by her husband who started plucking at her sleeve as if he were persuading her to be sensible. Sabri was not slow to notice this. "You tell her," he said to the man. "You are a man and these things are clear to you. She is only a woman and does not see the truth. Tell her what it is worth."

The cobbler, who quite clearly lacked spirit, turned once more to his wife and was about to say something to her, but in a sudden swoop she produced the key and raised it above her head as if she intended to bring it down on his hairless dome. He backed away rapidly. "Fool," she growled. "Can't you see they are making a fool of you? Let me handle this." She made another pass at him with the key and he tiptoed off to join the rest of her relations in the coffee-shop opposite, completely crushed. She now turned to me and extended a wheedling hand, saying in Greek, "Ah come along there, you an Englishman, striking a hard bargain with a woman. . . ." But I had given no indication of speaking Greek so that it was easy to pretend not to understand her. She turned back to Sabri, staring balefully, and banging the key down once more shouted "Six hundred," while Sabri in the same breath bellowed "Two hundred." The noise was deafening.

They panted and glared at each other for a long moment of silence like boxers in a clinch waiting for the referee to part them. It was the perfect moment for Sabri to get in a quick one below the belt. "Anyway, your house is mortgaged," he hissed, and she reeled under the punch. "Sixty pounds and three piastres," he added, screwing the glove a little to try to draw blood. She held her groin as if in very truth he had landed her a blow in it. Sabri followed up swiftly: "I offer you two hundred pounds plus the mortgage."

She let out a yell. "No. Never," and banged the key. "Yes, I say," bellowed Sabri giving a counter-bang. She grabbed the key (by now it had become, as it were, the very symbol of our contention. The house was forgotten. We were trying to buy this old rusty key which looked like something fitter for Saint Peter's key-ring than my own). She grabbed the key, I say, and put it to her breast like a child as she said: "Never in this life." She rocked it back and forth, suckled it, and put it down again.

Sabri now became masterful and put it in his pocket. At this she let out a yell and advanced on him shouting: "You give me back my key and I shall leave you with the curses of all the saints upon you." Sabri stood up like a showman and held the key high above his head, out of her reach, repeating inexorably: "Two hundred. Two hundred. Two hundred." She snapped and strained like a hooked fish, exclaiming all the time: "Saint Catherine defend me. No. No." Then quite suddenly they both stopped, he replaced the key on the desk and sat down, while she subsided like a pan of boiling milk when it is lifted off the fire. "I shall consult," she said briefly in another voice and leaving the key where it was she took herself off across the road to where her seconds waited with towels and sponges. The first round was a draw, though Sabri had made one or two good points.

"What happens now?" I said, and he chuckled. "Just time for a coffee. I think, you know, my dear," he added, "that we will have to pay another hundred. I feel it." He was like a countryman who can tell what the weather will be like from small signs invisible to the ordinary townsman. It was an enthralling spectacle, this long-drawn-out pantomime, and I was now pre-pared for the negotiations to go on for a week. "They don't know about the water," said Sabri. "They will let us have the house cheap and then try and sting us for the water-rights. We must pretend to forget about the water and buy the house cheaper. Do you see?" I saw the full splendour of his plan as it unfolded before us. "But," he said, "everything must be done today, now, for if she goes back to the village and makes the gossips nothing will be consum-mated." It seemed to me that she was already making the gossips in the café opposite, for a furious altercation had broken out. She was accusing her husband of something and he was replying waspishly and waving his arms.

After a while Sabri whispered: "Here she comes again," and here she came, rolling along with sails spread and full of the cargo of her misfortunes. She had changed her course. She now gave us a long list of her family troubles, hoping to soften us up; but by now I felt as if my teeth had been sharpened into points. It was clear that she was weakening. It was a matter of time before we could start winding her in. It was, in fact, the psychological moment to let out the line, and this Sabri Tahir now did by offering her another hundred ("a whole hundred," he repeated juicily in a honeyed voice) if she would clinch the deal there and then. "Your husband is a fool," he added, "and your family ignorant. You will never find a buyer if you do not take this gentleman. Look at him. Already he is weakening. He will go else-where. Just look at his face." I tried to compose my face in a suitable manner to play my full part in the pantomime. She stared at me in the manner of a hungry peasant assessing a turnip and suddenly sat herself down for the first time, bursting as she did so into heartrending sobs. Sabri was delighted and gave me a wink.

She drew her wimple round her face and went into convulsions, repeat-ing audibly: "O Jesus, what are they doing to me? Destruction has overtaken my house and my line. My issue has been murdered, my good name dragged in the dust." Sabri was in a high good humour by this time. He leaned forward and began to talk to her in the voice of Mephistopheles himself, filling the interstices between her sentences with his insinuations. I could hear him droning on "Mortgage . . . two hundred . . . husband a fool . . . never get such an opportunity." Meanwhile she rocked and moaned like an Arab, thoroughly enjoying herself. From time to time she cast a furtive glance at our faces to see how we were taking it; she could not have drawn much consolation from Sabri's for he was full of a triumphant concentration now; in the looming shadows he reminded me of some great killer shark—the flash of a white belly as it turned over on its back to take her. "We have not spoken of the water as yet," he said, and among her diminishing sobs she was still able to gasp out, "That will be another hundred."

"We are speaking only of the house," insisted Sabri, and at this a look of cunning came over her face. "Afterwards we will speak of the water." The tone in which he said this indicated subtly that he had now moved over on to her side. The foreigner, who spoke no Greek, could not possibly understand that without water-rights the house itself was useless. She shot a glance at me and then looked back at him, the look of cunning being replaced by a look almost of triumph. Had Sabri, in fact, changed sides? Was he perhaps also planning to make a killing, and once the house was bought. . . . She smiled now and stopped sobbing.

"All this can only be done immediately," said Sabri quietly. "Look. We will go to the widow and get the mortgage paper. We will pay her mortgage before you at the Land Registry. Then we will pay you before witnesses for the house." Then he added in a low voice: "After that the gentleman will discuss the water. Have you the papers?"

We were moving rather too swiftly for her. Conflicting feelings beset her; ignorance and doubt flitted across her face. An occasional involuntary sob shook her—like pre-ignition in an overheated engine which has already been switched off. "My grandfather has the title-deeds."

"Get them," said Sabri curtly.

She rose, still deeply preoccupied, and went back across the street where a furious argument broke out among her seconds. The white-bearded old man waved a stick and perorated. Her husband spread his hands and waggled them. Sabri watched all this with a critical eye. "There is only one danger—she must not get back to the village." How right he was; for if her relations could make all this noise about the deed of sale, what could the village coffee-shop not do? Such little concentration as she could muster would be totally scattered by conflicting counsels. The whole thing would probably end in a riot followed by an island-wide strike. . . .

I gazed admiringly at my friend. What a diplomat he would make! "Here she comes again," he said in a low voice, and here she came to place the roll of title-deeds on the table beside the key. Sabri did not look at them. "Have you discussed?" he said sternly. She groaned. "My grandfather will not let me do it. He says you are making a fool of me." Sabri snorted wildly.

"Is the house yours?"

"Yes, sir."

"Do you want the money?"

"Yes."

"Do you want it today?"

"Yes."

My friend leaned back in his chair and gazed up at the cobwebs in the roof. "Think of it," he said, his voice full of the poetry of commerce. "This gentleman will cut you a chekky. You will go to the Bank. There they will look with respect at it, for it will bear his name. They will open the safe. . . ." His voice trembled and she gazed thirstily at him, entranced by the story-book voice he had put on. "They will take from it notes, thick notes, as thick as a honeycomb, as thick as salami" (here they both involuntarily licked their lips and I myself began to feel hungry at the thought of so much edible money). "One . . . two . . . three," counted Sabri in his mesmeric voice full of animal magnetism. "Twenty . . . sixty . . . a hundred" gradually getting louder and louder until he ended at "three hundred." Throughout this recital she behaved like a chicken with her beak upon a chalk line. As he ended she gave a sigh of rapture and shook herself, as if to throw off the spell. "The mortgage will have been paid. The widow Anthi will be full of joy and respect for you. You and your husband will have *three hundred pounds*." He blew out his breath and mopped his head with a red handkerchief. "All you have to do is to agree. Or take your key."

He handed her the key and once more swivelled round, to remain facing the wall for a full ten seconds before completing the circle.

"Well?" he said. She was hovering on the edge of tears again. "And my grandfather?" she asked tremulously. Sabri spread his hands. "What can I do about your grandfather? Bury him?" he asked indignantly. "But act quickly, for the gentleman is going." At a signal from him I rose and stretched and said, "Well I think I . . ." like the curate in the Leacock story.

"Quick. Quick. Speak or he will be gone," said Sabri. A look of intense agony came over her face. "O Saint Matthew and Saint Luke," she exclaimed aloud, tortured beyond endurance by her doubts. It seemed a queer moment to take refuge in her religion, but obviously the decision weighed heavily upon her. "O Luke, O Mark," she rasped, with one hand extended towards me to prevent me from leaving.

Sabri was now like a great psychologist who divines that a difficult transference is at hand. "She will come," he whispered to me, and putting his fingers to his mouth blew a shrill blast which alerted everybody. At once with a rumble Jamal, who had apparently been lurking down a side street in his car, grated to the door in a cloud of dust. "Lay hold of her," Sabri said and grabbed the woman by the left elbow. Following instructions I grabbed the other arm. She did not actually resist but she definitely rested on her oars and it was something of an effort to roll her across the floor to the taxi. Apparently speed was necessary in this *coup de main* for he shouted: "Get her inside" and put his shoulder to her back as we propelled her into the back of the car and climbed in on top of her.

She now began to moan and scream as if she were being abducted—doubtless for the benefit of the grandfather—and to make dumb appeals for help through the windows. Her supporters poured out into the road, headed by a nonagenarian waving a plate and her husband who also seemed in tears. "Stop." "You can't do that," they cried, alerting the whole street. Two children screamed: "They are taking Mummy away," and burst into tears.

"Don't pay any attention," said Sabri now, looking like Napoleon on the eve of Wagram. "Drive, Jamal, drive." We set off with a roar, scattering pedestrians who were making their way to the scene of the drama, convinced perhaps that a shot-gun wedding was in progress. "Where are we going?" I said.

"Lapithos—the widow Anthi," said Sabri curtly. "Drive, Jamal, drive."

As we turned the corner I noticed with horror that the cobbler and his family had stopped another taxi and were piling into it with every intention of following us. The whole thing was turning into a film sequence. "Don't worry," said Sabri, "the second taxi is Jamal's brother and he will have a puncture. I have thought of everything."

In the brilliant sunshine we rumbled down the Lapithos road. The woman looked about her with interest, pointing out familiar landmarks with great good-humour. She had completely recovered her composure now and smiled upon us both. It was obviously some time since she had had a car-ride and she enjoyed every moment of it.

We burst into the house of the widow Anthi like a bomb and demanded the mortgage papers; but the widow herself was out and they were locked in a cupboard. More drama. Finally Sabri and the cobbler's wife forced the door of the cupboard with a flat-iron and we straggled back into the sunshine and climbed aboard again. There was no sign of the second taxi as we set off among the fragrant lemon-groves towards Kyrenia, but we soon came upon them all clustered about a derelict taxi with a puncture. A huge shout went up as they saw us, and some attempt was made to block the road but Jamal, who had entered into the spirit of the thing, now increased speed and we bore down upon them. I was alarmed about the safety of the grandfather, for he stood in the middle of the road waving his stick until the very last moment, and I feared he would not jump out of the way in time. I closed my eyes and breathed deeply through my nose: so did Sabri, for Jamal had only one eye and was unused to speeds greater than twenty miles an hour. But all was well. The old man must have been fairly spry for when I turned round to look out of the back window of the car I saw him spread-eagled in the ditch, but quite all right if one could judge by the language he was using.

The clerks in the Registry Office were a bit shaken by our appearance for by this time the cobbler's wife had decided to start crying again. I cannot for the life of me imagine why—there was nobody left to impress; perhaps she wanted to extract every ounce of drama from the situation. Then we found she could not write—Grandfather was the only one who could write, and she must wait for him. "My God, if he comes, all is lost again, my dear," said Sabri. We had to forcibly secure her thumbprint to the article of sale, which sounds easy, but in fact ended by us all being liberally coated with fingerprint ink.

She only subsided into normality when the ratified papers were handed to Sabri; and when I made out her cheque she positively beamed and somewhat to my surprise insisted on shaking hands with me, saying as she did so, "You are a good man, may you be blessed in the house."

It was in the most amiable manner that the three of us now sauntered out into the sunlight under the pepper trees. On the main road a dusty taxi had drawn up and was steadily disgorging the disgruntled remains of the defeated army. Catching sight of her they shouted vociferously and advanced in open order, waving sticks and gesticulating. The cobbler's wife gave a shriek and fell into her grandfather's arms, sobbing as if overtaken by irremediable tragedy. The old man, somewhat tousled by his expedition, and with grass in his eyebrows, growled protectively at her and thundered: "Have you done it?" She sobbed louder and nodded, as if overcome. The air was rent with execrations, but Sabri was quite unmoved. All this was purely gratuitous drama and could be taken lightly. With an expressive gesture he ordered Coca-Cola all round which a small boy brought from a barrow. This had the double effect of soothing them and at the same time standing as a symbolic drink upon the closing of a bargain—shrewdly calculated as were all his strokes. They cursed us weakly as they seized the bottles but they drank thirstily. Indeed the drive to Lapithos is a somewhat dusty one.

"Anyway," said the cobbler at last when they had all simmered down a bit, "we still have the water-rights. We have not yet discussed those with the gentleman." But the gentleman was feeling somewhat exhausted by now, and replete with all the new sensations of ownership. I possessed a house! Sabri nodded quietly. "Later on," he said, waving an expressive hand to Jamal, who was also drinking a well-earned Coca-Cola under a pepper tree. "Now we will rest." The family now saw us off with the greatest good humour, as if I were a bridegroom, leaning into the taxi to shake my hand and mutter blessings. "It was a canonical price," said the old greybeard, as a parting blessing. One could not say fairer than that.

"And now," said Sabri, "I will take you to a special place of mine to taste the *meltemi* wind—what is the time? Yes, in half an hour."

High upon the bastions of Kyrenia castle was a narrow balcony which served the police officers as a mess. Sabri, I discovered later, was a sergeant in the specials. Here, gazing across the radiant harbour-bar towards the Caramanian mountains, we sat ourselves down in solitude and space like a couple of emperors while a bewildering succession of cold beers found their way out on to the table-cloth, backed up by various saucers full of delicious Cypriot comestibles. And here Sabri's wind punctually arrived—the faintest breath of coolness, stirring across the waters of the harbour, ruffling them.

"You see?" he said quietly, raising his cheek to it like a sail. He was obviously endowed with that wonderful Moslem quality which is called *kayf*—the contemplation which comes of silence and ease. It is not meditation or reverie, which presupposes a conscious mind relaxing: it is something deeper, a fathomless repose of the will which does not even pose to itself the question: "Am I happy or unhappy?"

He had been jotting on a slip of paper and now he handed it to me, saying: "Now your troubles begin, for you will have to alter the house. Here, I have costed it for you. A bathroom will cost you so much. The balcony, at so much a cubic foot, should cost you so much. If you sell the beams—they fetch three pounds each, and there are eighty—you should have so much in hand. This is only for your private information, as a check, my dear." He lit a cigarette and smiled gently. "Now the man you want to build for you is Andreas Kallergis. He is good and honest—though of course he is a rogue like me! But he will do you a solid job—for much can go wrong, you know. You will find the cost of cement brick there, and rendering per cubic metre."

I tried to express my gratitude but he waved his hand. "My dear Durrell," he said, "when one is warm to me I am warm to him back. You are my friend now and I shall never change even if you do."

We drank deeply and in silence. "I was sent to you by a Greek," I said, "and now the Turk sends me back to a Greek."

He laughed aloud. "Cyprus is small," he said, "and we are all friends, though very different. This is Cyprus, my dear."

It seemed in that warm honey-gold afternoon a delectable island in which to spend some years of one's life.

YEAKUQUALAGELIS: YOU ARE PROUD
OF WHAT YOU HAVE DONE
IN POTLATCHING

I was born during the cold winter of 1913. My mother had been living with her father at Village Island and they came to Alert Bay. When I was about to be born they had to find someplace to take my mother where there would be no noise. So my grandfather, Jim Bell, made a small little tent for my mother up beside an old barn because she knew that I was going to be born. It was December 31, 1913. I was born in that little tent beside the barn. After I was born they just bundled me up and took me home to my mother's sister's house who was living in Alert Bay. She had married Ed Whanock and they had a house on the Nimpkish Reserve in Alert Bay. Of course my grandfather called all the people together right away and gave away some blankets and other things at a potlatch which was the way of my people. It was at that time that they gave me my baby names. I received my father's father's name from the Kwiksutainuk people, Owadzidi, which means "people will do anything for him because he is so respected." My mother's father, Jim Bell, was from the Mamalilikulla people and I received the name Poogleedee from him, which means "guests never leave his feasts hungry." I received the name Waltkeena which was from Chief Goatlas of the Mamalilikulla and means "something very precious has been given to us." I received the name Sewid after my father and his father, which means, "paddling towards the chief that is giving a potlatch." My father's father had taken the name James because he used to work for James Douglas, the first governor of British Columbia, and that was passed on to my father and at that time it was given to me.

My mother's name was Emma Sewid. When she was quite young she married my father James Sewid. I had an older sister but she died when she was only ten months old. My mother was from the Mamalilikulla tribe and my father was an important man in the Kwiksutainuk tribe. Just a couple of months before I was born my father was killed in an accident. A tree fell on him when he was logging. My father and mother had been living at Village Island where the accident happened and Lucy Sewid, my grandmother, was living with them. My grandmother was a very religious woman and when my father died she was all alone because my grandfather, James Aul Sewid, had died some years before. She just moved to Alert Bay then from Village Island because there was nobody for her to live with at Village Island since she had been living with my father. When he died she just left everything. She left the house and all the things in it and they just boarded up the windows and everything. She bought herself a little house, a little shack down on the beach at Alert Bay and stayed there all by herself. She was there when I was born.

Before my father had died he had begun to gather together some things in preparation for the potlatch that he would give when I was ten months old. That was the time that I was to receive my everyday names and my chief's names. I received names from the Mamalilikulla people through Jim Bell and from the Kwiksutainuk people through James Aul Sewid. Aul Sewid had an uncle who was also a very strong chief at that time and the two of them were always together. My grandfather and his uncle were so strong that nobody could pay them back when they broke a copper. They used to just refer to them as the "uncles." My grandfather had passed all his great names and positions on to my father but when he died they were to come down to me. I was the rightful owner because they could never take those names away. Those names will always be there. Chief Aul Sewid's uncle was named Yakatlnalis which means "the whale." His name was taken up by my uncle at Kingcome, Toby Willey. When my father died Toby announced that he was going to carry out what my father had started because he had been chosen to stand by me as I grew up to take all those names and positions.

So Toby Willey gave this big potlatch in favor of me when I was ten months old. He had quite a bit of money himself and everything that had been gathered for my father was given to him. All my grandparents and all my relatives at Village Island all added to this to make it a very big potlatch. Some of them gave coppers. It was going to be a great honor to my people and to my mother to receive a child in that position. That's why all my grandfather's relatives in the villages all gave something for it. Some gave canoes, some gave articles, and some gave money. They gave it all to Toby to make the thing real big. Toby was not going to just take what was coming in. He was going to put in what he can on it to make it a bigger potlatch. When everyone who knew my father was dead heard that I was born they just all moved in and helped to make it real big.

And the day came for this big do to be held in Alert Bay. They had sent out invitations some time before this. This thing goes on for a week or two. Something goes on every night, and everyone had to be given a present every night whether it was a cup or a canoe or money or something else. It had to go on for a couple weeks because there was lots to say every night. One day, when it was a very nice day in Alert Bay, all the people gathered outside. Toby Willey, the young new chief that had taken up Yakatlnalis' position and name, spoke. He held me in his arms. I was a little boy—a ten-months-old baby. He put the copper down on the ground and announced to the people: "Here is my great nephew and we are very proud to have him here. I am very proud to see him and stand by him and to be chosen to take this position to be with him. He is going to take everything. He is the rightful owner of everything his grandfather Chief Sewid owned." And he laid me on this copper, just a little bundle, and announced to the people: "This copper will be his strength." My grandfather, Jim Bell, had bought that copper for my mother. My grandmother, old Lucy Sewid, was there, and she had helped him buy that copper, and she was just full of tears. She was part of all of it. Then all the chiefs of the different villages all got up and praised me. They told everybody about this new chief that was coming up. Every chief was shouting loud with their voices. Afterward they gathered up all the stuff and put it together for me. This was all added to in order to expand it because they wanted it big for me.

That was the time that they gave me many of my names. From Chief Goatlas I received the name Yeakuqualagelis, which means "you are proud of what you have done in potlatching." I received the Kwiksutainuk everyday name Natlamutlas, which means "the other tribes all get their names and wealth from us." My father had the Mamalilikulla everyday name Glacoatlas, which was given to me at that time, and it means "where they can get copper." Another name I received which was one of Aul Sewid's positions was Hanesuqwelak, which means "he always wants to share his wealth with others." I received Aul Sewid's chief's name which was right at the top of the Kwiksutainuk people at Village Island. It was Maquacoatla, which means "always giving away wealth." Lucy Sewid was part Matilpi and her brother gave me the name Gostidzas, which means "when the guests arrive for a potlatch they are all welcomed at his house." I also received a Matilpi chief's name, Comanaquala, which means "he is wealthy from many generations back." I remember that I also got the Mamalilikulla name Lagius, which means "a very high ranking man," and there were others that I can't remember.

During the first few years of my life I lived with my mother in the big community house at Village Island that belonged to Chief Goatlas, who was my grandmother's brother. Some of the time we would live in Alert Bay with Ed Whanock, who was married to my mother's sister. There were five or six families living in that community house. It had a dirt floor and a big fire in the middle. We each lived in one corner of that house and had our own fire where we cooked most of our meals. We lived with Jim Bell's family.

In the evenings if there were any dances to be held in the village they would just come and ask Jim Bell if they could use the community house. I would just move up with the other kids to the bedrooms and just sit there watching these dances. We had big dances every winter and sometimes I would dance in them too. It was right about the time that the government had stepped in and said the potlatches and dances were forbidden. So the people had to be very careful about taking part in potlatches that were going on in the other villages. I remember we used to move around from one village to another and go to these potlatches almost every month in the winter. Village

Island was one place where they never used to bother us when we were having something going on. When my relatives would put on a potlatch they would ask me to take part in the dancing.

I remember one time there was a real big do held at Village Island. It was a big potlatch given by a fellow from Alert Bay. The people came from all over and must have stayed there for ten days or more. There was something going on every night and they held it in our house. When the Kwakiutl people from Cape Mudge and Campbell River arrived on the beach my grandmother, Mary Bell, called me over and said, "There is a gas boat that has come in down on the beach and they say it is the people from Cape Mudge and Campbell River. Go down there and ask (she named somebody that was related to them) to come up and stay with us." So I ran down to that boat that had just come in and spoke to them in our language, but I didn't know just what to say because I didn't know who it was that I was looking for. So I just said as a little boy, "You are wanted up at our house. Come on up to the house." Well, the whole works came on up to our house and my grandparents had to have them all stay there. My grandmother said to me later, "Why didn't you just call the person I wanted you to call to come up?" I told her that I didn't know who it was so I just told them all to come up to our house. Well, everybody went in there and there were quite a few people that stayed there. There must have been over twenty people.

•   •   •

When I was about seven years old I left my mother and went to Alert Bay to stay with my grandmother, Old Lucy, and go to school. That's how I got my little education because I stayed with her off and on until I was about ten years old. Actually I wasn't in school regularly during the time I was with my grandmother. When I was a little boy I more or less drifted from one grandmother to the other grandmother, so that while I moved to Alert Bay I wasn't there all the time. My grandmother, Mrs. Bell, was a very religious woman and used to try in her own way to tell me to believe in God. Of course my grandmother Lucy was very religious also and she was brought up in a Roman Catholic church in Victoria where she used to live with her oldest sister who was married to a white man.

Old Lucy was living alone when I went to be with her and go to school. She was staying by herself in a little shack down on the beach which she had bought. After her husband Aul Sewid had died and then her son James Sewid died she was just lost. Her husband was dead, she had lost her only child, and I wasn't born yet when she first came to Alert Bay. I used to ask her, "Why did you come here?" and she would say, "I like to be near the church, that is my only hope, I go to church every time the bell rings." At first she had been a Roman Catholic but when she came to Alert Bay she was an Anglican. Her older sister, who had married this white man in Victoria who owned a store there, had died and her younger sister and her brother had also died. She had no choice but to go and live by herself.

I stayed with her during that time and she encouraged me to go to school and stay with school as long as I could. She could see that education was necessary. But I found it awfully hard as a young boy with nobody to turn to to support me. We used to just look after ourselves, Lucy and I. Our relief at that time was only two dollars and fifty cents a month. We had to go down on the beach, especially during the winter months and before the winter had set in, to fill our little woodshed up and get ready for the winter. We had about half a dozen chickens and we sold the eggs to some of the people in the village. On Saturday when I wasn't in school I used to go down to the big sawmill that was in Alert Bay and get old pieces of wood to sell. There was an Indian teacher in the day school where I went, and I would go and borrow a wheelbarrow from him and take this wood around to different people in the village and sell it to make a little money.

We were living right near the Anglican church and the minister there and his wife, Mr. and Mrs. Corker, were very kind to us. When the berries were ripe I would go with my grandmother and pick berries for the minister as well as the Indian agent and his wife, Mr. and Mrs. Halliday. They were very kind to us. Every now and then they used to give us a loaf of bread or sometimes some cookies. Sometimes Mr. and Mrs. Corker would give me some clothes that were too small for their children and I used to be the happiest boy in Alert Bay when I wore those new clothes. Everything else that I had the old lady used to make for me. She used to knit me a sweater and a little hat and make other clothes for me. We stayed together for a long time, old Lucy and me, and she was a very religious woman.

Robby Bell, my uncle, had already left Village Island to go to the Anglican residential school at Alert Bay when I moved to live with my grandmother and told her I wanted to go to the day school. The kids in the Anglican residential school lived right there all the time, but those kids who were living at home in Alert Bay village would go to the day school. Every day after school I used to run to old Lucy's house. My grandmother had some hard-tack, this pilot bread or biscuit, and she would put it in a little bag for me and I would run up to the residential school. I would look all over for Robby and give him these biscuits and he really appreciated it. I was just like brothers with Robby. Everything he got he shared it with me and I tried to do the same thing.

The Indian teacher at the day school, George Luther, was a great friend of mine. He liked me somehow. If it was a snowy day, or if it had snowed at night, my grandmother would wake me up early and give me breakfast and then I would go up to the school before anyone else got there. The school had a long stairway, and she used to give me a broom to sweep off the snow to get it ready for George Luther when he came. He really used to like that. He just thought the world of me and I used to go and help him make the fire in the big drum stove that we had in the school. Going to school was new to me and I found it awfully hard, especially such things as adding and arithmetic. Somehow I just couldn't put it in my head and I used to find it awfully hard. I really enjoyed school and that was the main reason I came to Alert Bay. I wanted to go to school pretty badly, and there was no school in Village Island, and that is why I started thinking about going to live with my grandmother. I enjoyed school very much but I had a lot of enemies there as a small boy.

Alert Bay was a Nimpkish village and I was half-Kwiksutainuk and half-Mamalilikulla, so that when I was a little boy in school I was an outsider. The people that were there used to pick on me all the time. They did it just because I was an outsider and my grandmother used to tell me that they did the same thing to her when she came to live in that Nimpkish village. They didn't like her to be living on their reserve because she was an outsider and they used to make remarks to her. They were doing the same thing to me when I was in school. I was the only Mamalilikulla or Kwiksutainuk boy that was there at that time. Of course the schoolteacher was a Nimpkish man but he liked me very much and thought a lot of me. The other kids used to tease me and I had a lot of fights with them. I always was pretty big for my age and nobody could ever stand up to me even if there were two of them. I wouldn't hesitate to take on two of them at a time. Sometimes I wouldn't fight them because my grandmother used to tell me not to fight. She would say, "If anybody is picking on you, you leave them alone. Don't you ever pay no attention to those people. They are doing the same thing to me."

One day there were some bigger boys picking on me and making remarks to me that I wasn't accepted there because I was an outsider. So I just let them have it. I wasn't thinking of anything else right then. I thought there was a limit for everything and they had reached the limit. Of course they all went home and complained to their parents because I had licked them all. I just went home to my grandmother but that wasn't the end of it. The parents of those Nimpkish kids came and butted in and began saying things to my grandmother which I didn't like even though I wasn't sure I understood what it was all about. They talked to my aunt, Mrs. Ed Whanock, who was also living in Alert Bay. So, as a result of this, my grandfather, Jim Bell, had to come from Village Island and give a potlatch that night in Alert Bay. The reason for giving that potlatch was because they didn't want anybody to pick on me. It was the custom of the Indians that if anybody got into a fight like that or if anybody called me down, my grandfather was not going to stand for it. So the only thing he could do was to call the people together and give a potlatch. At this potlatch he stood up in public before the people that had been making these remarks about me and told them what he thought. I didn't go to this potlatch but I knew it was being given because my mother came with my grandfather and bawled me out. She said, "If you hadn't done that and gotten into that fight your grandfather wouldn't have had to go to all this trouble and spend all this money for your misbehavior." I didn't say anything at all but just sat there and took it. I tried to avoid getting into any fights after that. Of course I went back to school and they were still picking on me.

One day in about 1922, when I was eight years old, George Luther told the kids that there wasn't going to be any school for a few days because they were going to use that room for a courthouse. The law against the potlatch had been passed and the mounted police were beginning to enforce it. The government had sent out the word that if the people would give up all their

Subsistence and Economic Exchange

masks and coppers and their regalia and everything that they owned in connection with the potlatch they wouldn't be put in jail. There were only people from three villages who did what they were ordered, Cape Mudge, Village Island, and Alert Bay. They gave all their masks and regalia and everything they owned from the Indian way and they put it in a big building behind the Indian office. That was just full of all the masks and things from these three tribes and they took them away. And the people who had refused to give up their things were brought into Alert Bay and put on trial and they used that schoolroom for a courthouse. And some of them from Fort Rupert, Kingcome, New Vancouver, Turnour Island, and from all over the Kwakiutl nation were brought there. After some people had been tried on a certain day the ones who had been sentenced were just kept in the schoolroom and had to sleep on the floor. The mounted police would lock that place up and guard it at night. After they were sentenced they were sent down south to jail for about two to six months.

I heard that some of my relatives had been sentenced and were going to be sent to jail, so I crept around in back of that schoolroom and looked through the window. All the people were just sleeping there on the floor. I didn't realize everything that was going on at the time. Old man Whanock and old lady Whanock were in there and Herbert Martin who was a close relation of mine was in there. I felt very badly about it because they told me that they were all going to be in jail. Of course the mounted police were watching all the time and they used to chase me away from there. That was the time that we lost a lot of our masks and regalia and coppers and other wealth.

·　　·　　·

When I was sixteen my grandparents and my wife's parents had gotten enough stuff together so that we were ready to go home to Village Island. They had gathered some money and dishes and furniture together which they put on Moses Alfred's seine boat and they took us home. They called it the Indian custom of "taking you home." My grandfather called all the people from the different islands to come to Village Island for this big potlatch that was to be given in honor of me. When we arrived there my grandfather got all the people together and announced that I was home. Then they gave away some money, dishes, big pails, furniture, and some bedding. My grandfather was the main person that was arranging for that ceremony and I didn't take an active part in it because I was only a teenager. That was his glory and even though it was in my honor it wasn't up to me to give it. The people who were taking part in it were the chiefs and the other responsible men of my village and all the people they had invited from the other villages. After that we settled down to our new life in that village.

During those winters at Village Island the people from other villages used to come and invite us to go to a big potlatch somewhere. When they arrived to invite us there were usually twenty or thirty people who came and sometimes as many as fifty. It was customary when they arrived in our village to invite them up to have a big feast and give a small potlatch. We gave them a meal and then the leading men of the village would give some money away to the people that had come to invite us. I used to take part in that with what little money I had. I would gather up all I could and give it away in order to take part in what was going on because they looked upon me as a leader of the Kwiksutainuk people who were at Village Island. I was taking the place of my grandfather and my father and they looked upon me to do this whether I liked it or not. A lot of the time my mother would give away things and give me money to give away because it wouldn't be right if I didn't do it. If I didn't take part in that giving, then when the people went home they would talk about me and things like that. Sometimes I would be up in the woods working and I wouldn't even know that it was going on. Then my mother or my grandfather would give something away for me and mention my name that I was the one that was giving it.

The people didn't respect those young men who spent all their money on drinking and gambling and weren't able to give anything when the other tribes came to invite us to their village. There were two or three people in Village Island who used to make home brew and drink and play cards all night. One day after they had been at this the Kingcome people came and called all the Village Island people together. There were about 150 people that came into Jim Bell's big house when he called them. Jim Bell and others gave some things away and then he stood up and made a speech about these three fellows who had been drinking and didn't have anything to give away. He named them right in front of all those people and then said, "What's the matter with you? Why don't you do something for these people who have come to visit us? I thought that's why you were playing cards all night, to make all kinds of money. Why don't you give something to these people? You are an awful disgrace to this village. What would you do if we weren't here? People would just come into this village and nobody would look after them!" That was a strong speech to get from a man that was so respectable, and those three fellows didn't open their mouths. They just sat there and held their heads down almost between their knees. If it had been a white man talking to them they might have just said, "To hell with you," or something like that, but not to such a respectable Indian. It was the Indian custom in those days that if they argued back that would have cost them money. In those days there were only a few people who would get drunk every weekend. Jim Bell would take a drink once in a while or he might just "wash his stomach out" at the end of the fishing season, but that was all. It was a disgrace in those days for an Indian to be drunk, and nobody wanted to have anything to do with a drunk Indian who was just falling and staggering down the road. It was a big disgrace to be seen in such a condition by your father or mother or grandfather or uncle. All the time they would have been praising you as a young respectable person and if you got drunk it meant that they would have to call the people together and give a potlatch to make up for that disgrace. The people were very proud in those days and there were some great men among the Indians. They were so great and so respected that nobody could do anything to shame them. They were great and everything they did was the best, and they would call the people together and give really big potlatches. They were really big and the people just came together and would be happy because there was lots to eat and all kinds of articles and things to take home.

One time, during those early years at Village Island, my grandfather came to me and told me once again that he was going to put on a big do and it was going to be the last one. And he told me, "I want you to be my top dancer," because that is what they called it. The highest dancer had to be the oldest son or the oldest grandson because it would be a disgrace to him if he took one of the younger ones. And I told him, "No, I don't want to be the one. I've got a lot of cousins, why don't you take one of them?" And he said, "Oh, no, that's not allowed. You have got to be the one." Well, I just figured that I shouldn't do it because I already had a couple children and I guess I was afraid of the law at that time. It was against the law to have potlatches and put on those dances and I didn't want to break the law. I always liked to be on the right side of the law ever since I was a little boy.

Well, all the people got together right away and Jim Bell announced to them that I didn't want to go through with it. Well, the people all said to him, "You can't have anybody else, it has to be him. He is going to have to go through with it. He is the rightful owner of that dance that was given to him when he married Flora. That is the dance that was given by the great chief Odzistales." Well, I didn't have any sons old enough to take the place of the top dancer so I had to do it. Anyway, I gave in. It was the time to open that big chest which had all the regalia and different dances in it that had been given to me by the Fort Rupert Kwakiutl when I got married. My grandfather had been holding all those things for me and it was up to us to take them out of that box and perform those dances. It was time for me to become a hamatsa.

In our Indian way we had lots of important names for the positions in the clans of the various tribes of the Kwakiutl nation. During the winter time the people used to put on their dances, and there were also important names and positions for the groups of people who had the right to those dances. There were lots of different dances, and some were for people of low positions and others were for people who were in high positions. The highest dance group was the hamatsa or Cannibal society. In order for a person to become a hamatsa he had to have the right to a name and a position in that group given to him from his ancestors or his wife's ancestors. Then there was a long ceremony to go through in order to really become a hamatsa. I had seen many of these at Village Island when I was growing up, and all the leading men of the other villages would come there and a young man would become a new hamatsa. The older hamatsas were only the men in the highest positions in all the tribes, and they would teach these young men to go through this ceremony and help them to become hamatsas. It was a very important position and that was why Jim Bell wanted me to go through with that and all the other people that were around me. That ceremony would go on for two or three weeks and the people would come from all over the Kwakiutl nation. There was one man who would be the master of ceremonies and he would tell the different people when to do their dances. There were always other new dancers for the other groups which were not as important as the hamatsa, but everything started with the hamatsa and that was the center of the whole winter ceremony. I had already become a dancer in some of the other groups when I was younger. The first time I became one was for my uncle Spruce Martin when I danced for him in Alert Bay when I was about five years old.

As soon as I gave in and decided to go through with it my grandfather sent word out to the other villages inviting them to come to our village. The day before everyone arrived I was supposed to disappear into the woods and go and seek the supernatural power of the Cannibal Spirit. I lived up in the woods for about ten days. In the early days they used to stay up in the woods for three or four months. My grandfather had been out that long when he first became a hamatsa. On the day that I disappeared into the woods I left all my clothes in the village and just dressed in some hemlock branches that were put around me. Some of the older hamatsas were up in the woods and they all began to blow on the whistles which were supposed to be the voices of the supernatural beings in the woods. Although I disappeared into the woods I didn't actually live up there all the time. Alfred Dawson was also a new hamatsa at that time and one other fellow. We would go out in the woods all day and then sneak back into our houses at night. In the morning we would leave before anybody was up so that nearly everyone thought we were out in the woods the whole time. My grandfather told me to go up in the woods in the morning and bathe in a stream or pool of water because I would need the strength to dance at night. We used to just walk around in the woods and never go near the village because there were lots of things going on there. They were dancing and giving potlatches and all the other things that were part of that winter ceremony. They hired a couple of my close relatives to stay with me at all times to be sure that nothing happened to me while I was walking around up there in the woods. I used to ask them to bring me something to eat, but although they brought our lunch up there they didn't give us much to eat. They wanted me to reduce and thin down by fasting. So every morning I took a cold bath and rubbed myself down with branches where nobody could see me. It was winter time but that was supposed to make me tough and feel light so I would be ready when the day came for me to come back to the village and dance. Sometimes during the day I would come into the village and show myself to the public for a minute or two and then rush back into the woods. All I had around me was the hemlock branches and when I did this all the different kinds of whistles would be blowing. They all had different tones which imitated the raven and geese and all the different birds of the woods. In the early days they really lived up to this ceremony, and when they were in the woods getting the supernatural power they didn't eat hardly anything and became very light and thin. I didn't feel anything special when I was up there.

The day after we disappeared into the woods the people started arriving from the other villages. They used to take two or three canoes with little gas motors on the back of them and tie them together to make the trip. As the people came into the village they had their regalia on and would start singing. All of their dancers were ready. Then the Village Island people all went down on the beach and as soon as the people got out of their boats they performed some dances for these visitors. Then all the people came up into the village, and they had woven a long piece of cedar bark and all the people held onto it and formed a big circle all the way around the community house where the dances were going to be held. They walked around and around the house holding onto this cedar bark which formed a big ring. Then they laid it down on a large canvas and a special man cut it into pieces for all of the people to make smaller rings which they put on their heads. The hamatsas all got theirs first and then all the other people. The dance connected with the hamatsa is called the "cedar bark dance," and when it began later on all the people put these rings on their heads. Then my grandfather gave a big feast for all the people and gave some things away.

Every night the people were all called into the big house where different dances were performed. They did these dances each night in order to bring back the new hamatsas from the woods. While we were in the woods we were supposed to become wild men and they were trying to bring us back to civilization. At night after the dances were over the hamatsas would all stay in the big community house and eat and sleep there. It was at this time that all the retired hamatsas would come and teach me how to dance and the new songs. They kept all of this a secret and nobody else could watch except the retired hamatsas. It was awful hard for me to take because they just sat there watching me dance and if I made any mistakes they told me to do it all over again. They didn't like the way I was doing it. It was really something for me to learn because I had never been through it before and didn't know what I had to do. The people teaching and watching me all knew because they had all been through it before. It was very important to perform that dance exactly right and not to trip and fall when you were doing it. And they told me that when I came in I was to pretend that I was fierce and wild. In every dance I was supposed to just run around like I was wild.

My grandfather hired singers and composers for the songs that were sung each night. There were singers from all of the other villages. They picked all the best singers and they were getting paid every night. The most important singers were paid a couple of dollars each night and the others were paid a little less. These singers all knew my songs which had been given to me from my grandfather Aul Sewid as well as some new songs that had been composed for this particular time. My grandfather had hired three or four composers to make up these new songs and teach them to the singers. All these new songs were telling the history of my father's side of the family and my mother's side in our language. During the dances each night while I was out in the woods, these singers were singing other songs while certain men were beating on the drums and beating the sticks on a long wooden log that was partially hollowed out. They were saving my songs until I came back from being with the Cannibal Spirit.

Finally the night came when I was going to return and all the people from all over the Kwakiutl nation were giving their dances. They started about 7 that night and it went on until about 3 in the morning. Each tribe and clan and family had their own songs and different kinds of dances. I was watching through a crack in the wall from a little room in the back of the big community house where I was hiding. No one knew I was there except the hamatsas because everything was a secret, but I'm telling the truth now. And I watched as all the different dancers came in and did the feather dance and the ladies did the paddle dance. They stood in front of the singers and made motions like they were paddling a canoe. Others did the salmon dance and the ghost dance and many others. Nobody could ever do a dance that did not belong to them or to one of their relatives. If one of the leading men wanted to have a particular dance done for him he could only do it if one of his relatives had a right to that dance and then he could call them in and have it done. Some of the dances that were done had a lot of clowning in them. And they were doing all of this to attract me and the other new hamatsas to come back to civilization, which wasn't so easy.

I had been told to watch for a particular dance which was going to be the last one at the end of all this dancing. They warned me that when that dance came I had to sneak out of that little room and go up on top of the big house. I saw someone talking to my stepfather, my grandfather, and Ed Whanock from that place where I was hiding and knew that it was time to go up. It was important for them to help me get up on the roof because in the early days that was when your enemies would do something to cripple you while you were climbing up. Of course we all have enemies and I had heard about this sort of thing happening at those big dos. They would try to do something to you so that you couldn't come out or so that you might come out crippled, and this would disgrace your family and the chief who was giving the ceremony. I had to come out a perfect man in perfect health. So I went out to the back of that house and put only my hemlock branches on around my body and on my wrists, ankles, and head. I had nothing on but branches. It was a cold winter night and the snow was falling. Dave Matilpi held the ladder while I climbed up and then stayed there so that no one else could come up. Ed Whanock was up on the roof and he had several of the hamatsa whistles with him. Ed knew the exact spot where I would remove a couple of the boards on the roof and go in. I was waiting up there patiently for my time to come and I was very cold. So then a certain dance came in that was the cousin of the Cannibal Spirit, which was my dance. This person began dancing and every time he jumped he held his head up and shouted, calling for me to come. On his third time of jumping and calling he was right in the middle of the house and we removed a couple of the boards and Ed Whanock began to blow this whistle.

As soon as the people heard this whistle they knew I was coming. All the dancers got behind a great big curtain at the end of the house and they all stayed there until I came in, no matter how late it was. Everybody was looking up because they heard this whistle and the master of ceremonies quickly told everybody to get up. And everybody got up and there was a lot of commotion and it was just as if everybody was panicky. Ed Whanock held my legs and I lowered myself halfway into the house and showed half of my body to the crowd. I was making the hamatsa noise and I could see all the people standing up and swaying their hands, which is the way they would greet one another. Some of them were chanting and beating with the sticks and there was a terrific noise that I heard up there. I had a strange feeling when they received me that night as I was hanging down through the roof. They were all chanting the songs and swaying their hands. I don't know how to express it, but it was a wonderful feeling to see all the people swaying their hands at me. It was something that I was going through that not many persons could go through.

Then Ed and I moved over to another spot and removed some of the boards and I went through again. The people were all down there chanting and about thirty or forty people were beating the drums and sticks. It was out of this world what they were doing, and I can't express how I felt. It made me feel funny, made me feel out of this world, everything that was going on in there that I could see down below me in the big house. Then we moved to another place and at this last one there was a rope tied to the big log of the roof and that is where I slid in. And all the hamatsas from the different villages were there with a big strong blanket to receive me. I jumped onto this blanket from the end of the rope and I'll never forget that when I came through my mother was crying. She just cried and cried because I guess she thought it was so real that I had come back to civilization again after I had been away so long.

My grandfather had picked a group of prominent young men from all the different villages and paid them to look after me during the ceremony. They all came right close to me and didn't allow anybody to come near me while we began to go around the fire in the center of the big house. At the far end of the house from the door was where the singers sat and the people who beat the drums and the sticks. All of a sudden when we came near that end of the house I broke away from those boys who were with me and went under a place in that end of the house and disappeared again. Right away the master of ceremonies got up and told everybody to sit down. When they had quieted down he said, "He does not altogether like to come with us or to come near us. It is a good thing that he came and showed himself to us so that we were able to see him again. We wish to see him again tomorrow and to have him visit us. I'd like to thank you all for what you have done tonight." And then everybody went home and slept for a little while except for the hamatsas.

That night after they had gone out I came back to work with all the retired hamatsas putting up the screen. During the previous nights several good painters had been painting a figure on this big wooden screen. Sometimes these screens were made out of cloth but mine was a wooden one. They painted the form of a man on it and in the stomach of this man they had a little round door through which I would come when I was to dance. It took about three hours to get this screen all nailed together and the branches all put around it. It had to be placed at the end of the house. All the hamatsas were there working together to get everything ready. The Kwakiutl tribes were strong in those days and they really worked together. That is where I learned what it meant to have unity and work together. Some of them would be sleeping for a while as others took care of the fire, gathered branches, or worked on the screen. Every time somebody was going to pound a nail a group of them would pound the sticks and make the hamatsa cry so that it would drown out the sound of pounding. When the pounding stopped they would stop making noise until someone began pounding again. When everything was ready we all slept until daylight. Then we all got up and went into the woods after breakfast to our place where we practiced the songs and dances. It was a secret place and nobody could come there except the hamatsas. This was the second day of my return and we all got ready for that part of the ceremony.

Then the master of ceremonies notified one particular man to go around to all the houses and call everybody to come to a big field there in the village. It was about 8 or 9 in the morning and this was the time when I was supposed to come in on my own. Then they formed a big procession with all the people doing their dances as they approached the big community house. When they got to the house they all went in one at a time and did their dance and then sat down. I was supposed to be the last one to come in. When they were ready I came in just wearing the hemlock branches and also the large hamatsa mask. They referred to that mask and the others which would be used for me as "my children." Some of the masks had large beaks on them and these were clapping together and making a loud noise as we came in. There were about twelve to fifteen boys with me that had been hired by my grandfather. They were real strong boys with blankets around them and no shoes on. They had been picked to look after me each time that I came in and especially before I was tame. Well, as I came in that morning I didn't dance in the right way but just stamped and ran and pretended that I wasn't completely ready to be with them there. I danced for a little while and then I would just go wild again, which is the reason they call it the wild man dance. Oh, it was really a man-killer. There were two of those fellows pushing me while I ran and danced and I would just run away with them hanging onto my arms, pulling them along. And all the time I was going around, the hamatsa whistles were going and the singers were singing and others were beating the drums and sticks. Then I disappeared by running in behind the big screen that had been made especially for me. Then they told all the people that they could go home until that night.

That night as all the people gathered in the big house the whistles were being blown slowly and gently all the time. They were never supposed to stop. I was hiding behind the screen on that special night. It was going to be another big night for me because they were going to try to tame me. Then the door of the screen which was in the stomach of the figure opened up and I came out to be the first dancer of the evening. All the trained singers were lined up outside of that door where I came out and they were singing my songs. They knew all the songs both new and old that told the history of my father's side and my mother's side of the family. I had been told that when I came out I should never stop moving but just to pretend that I still didn't want to dance until they finally held me down. I didn't have any cedar bark on but only the hemlock branches, and I went running around the big house in the wrong direction, doing a few dance steps and then stamping and running again to show that I didn't have any sense. Then the master of ceremonies gave the order to the boys who were with me to try to hold me down. When they tried I just jumped up and ran around again. Finally they just really pushed me down and held me down on the dirt floor.

Then as they were holding me down a specially chosen retired hamatsa who had blackened his face came out with a long pole. This pole was about ten feet long, and they tore an old blanket in strips and tied them to the end of this pole. They dipped that end of the pole into some water so that when they set fire to the pieces of blanket it would just smoke and not burn. He held the stick over the fire until the blanket pieces began to burn and it really started to stink. They call this *nueelqual* in our language. Then he came over to where these boys were holding me down and sitting on me. All the whistles were going and the people were beating the sticks all the time. He took this burning rag which was smoking and smelling and swung it over my head one time. As soon as he did this I jumped up and gave my hamatsa cry and started to try to move around again. When they got me down again this fellow ran over and put this burning rag over me again and this time I became a little less wild. On the third time that he put it over me I didn't move too much and just pretended that I was getting weaker. It was part of the play that I would keep weakening each time that they put that smoking rag over my head. On the fourth time I didn't move at all and then the whistles became very faint. This man then threw the pole into the fire and all the retired hamatsas began to make their cries and came down around me making noise with their rattles. Then the whistles stopped and it was finished. They took off all the hemlock branches and put brand-new cedar bark on me that had been made by the experts.

Then I began to dance in the proper way while they were singing my songs. I was not quite tame so that after one or two dances I would run around a little again. Then some of my relatives who had been picked came out and danced some of those dances and showed some of the masks that belonged to me and had come in that chest when I was married. All the time I was dancing those boys who were looking after me stayed right close to me.

They sang four of my songs and on the fourth one, when I got over near the door, I just disappeared out of the door and left those boys standing there. They all began to push each other and cry out, "What happened to him?" Then they blamed each other real loud and said, "You shouldn't have let him go." One of them ran out after me and came back in a couple of minutes bringing my beautiful brand-new cedar bark. He brought it into the center of the big house and announced: "He is not quite ready to come to us yet and he is gone again. We have to expect and hope for the best." That ended the hamatsa dance and then all the different dances began. They did the swan dance and the ghost dance and many others until about 10 or 11, when everybody went home. As they were coming out of the big house to go home they could hear the hamatsa whistles way up in the woods. Those boys who were picked to be with me had come up there and were making the noises of the birds and then everybody knew that we were up there for something.

Just before daylight on the next morning I came in on my own free will with my mask that somebody had brought to me in the woods. I went behind that screen and stayed there all day until the big ceremony began that night. On this night I came out with the cedar bark on and danced many of my dances. I was the first one out and danced for a couple of hours. I was very tame then and was being very careful not to make any mistakes. The fourth night was the last one and I had to dance again for about the same length of time. They sang about eight of my songs that night. Each of these last two nights after I had danced the others all came out and danced too. All the masks and songs and dances that I had received from my ancestors were shown on those nights. Before any of those dances would be shown the master of ceremonies would announce where I got them from and tell everybody that I had a right to them. Some of my relatives came out and did different dances in my honor that they owned. In the early days the big chiefs had large dances because that showed what great men they were. That was why I used many dances, even some my grandfather didn't own but some other relative did, because my group of dances had to be large. Some of those dances were the ones that my grandfather Aul Sewid had received when he married into the Bella Coola people.

And when everything was completed on the fourth night they called everybody together to give us new hamatsas a bath. In my language they called us, "They're going to give you a bath." It wasn't really a bath in water but they used a great big circle of branches that was about five feet in diameter. All the chiefs were holding this ring of branches and I had to step inside of that circle and they rubbed me down with it. While they were rubbing me down it was the custom for them all to say something to me about my character. Some of the things they said were kind of like teasing me. I was the first one to be put through those branches and they told me to behave and to be kind to my friends and all sorts of things like that. I had to stand on my right leg all the time through that and then I stepped out. Right after the bath ceremony there was a big do and Jim Bell gave a lot of stuff away. He gave away money, clothes, shirts, pails, dishes, pots and pans, and many blankets.

He gave it to all the people that had been taking part in the ceremony. The chiefs from the different villages received some expensive gold broaches and bracelets and he gave them more than the other people. Those hamatsa positions were all in me then and I felt that I was honored in a high position because that was a very high dance. You had to be an honored and a respected man to go through that kind of thing and not very many people went through that. After that I had the right to do that hamatsa dance any time I felt like it and to take part in any ceremonies where some other young man was becoming a hamatsa.

Just a couple of days later, before any of the people had returned to their village, we heard that a sergeant of the mounted police was coming up to Village Island to investigate what was going on. They had heard about our dance there and that a young man had been put through it, which was against the law. That was why they sent this sergeant all the way from Ottawa. All the chiefs of the different villages were still all together when this mounted police came in. He told us, "I have been sent from the government to investigate what was going on in this village and I'd like to see what it is that you were doing." He demanded to see it that night, so we put on a good show for him. The dances we did were all mixed together and not in the right way we had been doing them. I was dancing with a fool's mask on along with a group of masks. The mounted police was standing to one side of the house while the big dance was going on and one of our people was interpreting to him what it was all about. And he asked him, "What is that dance there?" referring to me. "Well," he said, "he is supposed to be a person who doesn't know anything and just imitates anything he sees. We call it the fool dance because he is supposed to be a man that doesn't know anything." Then this mounted police said, "Oh, you people are all wrong. I think he is the smartest dancer in the whole works. He can dance any dance." Well, I was just giving it all I could. I was so strong that I was able to dance with that heavy mask on for over an hour.

When the announcer said that the ceremony was over the mounted police said, "I'd like to see the young man that went through this thing. I'd like to see him dance for me tonight because I was sent here to investigate this young man. I want him to dance with everything he had on, all his masks and everything. I want him to do it just like the way he did it last week." He was referring to me and the people named my name to him. Well, the chiefs of the village all come and looked for me and found me in the back of the big house and they said, "You have to come out and dance. The mounted police wants you to come and dance for him." So I got all my stuff on and the others who were dancing my dances and came out and started dancing. After I came out my masks came out and danced. At the end he got up and thanked the people and said, "It was a wonderful dance. I really enjoyed it. I can't see anything wrong with it." After that he went back to Ottawa. That was part of my becoming a hamatsa and it was a good thing they didn't lock me up.

·　　·　　·

In 1936 there was a strike in order to try to get better prices for the fish. We were all tied up in Alert Bay with our boats. They stopped everything and the company wouldn't give us any more groceries for our boats. Flora was up at the cannery and I didn't know how they were looking after the women up there. They didn't want the boats to move around but to just stay tied up in Alert Bay. We were all out of grub and all the men were getting kind of panicky. We weren't allowed to go up to Knight's Inlet to see our wives and children and we wanted to know how they were getting along. They finally settled it but we didn't make hardly anything at all because we had been tied up nearly all season. During the winter months some of the leading men called a gathering to talk about forming an organization on the coast. Chief Billy Assu from the Cape Mudge people was speaking our language while he talked to that meeting and encouraged all the people that were there to come forward and make up their mind for forming a fishermen's organization. George Luther was one of the ones who was really pushing it, and we formed the Pacific Coast Native Fishermen's Association. George Luther was elected to be the secretary of that association. I learned a lot about negotiating for the fish prices after that from George Luther since he used to ask me to sit in when they talked to the cannery people.

In the winters of those years that I was skipper on the "Annandale" there wasn't much to do so we stayed in Village Island most of the time. There were a lot of potlatches in our village as well as in some of the other villages but we had to be very careful because of the law at that time. Whenever a new hamatsa was dancing for the first time I would go there and help teach him what he was supposed to do. One of the most important things we did was practicing all the old songs. When I would go to a really big do at another village where a lot of the tribes gathered, the speaker for the ceremony used to call me in and say, "We are glad to see you, Jimmy. We welcome you, because we would like you to learn these songs, because we aren't going to be here very long to assist you when the time comes for you to lead them on your own." I used to like it whenever I had time, especially the singing. There was one old man named Jolof Moon who was the greatest composer I had ever known. Every tribe had their composers and singers but he was the leader of all the singers because he knew the songs of all the tribes. We used to get together before the big night when everybody sang all the songs in order to try to bring the wild man out of the woods. Since each tribe came in the order of their rank we had to know which songs would be sung and in which order. Old Man Moon would tell me to put down the first two words of the songs that he wanted to sing which belonged to the person dancing. Then that night I would sit real close to him all the time and he would ask me, "What is the first line of the next song?" And I would tell him and he would start singing right away. That was very important to him to have them in the right order and not to forget any of them so he always used to look for me. I didn't blame him because if he made a mistake the hamatsas would not like that.

One winter about this time my stepfather, David Matilpi, came to Village Island to invite the people to a big do at Turnour Island. Dave was a Maamtagila and he was getting ready to have his nephew Jimmy Wadhams become a new hamatsa. Dave had been loaning things out for a long time getting ready for this big potlatch. He had married my mother and Jim Bell had given one of his hamatsa positions to him and he was going to have his nephew take it. Everybody was expecting it because Dave was one of the leading men of his village. Jim Bell had about ten hamatsa positions and Dave was proud to have gotten one of them from the Village Island people to give to his nephew. When I arrived in Turnour Island to stay at my mother's house Jimmy Wadhams had already gone out in the woods. The whole village was quite busy and something was going on every night.

It was very important for me and the other hamatsas to be there because I had gone through that and could teach any of the new ones. All the different groups from the different dances were having their own gatherings and getting ready for the ceremony. I spent most of my time around the big fire in the big house where they had the dances every night. During the daytime all the hamatsas would be singing and dancing in order to practice. Some of the time we were teaching the new hamatsa how to dance. That's where I really learned how to sing the songs, especially the new songs that the new hamatsa was going to have. I never used to care about that. I used to sit and listen because I didn't think it was important. Of course they had a lot of good singers like Mungo Martin and Jolof Moon and some others. They are all dead now. Sometimes during the day they had a big feast. All they did was eat at those great big feasts. They would go out and get a big halibut and put it in a great big pot and everybody would come and eat. I had the right to be in that house during the day and at night after the big do was over because I was a hamatsa. I had gone through that before and it was in me. I was a hamatsa and that is the highest society and therefore we were entitled to go into the big house.

When Jimmy Wadhams came through the roof of the house on his first night I was down below dancing and cooperating with all the retired hamatsas. All of Dave's relatives danced because they had the right to. Then that night after it was all over we worked late getting the screen put up and all the branches around it. We had to be careful again to drown out the noise of pounding the nails into that screen. I often thought of the Bible days when we were doing that. They claim that when they built King Solomon's temple they did all the chipping and everything many miles away so that they wouldn't make any noise when they were building it. It was so sacred because it was God's house and nobody was allowed to make any noise. And then when everything was over Dave gave a lot of things away to all the leading people and after a few days we went back to Village Island.

It was somewhere around that time that I began to feel that it wasn't right to have these potlatches. When the people were invited to a potlatch they would be gone for ten days or two weeks and it would spoil it for the people who had jobs. I was busy logging and since I was so busy I didn't attend some of those potlatches. That was the downfall of the villages that started anything. I thought a lot about why I should give up the logging operation and go to a potlatch. We wouldn't be producing any logs during that time so I began staying right in the village even though the other people went. A few of the younger people would stay with me but about 80 percent of our people would go to the potlatch. The way I looked at it, it was more important to be on the job. I thought it was all right if it was a free time but not when there was a job to be done.

By that time I had been living in Alert Bay for nearly five years and I was really busy with all the things I was doing. We had our fishing business and our store and sawmill. I had finished my new house and our kids were going regularly to school although the older ones had already had to drop out. One thing that was quite different was putting on potlatches. The law against that was still strong and Alert Bay was really bad for that kind of thing. Even when the mounted police weren't very interested in whether we did those potlatches or not, there were too many old churchgoers who were squashing it. If you saw them in church after you had been taking part in it they would say, "There is the old devil." That was the kind of people that we used to have there, but they knew they were wrong because you couldn't judge people on their appearance or on whether they took part in those potlatches. Once in awhile, if I wasn't too busy, I would go to one of the other villages for some potlatch that was being put on, but I didn't do anything myself or put on anything at Alert Bay. Sometimes something would go on at Alert Bay in a very quiet way, and without calling all the people together someone would go around to the homes and give some things away.

For some years the white people in Alert Bay had formed a committee each year which tried to raise money to help support the hospital. This hospital week committee, as it was called, would meet during the spring and plan ways to raise money. That year I was asked to be on the committee. I was the only Indian on the committee and they elected me to be the chairman of that committee, which was the first time that an Indian had been the chairman. I called the committee together and we discussed different ideas for raising money. Mr. Cameron, a friend of mine who was the fisheries officer, used to watch me like an old watchdog to see if I did anything as the chairman that wasn't according to parliamentary procedures. He used to get after me and correct me if I did anything wrong, which was a wonderful experience for me. After we had met a few times I asked my committee to all come back to our next meeting with some definite suggestions of things that we could do.

Before we met again I thought a lot about what we could do, and it just came to me that it would be a good idea to bring the potlatch custom and the dancing out to the surface again and let the public see it because it had been outlawed and lost. I had the idea that we wouldn't go and do it the way they used to do it when they gave people articles to come and watch the dancing.

The way I figured it was going to be the other way around, like the theaters, operas, or a good stage program which was put on and the people had to pay money to get in. I knew it was going to draw the outside people like from Beaver Cove, Sointula, and Port McNeil. When our committee met there were several ideas that people suggested we try. One thing we decided to do was to sell tickets for our May Queen like they had done in previous years. Tickets are sold in the name of different girls and the people buy tickets for those girls. The girl who has the most tickets becomes the May Queen and all the proceeds would go into the hospital week fund. My job was to try to raise money, as the chairman, and the more money we raised the better it would be for the hospital. So I said to my committee, "Why don't we put on an Indian dance?" One of them said, "Well, you would have to be the one to do that." So I said, "Fine, I'll do it if you will pass it in a motion in this committee." So they passed it.

The first thing I did was to go and talk to Bill Scow, who was one of the leading men of the people. All the old people were still alive then and we wrote a letter to all the chiefs of the different tribes to come together and bring their dance regalia with them when they came. So when they came I called a meeting for all the chiefs in the community hall. There were a lot of them, about ten or fifteen of the leading men of each village. I was in the chair and Bill Scow was beside me because he had the responsibility as a member of a subcommittee to write to all of the chiefs. It was quite a big meeting and I got up and said, "The reason I brought all you people here, and I hope you brought your masks and stuff, is because we would like to put on a big do. We would like to put on a big Indian dance. I feel that you chiefs all did your duty and gave big potlatches in your days but now that is gone. But you are still the rightful owners of all your masks and things. I think it is a worthy cause to bring you here and we can all support St. George's hospital because we all use it. It will be good for the whole district if we can make some money to contribute to the hospital."

I must have been facing a couple of hundred people in that hall and they were all the chiefs and prominent men. None of the non-Indians on my committee had come with me and I was facing all those people alone. I didn't know what I was going to be up against until one fellow got up and spoke: "Oh, now that we are all here you think you are going to use all our stuff just like that! It cost us money to show it because we always gave away lots of things when we performed with our masks and other regalia. We have all spent all kinds of money to show our stuff before in the Indian way and you aren't going to just bring us here and ask us to show it in this new way." After he sat down a lot of other chiefs got up, and there were many who were against putting on that dance. I was just sitting there with Bill Scow at a little table facing the people. I let them get up one by one and say what they wanted. I was just sitting there and thinking, really deep thinking, that if I just sat there and took what they were saying I might as well quit my job. I might as well give it back to them in very harsh words. And that was the time that the potlatch came back to me while I was sitting there thinking and listening to them. I had some masks and other regalia but I had never given a potlatch to show it. That was the time that I decided that I was going to bring it to the public because they made me mad, really mad. Everybody knew that I owned those things but it was only a matter of showing them and then it would be announced that I was still the rightful owner of it all.

Well, after all the chiefs that wanted to had spoken and all had said the same old thing I got up and spoke. "Thank you very much," I said (of course I was speaking our language). "Thank you very much. You have come on your own expense to Alert Bay as I stated when I first welcomed you. You have come for a good cause to support our hospital. I don't want you to forget this. I'm not a prophet but I'm going to tell you something. Every one of you are going to go into that hospital before you go to the Happy Hunting Grounds. The reason why I brought you here was because I know that the hospital is good for you. It is not just for the Nimpkish people but for all the other people as well. I have been working for the hospital and raising money for the hospital and none of you have put one cent in there. This was the only time that you could have put something towards this hospital. Now, I have my boats ready and you can all go home. I'm going to take you back to where you came from and I'm going to pay for your expenses. You might as well get out of here. That is all I can say. I want you to go."

You could have heard a dime drop in there. It was real quiet for a minute, maybe five minutes. Everybody was just stopped. I was quite young too and I didn't want to get up again. I was sitting there thinking that if Jim Bell was alive that he could come in there and squash those people to pieces. He was that kind of man and he wouldn't want anybody to talk to me like that. Well, I knew I had some friends there somewhere. I had a lot of uncles and I would say that I was a lucky man. Spruce Martin was still alive and Mungo Martin was alive and Chief Tom Johnson and Ed Whanock were there. Billy Matilpi of the Matilpi people was there, and I think from the Scows at Gilford Island and with Toby Willey and his brothers from Kingcome I had about ten uncles. Henry Bell was there from Village Island as well as Tom Dawson. So Ed Whanock got up and I guess he knew that I was mad because I was really shouting at the top of my voice. "Well, Jimmy," he said, "put me on your list. I've got quite a few masks and I'm going to perform tomorrow night. I've got nothing to be ashamed of. I've been showing all my masks for many, many years and I've given away a lot of money and I will do it for nothing so that I can help this worthy cause of saving people." Oh, that was it! He really hit those chiefs when he said, "I've got nothing to be ashamed of." I just held my head down and was waiting. Billy Matilpi got up next. He was from the Matilpi people and related to me through my grandmother Lucy Sewid. "Jimmy," he said, "Put me on because I'm coming." Then there was Mungo Martin and Spruce Martin. Pretty soon all of them got up one by one and said, "Put me on," and they were just pleading!

The worst part of it was that some of them didn't bring their masks. They had to get a boat and get their masks and I had to pay money to hire speedboats for them to go and pick up their masks. It cost $15 or $20 to hire a speedboat, but that didn't stop me. The next day we all got together to practice and then all those people started fighting among themselves about who was going to be first and who was going to be next. The tribes of the Kwakiutl nation are all in order; the Fort Rupert Kwakiutl are first, then the Mamalilikulla, then the Nimpkish, and so on, and everybody wanted to be in the right order. For instance, there were four or five people who wanted to put on a dance from the Kwakiutl people at Fort Rupert and they wanted to be in order as well, so we had to be very careful. I whispered to Bill Scow, who was writing down what our program was going to be, to just go along with them, because we didn't want any more trouble in our family. I wanted to do this thing right because it was like a test case and was going to be the first one and it was going to be a big one. So we put everybody in order and they practiced all day. As they came in according to the rank of their tribe we gave each one so many minutes to do their dance and then we cut it off. There were some of the dancers that we didn't use because we only wanted to use the good ones.

That night the hall was really crowded with people from all over the area. As the chairman I got up and made a speech at the beginning of the evening. I said, "I want to welcome all you people from the white communities who have come tonight and I want to welcome all of my people who are going to put on this performance. In the early days when the Indian people used to put on this kind of dance, the chiefs used to call the people together to come and watch their dance and they paid them to come and watch. Tonight we are going to reverse it. You people that are here tonight have paid to come in to watch this wonderful performance that is going to be put on for you tonight by my people. I'm sure you are going to enjoy it and it is for a good cause." So then each dancer began coming out, and it was announced what dance he was doing and we tried to interpret it all to the white people as the dances were performed. We must have had a five-hour do there that night and I think it was one of the biggest dances because all the big chiefs were there, the prominent and noble men of all the villages. I brought out some of my masks that belonged to me and showed them for the first time that night. And that was the time that I made up my mind that I was going to learn my songs and make some masks, and if I wanted to put anything on I could just grab my sack and go to it. I had taken part in the small potlatches at Village Island and some other places but I hadn't given anything since moving to Alert Bay. And I lived to see all those people that were making those harsh words and remarks to me in that meeting go into the hospital before they died.

•   •   •

Shortly after I became a lay reader, I was elected again to be the chief councillor of the Nimpkish band. We elected five councillors and they were Alfred Hunt, George Cook, Herbert Cook, George Alfred, and Robby Bell. It wasn't very long after that election that my uncle, Chief Tom Dawson of the

Kingcome people, came to Alert Bay and invited me to attend a big do that he was going to put on, and he wanted me to bring some of the people up in my boat. So I went up with some of the people and he put on this big do that lasted for several days. On the final day after there had been many Indian dances and many things given away, he was giving away his personal belongings, doing what I think is called "making a will." He was sitting on a box up in front of all the people, and he called me up to where he was sitting after he was through telling what was going to belong to each of his own children.

When I went up he talked to me so that everyone could hear. "Jimmy," he said, "I am very proud of you and that is why I wanted you to come forward here today. I have been very proud of you and your work for our people. I have always thought that you have inherited what you have been doing through your mother's side and your father's side, especially Chief Odzistales of the Mamalilikulla people. He was a good leader of his people. Your grandfather, Chief Aul Sewid, was also a big man in his time during the potlatch days and a strong leader. He was well liked by the first governor of British Columbia, James Douglas, and he used to interpret for him and help him in many ways. That is why I think you are like you are today. It has been just natural for you to work through the Native Brotherhood in your own way for our people. I would like you to accept this gift, this little token from me, this talking stick. It was made especially for you by Benny Dick of Kingcome and I have paid him for doing this for you. This talking stick represents your crests on your mother's side and your father's side. I want you to take this talking stick and use it whenever you think you can.

"The first crest at the bottom is Tsunuqua who was a giantess. This is the crest of the Temltemlels clan from your mother's side. Temltemlels was the first man of that clan and he had the supernatural power to turn into the Tsunuqua. The second crest is Tselkamai which means 'owner of the cedar bark dances.' He was also a great man with many supernatural powers. The next one is the double-headed serpent Sisiutl, and I have put it on this talking stick because it represents the strength of the Kwakiutl people. The next one is the Cedar Man. In the early days when the people heard the flood was coming, he went inside of a big hollow cedar log and after the flood he came out. The next one is Yakatnalas which means 'The Whale' and comes to you from your father's side. The next one is Qolus and that is the same as Odzistales which means 'he is so big that he can hardly move around.' You have that name through your grandfather, Aul Sewid."

So I took the talking stick from him and said, "I thank you from the bottom of my heart because this will give me more strength in what I am doing. I will treasure this wonderful gift especially because I know that some people like yourself have been quietly standing by me in all that I have been trying to do for our people." It was awfully hard to talk when I answered him and I had tears in my eyes as I thought of my grandparents and my father and mother who had passed away many years before. When I returned to Alert

Bay after that do, I was really touched by that wonderful gift and I started to think about putting on a do myself.

The next year I talked it over with my wife and my in-laws about calling the people to Alert Bay for a do when they came for the sports day in the spring. The reason I wanted to do it was because when Chief Tom Dawson had given me that talking stick it made me feel that I should do something to show the people that I could do it on my own. Of course, in previous years when I was young, I was involved in many potlatches with the help of my grandparents and with the help of my uncle, Toby Willey. I had used my own money and belongings in a potlatch after my wedding, but I hadn't done any for over twenty years. I wanted to do it to announce that I had received that beautiful present from my uncle. I talked it over with my in-laws because the purpose of that night was going to be to announce and give my grandchildren names that were associated with the particular dances. The custom was that everything was to come to me from my wife's family and then I could pass it on to my children and grandchildren. Many of my relatives had given names to my older grandchildren, but that was to be the first time for some of the others and all the names that had been given to my children and grandchildren would be announced again. So I sent Simon Beans around in his boat because he was a very close relation of mine to invite the villages to come to Alert Bay. He went around to Village Island, Gilford Island, Turnour Island, New Vancouver, Fort Rupert, and Kingcome and invited all the people to come.

I asked my uncle, Chief Tom Dawson, to be the master of ceremonies, to announce the different names and dances. We met in the council hall at about 8 o'clock, and the first thing was some of the people of my wife's family got up and gave a speech and announced that the articles and some names for that do were coming from my wife's side of the family. Even though I was the one who gathered all the stuff together, it was the custom that it was supposed to come from them that night even though I had given it to them. After that Tom Dawson started announcing the dances, the singers who I had hired that day started singing, and different ones of my relatives there started coming out and dancing. I went out first and danced the hamatsa dance, and Herbert Martin was dancing right along with me as well as two or three hamatsas who were my relations from other villages. They usually did that just to show their appreciation of what I was doing there that night.

Then Tom Dawson announced the names that had been given to my children before and then they danced. Most of my children had danced before, like at Simon Beans' potlatch, but some of my grandchildren had never danced. Bobby's oldest boy danced the kind of dance that Aul Sewid had gotten for the first time among the Kwakiutl. Bobby was wearing the chilcat blanket that night because we had received that right from Odzistales of the Mamalilikulla. The dancing went on until nearly eleven o'clock, and they only stopped when it was announced that someone was going to dance and they told the name that he was going to receive.

My wife had gathered up some things like towels and small household articles and I took some money out of the bank to give out to the people. After the dancing was over, Tom Dawson announced that there was going to be a little intermission and Henry Bell and Simon Beans went around for me and gave out some money. My wife had given the articles to her family and they were passing the things out. I had taken about five or six hundred dollars out of the bank and I just gave that money to Henry Bell who gave it out along with Simon Beans. They gave out about ten dollars apiece to some of the chiefs and some of the younger men got two dollars and the women got a dollar each. Everybody got something but I considered them all just small presents, just tokens. While they were giving out the money and articles we served everybody coffee and sandwiches and cake. There were over two hundred people there including some of my non-Indian friends.

After we had given everything away, Chief Tom Dawson got up and gave all the other chiefs a chance to say what they wanted. Many of my uncles got up, like Mungo Martin and Henry Bell and Sandy Willey, and made speeches. They all thanked me for putting on that do and said they were all happy to see me do that thing that night. Then they each gave a wonderful speech about the history of my family, especially on my father's side about Chief Aul Sewid. They didn't have to tell it but they just liked to bring it out when they made their speech. All of the chiefs of the other villages already knew all about it anyway and they didn't have to be told, but they just wanted to say that. They thanked me for the wonderful hospitality that I had given them when they came to visit the village where I was chief councillor. Just before it was all over I got up and made the last speech. "I want you all to know," I said, "that this is not a big do as far as I'm concerned. It is not like the ones in the past, the real big potlatches. The reason I put on this do was to announce to you all that I have received this talking stick from my uncle, Chief Tom Dawson. I want to announce in public that he had it specially made for me. I want to thank you all for coming and to say that I'm not going to boast about what I have done tonight. It was just a small token and I just wanted to do it. I felt like doing it and I didn't have to trouble anybody or anyone else by borrowing from them to do this. I can do it on my own of my own free will. I want to make sure that nobody can think that I was just doing it because I felt like I had to pay for my name or anything like that. It is the duty of a descendant chief to do these things and I felt that it was my duty to go ahead and do it. Thank you all for coming."

In March 1964 we had the Native Brotherhood convention in Vancouver. Guy Williams was elected president again and I was reelected one of the vice-presidents. At that meeting one of the most important things that we discussed was the problem of Japanese and Russian fishermen catching fish along the coast. Many of the Japanese boats were catching salmon out in the North Pacific and we felt that this was reducing the number of salmon which returned to their spawning grounds. The Fisheries Department was concerned with conserving the salmon, but they usually only restricted fishing around the mouths of the streams where the fish spawned and that hit the native fishermen the hardest. Fishermen from France and the United States were also fishing right close to our shores and we felt that it would be best to establish a twelve-mile limit along the coast that would be only for the Canadian fishermen. Since there was a discussion going on in the House of Commons about the problem, it was decided at that convention to send Guy Williams back to Ottawa to talk to the government people and make known what the native people wanted. I was appointed to go along with Guy and talk to those leaders about our problems.

· · ·

When I got back from Ottawa my wife told me that Alvin, my youngest son, was going to get married. I didn't like it very much because the wedding was going to be in Saskatchewan. I knew Alvin was engaged to this girl from the Cree Indians and I wanted to do something for him when he got married, the same as I had done for my other children. They were all married in the church and I used to give them good receptions and big dos. It would cost us a lot of money to go back to where he was going to be married, and it would be kind of hard on her family if they got married in Alert Bay. So I decided that when Alvin returned from Saskatchewan, I would put on an Indian do. It wasn't the same as the receptions that I had put on for the other children when they got married. But when he came back it was just about time for the sports days in Alert Bay, so I invited all the people to come to the do the first night they arrived in our village. There were about two hundred people from all over the agency who gathered in the council hall that night.

I had received another chest with some dances in it from Moses Alfred. I had already used the earlier one he gave me with the hamatsa dance in it for Bobby. This second one had a different dance in it, the feather dance, which was for one of the other societies. I thought I was going to give the names and dances to my second oldest son that night but he didn't want to go. My oldest son already held the hamatsa cedar bark dance and according to the Indian way I couldn't mix them. So Alvin danced the feather dance that night. At the start of the evening my wife's people got up and made some speeches and announced that they were giving me that chest with the feather dances and the names for my grandchildren and all the money and things to give away. Of course I had gathered some money and my wife had gathered some articles to give away, but it was the Indian custom to receive it in public from my wife's people. Then the singers started to sing and the dancers began to come out and dance. We had been in such a hurry to get ready for that that we couldn't do it in the proper way, with all the dancers going out and coming in with their masks of the different animals. I did use the chilcat blanket because that was in my family and lots of button blankets and the headgear that went with the feather dance. All my relatives danced that night because when they felt happy they always liked to dance and perform for the people to show that they were part of my family and related to my grandfather. I had one of my uncles, Chief Tom Umpkeep, acting as master of ceremonies and he was announcing the names and the dances. Then he passed out money to all the people that were there. He gave ten dollars each to the leading chiefs from each of the villages and maybe two dollars to the young men and one dollar to the women. Then we gave away quite a lot of apples, oranges, and candy, and popcorn for the children. My wife gave away some articles but I didn't pay too much attention to what she gave away because that was her own doings. It cost me nearly two thousand dollars that night.

After they had given away all the articles and money I got up and made a speech. I said, "Thank you for coming tonight. The reason why I did this tonight was because I felt so happy that Alvin was married. I always liked to do a little bit for my children because that was what my family did for me when I was married, so I feel that I should do it for my children. This is the last of my boys. I always like to treat my children alike and I have done something for each of them when they were married, but Alvin wasn't married in Alert Bay and that is the reason why I have done this. I like to do this not only for my children but for my stepbrothers and stepsister. I have stood for the expenses of each of their weddings and it usually cost me between a thousand and fifteen hundred dollars. Usually we just put on a reception and a dance in the white man's way for the others but tonight I wanted to give this Indian do. I want to announce that I am doing this for Alvin because he has married this girl from the Cree people. I am happy that he has married into the Cree people, but according to the Kwakiutl custom I am not allowed to use their dances and regalia. I want to thank you all again for coming." After that everybody went home.

Early in December 1966 I made a trip down to Vancouver and when I returned I decided to put on a special kind of potlatch. When I was a little boy my parents and grandparents had told me about how they sometimes used to have a *gwomiass*, which is a play potlatch. I didn't actually see one but they used to talk about it and say that it was more or less like a social gathering with friends. It was different from the real potlatch where a big chief would give a lot of things away. The smaller the amount that one gave away the bigger he was in this play potlatch because it was just for fun. It was just a play. After I was married my wife's aunt and mother used to tell me about it and that anybody could give small things away to each person, such as a lot of candy, buttons, or nickels. They had little names that they gave to people, such as a fish, a rapid of a river, a tree, a bird, or a duck. They were not like the real chief's names but they were inherited from their ancestors to be used in the play potlatch. They also had songs which were handed from generation to generation which had pretty bad words in them. At the play potlatch they would divide up with the men on the one side of the big house and the women on the other, and they would sing these songs and give things away, and each side would try to beat the other side.

So I talked to some of my people and asked them if there was anything going on the day before Christmas Eve. They said that there was nothing going on and so I thought it would be good to have something going on for my people and for the non-Indians as well. I talked to some of the older people and some of the younger people to see if we could put on a play potlatch since it was Christmas time and everybody was happy together. Well, we sent word around in Alert Bay but we didn't invite any of the outside villages and it wasn't advertised too much. So we all gathered in the community house and there were about one hundred people there that night. The men were on one side and the women were on the other and the women started it off. Each side had their own master of ceremonies who announced what they were going to do. One of the older women got up and announced that a great chief was going to give a potlatch. Then a young girl got up and they mentioned her name, it was a funny little name, and they all started singing a funny little song. The words of that song were more or less calling the men's side down. After they sang that song someone danced and then that young girl gave away little pieces of candy to everybody that was there. Her friends were helping her give away those little presents.

When she was done then one of the men on our side got up and announced that a great chief, a non-Indian, was going to give a potlatch. We gave him a funny little name and then some of us helped him give out his presents. Then it just went back and forth from one side to the other and some of the people were dancing some of the time. Flora gave away a lot of little five-cent candy bars but I didn't give anything away that night. I danced the feather dance to show some of my non-Indian friends how it went. Some of the others danced the hamatsa dance and tried to imitate the regular hamatsas making noises and singing like the hamatsas do. The speeches that they made that night were more or less a joke, telling how great the person was and that they were going to sing the great songs of that great chief. It was all in our language but there were some who were interpreting it to the non-Indian friends of ours. We didn't measure who was the highest that night, but the women beat the men because there were more women that gave away than men. It went on until about eleven o'clock and then we all went home. It was quite a nice gathering and everybody was happy and laughing and dancing around all that evening.

That is the end of my story. As I think back over my life I think it was a full life and a wonderful life. I realize that I have gone through many things in my life and I think lots of my people can learn from my experiences. As a little boy I grew up in the Indian way and now our life has turned to the modern way. Many times I have talked to my people at gatherings on how to go about their own business and how to go about their family life and how to carry on the work for their tribe. I don't like to brag about anything that I have done because I'm not the judge as to what I have done. I have always tried to live up to all the things that I have done and I think that others can learn from hearing about my experiences. I thought that if I could put my life story in a written book then even people that I know in distant places could read about it and it might be a help to them. That was why I thought it was necessary to make this book.

THE GODFATHER

Amerigo Bonasera sat in New York Criminal Court Number 3 and waited for justice; vengeance on the men who had so cruelly hurt his daughter, who had tried to dishonor her.

The judge, a formidably heavy-featured man, rolled up the sleeves of his black robe as if to physically chastise the two young men standing before the bench. His face was cold with majestic contempt. But there was something false in all this that Amerigo Bonasera sensed but did not yet understand.

"You acted like the worst kind of degenerates," the judge said harshly. Yes, yes, thought Amerigo Bonasera. Animals. Animals. The two young men, glossy hair crew cut, scrubbed clean-cut faces composed into humble contrition, bowed their heads in submission.

The judge went on. "You acted like wild beasts in a jungle and you are fortunate you did not sexually molest that poor girl or I'd put you behind bars for twenty years." The judge paused, his eyes beneath impressively thick brows flickered slyly toward the sallow-faced Amerigo Bonasera, then lowered to a stack of probation reports before him. He frowned and shrugged as if convinced against his own natural desire. He spoke again.

"But because of your youth, your clean records, because of your fine families, and because the law in its majesty does not seek vengeance, I hereby sentence you to three years' confinement to the penitentiary. Sentence to be suspended."

Only forty years of professional mourning kept the overwhelming frustration and hatred from showing on Amerigo Bonasera's face. His beautiful young daughter was still in the hospital with her broken jaw wired together; and now these two *animales* went free? It had all been a farce. He watched the happy parents cluster around their darling sons. Oh, they were all happy now, they were smiling now.

The black bile, sourly bitter, rose in Bonasera's throat, overflowed through tightly clenched teeth. He used his white linen pocket handkerchief and held it against his lips. He was standing so when the two young men strode freely up the aisle, confident and cool-eyed, smiling, not giving him so much as a glance. He let them pass without saying a word, pressing the fresh linen against his mouth.

The parents of the *animales* were coming by now, two men and two

---

women his age but more American in their dress. They glanced at him, shamefaced, yet in their eyes was an odd, triumphant defiance.

Out of control, Bonasera leaned forward toward the aisle and shouted hoarsely, "You will weep as I have wept—I will make you weep as your children make me weep"—the linen at his eyes now. The defense attorneys bringing up the rear swept their clients forward in a tight little band, enveloping the two young men, who had started back down the aisle as if to protect their parents. A huge bailiff moved quickly to block the row in which Bonasera stood. But it was not necessary.

All his years in America, Amerigo Bonasera had trusted in law and order. And he had prospered thereby. Now, though his brain smoked with hatred, though wild visions of buying a gun and killing the two young men jangled the very bones of his skull, Bonasera turned to his still uncomprehending wife and explained to her, "They have made fools of us." He paused and then made his decision, no longer fearing the cost. "For justice we must go on our knees to Don Corleone."

Amerigo Bonasera followed Hagen into the corner room of the house and found Don Corleone sitting behind a huge desk. Sonny Corleone was standing by the window, looking out into the garden. For the first time that afternoon the Don behaved coolly. He did not embrace the visitor or shake hands. The sallow-faced undertaker owed his invitation to the fact that his wife and the wife of the Don were the closest of friends. Amerigo Bonasera himself was in severe disfavor with Don Corleone.

Bonasera began his request obliquely and cleverly. "You must excuse my daughter, your wife's goddaughter, for not doing your family the respect of coming today. She is in the hospital still." He glanced at Sonny Corleone and Tom Hagen to indicate that he did not wish to speak before them. But the Don was merciless.

"We all know of your daughter's misfortune," Don Corleone said. "If I can help her in any way, you have only to speak. My wife is her godmother after all. I have never forgotten that honor." This was a rebuke. The undertaker never called Don Corleone "Godfather" as custom dictated.

Bonasera, ashen-faced, asked, directly now, "May I speak to you alone?"

Don Corleone shook his head. "I trust these two men with my life. They are my two right arms. I cannot insult them by sending them away."

The undertaker closed his eyes for a moment and then began to speak. His voice was quiet, the voice he used to console the bereaved. "I raised my daughter in the American fashion. I believe in America. America has made my fortune. I gave my daughter her freedom and yet taught her never to dishonor her family. She found a 'boy friend,' not an Italian. She went to the movies with him. She stayed out late. But he never came to meet her parents. I accepted all this without a protest, the fault is mine. Two months ago he took her for a drive. He had a masculine friend with him. They made her drink whiskey and then they tried to take advantage of her. She resisted. She kept her honor. They beat her. Like an animal. When I went to the hospital she had two black eyes. Her nose was broken. Her jaw was shattered. They had to wire it together. She wept through her pain. 'Father, Father, why did they do it? Why did they do this to me?' And I wept." Bonasera could not speak further, he was weeping now though his voice had not betrayed his emotion.

Don Corleone, as if against his will, made a gesture of sympathy and Bonasera went on, his voice human with suffering. "Why did I weep? She was the light of my life, an affectionate daughter. A beautiful girl. She trusted people and now she will never trust them again. She will never be beautiful again." He was trembling, his sallow face flushed an ugly dark red.

"I went to the police like a good American. The two boys were arrested. They were brought to trial. The evidence was overwhelming and they pleaded guilty. The judge sentenced them to three years in prison and suspended the sentence. They went free that very day. I stood in the courtroom like a fool and those bastards smiled at me. And then I said to my wife: 'We must go to Don Corleone for justice.' "

The Don had bowed his head to show respect for the man's grief. But when he spoke, the words were cold with offended dignity. "Why did you go to the police? Why didn't you come to me at the beginning of this affair?"

Bonasera muttered almost inaudibly, "What do you want of me? Tell me what you wish. But do what I beg you to do." There was something almost insolent in his words.

Don Corleone said gravely, "And what is that?"

Bonasera glanced at Hagen and Sonny Corleone and shook his head. The Don, still sitting at Hagen's desk, inclined his body toward the undertaker. Bonasera hesitated, then bent down and put his lips so close to the Don's hairy ear that they touched. Don Corleone listened like a priest in the confessional, gazing away into the distance, impassive, remote. They stood so for a long moment until Bonasera finished whispering and straightened to his full height. The Don looked up gravely at Bonasera. Bonasera, his face flushed, returned the stare unflinchingly.

Finally the Don spoke. "That I cannot do. You are being carried away."

Bonasera said loudly, clearly, "I will pay you anything you ask." On hearing this, Hagen flinched, a nervous flick of his head. Sonny Corleone folded his arms, smiled sardonically as he turned from the window to watch the scene in the room for the first time.

Don Corleone rose from behind the desk. His face was still impassive but his voice rang like cold death. "We have known each other many years, you and I," he said to the undertaker, "but until this day you never came to me for counsel or help. I can't remember the last time you invited me to your house for coffee though my wife is godmother to your only child. Let us be frank. You spurned my friendship. You feared to be in my debt."

Bonasera murmured, "I didn't want to get into trouble."

The Don held up his hand. "No. Don't speak. You found America a paradise. You had a good trade, you made a good living, you thought the

Subsistence and Economic Exchange

world a harmless place where you could take your pleasure as you willed. You never armed yourself with true friends. After all, the police guarded you, there were courts of law, you and yours could come to no harm. You did not need Don Corleone. Very well. My feelings were wounded but I am not that sort of person who thrusts his friendship on those who do not value it—on those who think me of little account." The Don paused and gave the undertaker a polite, ironic smile. "Now you come to me and say, 'Don Corleone give me justice.' And you do not ask with respect. You do not offer me your friendship. You come into my home on the bridal day of my daughter and you ask me to do murder and you say"—here the Don's voice became a scornful mimicry—" 'I will pay you anything.' No, no, I am not offended, but what have I ever done to make you treat me so disrespectfully?"

Bonasera cried out in his anguish and his fear, "America has been good to me. I wanted to be a good citizen. I wanted my child to be American."

The Don clapped his hands together with decisive approval. "Well spoken. Very fine. Then you have nothing to complain about. The judge has ruled. America has ruled. Bring your daughter flowers and a box of candy when you go visit her in the hospital. That will comfort her. Be content. After all, this is not a serious affair, the boys were young, high-spirited, and one of them is the son of a powerful politician. No, my dear Amerigo, you have always been honest. I must admit, though you spurned my friendship, that I would trust the given word of Amerigo Bonasera more than I would any other man's. So give me your word that you will put aside this madness. It is not American. Forgive. Forget. Life is full of misfortunes."

The cruel and contemptuous irony with which all this was said, the controlled anger of the Don, reduced the poor undertaker to a quivering jelly but he spoke up bravely again. "I ask you for justice."

Don Corleone said curtly, "The court gave you justice."

Bonasera shook his head stubbornly. "No. They gave the youths justice. They did not give me justice."

The Don acknowledged this fine distinction with an approving nod, then asked, "What is your justice?"

"An eye for an eye," Bonasera said.

"You asked for more," the Don said. "Your daughter is alive."

Bonasera said reluctantly, "Let them suffer as she suffers." The Don waited for him to speak further. Bonasera screwed up the last of his courage and said, "How much shall I pay you?" It was a despairing wail.

Don Corleone turned his back. It was a dismissal. Bonasera did not budge.

Finally, sighing, a good-hearted man who cannot remain angry with an erring friend, Don Corleone turned back to the undertaker, who was now as pale as one of his corpses. Don Corleone was gentle, patient. "Why do you fear to give your first allegiance to me?" he said. "You go to the law courts and wait for months. You spend money on lawyers who know full well you are to be made a fool of. You accept judgment from a judge who sells himself like the worst whore in the streets. Years gone by, when you needed money, you went to the banks and paid ruinous interest, waited hat in hand like a beggar while they sniffed around, poked their noses up your very asshole to make sure you could pay them back." The Don paused, his voice became sterner.

"But if you had come to me, my purse would have been yours. If you had come to me for justice those scum who ruined your daughter would be weeping bitter tears this day. If by some misfortune an honest man like yourself made enemies they would become my enemies"—the Don raised his arm, finger pointing at Bonasera—"and then, believe me, they would fear you."

Bonasera bowed his head and murmured in a strangled voice, "Be my friend. I accept."

Don Corleone put his hand on the man's shoulder. "Good," he said, "you shall have your justice. Some day, and that day may never come, I will call upon you to do me a service in return. Until that day, consider this justice a gift from my wife, your daughter's godmother."

When the door closed behind the grateful undertaker, Don Corleone turned to Hagen and said, "Give this affair to Clemenza and tell him to be sure to use reliable people, people who will not be carried away by the smell of blood. After all, we're not murderers, no matter what that corpse valet dreams up in his foolish head."

PART THREE

SOCIAL ORGANIZATION—KINSHIP
AND GROUPS

Like other social animals, mankind's ability to exploit his environment and protect himself from predators is greatly increased by group life. But in contrast to ants, wasps, bees, horses, chimpanzees, and other social animals, human social organizations serve two other important functions. First, the human infant has the longest period of maturation, which requires a social group for it to depend upon. Second, even if we all reached physical maturity in two or three years, we would not be able to survive. Human survival depends upon learning our culture, acquiring a social inheritance; and that takes time. Therefore every human social organization has the important functions of preserving a cultural code and imparting that code to its dependent members. Fundamental to these requirements is the fact that human societies differ from all other animal societies because they are culturally constituted.

To accomplish the basic tasks of maintaining itself and transmitting a culture to the next generation, every social system divides up the work to be done and parcels it out among its members. Social organizations are composed of such positions or statuses as fathers, mothers, chiefs, story tellers, curers, soldiers, astronauts, and many more. A *status* is a relatively fixed category of positions in a social organization that are filled by individuals. People enter these positions, occupy them for a number of years, and then through death, retirement, promotion, or some other means leave them. The social system continues while individuals come and go.

Every status category has associated behavioral expectations or *roles*. If someone occupies the status of curer, chief, or airplane pilot, others expect that person to behave in some particular way. We do not all live up to the role-expectations for statuses we occupy; on the other hand, the extent to which we do conform to these expectations is far greater than we tend to think. Social systems can tolerate only so much deviation from role-expectations before there is serious conflict and breakdown. One source of deviation from our roles is the changing definition of what appropriate behavior should be.

The social organizations that man has created are organized around several universal principles including kinship. In small societies it has more importance than in our own industrial one, but we must not underestimate its significance even in the most complex societies. Groups are also formed on such principles as residence, age, religious beliefs and practices, occupation, and a wide variety of special interests.

Social organizations also give each of us the sense of who we are—our *identities*. The human self is constituted and defined by society, by the statuses we occupy and the roles we play. Each social system takes the principles of organization, weaves them together in a unique pattern of roles and statuses, and by this means gives each individual his or her identity. But our sense of self, our identity, is a fragile thing, on loan to us from our society. It is reinforced by the labels others use to address us, the sanctions they use to remind us to act our age, to act like sons or daughters, to fulfill the expectations that go along with who we are.

These selections illustrate different social organizations in operation, most often from the perspective of individuals who have assumed the identities their culture offers them.

PAPIK AND POWTEE—
ESKIMO KINSMEN

When in the gloom of fall they rejoined camp Ernenek let Asiak's parents have a lamp and they let him have Asiak.

He was proud that as a married man he now was in a position to repay other husbands for what little favors he had received from them. When he discreetly left the igloo, hinting that Anarvik might welcome a little laugh with Asiak, there was a new tilt to his head and a new squareness to his shoulders. At last, Ernenek was a full-fledged Man. He did not allow Siksik to be a spoilsport, ignoring her insinuations that for many seasons now Anarvik had been unable to laugh or even just titter with a woman.

Old Ooloolik died the following winter for no particular reason at all. He went to sleep and forgot to wake up. This was unfortunate. If his relatives had had an inkling of his impending death they could have dressed him in his burial clothes and moved him into a makeshift shelter, as the shade of the deceased contaminates an igloo and it has to be abandoned. So in the dead of the night they decamped, erasing their tracks as they went, and built fresh igloos far enough to be safe from the dead man's vengeance; even Ernenek, who was afraid of no man living.

For a dead Eskimo is a bad Eskimo. He is enraged that he is dead while his dear ones are alive and he will hurt them with all his power. And as the dread of Ooloolik's ghost was great, the wails of mourning were loud and plentiful in an effort to conciliate it. For further precaution everybody built sham snares and traps about their new dwellings in order to frighten away the ghost should it want to come back.

The dead made things hard for the living. But so did the living for the dead.

Anarvik and Siksik migrated to the southward at the break of day, but Asiak's mother, Powtee, felt too old to travel, and Ernenek and Asiak stayed on with her.

They were good to the old woman who had no one left after Ooloolik had died and Imina had gone to Kidok's tribe. For a whole year they tended her with care and affection, providing her with foods and garments although her stiff fingers were unable to sew or scrape, and her teeth, used down to the

From "The Facts of Life" (pp. 36–51 in hardcover edition) in *Top of the World* by Hans Ruesch. Copyright, 1944, 1946, 1947, 1950 by Hans Ruesch. By permission of Harper and Row, Publishers, Inc.

gums, were incapable of softening hides any longer. They gave her choice and tender morsels, and Asiak fed her mouth to mouth, thus paying her back what she had received from her in childhood—a fair exchange. But an end would have to be set to all this, sure as winter.

And it was.

The old woman knew what it meant when she was packed on the sled and driven out over the wind-harassed ocean, luminous with stars. Nobody talked on the ride, nor when a halt was called and Ernenek made the old woman sit on a dogskin he had spread in the midst of the sea field for her, so that she might die in comfort. Embarrassed, he had then waddled back to the sled, muttering to himself and feigning to be busy with the lashings.

Asiak, to conceal her own distress, was berating the huskies more than she was wont and kicking with great accuracy at their pointed snouts when they tore at one another's pelts.

Meantime, seated composedly on the dogskin, Powtee was watching her daughter with a worried eye.

Asiak was pregnant and probably had no inkling of how close to delivery she already was. She had never witnessed human birth, nor would there be anyone with her now who had, and Powtee wondered whether her daughter had learned enough about the facts of life from the husky bitches.

"Step close, little one. A useless old woman has something to tell you."

Asiak complied and respectfully listened to her mother's words.

"It is possible that you will soon bear a child. Now you must know the child is impatient to see the world—that's why you feel it toss in your belly —and you must do everything in your power to help it on its way. If you happen to be in the igloo when the moment comes, remove the hides from the ground so as not to soil them, then stand on your knees, which is the best position for childbearing, and dig a hole under you to make room for the child. But it happens that at the last moment the child gets afraid to come out and after it has already stepped into the world it still clings to you—unlike the dogs you have seen, that are born free. So you must cut it from you, and do it immediately, otherwise it will die, and you with it. Did you understand what somebody said?"

"Almost everything. How wise you are!"

"Now listen carefully: as soon as the child is born, look if it is a boy or girl. If it is a boy, everything is all right. Lick it clean with your tongue, then rub it with blubber. Don't be afraid to rub hard: it won't break. Only after a sleep or two may you start washing it in urine. But if it is a girl you must strangle her at once, before you get fond of her, or set her out on the ice, filling her mouth with snow so that she'll die quickly."

"Why must somebody do that?"

"Because during the time you give suck to a child you will be barren, which means that in order to raise a girl you will delay the arrival of a boy, and it is indispensable that you raise a male quickly in your family: it is he that will bring in the food when you and your husband grow old, which happens very, but very quickly. Once you have a boy you may raise a girl too, if you care. But you should know that many wise parents let their daughters live only if somebody has promised already before their birth to marry them, and provide for them while they grow. Is all that clear to you, little one?"

"Yes, little one."

"Somebody is glad it is." And so as to give her daughter a chance to depart she tore her gaze away from her and stared out across the lonely white reaches and toward the distant shadows, denoting land, blurry in the gloom of the Arctic night. She was a stickler for such old rules of *savoir-vivre* as demanded that departures should be ignored. So it would have been as impolite for Asiak and Ernenek to take leave as for her to take notice.

But as the young couple slipped out of her life's scene, it was only in sound. In sight they stayed with her, so familiar was she with the pattern of life which was unchanged since her childhood days, and unchangeable. And she was ashamed that at the end of a full life she should not yet be satisfied with her lot, but nurture one more desire—to see and hear and hold once more in her gnarled old hands a new-born babe. And as she sat waiting for death her thoughts went to the small igloo where even now the miracle of birth was taking place. She could picture accurately everything that was happening there in her absence.

Almost everything.

Even while Powtee was waiting for death on the dogskin the child was coming to Asiak, as if speeded on its way by her great sorrow. Already during the homebound ride was she assailed by the grip of labor, though not a sound came from her lips.

Sleepy-eyed puppies emerged yapping and stumbling from the tunnel, shaking the snow from their woolly hides. While Ernenek unharnessed the team Asiak did not tarry to unload the sled, but dropped prone in the snow and with some difficulty squeezed herself through the narrow tunnel. She discarded her outer suit, lit the lamp and stretched herself out on the snow couch.

Ernenek soon followed.

His presence disturbed her. She wished to be alone in what was about to happen. "Remember," she said, keeping her eyes closed, "the musk-ox flank we cached in the great gulf last spring?"

Ernenek exulted at the memory. "It was not a small musk ox!"

"Yes, you always have the biggest everything. It must be nice and mellow now. Maybe we could eat a piece of it."

Ernenek's big face grew serious. "It is a long trip and somebody is sleepy."

"A foolish woman wants some of that meat."

Ernenek shifted his squat, powerful frame, his head slightly bent under the ice vault. "There is fat, frozen seal in the larder," he said enticingly, "and liver that is rotting since summer."

"Somebody doesn't want fat, frozen seal," Asiak said, unimpressed, "nor liver, no matter how rotted it is, but musk-ox flank."

She had had many such sudden whims lately, and it would have been easy for Ernenek to silence her with a single slap—any time he was in good shape. He often wondered why he never did it, but found no answer. There were more things Ernenek couldn't answer than one could ask. He stamped and spat and snorted and cursed. Then he added grease to his face, reharnessed the team, and off he set for a musk-ox flank.

With her foot Asiak pushed into place the snowclod that sealed the entrance, for she had chills, though up to now her pregnancy had kept her warmer than a double bearskin; then she broke a piece of drinking snow from the block, melted it over the lamp in a vessel of hollowed soapstone and drank avidly, without ever leaving the couch. The impatient child drove daggers through her body, causing her to set her teeth while in her boots her toes curled in. The throes made her sick at her stomach and her damp hair clung to her brow. She bit her lips till they burst.

The wick of moss floating in the melting blubber of the lamp began to splutter, sending black coils of smoke toward the opening in the ceiling and calling her attention to the trimming, but she ignored it. She got up, removed the hides from the floor, and with a garment scraper gouged out a hole in the snow. She knelt over it, let her pants down to her knees and waited, resting one elbow on the couch and the other on the snow block. The apricot light mellowed, turning brown, purple, blue, gray, black.

And in the dark, Asiak's first-born dropped headlong into the snowhole.

Where there was something tugging at her she bent forward and chewed through it, and as soon as her child was free, a mighty squalling filled the igloo and she hurriedly lit the lamp to see what she had brought forth.

It was a male and the power of his voice made her guffaw a little, for it reminded her of Ernenek. She licked the soft heap of pale-brown flesh till it gleamed immaculate except for the blue Mongolic spot at the base of the spine, then dried it with a foxskin mop, smeared it with blubber, and quickly tucked it away into her deerskin bag because the pangs of the afterbirth were assailing her.

This over, she felt a reckless craving for food and wolfed a huge piece of frozen seal. After that a great quiet and contentment pervaded her. She undressed and crept into her bag.

The little hunter was squalling frantically. She stopped his mouth with her breast and he began to suck with all his might, hurting her a little but also giving her a sensation that vaguely resembled sexual pleasure.

And this also marked the reawakening of her sexual desires which, like in the animals of the wild, had gone to sleep the day of conception, causing her entire being to strive inward and to be on the defensive against the outer world.

And the long period of confinement had puzzled Ernenek who knew of the primal powers in Asiak's blood that commanded her as little as she did.

When Ernenek returned with the groceries he stayed rooted on all fours in the passageway, his big jowl unhinged, stilled in great wonder. A little crest of jet-black hair emerged from the sleeping bag beside Asiak's cheek.

"It came to pass that a woman has brought forth a child," she said shamefacedly. "But isn't he beautiful?" she added, holding it up triumphantly.

Ernenek wagged his head in doubt. "Somebody has seen bear cubs that were better looking." And he got to his feet, forgetting to beat the ice dust from his clothes.

"He will improve as he grows," Asiak said firmly. "But he has everything he needs. Even a name. His name is Papik."

"How do you know his name is Papik?" Ernenek asked, astounded.

"Because somebody happens to like that name."

So Ernenek sprawled Papik on the snow and watched him, wide-eyed, from the couch, not yet conditioned to fatherhood.

"He might not feel warm, all naked in the snow," Asiak suggested, and Ernenek lifted him up on his knees and began to inspect him from toe to top, shaking with laughter at the wee size of his parts, and Asiak felt slighted and a little angry. For, actually, the little hunter was powerfully built, with square shoulders, a big chest, short but strong arms and broad cheekbones, and his slightly slanting eyes shone black and lively in his greased face.

Ernenek made sure that every little thing was there. The tender, minute nails on the blunt-fingered hands. The short nose, almost disappearing between the bursting cheeks. The rich, round mouth and tiny tongue. . . .

"Asiak!" Ernenek rose bolt upright, hitting the ceiling and dangling his son by one foot, and the little one burst into a squall while his face grew crimson.

Asiak's eyes widened. "What is the matter?"

"It has no teeth!"

Consternation followed. Asiak probed her son's gums, unheedful of his squalls. Ernenek was right: no trace of teeth. And for the first time he saw tears on her that were not caused by laughter.

"You must have broken some taboo," he told her sternly.

"Not to my knowledge."

"Did you eat sea animals together with land animals? Or put the products of the sea and products of the land into one and the same pot?"

"Of course not."

"Then you must have tried to spear a seal, or killed a white caribou, or sewn out of season. Why don't you confess?"

"Because I didn't do it! How about *your* breaking some taboo? Think. Think hard!"

"A stupid woman talking thus to her husband! What is the world coming to?"

"The important thing is: what can be done about it?" She bit her finger sharply while fighting rivers; for of course she knew what had to be done.

And so did Ernenek. He shifted and coughed and cursed and muttered to himself. Then he laughed coarsely, feigning indifference.

Asiak anticipated him. "We'll set him out on the ice. The sooner the better."

Ernenek went to stroke her hair and snuff at her. "We'll have other children, and maybe they will have teeth in them."

Although a little numb from childbed, Asiak wanted to go along for the ride, and they traveled the same route they had come about one turn of the moon earlier. Powtee might still be alive, if a bear had not come to fetch her, and to Asiak the thought that little Papik would not step alone into eternity but in his grandmother's arms was somewhat of a comfort.

No bear had come to fetch the old woman and she was where they had left her, seated composedly in the midst of the white expanse like the Queen of the Sea. She was a little benumbed from such a lot of fresh air, but when finally she was able to unlock her leathery jaw it was to make a startling announcement:

"A useless old woman may know how to make his teeth grow."

It might take till summer, she explained, before the Powers of the Winds and Snows with which she, as an old woman, was on personal and excellent terms, would bow to her request; but in the end Papik would get his teeth. And although Asiak and Ernenek were not sure she knew what she was saying, for old women gibbered all sorts of things as remote from reality as the ice from the moon, they grabbed at the chance.

They drove back with her and the child, and Ernenek had to build another igloo of warm new snow leaning on and connected with their own, into which Powtee might retire with her grandchild, for she wished to be undisturbed in her conversations with the Powers of the Winds and Snows. And Asiak fretted behind the blocked entrance, waiting to be called in for the feeding.

Besides mother milk Papik got blubber to suck from Powtee's finger, and liver juice was squeezed into his mouth. The old woman barely took any nourishment herself. She became skinnier and her nose stood out more and more between the sunken and deeply furrowed cheeks. But her eyes showed more life than a brace of seal in the water.

The boy grew markedly, but as Asiak kept exploring his gums in vain, she became sullen and taciturn, and many a time Ernenek, waking to her quiet sobbing, would put out his small, rough hand from his sleeping bag and touch her wet face in the dark.

Listlessly she sewed with her triangular needle and caribou sinew the trundle hood in which to carry her son, his garments of young hide and the white boots of baby seal; listlessly she tanned the skins with human water and scraped them into softness. Whenever the north wind allowed, she stepped out into the starry night and waddled about pigeon-toed, and at times she caught herself talking aloud, like Ernenek.

Her squat but well-shaped body, grown hefty in the outdoor life of summer, fined down. This was normal in winter. But she should have got more sleep, as Ernenek and everyone else she knew did in this season. Instead, she dozed fitfully or not at all.

The little ice blister might have been a happy homestead. The igloo was small, for reasons of warmth, but it had every imaginable comfort: the larder contained plenty of blubber for fuel and light, and food enough to last all winter; and when through the thick ice wall one heard the gale lowing outside, this was a warm and cozy nook with its tender sunset light, the fragrance of burning blubber and mellowing meats, and such a fearless hunter as Ernenek snoring in the bag.

But Asiak yearned for the sun's summoning, when they could drive southward to meet the herds, and life would consist of excitement that might help her forget; of stalking the caribou and musk ox and setting snares and traps, and perhaps meeting large crowds of other men, possibly as many as eight or ten people, and with them hunt and make merry.

In her heart, hope for Papik's recovery had been short-lived and she regretted having taken him back.

Separation would be unbearable now.

Spring came, the long dawn, the slow aurora, paling the stars, turning purple, turning light, turning day, and at long last—the sun! And Asiak, after time-honored custom, extinguished the light, poured out the fuel, and rekindled the lamp with fresh blubber and a new wick.

And in stride with the breath of life reappearing from below the horizon, drowsiness dropped from the Men, their wasted bodies clamored for flesh and the blood pulsed faster through their veins, making them restless, causing them to inspect and reinspect the lashings of their sleds and whet the tips of spears and arrows and tighten the sinews that spanned their bows.

His muscular body glistening with grease, Ernenek stood amid the glowing ice walls. "At our first stop we'll abandon the two."

"But somebody has grown very fond of Papik," said Asiak, feeling her heart turn colder than an abandoned igloo. "Even as he grows bigger a silly mother could chew his food in her own mouth."

"And what when you die? The men will mock and the women scorn him, all his life. No, no. He is not fit to live." And he turned round and went to harness the huskies, muttering.

When the sled was packed and the huskies were barking impatiently, Powtee emerged from the igloo with Papik in her arms.

"You can take him along without me. It came to pass that his teeth have started to grow."

There they were, under Asiak's probing finger, two sharp, tiny chips of tooth, and Powtee promised that more would be forthcoming, a whole row of them, a full and straight and white team of them. How she had done it, what she had done, nobody knows. But the story is true, because Ittimangnerk, the trader, who saw Ernenek's family the following summer and bartered tea for some of their foxskins, told it to somebody who had never caught him lying, except for business reasons.

Asiak fell upon her mother's neck and snuffed at her walnut-stained face and rubbed her nose against it and washed it with tears, and Ernenek bounced higher than a young seal showing off before his first bride, and making very similar sounds.

"You must stay with us, little one," Asiak told Powtee. "What if our next children are born without teeth?"

"Do not worry. The Powers of the Winds and Snows have promised that all your children shall be provided with teeth, even if they don't show any at first. Some old woman is weary of these long journeys. She feels drowsy and wayworn and weak. The spring no longer stirs her blood."

Departure at this point being improper they opened a bundle and returned indoors to brew some tea and prattle and catch up on laughter and pull at Papik's teeth and drop tidbits into his mouth, and once Asiak had to reach deep into his throat where too big a morsel had got stuck. They gorged and guzzled and made merry till Asiak, who had slept little this winter, was overcome by sudden weariness and lay down to rest. Ernenek kept stuffing his face with meat and cracking bones for the marrow till he also grew sleepy and went down snoring.

Powtee rose and quietly slipped out. The team barked at her but she shushed them, clouting the more demonstrative ones vigorously over the head with the handle of her snow knife. She had left behind her inner suit of aukskins that might come in handy to Asiak or the little one, for it took a lot of sewing to fit so many small skins together, and wore her seediest dogskin garments with scarcely any hair left on them.

A rousing gale greeted her bluffly under a sulky sky. Progress was laborious to her leathered old body that had burned high energy all winter with barely any refueling. There was no sound but the crunch of her pads on the harsh snow, and way underfoot the muffled rumble of the sea, of the warm sea, the good rich sea filled with the good, fat fish.

She pressed on till she broke into a sweat, which she had been trained to avoid carefully since earliest childhood unless she was in her sleeping bag. But she kept on trudging with all her waning might, straining and perspiring. On an ice ridge in mid-sea she stopped. The igloo was no longer visible to her life-weary eyes.

She sat down and waited placidly for the sweat on her body to turn to ice.

Time passed. She didn't know how long, nor did anyone know or care, nor did it matter.

At first the frost about her body was painful. She felt the cast of ice chill her flesh, and bones, and thoughts. Sensation waned and departed, the mind grew sluggish in line with the slowing blood, and sweet drowsiness came. Before long she no longer felt cold, but cozy and contented.

She made out the shape of a bear jogging over the sea fields and thought of Ernenek's joy if he were to sight the great beast. It was approaching warily, restraining its nine hundred pounds of hunger, diffident of anything that had semblance of man, because man had so much the semblance of bear. It moved over the ice with a ponderousness that was only apparent, its small ears alert, its broad mobile nose and pin-point eyes alive in its jolly triangular face, making low, gurgling sounds and puffs of respiration in the cold.

Powtee couldn't help but grin a little with her toothless mouth about the fact that the mere human shape was sufficient to keep at bay so big a beast. And she reflected that the bear was right in being wary, for surely someday Ernenek would meet it face to face on the white sea, inveigle it into swallowing a ball of spring bait and follow it in its sickness till he could slay it. Before a new igloo the old shouts of joy would rise as the hunter skinned the kill and his mate removed the entrails before they froze and their son bit into the fuming liver with his row of perfect ivory teeth, till of the big white hunter nothing would be left but the blood stains on the wall.

Powtee knew the future because she knew the past, and her familiarity with the facts of life allowed her to understand, and therefore accept without bitterness, nature's eternal tragedy—that flesh must perish so that flesh may live. She was to die so that the bear might live for the day when Ernenek could slay it to feed Asiak and Papik.

And so she would return to them.

By the time the bear closed in, almost all feeling had left her, and it was with hardly any pain at all that she passed on to the regions of the constant and unruffled slumber.

CHAPTER 13   ELIZABETH MARSHALL THOMAS

THE HARMLESS PEOPLE

That year, in the Veld Food Season, there was a tragedy and also a wedding. The tragedy took place late one afternoon when a baby girl, playing house with a real fire, burned down her grandfather's grass scherm, thus destroying everything her grandparents owned, everything they had made over a lifetime. The two old people had been very industrious and the wife a prolific maker of ostrich-eggshell beads.

At the start of the blaze a great crowd of people gathered, arriving just in time to see the baby girl run out of the scherm as it collapsed in flames behind her. She ran straight to her mother and sat at her feet, ignoring the great crowd of people and placidly eating one of her grandfather's leather sandals which she had rescued from the fire and which, she found, had been cooked to a turn. No one was angry with the child, everyone was thankful that she had not been hurt. The people remarked at the size and the intensity of the fire and shook their heads at the destruction, each one telling someone else where he had been when he first had seen the blaze. They asked each other why no one put the fire out, as no one did, and soon the scherm was a heap of white ash and the old couple who owned it ruined materially, too old to start again.

A few weeks after that, two children were married. The groom was about sixteen and the bride was eight. It was considered to be an excellent match, as the bride was pretty and the groom was already becoming famous as a hunter. But even in these auspicious circumstances complications and involved negotiations arose, until, for a while, people began to think that no wedding would take place. The bride's aunt disliked the groom's mother, and recalled an old scandal that had shadowed the family for years. The groom's mother had divorced the groom's father long ago to marry her present husband, which in itself was altogether usual, but it came out that the man and woman had maintained an adulterous relationship before the divorce and furthermore were tabu relatives, which made their union incestuous—not as severely so as marriage between parent and child or brother and sister, but incestuous nevertheless—and it caused a scandal that reverberated throughout all of Nyae Nyae. The two were middle-aged when they married, and they had clung solidly together through the storm of scandal and disapproval, for it was truly a marriage of love.

The little girl did not want to be a bride. When we asked her how she felt about her wedding she hid her face in her hands and said that she was still a young child, too young to get married.

All in all, only the groom's family behaved well, showing patience and forbearance until at last the wedding took place. One day the young man killed a little buck and, according to custom, gave most of it to his bride's parents, thus proving that he hunted well and would provide for them and their daughter. With this the engagement was sealed. Shortly afterward the mothers of the bride and groom built a scherm for the young couple which they furnished with wood and water and enlivened with a fire, kindled by brands from their own fires. Very early the following day the bride's mother adorned the bride, washing her, hanging white bead ornaments from her hair, rubbing her clothing with red, sweet-smelling powder, a symbol to Bushmen of beauty. Then, sitting her upon one large kaross, they covered her with another and left her to spend the day motionless, waiting for evening, when the union would take place.

It is common in Bushman ceremonies for a person at a transitional moment of life to be raised from the ground and hidden from the sun, as though suspended between earth and sky. Young people on the day of their first marriage are protected in this way; so are newborn babies, and so are girls on the day of their first menstruation. At a funeral, too, the body before burial is covered and raised from the ground, and perhaps all this is because a person is especially susceptible to damage at times of life when change is taking place, when, perhaps, a person is as delicate and fragile as a new moth emerged from a cocoon.

Because the sun brings death, no ceremony or part of any ceremony is performed when the sun is strong; but when evening came and the sun itself was dying, the groom was led to his new home by his three brothers, who took him by the hands and pulled him there, forced him, for custom demanded that he show reluctance. The bride, according to custom, refused to go to her husband and had to be picked up by another little girl and carried to him. In the drama of reluctance the bride struggled while the other girl caught her. She lifted the bride and carried her on her shoulders, not upright as a figure of triumph but wrapped in the kaross and motionless, like a dead little animal, then put her shrouded body on the floor of the new scherm and left her there to lie quietly while the wedding guests arrived. Again according to custom, the groom seemed to take no notice of his new bride; the people in the werf paid no attention, and, in fact, all the people went about their business in such a matter-of-fact way that an observer would think that nothing had happened although the young people were now married, the wedding had taken place.

The parents of the couple could not attend the wedding, for the young bride and groom were so tabu to them at this time that they could not even mention their names. In fact, no older person could attend, and the guests who came were all children, three-year-olds to teen-agers, who sat by the young couple's fire decorously, the boys on the man's side, the girls on the woman's, and talked quietly for twenty minutes or so, the youngest guests leaving when their bedtimes came. That was all. In the morning the little girl and her young husband were anointed with fat by their mothers, and they lived together from that day on.

A month later the bride's mother, who was herself a young woman, bore another child, her second daughter. We were at her werf at the time, sitting in the shade. That day the young woman had not gone out for veld food, but was lying propped up on her elbow in front of her scherm when suddenly, without telling anyone what was happening, she stood up and walked into the bushes, only to come back some time later with her baby in the fold of her kaross. We might not have known what had happened except that she was smiling a sure, sweet smile because she was pleased with herself. Her belly was flatter, and a tiny foot with a pink sole and curled toes stuck out from her kaross.

Day or night, whether or not the bush is dangerous with lions or with spirits of the dead, Bushman women give birth alone, crouching out in the veld somewhere. A woman will not tell anybody where she is going or ask anybody's help because it is the law of Bushmen never to do so, unless a girl is bearing her first child, in which case her mother may help her, or unless the birth is extremely difficult, in which case a woman may ask the help of her mother or another woman. The young woman was only fifty feet from the werf when she bore her daughter, but no one heard her because it is their law that a woman in labor may clench her teeth, may let her tears come or bite her hands until blood flows, but she may never cry out to show her agony. Bushmen say a woman must never show that she is afraid of pain or childbirth, and that is why a woman goes alone, or why a young girl goes only with her mother, for then if she shows her pain and fear, only her mother will know.

When labor starts, the woman does not say what is happening, but lies down quietly in the werf, her face arranged to show nothing, and waits until the pains are very strong and very close together, though not so strong that she will be unable to walk, and then she goes by herself to the veld, to a place she may have chosen ahead of time and perhaps prepared with a bed of grass. If she has not prepared a place, she gathers what grass she can find and, making a little mound of it, crouches above it so that the baby is born onto something soft. Unless the birth is very arduous and someone else is with the woman, the baby is not helped out or pulled, and when it comes the woman saws its cord off with a stick and wipes it clean with grass. Then the mother collects the stained grass, the placenta, and the bloody sand and covers them all with stones or branches, marking the spot with a tuft of grass stuck up in a bush so that no man will step on or over the place, for the ground where a child has been born is tainted with a power so strong that any man infected with it would lose an aspect of his masculinity, would lose his power to hunt. The woman does not bury the placenta, for if she did she would lose her ability to bear more children.

The moment of birth is a very important one for the child and for the mother; it is at this moment that the child acquires a power, or an essence, over which he has no control, although he can make use of it. It will last him all his life; it is a supernatural essence that forever after connects the person born with certain forces in the world around him: with weather, with childbearing, with the great game antelope, and with death, and this essence is called the *now*.

There are two kinds of *now*, a rainy or cold one and a hot or dry one. If a person has a wet *now* and burns his hair in a fire or urinates in a fire, the person's *now* is said to make the weather turn cold (if it is the dry season) or bring rain (if it is the rainy season). If a person has a dry *now* and burns hair or urinates in a fire, the *now* is said to stop a cold spell or a bad storm. When a person dies, too, the weather changes violently according to the person's *now*. After a death, scorching droughts or devastating storms are sure to follow.

We knew a Bushman woman at Gautscha whose young son was living not with her but far away with the family of his infant wife, and once, when a rainstorm came so violently that branches were splintered from the trees and water ran in torrents like waterfalls over the rocks beside the pan, the woman began to pine and grieve for her son, who, she felt sure, was dead. At last a visitor came from her son's band who assured her that her son was safe and well, and she knew then that the storm was not for his *now*, loose in the air, but possibly for the *now* of someone else, though when she heard the news it did not matter to her who might have died, for she was happy.

The effect of *now* is simple when a person dies, or when a person burns his hair or urinates to change the weather. With childbearing for women and with killing the great antelope for men (as the great antelope also have *now*, although the small ones do not) the *now* has a larger, more complex effect. In these cases the *now* of the hunter interacts with the *now* of the antelope, the *now* of the woman interacts with the *now* of the child newly born, and when the blood of the antelope falls upon the ground as the antelope is killed, when the fluid of the womb falls upon the ground at the child's birth, the interaction of *nows* takes place, and this brings a change in the weather. In this way a mother may bring rain or drought when she bears a child, a hunter may bring rain or drought when he kills an antelope, no matter what kind of *now* the mother or the hunter may have. The mother or the hunter can only watch the weather to see what has taken place.

Now is intangible, mystic, and diffuse, and Bushmen themselves do not fully understand its workings. They do not know how or why *now* changes weather but only that it does. They watch the changes carefully, though, and by observing have discovered the limits of their own *nows*. When the fluid from a mother's womb falls upon the ground the child's *now* is determined, and it is partly for this reason that birth is such a mighty thing.

Birth is usually joyous. Bushmen of all ages adore their children and grandchildren, placing a child's health and wishes uppermost in their minds. Orphans are eagerly adopted by their aunts or grandparents, and a newborn baby is welcomed as though it were the first baby the werf had ever seen. Sometimes, though, a baby is born that cannot be supported, and if this happens the baby is destroyed. If a woman bears a child that is crippled or badly deformed, she is expected to destroy it, and if the season is very hard and she already has a baby under a year old depending on her milk, she is forced to kill her newborn child. Bushman women can hardly bear this, but they do.

If a woman knows that she must kill her baby, she braces herself for this as best she can, and when the time comes to do it she must act immediately, must take advantage of the moment after birth before the infant has "come to life," that moment between the time the baby is born and the time her love for the baby wells up in her so that the act would be impossible forever after. She must think of the child she has already and act quickly, before she hears her infant's voice, before the baby moves or waves its feet; she must not look at it for long or hold it, but must have a shallow grave ready for it and must put it in at once and cover it and never think of it again. In times of extreme deprivation she can do this, or she can wait to watch both her children die. All this is very hard, and Bushmen, who have no mechanical form of contraception and know no way to cause miscarriage or abortion, prefer to abstain from intercourse for long periods rather than to suffer such pain.

We knew one woman who had been forced to destroy a baby to save an older child, and we knew one woman who had borne a crippled child and had been persuaded to destroy it by her mother, who had been present at the birth. Such things are very rare, though, and this is fortunate.

•   •   •

When the young woman came back to the werf with her baby she sat down and calmly washed the blood from her legs with water from an ostrich eggshell. Then she lay on her side to rest with her baby beside her, and covered the baby from the sun with a corner of her kaross. She put her nipple in the baby's mouth and let her try to nurse. The young woman still said nothing to anyone, but she did open her kaross to show the baby, and one by one we all came by to look at her, and she was not brown, not gold, but pink as a pink rose, and her head was shaped perfectly. At the bottom of her spine was a Mongolian Spot, dark and triangular, and her hair, which she shed later, was finely curled and soft as eider down.

The father had been away, but he came home a little later and sat stolidly down on the man's side of the fire, his hands on his knees. He pronounced the baby's name softly to himself. Later, when he had no audience, he slipped his finger into the baby's hand. Of course the baby grasped it strongly, and the father smiled.

THE MARTÍNEZ FAMILY

CAST OF CHARACTERS

Pedro Martínez, age 59	*the father*
Esperanza Garcia, about 54	*the mother*
Conchita Martínez, age 29	*the eldest daughter,*
	married and living with
	her husband, Juan
Felipe Martínez, age 23	*the eldest son*
Martin Martínez, age 22	*the second son*
Ricardo Martínez, age 18	*the third son*
Machrina Martínez, age 17	*the younger daughter*
Moisés Martínez, age 13	*the youngest son*
Herman Martínez, age 7	*Conchita's*
	illegitimate son

The ancient highland village of Azteca lay quiet and serene on the mountain slope in the early morning darkness. The air was cool and fresh after the long night rain. Spreading from the top of the slope to the broad valley below, eight barrios, each with its own chapel and patron saint, formed little communities within the larger village. A paved road connecting Azteca with the main highway cut across the village and ended abruptly at the plaza. Here were the municipal building, the central church, the mill, a few small shops, and a bare park. Extending up and down the slope the old terraced streets, laboriously constructed of blue-gray volcanic rock, were lined by small, one-story adobe houses with their patios of semitropical plants and trees set behind low stone walls.

In the barrio of San José, halfway between the highest and lowest point in the village, stood the house of Pedro Martínez, almost hidden by the overhanging branches of the native plum trees in his orchard. The tile-roofed house was typical of those in San José, the poorest of the eight barrios, and consisted of one windowless room and an attached kitchen flimsily built of cane stalks. The house site was still called by its pre-Hispanic Nahuatl name, *Tlatlapancan,* or "the place where much was broken," referring to a local legend which told how the village god Azteco, said to be the son of the Virgin Mary, had broken one of his clay toys on this site. Forty-three years before, Pedro had thought the house site would be a propitious one and had bought it for fifty pesos.

Over the years Pedro had carefully worked on the little house and its neglected plot of ground, planting guave, coffee, avocado, hog plums, and other plants, all of which contributed to the family diet. Five years ago he and his sons had built the kitchen and had moved the simple hearth of three large stones from the smoky adobe room to the more airy kitchen where the smoke could filter through the spaces between the cane stalk of the walls. For all of its simplicity, it was the best house Pedro and his wife Esperanza had ever lived in.

It was still dark on this July morning when Esperanza opened her eyes. The house was quiet and no sounds came from the street. Esperanza got out of the hard bed in which she and Pedro slept, smoothed her dress, and wrapped a thin dark blue cotton shawl about her head and shoulders to ward off the morning chill. She walked barefoot across the dirt floor, found the big clay water jug, and dashed some cold water on her face; then she dried herself with the edge of her shawl.

Kneeling at the hearth, Esperanza uncovered the ashes of last night's fire and fanned some still glowing chunks of charcoal into flames. She didn't want to use a match to light the fire for a box of matches cost five centavos and was still a luxury. Now the big clock in the plaza struck four. It was a half-hour earlier than she had thought. Well, her daughter Machrina could sleep a little longer. It was the time of year when the men planted and cultivated the corn, and the women had to rise early to prepare food for them. In the winter months, during the harvest, when the men sometimes worked all night and the women had to give them food at any hour, Esperanza and her daughter had to snatch sleep sitting on the low stools. It was only in September and October when the men were harvesting plums that the women could stay in bed as late as six o'clock.

Esperanza filled the clay pot and set the cinnamon tea to boil. Over a hundred *tortillas* had to be made—twenty-five each for Pedro and for Felipe, Martin, and Ricardo, the three oldest sons who worked in the fields, and ten more for Pedro's dog. Esperanza lifted down one of the tin cans hanging from the rafters where she kept her supplies of food. It contained corn which had been ground at the mill the previous night. Before the coming of the mill, a few years back, Esperanza had got up at two in the morning during the farming season to grind soaked corn into a fine dough. Now the mill did most of that work for her; she had only to regrind the dough a bit to make it smoother and to give it the taste of the grinding stone. The men of the village had opposed the corn mill because, they said, hand-ground corn tasted better. But the women had won out; the mill was a success. Yes, it was good to have the mill. But all the same it was expensive. The thirty-four centavos paid to the miller would have bought half enough corn to feed the whole family for a meal. Machrina should do more grinding at home, Esperanza thought as she knelt before the grinding stone.

The first slapping of the *tortillas* into shape caused Pedro to stir, but the reassuring sound lulled him back to sleep. Their bed stood in the far corner of the kitchen behind an improvised wall of empty plum crates. This wall did not protect him from the noises of the kitchen but it did provide some privacy from the grown children, except during the plum season when the crates were used to haul plums. Until a year ago the whole Martínez family had slept in the other room, but Pedro had recently moved the metal, springless bed into the kitchen. It was embarrassing, he had come to realize, to lie down with one's wife in the presence of one's grown children. And the bed, which he had acquired almost as a gift from a soldier he had met when they were both patients in the military hospital, showed off to better advantage in the kitchen.

Pedro's wish for privacy, however, had been partially thwarted when Machrina announced that she too wanted to sleep in the kitchen "since it is not nice for a girl to sleep all alone with her grown brothers." Machrina and little Herman, who had shared her bed since infancy, now slept in a cold and draughty corner of the kitchen. The four sons slept undisturbed in the adobe room.

When the plaza clock struck five Esperanza awakened her daughter who quickly jumped up, fully dressed in a slip, plain cotton dress, and apron, and took her mother's place at the grinding stone. Machrina looked younger than her seventeen years. Her brown hair was parted in the middle and worn in two braids; her face was quiet and serious but during the day, when she chatted with a friend or with her brothers, it was often lighted up by a smile that revealed her tiny, childlike teeth. Now she tucked her bare feet under her short, plump body and began to grind the corn. Esperanza, too, was short and round, but she rarely smiled and her face generally had a drawn, dull expression.

Esperanza next woke Martin since it was his turn to go for water. He slipped into his soiled cotton pants and huaraches, washed his face in the cold water, and without a word shouldered the yoke with the two water cans and left for the fountain. The daily rains now watered the fruit trees and the garden, so Martin had to make only eight trips back and forth to fill the family water jug. In the dry season the boys had to make twenty trips.

Felipe, the eldest son, awoke before Martin had finished his chore. Felipe was the most fastidious member of the family and took longest to dress. At night he took almost all his clothes off under his blanket and hung them on a nail. He brushed his teeth (without toothpaste), washed his face and hands with soap every day, and used a rag to dry himself with instead of his shirttail. He had a small pocket mirror which he let no one else use. All this had come about since Felipe had found a sweetheart, a widow much older than himself. Now, seated on the iron cot frame which supported the *otate,* a hard mat made of bamboo-like stalks placed crosswise and lashed together, Felipe groped for his huaraches. His left eye was blind, due to a childhood fall from a plum tree, and he turned his head in a rather exaggerated manner to see to the left.

As the eldest son, Felipe tried to dominate his brothers and sister, but was generally unsuccessful, particularly with Martin, who was taller and stronger than Felipe and almost the same age. Martin had flatly refused to obey Felipe or to show him the respect due an older brother. For this Felipe blamed his father, who had never permitted him to exercise authority.

Pedro and his third son, Ricardo, were now getting up. Pedro was short and stocky and his paunch bulged as he dressed in his homemade, dirty, patched shirt and white, pyjama-like *calzones*. He slipped his blackened, calloused feet into heavy huaraches cut from an old rubber tire. A sparse, untrimmed mustache covered his upper lip and he almost always looked unshaven. On Saturdays when he bathed and changed into clean clothes or on the days he went to town or to Mexico City, Pedro wore a pair of dark store-bought trousers and looked more sophisticated. He usually wore his straw sombrero tilted down over his eyes, a rather cocky angle for a man of fifty-nine.

Felipe, Martin, and Ricardo all looked like their father and until recently had dressed as he did. Now they wore factory-made shirts which they had demanded, but none of them owned dark trousers. The youngest son and the grandson wore old-style, homemade white *calzones* and shirts, used small sombreros, and always went barefoot.

Esperanza began to serve the men cinnamon tea, *tortillas,* chile, and salt, while Machrina filled four hemp shoulder bags with the same food for their midday meal. She added a handful of acacia pods to each bag and poured tea into four gourds. The men ate quickly, without conversation. Speaking in Nahuatl, Esperanza asked Pedro to bring home some squash for the evening meal. When Ricardo coughed over his food she warned him to wrap himself well in his blanket when they passed by the stream, the abode of *los aires,* the spirits of the air.

The Martínez family had good reason to avoid these malign spirits; some years before Esperanza had become ill with a fever and had suffered a partial paralysis of the legs after having washed clothes in the stream. *Los aires,* as everyone in her village knew, could sometimes take the shape of winds, sometimes spirits, sometimes little malign people who could cause sores, pimples, paralysis, and other illnesses. One had to be on one's guard against offending them near anthills, stream beds, ravines, in stagnant pools, and atop the highest hills. Sometimes it helped to ask their permission in Nahuatl before taking water from a stream, but in any case it was safest not to venture too near them without being well wrapped up. Many men took a morning drink of alcohol to protect them from *los aires* before they started out to the fields, but Pedro preferred to take his when he came home at night.

By five-thirty the men were ready to leave. Each slung a bag and a serape over his shoulder. Pedro called to his dog in Nahuatl, "Now let's go."

He used the old tongue with his wife and his dog, but he spoke to the children in Spanish except when he was angry. When Martin, on the other hand, said, "We're going, mamá," it was in Spanish.

The men set off in silence. Pedro walked with his dog a few paces behind the boys. When neighbors saw them walking along in this formation they would say that Pedro looked like a veritable *patrón* striding behind his peons. Yet there were mornings when Pedro talked to the boys in the course of their two-hour walk to the fields, giving advice or telling what work had to be done. The boys, however, spoke only in answer to a question. Out of their father's earshot they would joke about their sweethearts or visits to the saloons of Cuahnahuac. But this morning they moved silently down the road.

It was still barely light. All around them, just beyond the far edges of the fields, the blue-green slopes of the pine-covered mountains rose through the morning mist. Pedro and Ricardo were headed for the mountain slope corn-field which they had cleared the year before. This was communal land belonging to the municipality which consisted of seven villages; anyone could work it. New clearings had to be made every two or three years, for heavy rains washed the topsoil away. To acquire new fields Pedro and his sons burned the brush and weeds, cut down young trees, and built new stone fences. The boys worked well; they had the largest mountain clearing in Azteca. But the crops could supply enough corn and beans for only three or four months. So Pedro had to try other means of earning a living as well—making rope from maguey fiber, selling plums, hiring out his sons as farm-hands. One thing he would not do to earn money was to make charcoal for sale, as so many of his neighbors did. This practice, he knew, was wasteful of the precious oak and pine forests and ultimately ruined the land. He had been one of the leaders in the struggle for the preservation of the communal forest lands. So he made charcoal only once a year and only for the use of his family.

Felipe and Martin were on their way to Don Porfirio's fields where they were working as peons. These fields, located on fairly level ground, were cultivated by plow rather than by the ancient *coa* or hoe which Pedro used on his mountain strip. The land was easier to work than the mountain clearing and Don Porfirio was less of a taskmaster than Pedro. So the boys were glad of a chance to work for Don Porfirio and to earn some cash for the family. Pedro could be expected to give them something later on—a new shirt or a sombrero or some pocket money.

When they got to Don Porfirio's field the two older boys left the road. Pedro nodded in parting and walked on in silence with Ricardo, absorbed in his own thoughts. He had sold a mule to Don Gonzalo the day before in order to pay off his debt to Doña Conde, and it infuriated him to think that he had had to sell it for only 300 pesos when it was easily worth 450. And now he had only one mule left. This meant that the boys could bring only half the usual amount of wood down from the mountains and that there would be little left to sell after Esperanza took what she needed. Besides, during the plum season the boys could earn only half of what they had made the year before hauling crates of fruit to the railway station. And at harvest twice as many trips would have to be made to bring the corn down from the fields.

Pedro couldn't remember a time when he hadn't been in debt. Early this past year, after he had come out of the hospital where he had had surgery, he had borrowed 300 pesos from the widow Isabel to pay medical bills. Then, finding his indebtedness to her irksome because she expected free "legal" advice from him, he had borrowed 150 pesos from a wealthy politico to help pay her back, and 300 pesos from Asunción to pay other bills. And all this time he was paying back, at eight per cent monthly interest, a loan of 200 pesos from the previous year. At times it seemed as if he were walking forever in a treadmill of old obligations. "The debt remains; only the creditors change."

For Pedro as for most of the inhabitants of Azteca, getting enough money for food and clothing from one harvest to another was the all-absorbing, never-solved problem. At best Pedro, with the assistance of his wife and sons, earned 2,400 pesos a year ($300 at the 1948 rate of exchange). The boys earned about half of this by hiring out as peons and by gathering and selling firewood. Another third came from plums, rope-making, and corn. A small amount, hardly more than 60 pesos, came from fees the villagers paid to Pedro for going with them to see a lawyer or to attend a court session in Cuahnahuac. Pedro had learned something about legal matters during his years of political activity and had gained the reputation of being "half a lawyer." However, his income from "legal" advice was no greater than that from Esperanza's occasional small sales. Pedro could have doubled his income if he and the boys had worked as peons throughout the year at the local rate of four pesos a day, but he refused to work or permit his sons to work on haciendas which were still a symbol of oppression to him. Steady, year-round work was not available in the village, and in any case Pedro preferred to work as an independent peasant.

It was to become an independent peasant with a parcel of land of his own that Pedro had fought with Zapata in the Revolution. Pedro had worked for others since he was eight years old, first tending cattle for his Uncle Agustín who often beat him, then from age ten until after his marriage as a servant and peon on haciendas where he also had been beaten. Even during the brief, happy period when his mother had brought him and his sister to live with her and their stepfather in the large town of Tepetate and he had entered a public school, Pedro had had to defend himself from his "superiors." At that time he spoke only Nahuatl, the language of the Aztecs, and he would get into fights because his schoolmates called him "Indian," in an insulting manner.

"I did not know how to speak Spanish, but I knew how to fight. Then they would go crying to the teacher and he would come out and give me more strokes. I had a lot of trouble but I really liked school. One day when it was almost time to go home at noon the teacher was out of the room and the boys began to say to me in low voices, 'Indian, Indian.' I just raised my elbow up a little and hit one of them right where it hurt. Uy! He began to yell and the teacher came running, saying, 'What's going on here?'

"Well, all of them told on me and he hit me twelve times with a stick. Zas! Poor me! He even pushed me around on the floor. He threw me around until I urinated. Then, since it was time to go and the doors were being closed, he took me and made me kneel on a table with my arms stretched out and a stone on each hand. I tell you I was scared. They were leaving me a prisoner! But just as the last teacher was leaving I jumped off that table and began to yell and ran all the way to my house. I told my mother and stepfather what had happened. My mother said, 'Well, you may be ignorant, but you *did* stand up for yourself.' "

Pedro did not finish the first grade and barely learned to read because his stepfather took him out of school to begin to earn eighteen centavos a day at a nearby hacienda. When the Revolution came Pedro was already married and the father of a child; it was natural for him to sympathize with Zapata and he joined the fight. Later, he worked for the improvement of his own village, taking part in the rebuilding, in the new elections, in the local government, in the fight for the conservation of the forests, and in the construction of the road. And old abuses had been ended. The village regained the right to use its communal hillside land and some fortunate peasants received *ejido* land reclaimed from the haciendas. Indebtedness and acute poverty were lessened, the pawning of children as servants was abolished, school attendance increased, and there was more personal freedom. But for Pedro the Revolution was a failure. He believed that he did not live much better than he had under the pre-Revolutionary government of Porfirio Díaz. High prices and the increasing need for cash made life difficult. "What good is it to have freedom if we don't have enough to eat? Before it was the hacienda owners who exploited us, now it's the government and the bankers. It's all the same."

Yes, Pedro felt defeated. For him the Revolution had ended with the death of Zapata. His twenty-five years as a politico had gained him little more than prestige. His laborious effort to teach himself to read and write and to educate his eldest daughter had not "raised up" the family as he had hoped. Even his conversion, fifteen years ago, from Catholicism to Seventh-Day Adventism had left him dissatisfied. Pedro's life had been a search for ideals and causes rather than a struggle for personal aggrandizement. He did not understand the changing times, the money economy, or the business values of post-Revolutionary Mexico. He knew only that he was still a poor, landless peasant who depended heavily upon the labor of his sons to make ends meet.

Pedro was worried because his two older sons had begun to resist his plans for them. Felipe complained that too hard work was ruining his health. He wanted to learn a trade! Martin wanted to become a baker. When he had turned eighteen his godmother had offered to take him as an apprentice in her bakery and he had been eager to accept. Pedro had firmly forbidden it.

He needed his sons to work in the fields. But as soon as Martin became of age he apprenticed himself to the godmother without consulting anyone. He had worked for six months without wages, and Pedro had scolded him until Martin wept in desperation. Whenever Martin missed a meal at home Pedro became enraged and shouted, "I don't want you to work for that piece of *tortilla* they give you." He ordered Martin to refuse all food at the bakery and to take his meals in his father's house. When the planting season started Martin returned to work in the fields, but Pedro feared that he intended to go back to the bakery when the harvest was over.

Pedro had different plans for his youngest son, Moisés, who was too delicate to bear up under the life of a peasant. With God's permission and the help of his older sons, Pedro hoped to educate Moisés to be a teacher "or perhaps even a lawyer." Pedro would be happy if one of his children could have a "career." It would benefit the whole family.

The path was lighter now and Pedro came out of his reverie to realize that the walk to his field was nearly over. He caught up with Ricardo and began to tell him just where to begin the weeding for the day.

When the men had gone Esperanza took stock of the day's food supply. There was only a little corn dough left, barely enough for the two boys still asleep, and some chile, cinnamon, sugar, and salt. There was no money because Pedro had used the mule money to buy huaraches for Felipe, a sombrero for himself, and a machete for Ricardo—all badly needed for work in the fields. The rest of the money had gone to the hateful Doña Conde. Where could she borrow now? What small thing could she sell?

These were the questions that faced Esperanza nearly every day. Yesterday's money was usually gone by the next morning except when she put away a small sum in one of her hiding places around the house. Even when Pedro gave her larger sums it would usually be spent quickly, either to repay debts or to buy something they urgently needed. But the really bad times were when there was a serious illness in the family. Then they had to sell nearly everything, sometimes all their young turkeys or a grinding stone, sometimes a mule.

Esperanza wondered from whom she could borrow. She could not ask her cousin Maria for a loan, for she had not paid back the ten pesos borrowed a few days ago. Nor could she approach her Aunt Gloria: she had herself stopped by yesterday to ask for a small loan. There were her neighbors to the right but they had spoken badly about Pedro ever since he had become a politico. Why they were so resentful Esperanza could not see, for his political activity had certainly not made the family "even a little rich." No one else nearby ever had enough money to lend, and Esperanza did not want to borrow a small sum at interest from those who had plenty. It was better to sell the turkey even though it would be a long time before she would be able to buy another baby turkey to raise. Esperanza drank her cinnamon tea and went to look for the bird. It was seven when she put on her shawl, hiding her turkey under it (why should her neighbors know her business?) and left for the barrio of San Martín where she knew of several houses where they ate well.

Machrina went out to the back of the orchard. The younger boys were still asleep and there was no danger that they would spy on her through the bushes as they sometimes did. Like most of the villagers, the Martínez had no toilet and no outhouse. When she came back Machrina washed her hands before she knelt at the grinding stone to begin making *tortillas*. She called sharply to Moisés and Herman and told them to wash. She generally adopted a scolding tone toward the younger boys, particularly to Herman, her special charge. She had taken care of him ever since her sister Conchita had come home from school and given birth to the fatherless boy. Even during the six months when Conchita was nursing him and still stayed at home, it was Machrina (then ten years old) who had carried Herman about, bathed him every three days, swaddled him carefully so that he would grow up to be quiet and well-mannered, and washed his soiled clothes. But during the past few years Machrina had gradually stopped playing with him and picking him up and had begun to scold him often. When he misbehaved she spanked him. It didn't trouble Machrina that Herman now avoided her and seemed to prefer Moisés' company to hers; it was right that he should keep his distance and respect her.

The boys had finished eating and were playing in the patio when Esperanza returned an hour later, still carrying the turkey. While she ate the two *tortillas* Machrina had made for her, she told her daughter she had been offered only two and a half pesos for the turkey. There was nothing to do now but go to Señor Don Porfirio and ask for an advance on the boys' wages.

Before she left again Esperanza reminded Moisés to bring water from the fountain and then to go to school. She sent Herman to her cousin's house to bring back the scissors she had borrowed. Machrina knew her work and needed no instructions. Ever since Esperanza's illness of the year before Machrina had shown that she could be depended upon. To show her family, particularly her father, that she could be depended on seemed in fact to be Machrina's only goal nowadays. She had gone to the local school through the fifth grade and had wanted to become a teacher, or at least a seamstress. But suddenly Pedro took her out of school to help her mother and no one dared say a word in protest. It was true that Esperanza had not been well and that looking after so many men and her little grandson seemed to be too much for her.

Alone now, Machrina folded the blankets on the two beds, then picked up the twig broom and began to sweep the dirt floor. She swept unhurriedly, taking special pains with the corners, for her father noticed whether or not the work was well done. She had often heard him speak, half jokingly, half scornfully, of how ignorant her mother had been when he had married her: "She didn't know how to sew, nor sweep, nor iron, nor wash clothes. She hardly knew how to grind corn or make *tortillas*." Pedro had showed Esperanza how to do much of the housework; he had taught her even how to sweep because at first she always missed the corners. When she had tried to make him his first pair of *calzones* she had had to call in her mother to help. Actually, as Pedro himself knew, this was not Esperanza's fault. Formerly parents did not teach their daughters many domestic skills because girls married very young and the mother-in-law was obliged to teach the daughter-in-law. Esperanza was about fourteen when she married and her mother-in-law was dead.

Machrina went to clean the room where her brothers slept. She folded the blanket and straightened the straw mat on the *otate* shared by Martin and Moisés. The other boys had taken their blankets with them. The blankets were almost the most expensive things in the house; each one had cost about fifty pesos. She then piled up the rough plum crates which served as a bed for Ricardo. For a while he had shared the cot with Felipe, but Felipe had wanted it all to himself and had quarreled and complained so much every time Ricardo lay down on it that he had finally rigged up eight plum crates, two across and four down, to make a bed of his own. With a straw mat and a rag-stuffed pillow under him, and a blanket, this new bed was only a little more uncomfortable than the cot. But the crates were heavy and made more work for Machrina; they had to be piled one upon the other during the day because they took up too much space.

The adobe walls, papered here and there with old newspapers, religious posters, and calendars, had nails jutting out to hold extra clothes and sombreros. The room had little furniture and did not take long to clean. Machrina dusted the wooden chest where her father kept his most prized religious books, a copy of the Constitution of Mexico, and the Civil Code of Morelos that he referred to when neighbors consulted him about legal problems. Here too were kept important papers and a few pieces of good clothing. Machrina lined up against the wall seven stools and two reed chairs that her father had bought in the past few years. Formerly the family had used the plum crates as chairs. She also arranged three small benches that Martin had made when he studied carpentry in a class held by a recent government cultural mission.

Machrina dusted the remaining piece of furniture, a wooden table that had served as an altar when the family was Catholic. It now held small piles of old, worn school texts that Conchita had used when she taught school, some religious pamphlets, and a little frivolous reading matter which Pedro hardly approved of: several sheets of popular songs, the comic books "Chamaco" and "Paquín," and three paper-covered novels which the older children had read and reread. This was more reading matter than could be found in most Aztecan homes. In addition, there was a special pile of six Bibles, one for each member of the family who could read. Machrina carefully dusted these and when she lifted Felipe's copy a folded paper, a note from the widow, fell to the floor. "Widows are bold," she thought as she put back the note. "With no man at home to tell them what to do they can have lovers and go to all the fiestas."

Machrina went back into the kitchen, wiped the low table where Pedro and the three oldest boys ate, and picked up some plum pits from the floor. From force of habit she looked into the table drawer to see if there was a little money there that Esperanza could use for food. There was nothing, not even Pedro's toothpicks or the aspirins that Esperanza took for her headaches.

At half past nine Esperanza returned empty-handed. Don Porfirio had gone to the courthouse and would not be back until about ten. It would have been humiliating to wait for him so Esperanza returned home, sat and talked with her daughter for fifteen minutes, and then climbed the steep hill once more to Don Porfirio's house. At ten-thirty she was back again, this time with four pesos in cash and twelve *cuartillos* of corn which Don Porfirio had given her. Tired from having walked so much, she lay down to rest for half an hour.

Esperanza had noticed that she tired more easily than she used to. Maybe she was getting old, but in truth she could not say what her real age was since her mother had never told her just when she was born. Or perhaps she drank too much alcohol, as her Aunt Gloria thought she did. The tiredness had grown upon her since her long illness of the year before. Perhaps she was being bewitched by some enemy of hers or Pedro's. Pedro, who studied the Bible, had taught her not to believe in that sort of thing unless it was an absolutely clear case of sorcery. She always tried to please her husband, but if it were sorcery should she not go to a *curandero* before it was too late?

While her mother rested Machrina washed the few breakfast dishes, cleaned the grinding stone, and prepared half of the corn by soaking it in water and lime. She revived the fire with a straw fan and placed two iron bars across the hearth to hold the tin can in which the corn would be boiled.

At eleven Esperanza got up and left for the plaza to do the day's marketing. She hurried down the hill, turned left, and walked along an unpaved street heedless of the mud and deep puddles of water left by the daily heavy rains. In fact the water felt good to her bare feet for it was almost noon and the ground was getting hot. At the end of this long street she turned right onto a steep, stone-paved street that was lined with houses, several of which had windows and were smoothly plastered and whitewashed and much finer than any in her barrio. She was now in the larger barrio of San Martín where some well-to-do peasants lived.

Esperanza quickened her step, pulled her shawl more tightly around her shoulders, and, as any good Aztecan wife would, kept her eyes to the ground except for an occasional swift glance when she passed a house or looked up to see who was coming her way. The street was quiet and empty except for a few pigs and chickens. Two women, still in the distance, were returning from the plaza. Esperanza could hear the slapping of *tortillas* in the houses and regretted that she had made such a late start. Her head ached, she was thirsty; and for the first time in a long while she felt that she wanted a drink of alcohol.

Actually, things at home had been peaceful for a time. Pedro had not scolded her since he had taken the widow Eulalia of the barrio of Santo Domingo to the fair two weeks ago. Esperanza had been resentful when Pedro told her to prepare food for the widow and she couldn't hide how she felt when she was serving him his dinner. Pedro had picked up the plate and thrown it at her, food and all, scattering beans and *tortillas* on the floor. And the flow of ugly words that followed! He had said that she was ignorant and he didn't know how he had come to marry her. He needed a woman who could read and write and who was able to earn money—like Eulalia! He said that he was a man and had the right to do what he pleased, that she, being a woman and a very stupid one, would have to bear anything he did or said to her, even if he should decide to bring the widow to live in the same house. Better yet, he would go away with the widow who also knew how to cook and serve him and who would be of more help to him because she was clever. Then Pedro had forced Esperanza to scrape up the beans and eat them while he sat and watched her. After he left she cried and took out her bottle and drank. The children didn't like to see her drink alcohol but sometimes she had to. Three days later Pedro returned and ever since he had been quiet and had not lost his temper. He had brought home some sweet chile, dried cod, salt, and sugar, and everyone had been pleased.

Esperanza knew her husband was hot-tempered and sometimes treated her and the children unjustly. But he was kind too, and she knew he loved her. When they were young he used to console her after he had made her cry by taking her in his arms and saying, "Come on, don't get mad." Yes, she had had a better life with him than with her mother and elder half brother.

"In my house my brother scolded me and my mother hit me and I never talked back. Once I said, 'You hit me so much that I would rather go to my godmother.' My *madrina* liked me a lot and gave me many things. Then my mother hit me more, hard with a rope. I ran out into the street to look for my *madrina's* house. My mother followed me and threw a stone at me. Possibly she just wanted to frighten me for it fell to one side. Later my brother came and defended me. 'Why do you hit her so much?' he said to my mother. I had no liberty whatsoever then. In truth I never went anywhere. Many times people wanted to hire me to watch their children but my brother never wanted me to. He never wanted me even to go to school."

Esperanza had never learned to read or write and could not defend herself when Pedro accused her of being ignorant and stupid. But she would say, "Didn't you know what I was when you sent your mother to ask for me?" Indeed, when Pedro had looked about for a wife he had decided that the young Esperanza, who was virtuous and innocent and poorer than he, was the ideal girl for him. Esperanza had not wanted to marry him or anyone else, but when his mother died and he was left an orphan with no one to make his *tortillas,* she took pity on him and consented.

A few days before the marriage her mother had given her advice: "Now that you are going to marry you must have a different character. Here you have one character but there you must have the character of your husband. If he scolds you, do not answer. If he beats you, bear it because if not your husband is going to say, 'What kind of upbringing did we give?' " Esperanza had followed her mother's advice. "And I was always that way," she thought. "When Pedro hit me I only sat down and cried."

The marriage took place in the village church in 1910. Pedro gave Esperanza the first dress she had ever had (before that she had always worn a blouse and long skirt). He gave her a fifty-centavo piece to spend. He took her to live with him and his aunt in his one-room house.

"I remember the night we married. I was terribly afraid. Pedro still bothers me sometimes when he says jokingly, 'Why were you so frightened that night?' In reality I do not know what it was that troubled me. Chills came over me. I was terribly afraid, for never, never had we spoken to one another. After we ate dinner Pedro's aunt went to bed and so did he. He had gone to bed with his clothes on. He has always done that. I also always go to bed with my clothes on. The aunt told me that for this I had got married and that I should go to bed. I was very afraid and ashamed. Pedro covered me with the blanket and then began to embrace me and touch my breasts. Then he went on top of me. I didn't know what the men did to one, and I said to myself, 'Maybe it's like this.' I felt like crying or going to my mother, but I remembered that they had married me and then I said, 'If I die, I'll die. I have to go through it here even though he kills me.' And I closed my eyes and waited for the worst. Pedro already knew how these things were done because he had even had a daughter by a married woman. I don't remember that I bled, but I know that it hurt a lot, and I didn't cry because there was someone else there and it would make me ashamed if she heard.

"Two weeks later I was still afraid. Little by little one picks up confidence. I didn't even tell anything to my mother. I only told a cousin of my husband. I said: 'Men only play with one. Why do they have to get married?' Then she said, 'That's the way they are and you have to let him.' After about two months I was feeling pleasure and then I began to love my husband."

Esperanza hurried down the street and without slackening her pace said *"Buenos días"* to two women whom she passed. One of the women was her former *comadre,* the godmother of her little dead son Angel, the last of her children to have been baptized in the Catholic faith. When Pedro turned Protestant all their Catholic *compadres* had broken off the relationship with them. Esperanza had become Protestant because of Pedro's insistence and because "no one recognizes me any more anyway." That had been eighteen years before but it still upset Esperanza to meet her former *comadres* and *compadres.*

Why Pedro, when he was forty years old, had decided to abandon his old faith and incur the wrath of the village, Esperanza had never clearly understood. She was only dimly aware that he had been disillusioned with the Mexican Revolution and that his defeats in the post-Revolutionary political struggles in Azteca had been hard for him to bear. Then several things had happened all at once which led to his conversion. He was given a Bible which seemed to him the great revelation of his life. He treated it "like a saint," and when a Protestant missionary came to the village he was ready to listen to him. One night at a wake he denounced priests and Catholicism to his Uncle Agustín who was a devout Catholic and who, moreover, had treated Pedro cruelly as a child. When Agustín berated Pedro for his anti-Catholicism and taunted him about his ignorance, Pedro vowed to make a serious study of one of the Evangelical faiths. After a year the two met again for a debate which lasted throughout a night, and Pedro argued down this uncle who had once been such an authoritarian figure to him. He told his wife, "I really gave it to him good. I showed him all the lies. I fought my uncle with his own books. I showed him that the dead don't return, that Sunday isn't the day of rest, that baptism is done by immersion, that confession and communion are useful but not if done to another human being, that purgatory and hell are lies, all lies. The saints, too, these pictures before which they cross themselves, it's all a lie." He was so hard on his uncle that "the poor old man even cried."

Then Esperanza, Pedro, and a daughter Rufina fell ill. The villagers interpreted these calamities as his punishment from God and Pedro grew angry. "Now that people are talking so much," he had said, "I'm going to become a Protestant so that they will be speaking the truth. I'm going to take down all the religious pictures and saints we have. In this way once and for all we'll die or we'll be saved."

Rumor of Pedro's intention to "burn the saints" traveled through the village. Friends and relatives came to protest; other people stopped speaking to the family. This was the beginning of several years of ostracism. The Martínez boys had to sell their firewood in Tepetate; Esperanza went to more distant parts of the village to sell her chickens and eggs. Pedro was once stoned, and when Rufina died her godfather refused to make her coffin. At school the children were shunned or tormented. Conchita's classmates once dragged her by her hair toward the church to force her to kiss the priest's hand, and two boys nearly strangled her with her own braids because, they said, she had been trying to convert them. One rumor which persisted for many years was that Pedro had been seen kneeling before his eldest daughter who stood on a table "like a saint" surrounded by flowers.

Although Esperanza was greatly disturbed when she realized that her husband was approaching conversion, she felt helpless to prevent it. She did nothing but weep and avoid people. Her relatives came and warned her not to leave the religion of their fathers. "Protestantism has just come out," they told her. "It is something new. Besides, Protestants don't believe in God." Pedro's sister urged her to leave Pedro. "It's awful, what he has done," she said, "to remove the saints and have those devils meeting in my mother's house. Leave him and his children and then you'll see how he will leave the Seventh-Day Adventists." But Esperanza had answered, "What can I do? He's the boss."

It had been more difficult for Esperanza to adjust to the change of religion than it had been for Pedro. He had always been ardently interested in religion and as a Catholic had been a prayer-maker and twice a *mayordomo* of the barrio. He was used to going to church often, especially on all the feast days. He had prayed all night on Good Fridays, fasted during Holy Week, and confessed and took communion once a year. When he became an Adventist, he threw himself into it just as passionately, reading and joining a study group, converting others, and conducting services in their home. He even seemed to enjoy standing up against the whole village!

Esperanza, who believed in a vague mixture of Catholic and pagan concepts, had never been deeply involved in the Christian religion. Once when she needed firewood in a hurry she had burned a cross which Pedro had set up in their patio to protect the house! She actually saw little difference between the new and old Christian faiths and even after her conversion she did not make a clear separation between them. Once, on the Day of the Dead, she "felt sorry for our dead little ones" and put a candle and flowers in the barrio chapel for them. Another time she went to the chapel of San José "to pray to God to give me peace in my home because Pedro was insupportable. And he really did calm down after that." On the whole the conversion brought Esperanza only confusion, inconvenience, and ostracism, and made it less possible for her to find comfort in her old folk beliefs.

The family did benefit, however, from a spiritual change in Pedro and for this reason was able to accept his conversion in spite of the severe social disapproval. Pedro dropped out of politics, stopped drinking, and turned to work and religion. As part of his faith he tried to control his temper and speak humbly in the face of provocation. "If we fight, everyone criticizes us." The family began to eat better and to have a more peaceful domestic life. In fact, at no time was the family so united and contented as during this period when Pedro devoted himself to their physical and spiritual well-being. For his part he was repaid for his efforts by the support and admiration of his children and, to some extent, of his wife.

In recent years Esperanza had been aware that Pedro was slowly but unmistakably drifting back toward Catholicism. He had become disillusioned, little by little, by the behavior of some of his co-religionists. He had hoped that the high moral principles of the Adventists and their emphasis upon brotherhood would give him the trust and love he wanted. The first jolt came when the man who had converted him attempted to seduce his daughter, Conchita, while he was a guest of the family for a night. Pedro also had been hurt by being treated as an inferior by some of the Protestant ministers. One incident had been crucial and stood out as a turning point. Conchita wanted to study in Mexico City and Pedro had taken her to the city to the home of a Protestant pastor who had promised to give her room and board in exchange for work.

"Conchita had malaria at the time," Pedro said, "but she was so enthusiastic about studying that she wanted to go anyway. So I brought her. It was a two-story house. It was beautiful, like heaven. I only saw it from a distance, like Moses when he went to . . . just from a distance, that's as much as I saw of it. Yes, the house was pretty but they took me into the kitchen and I never got any further than that. That so-and-so treated me like dirt. My poor daughter started right in helping his wife even though she was very sick. I said to her, 'Come on, let's go. I don't like this man's character and you're sick. I can tell he's very harsh and his two children are even worse.' She answered, 'I'm not leaving even though I die here.' Hmmm, what could I do? The pastor invited us to the evening service and said I could sleep there that night. They gave me a cup of coffee and when it was time to go to bed they took Conchita upstairs to sleep on a dirty carpet in their daughter's room. The pastor told me to make myself comfortable in the kitchen. But how could I make myself comfortable? They didn't give me anything, not even an old rug did they throw at me. The floor was made of cement and was still wet from being washed. It was very cold. I thought, '*Caray!* Are these people Christians?' That's how I began to lose faith.

"So I said to myself, 'This isn't right but what can I do? I'll stay this once. After all, it means her future.' Well, I suffered through it. I didn't sleep the whole night long. I just sat down on my pack and leaned against the edge of the charcoal burner. As bad luck would have it I had to go to the toilet but I couldn't find a place to go. There was a great big dog outside the kitchen door in the patio and as soon as I opened the door a bit he would start to growl. He was an enormous dog and angry. That was worse. Now I was a prisoner! The animals there were just as bad as their master. God was punishing me, I was really in a fix.

"At about four-thirty in the morning the mother came downstairs to sweep the street. She was so much of an Indian that the children treated her like a servant. Just imagine! The children and the husband sleeping and the poor mother out in the street sprinkling and sweeping. And these people were Christians! The son came into the kitchen at night and didn't even speak to me. Just walked past me. What kind of upbringing do these people have? At five o'clock my daughter came down. She saw me sitting there and said, 'Papá, let's go.' I said, 'Yes, these bourgeois! the kind who won't work!'

"That was the way they treated me. It entered like a big thorn and hurt a lot. That man a Christian? A lie! That man a brother? A lie! I hated him. May God forgive me but I still hate him. I wrote him a strong letter saying, 'You are not a Christian, you are a king bee who doesn't work. You are nourished by the health of the faithful. You are even worse than the priests.' "

After that Pedro participated less in the affairs of the Adventist church, although he continued to attend Saturday services fairly regularly. In 1943 he stopped contributing tithes (one-tenth of his crop) to the church. He prayed but no longer underwent penitential fasting. He drifted back into politics and because of politics began to drink again. Also "because of politics," he began to attend wakes and fiestas with his Catholic supporters. He grew more tolerant of Catholicism and in fact took pleasure at being accepted again by the Catholic community. Yet he believed at the same time that his

Protestant faith and his high standard of morality had gained him more respect from the villagers than they had had for him before.

But it was too late for Esperanza. She was too far withdrawn from social and community life to pick it up where she had left it eighteen years before. She was unprepared to build anything new. Her conversion had been one more traumatic experience in a lifetime of traumas. She would be content, so long as God gave her life, to keep on working for her family, accepting whatever fate brought her and asking for nothing.

From the paved road Esperanza made another left turn and walked quickly past a few more houses, past the park, and across the plaza to the archway where the women waited in the shade to sell their little piles of food. From them Esperanza carefully made her small purchases—one-fourth of a kilo of rice at thirty-five centavos, ten centavos' worth of coffee, fifteen centavos' worth of lard, fifteen centavos for tomatoes, and twenty for chile. The rice and lard were wrapped in little cones of paper which Esperanza placed along with the other articles in the basket which she carried under her shawl. She then went into one of the small dark stores under the archway and bought one-tenth of a liter of drinking alcohol and twenty centavos' worth of kerosene for the lamp. On the way home she stopped at the drug-store for two aspirin.

The noon church bells were ringing when she reached home after the long climb up the hill. Without sitting down to rest she gave the basket of food to Machrina, took up the can of boiled corn, and hurried back to the plaza, this time to the corn mill. The corn was still too hot to be ground but it was already late, and even though the dough would be tough and rubbery it was needed for the noon meal for those at home. Machrina had put aside some corn to cool for the evening meal. It meant another trip to the mill but that was better than giving the men inferior *tortillas*. Like all men, they had bad tempers and had to be served properly.

Esperanza looked expectantly at the mill entrance to see who was waiting there. She enjoyed standing in the long queue; it was one of her few chances to chat with the women she knew. But at this hour the mill was empty and the miller put her corn through the noisy machine without delay.

Machrina was preparing the rice when Moisés came home from school. Without greeting his sister he sought out Herman, who had been playing quietly in the patio all morning. Herman's face lit up when he saw Moisés, but he did not move away from the little pile of stones he had gathered. When Esperanza came in she called to Moisés to take the mule to pasture. This was one of his daily chores. He also brought some water from the fountain every morning, picked fruit for his mother, ran errands, and every afternoon after school he went back to the plaza with a small can of corn for the mill. During school vacations he had more responsible jobs, selling a little corn or wood, cleaning the maguey fiber, and helping his brothers make rope.

Herman also had regular chores since everyone was expected to work.

He had to make five daily trips to the fountain with two small water pails, bring in firewood as it was needed, and run errands for Machrina or his grandmother. Herman liked to go with Moisés to pasture the mule and asked Machrina to let him go. She said no because it looked like rain. Herman then appealed to Esperanza, who said yes. Since the food was not quite ready, the boys were sent to pick a few hog plums to stay everyone's hunger. Then, after a lunch of rice, *tortillas,* and coffee, the boys set out with the mule. Machrina shouted to them from the door not to loiter because if they came home wet she was going to hit them.

At one o'clock the two women sat down to eat. Esperanza was too tired to talk about the people she had seen in the plaza and fell asleep, still seated on the low bench. Machrina washed the few dishes and then took a can to fill at the fountain. The men of the barrio had built a new fountain near the house. Machrina was proud of it because it was largely due to her father's efforts that the fountain had been built. He was the only man in the barrio who wanted to advance and who could get things done. It had taken him more than a year to persuade his neighbors to form a *cuatequitl* (a cooperative work party) to build the fountain. Pedro might be poor, but he was a man of importance not only in his own barrio but in the village. Machrina had often heard her father call men who did not take part in politics "stones," "balls of flesh with eyes," or simply "women!" and she judged her neighbors by his standards.

Machrina was too young to remember how the family had suffered because of Pedro's political activity. He had been jailed three times and twice he had had to flee the village for his life. When he worked during elections he forgot his family entirely and left them to shift for themselves. He drank with his friends, had love affairs, and got into debt. That was why Esperanza said that, "Politics only grinds one into dust."

Down the street Machrina saw Elena, the daughter of the widow Gloria, sweeping her patio. Elena put down her twig broom and leaned over the stone wall. "I have something to show you," she said. She pulled a folded letter from her blouse. "A little girl ran over and gave me this letter at the mill this morning. It's a love letter." Love letters were very much prized by the young people in Azteca and severely frowned upon by the adults. This form of courtship, indeed courtship itself, was a recent phenomenon.

"Who sent it?"

"Who knows? There is no name."

Machrina read the letter carefully:

> *Most Beautiful Señorita:*
> *It is impossible to see you and not to love you and that is what has happened to me. Your beautiful image is engraved on my heart, so deeply do I see you every- where and, in the same way, I hear your sweet harmo- nious voice which shatters my whole being. If I contem-*

plate the countryside, it appears to resemble you, so beautiful is it; its odor carries a memory of a divine vision. Upon looking straight at the sun, my eyes become wounded; so do your beautiful eyes equally wound me. When I hear the song of the birds, it seems that I hear your divine voice. I beg only one word of you to indicate that you are not indifferent to the sensations of my heart; tell me this word which will make me think of myself as the happiest man on earth and which will make me fall upon my knees at your feet. If you are utterly disinterested, then I will die little by little as a flower dies on being plucked. But in my agony I shall always say I love you, I adore you.

"He must be very cultured," Machrina said.

"*Que va?* He probably copied it out of a book." Elena, who was eighteen, had a reputation of being *loca*, crazy about men. The year before she had gone to Cuahnahuac to be a servant in a doctor's house, but it was not long before the doctor's wife had managed to send her back home.

Machrina went on to the fountain to fill her water can. She thought about the letter and wondered whether she would ever receive one like it. And would she ever marry? Machrina was not sure. Where would she meet a young man who was not a Catholic? She would be glad to marry a Protestant and be able to keep her father's religion. If she married a Catholic she would have to become a Catholic and go to church to confess. She didn't want to do that. Better to stay at home with her parents.

When Machrina came home her mother was asleep in bed. Machrina poured the water into the water jug and sat down to read the Bible. The conversation with Elena had somehow disturbed her and reading the Bible made her feel better. She dozed off; with a start she heard the village clock strike three. She got up to sweep the patio and was watering the plants when Esperanza joined her, yawning and combing her hair. Esperanza said there was some mending to do. Without a word Machrina went into the kitchen for needle and thread and brought out the clothes. She always sewed under a tree in the patio because it was too dark to sew in the house. From the patio she could also see what was going on in the street.

Esperanza left to visit Conchita, her oldest daughter. During the morning she had twice passed Conchita's house on the way to the plaza, but she hadn't gone in because Juan, her son-in-law, might still have been home. He had forbidden Conchita to see her family, and Pedro had forbidden anyone in the family to visit Conchita. So Esperanza had to choose her hours carefully.

Conchita's troubles had begun eight years before when she left home to study to become a teacher. She had attended the State Normal School and a lot of money had gone into her education—for books, clothing, and transportation. For three years her father had given up planting and worked as a peon to earn cash for her expenses. Of course the neighbors had been critical from the very beginning. They had warned Pedro that he was striving too high for a poor man. They said that a girl could not be trusted away from home and least of all Conchita, who was "hot-blooded." Pedro ignored them. He had faith in his favorite daughter. Conchita had been born after the first children had died, and for five years she was an only child. Both Esperanza and Pedro had babied her, played with her, and enjoyed her more than they did any of their later children. Pedro gladly spent the money on her schooling in the hope that when she became a teacher she would help raise the economic and social standing of the entire family. Then she had had to come home from her very first position even before she had begun to earn any money. The school principal had made her pregnant.

It was a terrible blow to Pedro. He gave Conchita a merciless beating and did not speak to her for months. But he let her stay home and have her baby. After Herman was born Pedro ignored his presence; even now he seldom spoke to his grandson. Conchita went off to teach again when she was well, and sent home thirty pesos a month to help with expenses. She also brought little gifts from time to time, and everyone liked her for that. Pedro had begun to forgive her too. She had her father's temperament, he said; she couldn't help herself.

About a year before Conchita had first gone away to study, Pedro had met a young man named Juan who was an orphan born out of wedlock and unrecognized by the relatives of both his dead parents. At twenty-two Juan was still a bachelor with no home of his own. Pedro took a liking to the young man and invited him to live with the family for a year. Conchita was fourteen then and soon became Juan's secret sweetheart. The following year Conchita left the village, but for the next ten years she and Juan managed to be together whenever she returned home. Meanwhile he had other sweethearts and began to have children by several women. Conchita too had other sweethearts at school, but she liked Juan best. When her high status as a teacher was diminished by the appearance of Herman, Juan felt that he could ask her to marry him. She agreed, and her father quickly accepted. After a civil marriage ceremony the couple went to live with Juan's married half sister, leaving Herman with his grandparents.

But things had not gone well. Conchita could not adjust herself to being the wife of a peasant and there were many quarrels. When Conchita became pregnant she felt that Juan did not take proper care of her. He refused to hire a servant when the baby was born and she was not able to rest for the traditional forty days. The baby was only a month old when Conchita asked her father to take her home because Juan was neglecting her. Pedro took her home and because of his experience with legal matters he had his son-in-law brought to court on a charge of neglect. All this, of course, caused antagonism between the two men. Conchita later returned to her husband, but he began to get drunk frequently and to beat her. Just before the birth of their second baby he beat her so badly that Pedro took her home again. Pedro said, "While I live, your husband won't abuse you." Again there was a reconciliation and again Conchita became pregnant. Now her husband was even more violent and she went back to her father's house. This time Pedro demanded that Juan pay for the children's maintenance. Juan refused. Pedro had him arrested. Juan charged Conchita with abandonment.

Conchita gave birth to a healthy looking girl who died in a few days. The midwife accused Esperanza of having killed the baby through carelessness—she had attended a wake and then had sat in the kitchen near the baby without first having washed and changed clothing. Juan heard the accusation and refused to go to the child's funeral or to contribute to the expense.

Pedro wanted his daughter to stay home for good, and she seemed to agree. Actually she was not happy in her parents' home. Pedro made her work all the time and sometimes struck her in her children's presence. Conchita got in touch with her husband and he consented to take her back provided she would never again speak to her family. When Pedro came in from the fields one day and found that Conchita and her children were gone, he disowned her in a rage and forbade the rest of the family ever to see her again.

That was why Esperanza had to make secret visits to her daughter nowadays. And not only she: Machrina and the boys visited her too, for everyone missed Conchita at home. She had helped with the housework, had sympathized with her brothers, and had given each of them gifts. From Conchita, Esperanza had received her first silk dress, Machrina her first pair of shoes, Felipe a mirror, Martin a flashlight, Ricardo a pocket comb, Moisés his first toy. And Conchita had never come without a present for her son Herman.

When the dogs announced Esperanza's arrival, Conchita came out of her dark little one-room house with her sons beside her. Her long hair was uncombed, her clothes looked old and torn, and she limped from an infection in her foot. Partly because of her husband's jealousy and partly from pride, Conchita seldom left the house. She preferred to grind corn on her own grinding stone rather than walk to the mill.

"Come, greet your little grandmother," Conchita said to her sons.

With no change in expression each boy walked up to Esperanza, pressed his lips to her outstretched hand, then ran off to the rear of the patio to play among the chickens. Esperanza wiped the back of her hand with her shawl and, still standing, said, "Just imagine, I could not sell the turkey today. They offered only two and a half pesos for it." Conchita went into the house and came out a moment later with a sardine tin full of beans. Esperanza dropped the beans into her shawl and returned the measuring tin. They exchanged a few words, Esperanza said, "Thanks, little daughter," and quickly left.

It was five o'clock, not much time to prepare the beans for the men. At home Esperanza found that Machrina had stirred up the fire and put on the large bean pot full of water. Esperanza picked over the beans, washed them, and dropped them into the boiling water. Machrina went on mending clothes.

At five-thirty Moisés and Herman came back with the mule. Moisés was sent off at once to the mill with the can of boiled corn which this time was properly cooled. Herman went back to play with his pile of stones in the patio. Esperanza put up water for coffee, stirred the beans, added some *epazote* leaves and salt for taste, and prepared a sauce of onion, tomato, and chile to be eaten with the *tortillas*. Then she sat beside her daughter to mend an old shirt. They talked about Conchita, the evening meal, and what new clothing each might receive at harvest time.

When Moisés came back with the ground corn an hour later it was Machrina's turn to get up and make the *tortillas*. She complained that Moisés had taken so long she wouldn't have the *tortillas* ready in time. To make matters worse the corn was poorly ground and would have to be reground by hand. Esperanza went on calmly sewing. "Don't upset yourself, little daughter," she said. "There's no help for it. That's how it is."

Machrina was still grinding corn when her father and three brothers walked in at seven o'clock. Obviously tired, they went to lie down. Esperanza went to sit on a plum crate beside Pedro's bed, to recount to him her efforts to get money for the day's food. Pedro nodded approvingly when she told him that she had refused to let the turkey go at the low price offered and that she had succeeded in getting an advance on the boys' wages from Don Porfirio. She said nothing about her visit to Conchita and the gift of beans. She complained that her head ached and Pedro told her to go to bed early to avoid getting ill. She got out the alcohol and gave her husband his evening drink; this was to guard him from the ill effects of the winds which had blown against him as he had walked home hot and tired. She too took a short drink and then joined her daughter.

Machrina was kneeling at the grinding stone, working quickly now because the men did not like to be kept waiting long for their meal. She already had a little pile of *tortillas* which she kept warm in a napkin near the hearth. For each *tortilla* Machrina rolled a ball of corn dough between her hands, then slapped it out flat with a quick pat-a-cake movement. She was justly proud of her ability to make fine *tortillas*. When she was only eleven she had made them better than her older sister, and now her father and brothers said that she made them better than her mother.

Esperanza examined the young squash her husband had brought home from the field and prepared it for cooking. By eight o'clock it was done, and by then also Machrina had a large pile of toasted *tortillas*. Esperanza called out, "Pedro, come to eat!" More affectionately she said to the boys, "Come, little fathers, it's ready." Pedro and his sons washed, then straggled into the kitchen one by one, still drying their hands on their shirttails. The four men sat down on low benches on either side of the small table. Esperanza placed a pile of *tortillas* in the center of the table and handed each one a plate of beans. The boys waited for their father to take a *tortilla* before they took one, rolled it, and expertly scooped up mouthfuls of beans with it. The only sounds in the kitchen for some time were the noises of chewing, the slap of Machrina's hands making more hot *tortillas,* the crackle of the fire, and Moisés and Herman laughing in the patio. The older boys had talked and joked with each other in their bedroom, but now they sat eating soberly, as though wrapped in their private thoughts.

Pedro gave full attention to his food but he took everything in with his alert, small eyes. He noticed the pile of unmended clothes, the swept floor, the marketing basket with its little rolled paper packages, the basket of corn from Don Porfirio, and he mentally checked these things with Esperanza's tale of the day. He saw the Bible still opened on Machrina's bed in the corner and for a brief moment he permitted himself to glance affectionately at his youngest daughter. She was a good girl and a serious one, he reflected. She accepted wholeheartedly her father's new religion. She worked hard and was obedient. She might not be as intelligent or well educated as her sister but at least she would stay out of trouble and behave as a woman should. "Little daughter, how good these *tortillas* are!" Pedro said.

Machrina smiled. The boys nodded assent. Esperanza added some hot *tortillas* to the pile. Everyone was at ease for Pedro was in a good mood. There would be no ugly words tonight. Esperanza gave a dish of rice to Pedro, then one to her eldest son. Felipe was annoyed if she served any of his brothers before him. For Martin, her favorite, she spooned out a little more rice. Little was said. While the men drank their coffee Esperanza called to Moisés and Herman to come in, wash their hands, and be quiet. Before eating the two boys greeted Pedro silently, brushing their lips against his outstretched hand. They ate their beans, rice, and squash sitting on the floor near the hearth where Esperanza also sat.

The three older boys left the kitchen as soon as they had finished eating and went to lie down on their cots. They lay talking and laughing together. Moisés and Herman soon followed them. Martin and Felipe took out little bags of candy which they had bought on their way home from work. Machrina, who ate last since she had to keep providing hot *tortillas* for the others, hurried through her meal in order to join them before all the candy was gone. Soon Esperanza and Pedro were left alone in the kitchen. They listened to their children, who were now singing songs from the song sheet that Machrina had borrowed from her friend Elena. Pedro made a move of displeasure.

"Let them sing," Esperanza said. "It makes me feel a little happy."

But Pedro went to the boys' room. As soon as his children saw him in the doorway the singing stopped. "There is always High Mass among my poor children when he appears," Esperanza thought.

"Be quiet," Pedro said sternly. "The people will think we are a house of crazy ones. If you want to sing, sing a hymn. Let them see that we take our religion seriously." But when Pedro left there was no more singing. Herman came out and went to bed. Machrina helped her mother with the dishes. Felipe said that he was going out for a walk. Now that he was twenty-three years old he no longer asked his father for permission to go out. Nor did either of his parents demand to know where he was going as they had formerly done. Pedro merely called after him not to stay out late. Felipe did not reply.

At about nine o'clock Machrina climbed into bed and settled herself next to Herman, who was already asleep. She covered her face with the blanket and lay quietly on her back with her legs demurely stretched out before her as her mother had taught her to do when she was a little girl. Pedro and Esperanza sat near the fire occasionally saying something in a low voice. "Do you have money for tomorrow?" asked Pedro. "Who knows if it will be enough?" Esperanza said. They heard the sound of coughing in the other room. "Ricardo has a cough," said Esperanza. "I'll rub his chest with alcohol." She took the bottle and went into the boys' room. A few minutes later she came out. "He says that his lungs hurt. His body is hot. I think the spirits have hit him." Esperanza was worried; for her illness in the family was always a serious matter. She had given birth to twelve children and only six were alive. Their first child had died at eight "of the stomach," the second at eight months of smallpox, the third at two of a scorpion bite. Later two more children, aged seven and three, died "of the stomach." The last child, a daughter born in 1940, had died at ten months of "bronchitis."

Pedro was impatient with his wife. "It's a little thing. Don't make a woman out of him. Just give him some lemon tea and he will be better by tomorrow."

Esperanza stirred up the dying fire and put on the water to boil. She took a candle out with her into the garden and after groping about for a moment came back with a few blades of lemon grass which she dropped into the water. When the tea was ready she added some drinking alcohol and took it to her son. "That will cure him," Pedro said when she returned. But Esperanza said, "He has chills now. Let him stay in bed tomorrow. He is barely eighteen and still but a boy." Pedro looked at her with annoyance. "Be quiet!" he said. "What do you know, woman? When I was ten, I was working like a man, supporting my mother and my sister. He must learn what it means to be a man."

At nine-thirty Felipe walked in. His father said, "Now you are here." Felipe nodded and went to bed. He had never been one to talk much but for the past two weeks he hadn't addressed a word to his father. "He is angry again," observed Esperanza. "Who knows why?" Pedro knew why. It was because of the girl in Mexico City whom Felipe had decided he wanted to marry. He had met the girl only once for a few moments when he and his father had gone to the city to arrange for a sale of plums. She was an Aztecan girl but she had gone to school in Mexico City and was now a "lady of fashion." She wore shoes and stockings all the time and had cut off her braids. But she had smiled at Felipe and although he was a poor country boy he had dared to hope that she liked him. Felipe did not sleep well for a whole week after he had seen her. Finally he had asked his father to arrange the marriage with the girl's family.

Pedro had been against it from the start. "Think well," he had argued. "She lives in the city and we don't know her habits. She might even be a street woman and we wouldn't know." Pedro had really been taken aback by Felipe's request. Nowadays young people arranged their own marriages in secret before their parents were called in to carry out the traditional steps. If the parents objected the young couple usually eloped and made peace with their families later. But Felipe, who had never been fortunate with girls, did not smooth out the path for his father, and Pedro, although he had agreed to ask for the girl's hand, kept putting it off. Sometimes he growled at Felipe, "Do you still want to marry that girl in Mexico City?" He succeeded in turning the whole thing into a joke and Felipe was furious. So now the boy wouldn't speak to his father at all.

Pedro did not mind. The financial burden of the wedding, the gifts to the bride and her family, the support of his daughter-in-law while Felipe lived with them—all this would be more than he could manage. In the old days a son might live on with his father and more than repay these expenses by working for him, but nowadays young couples generally moved away after a year, leaving the parents with all their debts. The worst blow of all would be to lose a good worker. So Pedro kept his sons under close watch and saw to it that they worked hard and did not spend much time in the streets with the other young men. He discouraged them from thinking of having a good time or spending money on clothes, diversions, or other vanities. He also discouraged Machrina's attempts to look smart and pretty. Actually, marriage was the last thing he wanted for his children. Esperanza had much the same attitude. If she had needed a daughter-in-law to help take care of the menfolk, it might have been different. But she had a good worker in Machrina.

At ten o'clock Esperanza and Pedro got up from the low kitchen benches and went to bed, carrying a lighted candle. Pedro adjusted the wooden board which served as a door at night to keep out the animals. Without removing their clothes they got into bed and were soon alseep.

THE LAST RITE

Chou nan-an reached home before sunset. In the first courtyard he did not meet anyone. At the threshold of the second court his heart beat faster. The place looked unusually empty without his grandmother sitting in the low bamboo chair on the broad veranda. A pungent sensation crept up his nose. As long as he could remember she had been sitting there, rain or shine, ready to greet anyone who walked into the court. In his childhood this was the heart of the house. He was always sure that his grandmother would be there to receive him, and inside the wide folds of her sleeves, he would find cookies, candies or fruits of the season.

He ran through the stone-paved courtyard and up the few steps to the raised veranda. He was met by his mother who had just come out of the room to the right of the center altar room.

"Is she . . ." he asked.

She nodded and held him for a moment to look at him; she had not seen him in three years.

His grandmother's bedroom seemed full of silent women, her kinfolk, there to sit with her, according to custom, taking turns at night, until she either recovered or passed away in their loving care. The women all looked up when he entered. He followed his mother on tiptoe to the big built-in bed lit by an oil lamp on a nearby table. His grandmother was resting with her eyes closed. Her brown face was furrowed and her features sunken.

It seemed a long time before his grandmother stirred and asked for tea. Someone quickly handed his mother a bowl of the pale clear reddish broth of dried dates, believed to have the power of fortifying a weakened life. His mother kneeled on the low bench in front of the bed to feed the broth to the old woman. The old woman drank the broth with her eyes closed. After a few spoonfuls she asked, "Has my son come home yet?"

"Not yet. Shio-An-Erh is here. He has come home to see you, grandma."

The old woman opened her eyes slowly. Chou's mother got up quickly and stepping back, pushed her son to the foreground. He knelt on the low bench and took his grandmother's hand.

"I am home, grandma."

"Shio-An-Erh, I did not think I would see you again. You took a long time to come home." She spoke slowly and with great effort, then she nodded agreeably and closed her eyes, her hand clasping his.

His grandmother fell asleep with his hand in hers. He patiently kept his kneeling pose so as not to disturb her sleep. He loved his grandmother more dearly than he did his parents. In his childhood his mother was always too busy with housework to play with him, and his father had always treated him in the traditional way, serving as his strict disciplinarian. His grandmother had for him all the leisure and the unrestrained affection privileged to grandparents. It was to his grandmother he had made his childish vows to love her always. The memories of these vows brought him back home to her bedside. Watching the old woman sleeping with a sweet smile on her face, he was glad that he had come home.

In her sleep his grandmother frowned, made a little frightened sound and grasped his hand hard as if she had had a bad dream. Chou patted her hand with his free hand. She opened her eyes with a far-away look and when she finally focused them on him, she smiled. "I knew you would come home, I told them so," she said, pleased and somewhat boastfully.

In the evening his father walked in, still in his street robe, and kneeled on the low bench to have a look at his grandmother who was now asleep. When his father got up, his eyes swept about the room for Chou. He nodded to Chou and went out.

Chou delayed as long as possible leaving his grandmother to go to his father as requested by that look. He had hoped that his grandmother would wake up in time to furnish an excuse for him to postpone seeing his father alone. But since his grandmother went on sleeping peacefully and his mother kept casting worried glances at him, he got up and left.

As he came down the steps of the raised veranda and drew close to his father's room, Chou became panicky. He had to check his impulse to run back to his grandmother's room, his sanctuary in childhood. He was seized by that old familiar fear that he was not going to be able to speak clearly. Words would get stuck in his throat as in the old days whenever his father shouted at him. And his conversation with his father had never failed to produce thunder.

Yet in the years he had been away he had come to see his father in a different light. His father was not, as he had thought, his tormentor, nor was his father so staunch a believer in the old system. He did not oppose the new ways and the new people for what they were. He had not really had a taste of the good old days under the rule of the emperor. Just under twenty when the revolution of 1911 broke out, he had never had the chance to take the Imperial Civil Service Examinations and be appointed to an office, the first proof of a man's ability in his times and the first reward for his years of diligent study. The overthrow of the emperor nipped his budding dream of a useful successful life. If the revolutionists had made Sun Yat-sen an emperor, things would have been fine, his father had often said. When Chou had been away from home, away from his father, he read a deeper meaning

The Last Rite   191 into this comment of his father's. His father did not really care that the emperor had been overthrown or that the revolution had taken place. All he wanted was that there should be another emperor to hold the world together which he was born to and educated for. This personal disappointment made him hostile to the new world and the new people of whom Chou was one. It was a very tragic thing that happened to his father; the revolution had reduced him from a young man with as big a future as he could make it to a man who spent his life taking care of the family land. "A housekeeper," his father often called himself. When he understood this, Chou was sorry for his father and forgave him for the unfair treatment he had suffered at his hand.

During the last two days on the boat trip home Chou often thought that with this new understanding of his father he would have known how to handle him. In a way his father was like a disturbed youth who had not yet out-grown his young manhood's disappointment. Chou even went further towards this dream of reconciliation with his father. He had imagined many dialogues to convert his father, keyed to the various philosophical views of his father's that were familiar to him. Now in the grips of his fear to meet his father alone, he hoped only to summon enough courage to lift up the door drape and step over the threshold, let alone engage in conversation.

His father was in the study, actually the bookkeeping room where he went over the domestic accounts with the servants and kept no books worth reading. He had removed his street robe, rolled the sleeves of his white silk undergarment above the elbows, and was washing his face and hands in a porcelain basin. He dried his face with a plain cotton cloth. His eyes were bloodshot and his square jaw jutted out under the two strokes of a black mustache. He studied his son attentively.

Dinner was set in the center of a long table, at one end of which were a blue cloth-bound ledger, abacus, brushes and an inkstone. His father sat at the table and rolled down his sleeves. At a slight motion of his hand, Chou hurried forward to pour tea, holding the cup respectfully in both hands and at chest-level while his father took his time fastening the top button of his underjacket and gave his collar a few pulls to make it stand upright. When he took the cup his head bent a trifle to acknowledge the courtesy his son had shown him.

"Sit down," his father said as he picked up his chopsticks.

In the silent room the clinking of chinaware was exaggeratedly and uncomfortably loud. Chou sat straight on the edge of his chair. He wanted to lean back but could not move. His body seemed to be better disciplined than his mind; in the presence of his father, it behaved independently from his will, in compliance with his childhood training. He remained sitting respectfully on the edge of his chair.

His father did not seem to enjoy his dinner. He ate absentmindedly, absorbed in his own thoughts. Occasionally his eyes would rest on his son, but gave no indication of recognition. When he finished his dinner, Chou, again according to custom, got up and poured him fresh tea. His father's intent stare made him tremble and spill some tea in the saucer.

"What did they teach you in the last three years?" his father asked, sipping his tea.

"English, chemistry, physics . . ."

Before he could finish recounting the curriculum, his father waved for him to stop. He was not impressed by the titles of these strange foreign studies.

"I mean what have you learned? What knowledge is taught in the modern school?"

"It is complicated to explain . . ." The frown on his father's face cut Chou short. He paused and thought for a second. "In the modern school knowledge is much broader. The students are taught a general understanding of the cultures of various peoples and a fundamental knowledge of science—studies made on the natural aspects of the universe. And then the student proceeds to specialize in a branch of study chosen according to his interests and ability."

"Complicated and broader! Hern!" His father sneered. "What can be more complicated than to live the life of a man? Incidentally, in case they did not tell you this at school, let me tell you that the old-fashioned Chinese education teaches one to be a man."

Chou did not retort; again he had to face up to the impossibility of discussing anything with his father.

"We were taught our duties, duties to the emperor and duties to our parents. And we live by them." His father waited and then impatiently shouted, "What do you have to say for yourself?"

"Things are changing . . ." Chou faltered.

"What is changing and who does the changing? The same things go on: spring planting, fall harvest, rent collecting, paying taxes, feeding the family and going to the post office to send you money. Nothing is changing here."

Chou withdrew to greater depths of silence.

"You have been gone three years and you come home without having learned a thing. If good money was wasted to buy you common sense, I will teach you myself. The first duty you owe to me and to the old woman who is lying there dying, waiting for you, is to get yourself married. I do not want to remind you of the agony and humiliation you have inflicted upon your fiancée and her family because you do not understand—you never had any understanding."

"I cannot . . ." Chou's voice failed him in the middle of the sentence.

"I know. You never could do a good thing." His father snorted. "But you do not have to trouble yourself. I have taken care of everything, and I have checked the calendar, too. The day after tomorrow is a fair day and I only hope your grandmother can last that long to see you married." His father dismissed him with a wave of his hand.

Next morning after breakfast his sister came to see him. She filled in the details of the wedding arrangements. The family had been waiting for him to come home after the alarming telegram about their grandmother's illness had been sent to him. They had prepared everything, since it was also the grandmother's wish for him to get married on the first propitious day after his arrival. There would be no celebration or wedding party. These would follow either when his grandmother got well or on the hundredth day after her funeral. The east wing chambers were decorated as a bridal suite. From his room he could see that the windows were done up in red paper.

"Why are you so excited?" he said.

"I shall have someone to talk to and to sew with. She is so very nice, she really is."

"What do you know about her? You hardly ever had a chance to see her." Chou was surprised, since according to tradition his fiancée should not have come in contact with any member of his family until the wedding.

"But I do know her well," his sister said. "Since last year we have been going to the same school."

"School! What for?"

"What does anyone go to school for?" Her voice came quick and angry.

He ignored her anger, since they both knew his fiancée's purpose in obtaining an education was to raise his estimation of her.

"She wants me to give you this." His sister pointed to the package which she had put on his desk when she came in.

Shooting a glance at the tissue-wrapped package he said, "I cannot marry her. Doesn't anyone understand that is why I have not come home in three years?"

"What should she do?"

"It is not my concern."

"She is your fiancée."

"You, too! Have you forgotten what we used to talk about before I went away?"

"I remember. But I have grown up and understand things better. She is your fiancée, you have responsibilities towards her."

"Responsibilities and duties! That is all I have been hearing. And false responsibilities and duties at that! Of course, I have a great sense of responsibility and duty, but only to myself, as an individual, and to a better future for mankind. My utmost responsibility and duty are to destroy your type of responsibility and duty."

"But why destroy her?"

"She must fight her own way out!"

"How?"

"First and foremost by freeing herself from this feudalistic culture, rejecting the teachings and patterns of living formed and arranged for her before she was born and then by firmly insisting on her individual rights."

"Do not make speeches! You are not on a platform," his sister said.

"Just tell me how is she going to accomplish all this? She cannot set foot outside her house without her parents' permission."

"They have done a lot of harm to you. You have learned to yield and to compromise," Chou said regretfully. "I will take you with me this time when I leave. I shall introduce you to new friends who will help you to consolidate your thinking."

For reply his sister looked at her bound feet. "Their feet are not like mine."

An awkward moment lapsed as Chou was reminded of this overlooked impediment to his sister's emancipation.

"Mind is more important than physical appearance. You must not let this small hindrance prevent you from living a full life."

"Without this small hindrance your fiancée would stand more of a chance to please you."

"Your mind is poisoned. I do not wish to marry her because she is not the type of woman I would choose." His voice was raised to the pitch of impatience and temper, characteristic of student debates. "I do not care for women who consider uppermost the task of pleasing their husbands."

"But you can teach her new ways and new ideas. She is just as bright and willing to learn as I am."

"It is not a question of my willingness to help her. I would like to help her if at the same time I can preserve my independence, my freedom and my integrity."

"I used to think new ways and people with new ideas were better. But now I am grateful that my fiancé does not mind my bound feet and wants to marry me." She burst into tears and ran out of the room.

His talk with his sister was not what he had expected. He had counted on her as a mediator between him and his parents. And if that were to fail, he had taken it for granted that she would help him run away.

His father had taken, as expected, the precaution of posting a servant near him. On the pretext of being waited upon, he found that he was not left alone. While he was in his room the servant stayed in the room next to his, and when he walked about the house, he was followed.

A servant brought him a silk robe and said that his father wished him to wear it. He removed his student's cotton suit. He came out to the courtyard, went up to the broad veranda and lingered a moment near his grandmother's chair, his early refuge. Thousands of times he had run here to enlist her power against unpleasant orders from his parents. He touched the worn arm of the low chair and wished that once more his grandmother would exercise that authority on his behalf.

He sat down in her chair, the big square courtyard bare before his eyes. He saw every open and shut window and door and anyone who came in or went out of the gate. He realized that this was how the feeble old woman had participated in the activities of her household and knew so much about them.

His eyes dwelt upon the suite of three rooms at the upper end of the east chambers. How many hours, he asked himself, had his grandmother spent looking at the lattice windows and hoped to see them papered red.

His mother came out to the veranda and took the low roomy cushioned chair of the grandmother which he vacated for the stool that used to be his mother's.

"Grandmother is taking a nap. You have done her good. The doctor said this morning that her pulse is stronger."

"Good! Then we do not have to rush into this thing."

"It will be tomorrow. Your grandmother and father agreed," his mother said gravely. "It is not rushing. Your fiancée's getting to be an old maid. Eighteen years old and still she stays at home and braids her hair. Besides, there is your sister. You are holding up her wedding, too. Her fiancé's family is anxious to have a daughter-in-law."

"If I had known this, I would not have come home. No one cares about what happened to me."

His mother looked at him curiously and warily.

"No one wants to listen to me. I cannot marry this girl because I am already married. Now, do you understand?"

"Married," his mother repeated dubiously and then corrected him, "you mean you have taken a woman."

"I said I am married, married to a girl who goes to the same college with me."

"Ah, a modern girl," his mother said. She looked thoughtful. He waited impatiently for the serious nature of his marriage to penetrate her mind. "Do not tell your father," she said finally, "till this is over." She jutted her chin towards the red-papered lattice windows.

He walked angrily away from his mother. He had been away too long and had forgotten the paradoxical aspects of their morality. Laxity and indulgence loopholed a rigid code of behavior. His mother's attitude represented that of his family. To divulge his marriage to them would not matter in the least so far as their preparations to celebrate his wedding were concerned. A marriage which was not arranged by the family was not a marriage. And a girl, despite her upbringing and the prestige of her family, was not respectable if she entered into marriage unauthorized and unrecognized by the families of both sides. The most his wife could hope for was to come and beg humbly for recognition as his second wife.

His talk with his mother ended all hope of understanding from his family. Were he to tell his father of his marital status, his father would ignore him and send him tomorrow anyhow, on schedule, in a green sedan to bring home his childhood betrothed.

He had not written his family earlier of his marriage because he had thought it was the only way to avoid a break in relations—his father would instantly have cabled back cutting off his allowance and threatening to disown him. But as he now realized, it was a dimly felt distrust of his family that had prevented him from announcing the marriage. The repercussions of this great offense and disobedience, he must have subconsciously felt, would be more than disinheritance. His marriage could not alter the fact, in his parents' eyes, that he, their son, was meant to fit in their scheme of things and should be brought around to marry the girl they had engaged him to in his childhood. And his father was capable and unscrupulous. He had not been able to score an easy victory over him.

In the evening Chou had dinner with his cousins. One of them brought along a jug of wine. The excuse for their merry-making was that their grandmother rejoiced in it, too. After dinner, they all crowded into the grandmother's room. The old woman looked over the Chou descendants and signaled Chou to come forward. He knelt on the low bench, but his grandmother gestured for him to sit on the edge of her bed.

"They say I have spoiled you, but I know you will make up for everything. I will hang on—" she pointed in mid-air as if her life were being dispersed there, "till tomorrow."

"Do not talk like that! You will live for many, many years yet."

Tears rushed down Chou's cheeks.

"Not many years but . . ." The old woman paused to gather strength and smiled sweetly at her last wish. "The last banquet and all the friends and relatives to celebrate it."

Chou nodded; he had lost his voice.

He was sent to sleep in his own room and did not stay up to care for the sick woman. The lingering effects of the dinner wine made him sleep soundly.

In the morning when he woke up he noticed the package on the desk. He picked it up and opened it. It was an embroidered writing brush-holder, a pet souvenir women gave to men. Inside the brush-holder he found a letter from his fiancée. She acknowledged her awareness of his reluctance to marry her, begged for tolerance and thanked him for being merciful to allow her to assume his name. "I know only," she wrote, "of the traditional way of living. I shall be obedient to you as I am obedient to my parents. And I shall not question the propriety of anything you do since I cannot question what I do not understand."

He put the letter aside and concluded that she was a cunning woman. She pleaded for his sympathy and affection and at the same time hinted that he was free; she would not hold him to the conventional responsibilities of a husband.

There was much activity in the suite with the red-papered lattice windows. The door was open and the windows propped up. The servants kept going in and out.

After his visit to his grandmother he was sent to bathe and dress in formal gowns. At the propitious hour he was carried in a green sedan to his bride's house and came home followed by her red sedan. They held a simple ceremony without music. Afterwards, when they went to the grandmother's room, the sick old woman was propped up on pillows to receive them. Chou's parents stood by the bed and behind them stood the uncles, aunts and cousins. The crowded room was hushed; only the sound of the dangling pearls of the bride's headdress and the rustling of her stiff brocade were heard when they kowtowed to the grandmother.

During dinner he drank rounds of drinks with his cousins. Tottering, he was helped into the bridal chamber. He sat down in a red-lacquered arm-chair by a long red-lacquered table on which two thick red columnar candles were burning. The candles were to last out the night. So was the oil lamp under the bed. They were symbols of their long life together. Placed around the oil lamp were five kinds of nuts, symbolic of their prosperity. A red silk quilt was spread on the bed. His bride, still in her wedding gown, sat on the edge of the bed, her head bowed a little. A servant brought in strong tea, good for sobering up, and fastened the door on the outside. Chou drank two cups of tea.

"Go to sleep," he said to the girl who sat so still amidst the blazing red of the room. This was the one thing they could not force him to do, he said to himself. Yung-Chu, his wife by choice, might understand, he persuaded himself, if he held out at the last step and proved that he gave in to his family only on superficial grounds. He fulfilled his obligation to them as their son to take this woman into their house to be their daughter-in-law. She was as much his wife as he was their son, by circumstances and not by affection or choice.

Besides there was no other way for him to leave home and to go back to the city except through this compromise. But compromise was one word that Yung-Chu was afraid of. One compromise led to another, she had often warned him. She, too, was a student from a distant county who had come to the city to study. Like many young people around her, she lived as though she had no family and no awareness of the society around her. She cared for her approval of herself and for the approval of those who shared similar rebel-lious thoughts with her. When he first knew her, he was awed and, in turn, admired her for her advanced views and her resolution and courage to act upon them. When she found herself responding to his love, she came to live with him. There was no fuss and no bother about the significance of their union in relation to society. She did not tell him whether she had written her family about her marriage nor did she inquire about what he had done concerning his. The Chinese family, to her, was the remnant of a bankrupt society and the last restraint to young Chinese attempting to find a new life for themselves. When he showed her the telegram about his grandmother's illness, she merely looked at him, offended, and said in a challenging tone, "You must deal with it yourself. It is your own affair."

Chou understood and approved of his wife's attitude but at the same time he could not pretend that he was not hurt by it nor could he pretend that it was easy to live with a woman who constantly imposed upon themselves such unprecedented views. With her he had had some of the grandest moments of his life. Their visions of life conveyed him to a state in which he believed that life as it ought to be was within their reach, and they and their friends, undamaged and unspoiled by society, were the ones to live this good life, although in reality his life with Yung-Chu was very painful. When they were not talking about ideas, they seemed to be lost. They did not know how to do the least little thing without getting into a serious argument with each other. She refused to be addressed as Mrs. Chou, using only her own name, Lu Yung-Chu, if she had to assume a family name, and as a result involved themselves in needless and endless explanations to the conventional. She did the cooking and cleaning one week and he did it the next. This judicious distribution of housework afforded a good source of friction and Yung-Chu fought vigorous and valiant battles against the opposite sex in her own home. But all in all, she was the woman he loved and valued and he had admitted that his conventional male prerogatives were much at fault for the difficulties in his life with a woman like Yung-Chu. There was no doubt in his mind that she was the woman he wanted to go back to and the life with her was what he had chosen through his own free will.

Turning his chair away from the woman dressed in red who sat on the bed spread with red silk, he cushioned his head with his folded arms on the table and calculated the earliest possible date when he could leave. His grandmother was expected to die within a few days—the family had prepared for his wedding in the first and second main courts while in the third court preparations for the funeral went on steadily. In that case he had no choice but to wait till she died. But if the doctor gave a contrary prediction, then he would leave as soon as he could persuade his parents of his urgent desire to go back to school. He expected them to be lenient since he had compromised in marrying this woman, even though his father had hinted that he needed someone to help him manage the family estate and that his son had had enough education. Chou took this as another outburst of his father's hostility towards the new world; without the emperor there was no career worthwhile for a man to work at.

The sooner he could get back to the city, the better chance Chou had to explain to Yung-Chu what had happened. It would not be an easy task. He did not see how he could manage to convey to her his intricate relationship with his family, no more than he could explain to his family how he and Yung-Chu had been thinking and living. In some ways Yung-Chu was just as dogmatic as his father. She would judge him harshly and call his sympathy and love for his family cowardice. If she should condemn him as a coward and a renegade to their ideas, she would leave him. She and the friends they both had were, so he often felt even when he was with them, like the mules in a mill; they wore blinders in order to pursue without distraction their singleminded purpose of finding a new pattern of living for China. They would have wanted him to ignore, to destroy and to deny his feelings for everybody in this house where an old woman lay dying and a young girl waited to be made into a woman. But he did have feelings for them all, even for this girl whom he had just turned his back on. He was responsible for her, as his sister had said. If he did not go to take her home in the red sedan today he would have abandoned her to the sad life of an old maid. She would never be able to marry again and would be disgraced all her life through no fault of her own.

He turned around and saw that his bride had not moved. She sat in exactly the same pose, almost a part of the red decorations of the room, as though she were going to sit there guarding the edge of the bed throughout the night.

The red candles flickered and he had an impulse to blow them out. But this would have given alarm if someone were watching his windows.

"Go to sleep," he said.

The girl in red did not move.

Fine obedience! Chou was getting angry at her. It was not only his name she wanted, she was waiting for him to lift her headdress, to exercise his right as her husband.

"I said go to sleep!"

She trembled but made no move. The pearl curtain of her jeweled headdress was shaking. He went to her and parted the strings of pearls hanging down from her headdress. She was weeping quietly. Her eyes were downcast and tears were streaming down her powdered and rouged cheeks. She looked exceedingly beautiful in the candle light.

He let fall the strings of pearls and walked away from her. He knew that she was worrying about the next morning's questioning by her mother-in-law of the evidence of premarital chastity. He went back to her and took off her jeweled headdress. She had not raised her eyes but her tears had stopped, her lips were parted slightly and the rouge on her cheeks had deepened in color. His hand touched her black silky hair, which, for the first time in her life, was combed back and knotted into a chignon, and he felt for the essential gold pin that held the chignon in place. When he pulled the gold pin her hair fell loose and hung down her back, scattering the rest of the ornamental jeweled pins on the embroidered red silk quilt.

THE FAMILY DINNER

They were speaking in low voices in the kitchen.

"How is he? Has he said what he is going to do?" she asked her husband. "Is there any news?"

"None at all," the husband whispered. "He's coming down now. He says he just wants a house by the sea, in a place where the air is bracing and the water's soft and there's a good variety of fish."

"Sh-h-h! Why do we whisper like this? Here he comes. Get the plates."

A moment later, the very old gentleman, her father-in-law, was standing in the doorway, staring and smiling. He was short and very fat, and one of the things he liked to do was to pause in the doorway of a room and look it over from ceiling to floor. In the old days, his family or his workers at the factory used to stiffen nervously when he did this, wondering where his eye would stop.

"Excuse me being rude," he said at last. "What a lovely smell."

"Take your father in," the wife said. "These plates are hot. Go into the dining room, Grandpa."

"I'm just looking at your refrigerator, darling," the old gentleman said. "Very nice. It's a Pidex, I see. Is that a good make? I mean is it good—does it work well? . . . I'm glad to hear that. Did you get it from the Pidex people? . . . Ah, I thought you did. Good people."

The son, who was in his fifties, took the old gentleman by the elbow and moved him slowly into the dining room. The old gentleman blew his nose.

"No. Your mother's hands were as cold as ice when I got to her," said the old gentleman, astonished by a memory. "But she had gone. Where do I go? Do I sit here?"

He sat down very suddenly at the table. Although he weighed close to two hundred pounds, his clothes hung loosely on him, for he had once weighed much more. His nostrils had spread and reddened over a skin that was greenish and violet on the cheeks but as pale and stringy as a chicken's at the neck.

His daughter-in-law and two grandchildren brought in the joint and the vegetables. The grandchildren were called Richard and Helen. They were in their teens. Their mouths watered when they saw the food on the table, and they leaned toward it, but kept their eyes politely on the old man, like elderly listeners.

"I hope you haven't cooked anything special for me," the old man said. "I was just saying I talk too much when I come for a weekend here, and I eat too much. It's living alone—having no one to talk to, and so forth, and you can't be bothered to eat—that's the point. What a lovely piece of beef that is! Wonderful. I haven't seen a joint of beef like that for centuries. A small bit of loin of lamb we might have, but my wife can't digest it." He often forgot that his wife was dead. "And it doesn't keep. I put it in the larder and I forget and it goes wrong." His big face suddenly crinkled like an apple, with disgust.

"Well, well, I don't know, I'm sure," he went on, gazing at the beef his son was now carving. "I suppose it's all right. What do you call a joint like that?" He pointed across the table to his grandson. "We used to have beef when your father was a boy, Richard. Your father was a boy once. You can't imagine that, can you? Aitchbone, was it? I can't remember. I don't know where your mother used to get it. Bell's, I suppose. I don't know what we paid for it. Sixpence a pound, perhaps. We can't do it now; it's the price."

His son passed him a plate. The old man hesitated, not knowing whether to pass it on and not wanting to. "If this is for me, don't give me any more," he said. "I hardly eat anything nowadays. If I could have just a little fat . . ." Relieved, he kept the plate.

"Pass the vegetables to Grandpa," said his daughter-in-law to Helen.

"Grandpa, vegetables?" Helen said, looking younger now as she spoke.

"Oh," said the old gentleman. He had gone into a dream. "I was just watching you carving," he said to his son. "I was looking at your face. You've got just the expression of your Great-Grandfather Harry. I remember him when I was a little boy. Father took me to see him—it was one morning. He took me down to a warehouse, would it be?—in the docks or harbor—a factory, perhaps—and he lifted me up to a window and I saw him, just his face, it was only a minute. He was slitting up herrings; it was a curing place."

"Fish! I knew it." His daughter-in-law laughed.

"The sea is in our blood," said her husband. Everyone was laughing.

"What is this? What are you laughing at? What have I said?" the old gentleman asked, smiling. "Are you getting at me?"

"That is where you get your taste for kippers," said the daughter-in-law to her husband.

"Ah, kippers!" said the old gentleman, delighted by his strange success. "How are you for fish in this neighborhood? Do you get good fish? I sometimes feel like a piece of fish. But there doesn't seem to be the fish about, these days. I don't know why that is. No, I went up to the fishmonger on Tuesday and I looked. He came up to me and I said, 'Good morning.' 'Good morning, Mr. Hopkins,' he said. 'What can I do for you?' 'Do for me?' I said. 'Give me a fortnight in Monte Carlo.' He exploded. I said, 'What's happened to you? What's wrong?' 'What do you mean, Mr. Hopkins?' he said. 'I mean, where's your fish?' I said. 'That's not what I call fish. Not f-i-s-h.' He knew what I meant. 'Sole,' he said. 'Dover sole,' I said. 'Mr. Hopkins,' he said, 'I haven't had a Dover sole for a fortnight. Not one I'd sell *you*. Lemon sole,' he said, and something—grayling, did he say? Well, that's the way it is. And so we go on.

"No," the old man said after a moment. "Kitty, your mother, my wife, was very fond of fish. When we were first married, and so forth, we came down from the north—How old are you, my boy? Fifty-seven? You're not fifty-seven!—it was just before you were born, and my wife said, 'I'd give anything for an oyster.' The train didn't get in till eight, but we were young and reckless in those days. I didn't care a damn for anyone. I was ready to knock the world over. I was in a good crib, five pounds a week at Weekley's—before Hollins took them over. All expenses. I thought I was Julius Caesar— marvellous, isn't it? Do I mean him? And we went across the road and your mother said, 'Come on—' "

The son interrupted, picking up the story. "And a busdriver leaned out of his cab and said, 'Watch out, lady. Babies are scarce this year.' Mother told me."

"I'm sure she didn't," said the old gentleman, blushing a little. "Your father's imagination, Richard!"

"Yes, but what happened?" asked his daughter-in-law.

"And there was a little place, a real old London fish place—sawdust on the floor, I suppose they had in those days. Crossfield . . . Cross . . . Crofty—I forget the name—and we had a dozen oysters each, maybe I had a couple of dozen; I don't remember now, I couldn't say. Frederick's—*that* was the name of the place. Frederick's. And I suppose we must have followed it with Dover sole. They used to do a wonderful Welsh rabbit."

"And that is how I was born," said the son. "Let me give you some more beef, Father."

"Me? Oh, no. I don't eat what I used to. It's living alone, and these new teeth of mine—I've had a lot of trouble with them. Don't give me any more. I don't mind a couple of slices—well, just another. And some fat. I like a piece of fat. That's what I feel. You go home and you get to the house, and it's dark. And it's empty. You go in and the boiler's low—I don't seem to get the right coke. Do you get good coke here? You look at it all and you look in the larder and you can't be bothered. There's a chop, a bit of bread and cheese, perhaps. And you think, Well, if this is all there is in life, you may as well finish it. I'm in a rut down in that place. I've got to get away. I can't breathe there. I'd like to get down to the sea."

"I think you ought to go where you have friends," said his daughter-in-law.

The old gentleman put his knife and fork down. "Friends?" he said, in a stern voice, raising his chin. "I have no friends. All my friends are dead." He said this with indignation and contempt.

"But what about your friend Rogers, in Devonshire?" said his son.

"Rogers? I was disappointed in Rogers. He's aged. He's let himself go. I hadn't seen him for twenty-five years. When I saw him, I said to him, 'Why, what's the matter with you? Trying to pretend you are an old man?' He looked at me. He'd let his mustache go long and gray. I wouldn't have known him. And there was something else. A funny thing. It upset me." The old gentleman's jolly face shrivelled up again, with horror. "The hairs in his nose had gone gray!" he said. "I couldn't bear it. He was very kind, *and* his wife was. We had lunch. Soup of some kind—tomato, or maybe oxtail—and then a piece of lamb, potatoes, and cauliflower. Oh, very nice. I've forgotten what the dessert was—some cream, I suppose, they have good cream there—and coffee, of course. Cheese . . . I don't remember. Afterward—and this is what upsets me about old people—they wanted a rest. Every day, after lunch, they go off and have a sleep—every day. Can you imagine that? I couldn't stand that. Terrible."

"It's good to have a siesta," said the son.

"I couldn't. I never have. I just can't," said the old gentleman, in a panic. "The other afternoon after lunch. I forget what I had, a chop, I think—I couldn't be bothered to cook vegetables, well, on your own you don't, that's the point—I dropped off. I don't know how long, and when I woke up it was dark. I couldn't see anything. I didn't know where I was. 'Where am I?' I said. 'What day is it?' And I reached out for my wife. I thought I was in bed, and I called out 'Kitty, Kitty, where are you?' and then I said, 'Oh.' It came back to me. I'm here. In this room. I couldn't move. I got up and put on the light. I was done up. I poured myself out a small glass of port. I felt I had to. It was shocking. And shocking dreams."

He stared and then suddenly he turned to his daughter-in-law and said, in another voice, "Those sandwiches I shan't forget. Egg, wasn't it? You remember." He wagged a finger at Helen. "Helen, your mother is a wonder at egg sandwiches. It was the first time in my life I'd ever eaten them. The day we put Kitty away, you remember, she came down and made egg sandwiches. What is the secret of it? She won't tell. Butter, I suppose? Richard, what is the word I want? You know—'smashing,' I suppose you'd call them."

He paused, and his eyes grew vaguer. "No," he went on, "I don't know what I'll do. I think I shall go to the sea and look around. I shall get a list of houses, and put my furniture in store. I could live with your brother John, or you. I know I could, but it would be wrong. You have your own lives. I want my independence. Life is beginning for me—that is what I feel. I feel I would like to go on a cruise round the world. There was a house at Bexhill I saw. They wanted seven thousand for it. I felt it would suit me."

"Seven thousand!" said his son, in alarm. "Where would you get seven thousand from?"

"Oh," said the old gentleman sharply, "I should raise it."

"Raise it!" exclaimed the son. "How?"

"That's just it," said the old gentleman cheerfully. "I don't know. The way will open up. You, perhaps, or John."

Husband and wife looked down the table at each other in consternation.

"Shall we go upstairs and have some coffee?" she said.

"That son of yours, that Richard—did you see what he ate?" said the old gentleman as he got up from the table. "Marvellous, isn't it? Of course, things are better than when I was a boy. I feel everything is better. We used to go to school with twopence for a pie. Not every day— twice a week. The other days, we just looked at the shopwindow. Pies piled up. And once a week—Friday, I expect—it was herrings in the evening. The fisherwomen came calling them in the street, eighteen a shilling, fresh fish out of the sea. Salmon I used to be fond of. D'you ever have salmon?"

He paused in the doorway and looked at the carpet on the stairs and at the wallpaper. "I like rich things," he said, nodding to the carpet. "That gravy was good. Luscious grapes, pears, all large fruits I like. Those Christmas displays at the meat market—turkeys and geese by the thousand there used to be. I always used to bring your mother something. A few chops, two or three pairs of kippers. And so forth. I don't know what."

"Upstairs to the sitting room, Father," said the son. "I'm coming in a minute with the coffee."

The son went into the kitchen, and the whispering began again.

"Seven thousand!" he said. "Seven million wouldn't keep him!"

"Sh-h-h," said his wife. "It's a daydream."

"But what are we going to do?"

In a few minutes, he took the coffee upstairs. The old gentleman was sitting down, with his waistcoat undone and his thumbs twiddling on his stomach.

"I've been thinking about you," the old gentleman said rebukingly. "You've lost weight. You don't eat. You worry too much. My wife used to worry."

The son passed a coffee cup to him.

"Is there a lot of sugar in it? Thank you," the old man said. He gave it a stir, took a sip, and then held the cup out. "I think I'll have a couple of spoonfuls more."

BEING REFINED

Being refined is a very nice thing, and I have had some happy times noticing refinement in the members of my family, most of whom, especially those who were born in the old country, in Bitlis, finally learned that vocal modulation, for instance, constituted one of the many signs of being refined. Shouting was all right in the family, but out among Americans and people like that it was always a good idea to modulate the voice, at least until you found out that the Americans themselves weren't very refined, which my Uncle Shag seemed to be finding out all the time.

Another good sign of being refined was to look at a painting and not have your mouth hanging open in wonder because the fruit on the plate seemed so real you wanted to reach out and take some, which was pretty much the way paintings were appreciated by the immigrants who had only recently arrived in America.

Still another good idea was not to ask priests difficult questions about God, or biology, or about a stick becoming a snake, or a body of water dividing itself so that there would be a dry road running through it, or a dead man coming to life. Asking such questions really didn't demonstrate that you were an intelligent man, or that you had safely emerged from the Dark Ages, or that you knew how to think for yourself; all it seemed to do was make refined people look at you sideways, cockeyed-like, by which they meant that you must be some sort of unrefined person, all of your success as a lawyer, for instance, and all of your wealth notwithstanding. In the presence of music you hated, something classical by Ethelbert Nevin, being played on the piano by somebody's wife, accompanied by somebody else's daughter on the cello, it was not a sign of refinement to blurt out, "Can't you play something lively, like *Dari Lolo?*" Or if somebody you had just met looked ill, worn-out from worry of some sort, sunk in spirit, it was not courteous to say, "What's the matter with you? Why don't you stand up straight?"

Shag, or as he had it in full on his card and on the door of his office, Arshag Bashmanian, by the time he was 55 and all the rest of us were in our early 20s, had picked up a wide variety of pointers, as he put it, on how to be refined; and whenever it was in order to demonstrate his refinement, he hardly ever failed to do so.

The year his first daughter, named by her mother Genevieve because the name was refined, became engaged to an American boy named Edmund Armbruster who was a premed student in San Francisco, Arshag was obliged to drive there from Fresno, so that Mr. and Mrs. Armbruster, the boy's father and mother, could meet Arshag and his wife Shushanik, who had a wide circle of friends disciplined to calling her Susan because Shushanik just wouldn't do. And of course the Armbrusters were dying to have a look at the girl their boy had fallen in love with.

Taking his wife and daughter in the Cadillac to San Francisco didn't appeal to Shag, so he asked me to sit up front with him, while they sat in the back, where they belonged, and somehow I wasn't able to get out of it.

"Be in front of your house at five minutes to six," he said. "I'll pick you up, and we'll go right on."

"Isn't that a little early? It's only a five-hour drive, with one stop for gasoline, comfort, and maybe a cup of coffee."

"The earlier we start the better," Shag said. "I've always believed that."

"Are they expecting you at ten in the morning?"

"Well, don't argue," Shag said. "Don't argue about *everything.* Just be in front of your house in your best suit at five minutes to six, and I'll pick you up."

"How long will we be gone?"

"Well, we don't know yet. These people want to see if I pass the inspection. If I do, *that* will be *that,* and we'll come right back. If I don't, we'll come back the next day. If you ask me, I think they're going to have a very pleasant little surprise for themselves. I suppose they think we're country people. I don't suppose they expect to see somebody like me, in the kind of clothes I wear, driving a Cadillac."

"OK, I'll be standing there."

"A white shirt, a tie, and shine your shoes. And when we get up there and go into their house, don't all of a sudden say, 'I'm so hungry I could eat a horse,' or hint around that you want them to give us lunch. I think they'll give us lunch anyway."

"OK."

"And if any of their women—besides the boy, I think they've got two daughters—are beautiful, just compliment them in a nice way, and if they like it and start flirting, flirt back, but *politely.*"

"OK."

"I don't like the idea of driving two hundred miles to have some people I don't know inspect me, but what are you going to do when you've got a daughter who's in love and a wife who wants her daughter to marry into the the best possible family? You've got to go, that's all. What kind of a father would I be if I wouldn't do my daughter and my wife a little favor like that? I've met the boy, Bobby, and he's got class, there's no question about that, and if his people are anything like him, *they've* got class, too."

"Isn't his name Edmund?"

"Is that what it is? Well, anyway, he's a nice boy, a slow boy, slow in the head, but nice. Every time he said Bashmanian, I almost didn't know what he was saying. He took too long. It's not a complicated name, all you've got to do is say Bashmanian, not Bash Man Ian. But Jenny thinks she loves him, so maybe she does, so maybe you better go get a haircut, too, and be sure to shave real neat. Here's fifty cents for the haircut, give the barber a dime tip, keep the rest."

"OK."

I didn't get a haircut, but I did all the other things he said, and I was in front of my house at five minutes to six. Less than two minutes later the big sky-blue Cadillac drew up and I got in and sat beside him. His wife and daughter looked very nice in their new dresses and coats, and Shag himself looked all right, too. He was wearing everything. Diamond stickpin in his tie. Silk handkerchief in his jacket. Gold watch chain across the vest, gold watch attached to the chain. Red rose in the lapel buttonhole. Haircut, shampoo, manicure, shoeshine, Sen-Sen in his mouth—the damned smell nearly knocked me over.

We stopped for gas, comfort and coffee in Modesto, and we were in San Francisco at a quarter to eleven. At four minutes to eleven the Cadillac drew up in front of the house, which was in a neighborhood called Seacliff, where only rich people could afford to live, or as Shag put it, "They've got money all right, but let me tell you something. I can buy and sell them any day in the week, and don't ever forget it."

"Poppa," his daughter said. "Please don't talk that way. Just, please, forget that they've got money and that we've got money."

"All right, honey, for your sake I'll let it go this time, but I don't want these people putting on a lot of airs with *me*. I'm Arshag Bashmanian, who the hell do they think they are? Three-car garage. Why three? Why not make the whole house a garage?"

"Poppa, please."

"All right, all right, don't worry about your father."

The door was opened by a rather handsome woman in her late 40s, and from the expression of surprise on Shag's face I was sure he imagined that this was the mother of the boy his daughter had fallen in love with. He had never before visited anybody who had had a servant.

"Yes?" she said.

"Are you sure this is the right address?" Shag said to his daughter, who instead of answering him said to the woman, "I'm Genevieve Bashmanian, and this is my father, and my mother, and my cousin."

"Oh, yes, of course," the woman said. "Won't you please come in and sit down."

Well, the place was really swank. It was certainly the swankest place I had ever walked into, but it gave Shag an awful pain, because by comparison his mansion on Van Ness Avenue in Fresno was a remodeled barn full of Grand Rapids furniture and an original oil painting for which he had paid

$1000 by somebody named Gaston Voillard, 1874—a meaningless landscape in dull colors. Three years before when Shag had asked me over to the house to see how a successful man was entitled to live, so that it would be a lesson to me, he showed me the picture, told me how much he had paid for it, and then said, "This Gaston Voillard, 1874, he's one of the *greatest* painters, isn't he?"

"Yes, he is," I said.

Encouraged by my lie, Shag then said, "For God's sake, look at that picture, will you? Look at those leaves on those trees. The man's a genius. I wouldn't take *five* thousand dollars for that picture, if you want to know the truth."

But of course I didn't want to know the truth, so the conversation collapsed and we went to the little bar just off the kitchen, where he poured each of us a drink of raki.

Well, on the walls of the room in which we were now sitting there was an original Cézanne, an original Matisse and an original Picasso. Shag looked from one to the other, and then at me. He leaned his head over slowly to the right, and at the same time lifted his eyebrows, by which he meant, "What kind of cockeyed paintings do you call those?"

Soon the father, the mother, the son and a daughter of 11 came into the room. They were nice people, very gracious, very warm, and yet somehow in spite of everything, even in spite of the fine paintings they owned, they seemed to lack something. I really didn't know what it was, but it was a rather large thing. I suppose it might have been wit of some kind, or maybe health of some kind, or maybe humor. At any rate, it was impossible to be really at ease with them.

The boy's mother said lunch would be at one, and she would be terribly let down if we had made other plans. As a matter of fact, she would insist that we change our plans. In the meantime, perhaps we'd like to see the rest of the house, and then the garden, and after that we might enjoy taking a short drive up to the Legion of Honor Palace to see the new show.

"What kind of a show is it?" Shag said, as if it just might unaccountably be burlesque or something, in which case he would let these people know he didn't take his women to places like that.

"Well, it's the Second Winter Invitational, and I think even better than the first, which was an enormous success."

Shag looked at me, so I said, "*California* painters?"

"Well, actually, *Northern* California painters."

"Oh, paintings," Shag said. "Sure, let's go see 'em."

And so first we saw the house, and then the garden, and every bit of each burned hell out of Shag, and then we were all asked to get in the chauffeur-driven Rolls, but Shag said, "No, let's not all of us try to get into one car. I'll drive up with my nephew."

"Just follow us, then," the father of the boy said, "unless you know the way."

Following the Rolls, Shag said, "What do you think?"

"They're nice people all right."

"No, I don't mean *them*. What do you think of the impression I've made so far?"

"So far it's pretty good, I must say."

"Voice modulated, smiles, politeness?"

"Yes, you showed them all those things all right."

"I'll show them plenty more, too."

At the museum the Second Winter Invitational wasn't bad, although not much good, either, mainly a lot of stuff without any style of any kind, most of it experimental and messy. Not one picture like the one painted by Gaston Voillard, 1874.

"Shall we look at the permanent collection as well?" the mother asked. Shag said, "Why not?"

Well, it was the older stuff, an El Greco, a Rembrandt, a Rubens, but none of it especially exciting, certainly not to Shag; but then in the first of the five small rooms just off the main hall, to the left, there was a painting that really impressed him. Years later I made a point of going back and getting the name of the thing, and of the painter. His name was Jean Marc Nattier, French, 1685–1766, and the name of the picture was *The Duchess of Chateauroux as Thalia, Muse of Comedy*. It was a rather big picture of this pretty girl whose right breast was delightfully exposed. It was as big as life, very white, with a nipple the size and color of a pink rosebud. The girl's face had a twinkle to it, as of mischief. All around her were foldings of dark velvet, and in the background was a small stage with actors upon it.

We all stopped in front of the picture, and after a moment, Shag said, "My goodness, that girl's chest is so real you could reach out and touch it."

Lunch was soup, fish, meat, raspberries with ice cream and coffee.

Somewhere near the end of lunch there was a moment of silence, whereupon Shag said, "I don't think I've ever seen anything more real than that girl's chest."

Less than an hour after lunch we got back into the Cadillac, and Shag began to drive back to Fresno. He had been refined every minute he had been with the elegant people. He had worked very hard at it, saying, for instance, my goodness, and chest, for instance, but what is a man to do about a daughter? A daughter is always a lot of trouble, and now all of a sudden she was crying.

The upshot of the whole thing was that the engagement was slowly broken, or possibly it was simply permitted by time and silence to fade away, and a year later Genevieve married a poor but ambitious boy, by whom she now has four sons and three daughters.

As for Shag, one day he said, "I never did like those Armstrongs."

"Isn't the name Armbruster?"

"That's *exactly* what I mean. There's such a thing as a name like Armstrong but whoever heard of a name like Armbruster? Those people were phonies. They weren't *really* refined. They were performing, like those little trained dogs at vaudeville shows, and one thing I can't stand is a lousy performance."

THE REVOLT OF
THE EVIL FAIRIES

The grand dramatic offering of the Booker T. Washington Colored Grammar School was the biggest event of the year in our social life in Hopkinsville, Kentucky. It was the one occasion on which they let us use the old Copper Opera House, and even some of the white folks came out yearly to applaud our presentation. The first two rows of the orchestra were always reserved for our white friends, and our leading colored citizens sat right behind them—with an empty row intervening, of course.

Mr. Ed Smith, our local undertaker, invariably occupied a box to the left of the house and wore his cutaway coat and striped breeches. This distinctive garb was usually reserved for those rare occasions when he officiated at the funerals of our most prominent colored citizens. Mr. Thaddeus Long, our colored mailman, once rented a tuxedo and bought a box too. But nobody paid him much mind. We knew he was just showing off.

The title of our play never varied. It was always Prince Charming and the Sleeping Beauty, but no two presentations were ever the same. Miss H. Belle LaPrade, our sixth-grade teacher, rewrote the script every season, and it was never like anything you read in the storybooks.

Miss LaPrade called it "a modern morality play of conflict between the forces of good and evil." And the forces of evil, of course, always came off second best.

The Booker T. Washington Colored Grammar School was in a state of ferment from Christmas until February, for this was the period when parts were assigned. First there was the selection of the Good Fairies and the Evil Fairies. This was very important, because the Good Fairies wore white costumes and the Evil Fairies black. And strangely enough most of the Good Fairies usually turned out to be extremely light in complexion, with straight hair and white folks' features. On rare occasions a darkskinned girl might be lucky enough to be a Good Fairy, but not one with a speaking part.

There never was any doubt about Prince Charming and the Sleeping Beauty. They were always lightskinned. And though nobody ever discussed those things openly, it was an accepted fact that a lack of pigmentation was a decided advantage in the Prince Charming and Sleeping Beauty sweepstakes.

And therein lay my personal tragedy. I made the best grades in my class, I was the leading debater, and the scion of a respected family in the community. But I could never be Prince Charming, because I was black.

In fact, every year when they started casting our grand dramatic offering my family started pricing black cheesecloth at Franklin's Department Store. For they knew that I would be leading the forces of darkness and skulking back in the shadows—waiting to be vanquished in the third act. Mamma had experience with this sort of thing. All my brothers had finished Booker T. before me.

Not that I was alone in my disappointment. Many of my classmates felt it too. I probably just took it more to heart. Rat Jointer, for instance, could rationalize the situation. Rat was not only black; he lived on Billy Goat Hill. But Rat summed it up like this:

"If you black, you black."

I should have been able to regard the matter calmly too. For our grand dramatic offering was only a reflection of our daily community life in Hopkinsville. The yallers had the best of everything. They held most of the teaching jobs in Booker T. Washington Colored Grammar School. They were the Negro doctors, the lawyers, the insurance men. They even had a "Blue Vein Society," and if your dark skin obscured your throbbing pulse you were hardly a member of the elite.

Yet I was inconsolable the first time they turned me down for Prince Charming. That was the year they picked Roger Jackson. Roger was not only dumb; he stuttered. But he was light enough to pass for white, and that was apparently sufficient.

In all fairness, however, it must be admitted that Roger had other qualifications. His father owned the only colored saloon in town and was quite a power in local politics. In fact, Mr. Clinton Jackson had a lot to say about just who taught in the Booker T. Washington Colored Grammar School. So it was understandable that Roger should have been picked for Prince Charming.

My real heartbreak, however, came the year they picked Sarah Williams for Sleeping Beauty. I had been in love with Sarah since kindergarten. She had soft light hair, bluish-gray eyes, and a dimple which stayed in her left cheek whether she was smiling or not.

Of course Sarah never encouraged me much. She never answered any of my fervent love letters, and Rat was very scornful of my one-sided love affairs. "As long as she don't call you a black baboon," he sneered, "you'll keep on hanging around."

After Sarah was chosen for Sleeping Beauty, I went out for the Prince Charming role with all my heart. If I had declaimed boldly in previous contests, I was matchless now. If I had bothered Mamma with rehearsals at home before, I pestered her to death this time. Yes, and I purloined my sister's can of Palmer's Skin Success.

I knew the Prince's role from start to finish, having played the Head Evil Fairy opposite it for two seasons. And Prince Charming was one character whose lines Miss LaPrade never varied much in her many versions. But although I never admitted it, even to myself, I knew I was doomed from the start. They gave the part to Leonardius Wright. Leonardius, of course, was yarrler.

The teachers sensed my resentment. They were almost apologetic. They pointed out that I had been such a splendid Head Evil Fairy for two seasons that it would be a crime to let anybody else try the role. They reminded me that Mamma wouldn't have to buy any more cheesecloth because I could use my same old costume. They insisted that the Head Evil Fairy was even more important than Prince Charming because he was the one who cast the spell on Sleeping Beauty. So what could I do but accept?

I had never liked Leonardius Wright. He was a goody-goody, and even Mamma was always throwing him up to me. But, above all, he too was in love with Sarah Williams. And now he got a chance to kiss Sarah every day in rehearsing the awakening scene.

Well, the show must go on, even for little black boys. So I threw my soul into my part and made the Head Evil Fairy a character to be remembered. When I drew back from the couch of Sleeping Beauty and slunk away into the shadows at the approach of Prince Charming, my facial expression was indeed something to behold. When I was vanquished by the shining sword of Prince Charming in the last act, I was a little hammy perhaps—but terrific!

The attendance at our grand dramatic offering that year was the best in its history. Even the white folks overflowed the two rows reserved for them, and a few were forced to sit in the intervening one. This created a delicate situation, but everybody tactfully ignored it.

When the curtain went up on the last act, the audience was in fine fettle. Everything had gone well for me too—except for one spot in the second act. That was where Leonardius unexpectedly rapped me over the head with his sword as I slunk off into the shadows. That was not in the script, but Miss LaPrade quieted me down by saying it made a nice touch anyway. Rat said Leonardius did it on purpose.

The third act went on smoothly, though, until we came to the vanquishing scene. That was where I slunk from the shadows for the last time and challenged Prince Charming to mortal combat. The hero reached for his shining sword—a bit unsportsmanlike, I always thought, since Miss LaPrade consistently left the Head Evil Fairy unarmed—and then it happened!

Later I protested loudly—but in vain—that it was a case of self-defense. I pointed out that Leonardius had a mean look in his eye. I cited the impromptu rapping he had given my head in the second act. But nobody would listen. They just wouldn't believe that Leonardius really intended to brain me when he reached for his sword.

Anyway, he didn't succeed. For the minute I saw that evil gleam in his eye—or was it my own?—I cut loose with a right to the chin, and Prince Charming dropped his shining sword and staggered back. His astonishment lasted only a minute, though, for he lowered his head and came charging in, fists flailing. There was nothing yellow about Leonardius but his skin.

The audience thought the scrap was something new Miss LaPrade had written in. They might have kept on thinking so if Miss LaPrade hadn't been screaming so hysterically from the sidelines. And if Rat Joiner hadn't decided that this was as good a time as any to settle old scores. So he turned around and took a sock at the male Good Fairy nearest him.

When the curtain rang down, the forces of Good and Evil were locked in combat. And Sleeping Beauty was wide awake and streaking for the wings.

They rang the curtain back up fifteen minutes later, and we finished the play. I lay down and expired according to specifications but Prince Charming will probably remember my sneering corpse to his dying day. They wouldn't let me appear in the grand dramatic offering at all the next year. But I didn't care. I couldn't have been Prince Charming anyway.

AN ANTHROPOLOGY DEPARTMENT

The possibility that Dr. Hillebrand was developing kleptomania caused a good deal of pleasure among his younger colleagues—that is, the entire personnel of the Department of Anthropology, including its director, Walter Klibben. It was not that anybody really disliked the old boy. That would have been hard to do, for he was coöperative and gentle, and his humor was mild; he was perhaps the greatest living authority on Southwestern archeology, and broadly learned in the general science of anthropology; and he was a man who delighted in the success of others.

Dr. Hillebrand was the last surviving member of a group of men who had made the Department of Anthropology famous in the earlier part of the twentieth century. His ideas were old-fashioned; to Walter Klibben, who at forty was very much the young comer, and to the men he had gathered about him, Dr. Hillebrand's presence, clothed with authority, was as incongruous as that of a small, mild brontosaurus would be in a modern farmyard.

On the other hand, no one living had a finer archeological technique. Added to this was a curious intuition, which caused him to dig in unexpected places and come up with striking finds—the kind of thing that delights donors and trustees, such as the largest unbroken Mesa Verde black-on-white jar known up to that time, the famous Biltabito Cache of turquoise and shell objects, discovered two years before and not yet on exhibition, and, only the previous year, the mural decorations at Painted Mask Ruin. The mural, of which as yet only a small part had been uncovered, compared favorably with the murals found at Awatovi and Kawaika-a by the Peabody Museum, but was several centuries older. Moreover, in the part already exposed there was an identifiable katchina mask, unique and conclusive evidence that the katchina cult dated back to long before the white man came. This meant, Dr. Klibben foresaw gloomily, that once again all available funds for publication would be tied up by the old coot's material.

The trustees loved him. Several years ago, he had reached the age of retirement and they had waived the usual limitation in his case. He was curator of the museum, a position only slightly less important than that of director, and he occupied the Kleinman Chair in American Archeology. This was an endowed position paying several thousand a year more than Klibben's own professorship.

From *The Resting Place*, originally published in *The New Yorker*. Copyright © 1954 by Oliver La Farge. Reprinted by permission of Mrs. Oliver La Farge.

Dr. Hillebrand's occupancy of these positions, on top of his near monopoly of publication money, was the rub. He blocked everything. If only the old relic would become emeritus, the younger men could move up. Klibben had it all worked out. There would be the Kleinman Chair for himself, and McDonnell could accede to his professorship. He would leave Steinberg an associate, but make him curator. Thus, Steinberg and McDonnell would have it in mind that the curatorship always might be transferred to McDonnell as the man with senior status, which would keep them both on their toes. At least one assistant professor could, in due course, be made an associate, and young George Franklin, Klibben's own prized student, could be promoted from instructor to assistant. It all fitted together and reinforced his own position. Then, given free access to funds for monographs and papers . . .

But Dr. Hillebrand showed no signs of retiring. It was not that he needed the money from his two positions; he was a bachelor and something of an ascetic, and much of his salary he put into his own expeditions. He loved to teach, he said—and his students liked him. He loved his museum; in fact, he was daffy about it, pottering around in it until late at night. Well, let him retire, and he could still teach a course or two if he wanted; he could still potter, but Klibben could run his Department as he wished, as it ought to be run.

Since there seemed no hope that the old man would give out physically in the near future, Klibben had begun looking for symptoms of mental failure. There was, for instance, the illogical way in which Dr. Hillebrand often decided just where to run a trench or dig a posthole. As Steinberg once remarked, it was as if he were guided by a ouija board. Unfortunately, this eccentricity produced splendid results.

Then, sometimes Hillebrand would say to his students, "Now, let us imagine—" and proceed to indulge in surprising reconstructions of the daily life and religion of the ancient cliff dwellers, going far beyond the available evidence. The director had put Franklin onto that, because the young man had worked on Hopi and Zuñi ceremonial. Franklin reported that the old boy always made it clear that these reconstructions were not science, and, further, Franklin said that they were remarkably shrewd and had given him some helpful new insights into aspects of modern Indians' religion.

The possibility of kleptomania was something else again. The evidence—insufficient so far—concerned the rich Biltabito Cache, which Dr. Hillebrand himself was enumerating, cataloguing, and describing, mostly evenings, when the museum was closed. He was the only one who knew exactly how many objects had been in the find, but it did look as if some of it might now be missing. There was also what the night watchman thought he had seen. And then there was that one turquoise bead—but no proof it had come from that source, of course—that McDonnell had found on the floor near the cast of the Quiriguá stela, just inside the entrance of the museum.

The thefts—if there had been any—had taken place in April and early May, when everyone was thinking of the end of the college year and the summer's field trips. A short time later, and quite by accident, Klibben learned from an associate professor of ornithology that old Hillebrand had obtained from him a number of feathers, which he said he wanted for repairing his collection of katchina dolls. Among them were parrot and macaw feathers, and the fluffy feathers from the breast of an eagle.

Klibben's field was not the American Southwest, but any American anthropologist would have been able to draw an obvious conclusion; turquoise, shell, and feathers of those sorts were components of ritual offerings among the modern Hopis and Zuñis, and possibly their ancestors, among whose remains Dr. Hillebrand had carried on his lifework. Dr. Klibben began to suspect—or hope—that the old man was succumbing to a mental weakness far more serious than would be evidenced by the mere stealing of a few bits of turquoise and shell.

The Director made tactful inquiries at the genetics field laboratory to see if the old man had been seeking corn pollen, another component of the ritual offerings, and found that there the question of the evolution of *Zea maiz* in the Southwest was related to the larger and much vexed question of the origin and domestication of that important New World plant, so interesting to archeologists, botanists, and geneticists. Dr. Hillebrand had been collecting specimens of ancient corn from archeological sites for a long time—ears, cobs, and grains extending over two millenniums or more, and other parts of the plant, including some fragments of tassels. It was, Klibben thought, the kind of niggling little detail you would expect to find Hillebrand spending good time on. Dr. Hillebrand had been turning his specimens over to the plant and heredity boys, who were delighted to have them. They, in turn, had followed this up by obtaining—for comparison—seed of modern Pueblo Indian, Navajo, and Hopi corn, and planting it. It was natural enough, then, that from time to time Dr. Hillebrand should take specimens of seed and pollen home to study on his own. It might be clear as day to Klibben that the old boy had gone gaga to the point of making ritual offerings to the gods of the cliff dwelling; he still had nothing that would convince a strongly pro-Hillebrand board of trustees.

Even so, the situation was hopeful. Klibben suggested to the night watchman that, out of concern for Professor Hillebrand's health, he keep a special eye on the Professor's afterhours activities in the museum. Come June, he would arrange for Franklin—with his Southwestern interests, Franklin was the logical choice—to go along on Hillebrand's expedition and see what he could see.

Franklin took the assignment willingly, by no means unaware of the possible advantages to himself should the old man be retired. The archeologist accepted the addition of the young man to his staff with equanimity. He remarked that Franklin's knowledge of Pueblo daily life would be helpful in interpreting what might be uncovered, while a better grounding in Southwestern prehistory would add depth to the young man's ethnographic perceptions. Right after commencement, they set out for the Navajo country of Arizona, accompanied by two undergraduate and four graduate students.

At Farmington, in New Mexico, they picked up the university's truck and station wagon, and Hillebrand's own field car, a Model A Ford as archaic as its owner. In view of the man's income, Franklin thought, his hanging on to the thing was one more oddity, an item that could be added to many others to help prove Klibben's case. At Farmington, too, they took on a cook and general helper. Dr. Hillebrand's work was generously financed, quite apart from what went into it from his own earnings.

The party bounced over the horrifying road past the Four Corners and around the north end of Beautiful Mountain, into the Chinlee Valley, then southward and westward until, after having taken a day and a half to drive about two hundred miles, they reached the cliffs against which stood Painted Mask Ruin. The principal aim of the current summer's work was to excavate the decorated kiva in detail, test another kiva, and make further, standard excavations in the ruin as a whole.

By the end of a week, the work was going nicely. Dr. Hillebrand put Franklin, as the senior scientist under him, in charge of the work in the painted kiva. Franklin knew perfectly well that he was deficient in the required techniques; he would, in fact, be dependent upon his first assistant, Philip Fleming, who was just short of his Ph.D. Fleming had worked in that kiva the previous season, had spent three earlier seasons with Dr. Hillebrand, and was regarded by him as the most promising of the many who had worked under him. There was real affection between the two men.

Two of the other graduate students were well qualified to run a simple dig for themselves. One was put in charge of the untouched second kiva, the other of a trench cutting into the general mass of the ruin from the north. Franklin felt uncomfortably supernumerary, but he recognized that that was an advantage in pursuing his main purpose of keeping a close watch on the expedition's director.

After supper on the evening of the eighth day, Dr. Hillebrand announced rather shyly that he would be gone for about four days, "to follow an old custom you all know about." The younger men smiled. Franklin kept a blank face to cover his quickened interest.

This was a famous, or notorious, eccentricity of the old man's, and one in which Drs. Klibben, McDonnell, and the rest put great hope. Every year, early in the season, Dr. Hillebrand went alone to a ruin he had excavated early in his career. There was some uncertainty as to just where the ruin was; it was believed to be one known to the Navajos as Tsekaiye Kin. No one knew what he did there. He said he found the surroundings and the solitude invaluable for thinking out the task in hand. It was usually not long after his return from it that he would announce his decision to dig in such-and-such a spot, and proceed to uncover the painted kiva, or the Kettle Cave fetishes, or the Kin Hatsosi blanket, or some other notable find.

If Franklin could slip away in the station wagon and follow the old man, he might get just the information he wanted. So far, Dr. Hillebrand's activities on the expedition had evidenced nothing but his great competence. If the old

Social Organization—Kinship and Groups

man ever performed mad antique rites with stolen specimens, it would be at his secret place of meditation. Perhaps he got up and danced to the ancient gods. One might be able to sneak a photo . . .

Dr. Hillebrand said, "I shan't be gone long. Meantime, of course, Dr. Franklin will be in charge." He turned directly to his junior. "George, there are several things on which you must keep a close watch. If you will look at these diagrams—and you, too, Phil . . ."

Franklin and Fleming sat down beside him. Dr. Hillebrand expounded. Whether the ancient devil had done it intentionally or not, Franklin saw that he was neatly hooked. In the face of the delicacy and the probable outcome of the next few days' work, he could not possibly make an excuse for absenting himself when the head of the expedition was also absent.

Dr. Hillebrand took off early the next morning in his throbbing Model A. He carried with him a Spartan minimum of food and bedding. It was good to be alone once more in the long-loved reaches of the Navajo country. The car drove well. He still used it because, short of a jeep, nothing newer had the clearance to take him where he wanted to go.

He drove slowly, for he was at the age when knowledge and skill must replace strength, and getting stuck would be serious. When he was fifty, he reflected, he would have reached T'iiz Hatsosi Canyon from this year's camp in under four hours; when he was thirty, if it had been possible to travel this country in a car, he would have made even greater speed, and as like as not ended by getting lost. He reached the open farming area outside the place where T'iiz Hatsosi sliced into the great mesa to the south. There were nearly twice as many hogans to be seen as when he had first come here; several of them were square and equipped with windows, and by some of them cars were parked. Everything was changing, but these were good people still, although not as genial and hospitable as their grandparents had been when he first packed in.

He entered the narrow mouth of T'iiz Hatsosi Canyon in the late afternoon, and by the exercise of consummate skill drove some four miles up it. At that point, it was somewhat wider than elsewhere, slightly under two hundred feet across at the bottom. The heavy grazing that had so damaged all the Navajos' land had had some effect here. There was less grass than there used to be—but then, he reflected, he had no horses to graze—and the bed of the wash was more deeply eroded, and here and there sharp gullies led into it from the sides.

Still, the cottonwoods grew between the occasional stream and the high, warmly golden-buff cliffs. Except at noon, there was shade, and the quality of privacy, almost of secrecy, remained. In the west wall was the wide strip of white rocks from which the little ruin took its name, Tsekaiye Kin, leading the eye to the long ledge above which the cliff arched like a scallop shell, and upon which stood the ancient habitations. The lip of the ledge was about twenty feet above the level of the canyon, and approachable by a talus slope that was not too hard to negotiate. Some small evergreens grew at the corners of the ledge. From the ground, the settlement did not seem as if it had been empty for centuries, but rather as if its occupants at the moment happened not to be visible. The small black rectangles of doorways and three tiny squares of windows made him feel, as they had done over forty years ago, as if the little settlement were watching him.

South of the far end of the ledge, and at the level of the canyon floor, was the spring. Water seeped richly through a crack in the rock a few feet above the ground and flowed down over rock to form a pool at the base. The wet golden-brown stone glistened; small water growths clung to crevices. In the pool itself, there was cress, and around it moss and grass rich enough to make a few feet of turf.

Here Dr. Hillebrand deposited his bedroll and his food. He estimated that he had better than two hours of daylight left. He cut himself a supply of firewood. Then he took a package out of his coffeepot. The package was wrapped in an old piece of buckskin. With this in hand, he climbed up the slope to the ruin.

The sense of peace had begun once he was out of sight of the camp at Painted Mask Ruin. It had grown when he entered T'iiz Hatsosi Canyon; it had become stronger when he stepped out of the car and glimpsed through the cottonwoods his little village, with its fourteen rooms. By the spring, it had become stronger yet, and mixed with a nostalgia of past times that was sweetly painful, like a memory of an old and good lost love. These feelings were set aside as he addressed himself to the task of climbing, which was not entirely simple; then they returned fourfold when he was in the ruin. Here he had worked alone, a green young man with a shiny new Doctor's degree, a boy-man not unlike young Fleming. Here he had discovered what it was to like to step into a room that still had its roof intact, and see the marks of the smoke from the household fire, the loom ties still in place in the ceiling and floor, the broken cooking pot still in the corner.

He paid his respects to that chamber—Room 4-B; stood in the small, open, central area; then went to the roofless, irregular oval of the kiva. All by himself he had dug it out.

Could Dr. Franklin have been there then, spying unseen, he would have been most happy. From under a stone that appeared firmly embedded in the clay flooring Dr. Hillebrand took an ancient, crude stone pipe fitted with a recent willow stem. He filled it with tobacco, performed curious motions as he lit it, and puffed smoke in the six directions. Then he climbed out of the kiva on the inner side, and went behind the double row of habitations, to the darker area under the convex curve of the wall at the back of the cave, the floor of which was a mixture of earth and rubbish. Two smallish, rounded stones about three feet apart inconspicuously marked a place. Sitting by it on a convenient ledge of rock, he puffed at the pipe again; then he opened the buckskin package and proceeded to make an offering of ancient turquoise beads, white and red shell, black stone, feathers and down, and corn pollen.

Sitting back comfortably, he said, "Well, here I am again."

The answer did not come from the ground, in which the bones of the speaker reposed, but from a point in space, as if he were sitting opposite Dr. Hillebrand. "Welcome, old friend. Thank you for the gifts; their smell is pleasing to us all."

"I don't know whether I can bring you any more," the archeologist said. "I can buy new things, of course, but getting the old ones is becoming difficult. They are watching me."

"It is not necessary," the voice answered. "We are rich in the spirits of things such as these, and our grandchildren on earth still offer them to us. It has been rather for your benefit that I have had you bringing them, and I think that that training has served its purpose."

"You relieve me." Then, with a note of anxiety, "That doesn't mean that I have to stop visiting you?"

"Not at all. And, by the way, there is a very handsome jar with a quantity of beans of an early variety in it where you are digging now. It was left behind by accident when the people before the ones who built the painted kiva moved out. It belonged to a woman called Bluebird Tailfeather. Her small child ran off and was lost just as they were moving, and by the time she found him, the war chief was impatient. However, we can come back to that later. I can see that you have something on your mind."

"I'm lonely," Dr. Hillebrand said simply. "My real friends are all gone. There are a lot of people I get on nicely with, but no one left I love—that is, above the ground—and you are the only one below the ground I seem to be able to reach. I—I'd like to take your remains back with me, and then we could talk nights."

"I would not like that."

"Then of course I won't."

"I was sure of that. Your country is strange to me, and travelling back and forth would be a lot of effort. What I saw that time I visited you was alien to me; it would be to you, too, I think. It won't be long, I believe, before I am relieved of attachment to my bones entirely, but if you moved them now, it would be annoying. You take that burial you carried home ten years ago—old Rabbit Stick. He says you treat him well and have given him the smell of ceremonial jewels whenever you could, but sometimes he arrives quite worn out from his journey."

"Rabbit Stick," Dr. Hillebrand mused. "I wondered if there were not someone there. He has never spoken to me."

"He couldn't. He was just an ordinary Reed Clan man. But he is grateful to you for the offerings, because they have given him the strength he needed. As you know, I can speak with you because I was the Sun's Forehead, and there was the good luck that you were thinking and feeling in the right way when you approached me. But tell me, don't the young men who learn from you keep you company?"

"Yes. There is one now who is like a son to me. But then they have learned, and they go away. The men in between, who have become chiefs, you might say, in my Department, have no use for me. They want to make me emeritus—that is, put me on a pension, take over my authority and my rewards, and set me where I could give advice and they could ignore it. They have new ways, and they despise mine. So now they are watching me. They have sent a young man out this time just to watch me. They call him a student of the ways of your grandchildren; he spent six weeks at Zuñi once, and when even he could see that the people didn't like him, he went and put in the rest of the summer at Oraibi."

"New Oraibi or Old Oraibi?" the Sun's Forehead asked.

"New Oraibi."

The chief snorted.

"So, having also read some books, he thinks he is an ethnographer, only he calls himself a cultural anthropologist. And he is out here to try to find proof that my mind is failing." He smiled. "They'd certainly think so if they saw me sitting here talking to empty air."

The Sun's Forehead chuckled.

"They certainly would. They wouldn't be able to hear me, you know." Then his voice became serious again. "That always happens, I think. It happened to me. They wanted to do things differently, when I had at last come to the point at which an Old Man talked to me. I reached it in old age—not young, as you did. They could not take my title, but they wanted to handle my duties for me, bring me enough food to live on, hear my advice and not listen to it. Struggling against them became wearying and distasteful, so finally I decided to go under. At the age I had reached—about your age—it is easy to do."

"And now you say that you are about to be detached from your bones entirely? You are reaching the next stage?"

"Let us say that I begin to hope. Our life is beautiful, but for a hundred years or so now I have been longing for the next, and I begin to hope."

"How does it happen? Or is it wrong for me to know?"

"You may know. You are good, and you keep your secrets, as our wise men always did. You will see a man who has become young, handsome, and full of light. When we dance, he dances with great beauty; his singing is beautiful, and you feel as if it were creating life. Then one time when the katchinas themselves are dancing before us—not masks, you understand, the katchinas themselves—you can't find him among the watchers. Then you seem to recognize him, there among the sacred people, dancing like them. Then you think that the next time our grandchildren on earth put on the masks and dance, that one, whom you knew as a spirit striving to purify himself, who used to tell you about his days on the earth, will be there. With his own eyes he will see our grandchildren and bless them." The chief's voice trailed off, as though the longing for what he was describing deprived him of words.

"To see the katchinas themselves dancing," Dr. Hillebrand mused. "Not the masks, but what the masks stand for . . . That would keep me happy for centuries. But then, I could not join your people. I was never initiated. I'd be plain silly trying to dance with them. It's not for me."

"For over forty years I have been initiating you," the Sun's Forehead said. "As for dancing—you will no longer be in that old body. You will not be dancing with those fragile, rheumatic bones. There is room for you in our country. Why don't you come over? Just lie down in that crevice back there and make up your mind."

"You know," Dr. Hillebrand said, "I think I will."

Both the Kleinman Professor of American Archeology and the spirit who once had been the Sun's Forehead for the settlements in the neighborhood of T'iiz Hatsosi were thoroughly unworldly. It had not occurred to either of them that within six days after Dr. Hillebrand had left camp Dr. George Franklin would organize a search for him, and that four days later his body would be found where he had died of, apparently, heart failure. Above all, it had not occurred to them that his body would be taken home and buried with proper pomp in the appropriate cemetery. (But Philip Fleming, close to tears, resolutely overlooked the scattering of turquoise and shell in the rubbish between the crevice and the kiva.)

Dr. Hillebrand found himself among people as alien to him as they had been to the Sun's Forehead. They seemed to be gaunt from the total lack of offerings, and the means by which they should purify and advance themselves to where they could leave this life for the next, which he believed to be the final one, were confused. He realized that his spirit was burdened with much dross, and that it would be a long time before he could gather the strength to attempt a journey to the country of his friend.

His portrait, in academic gown and hood, was painted posthumously and hung in the entrance of the museum, to one side of the stela from Quiriguá and facing the reproduction of the famous Painted Kiva mural. Dr. Klibben adroitly handled the promotions and emoluments that fell under his control. Philip Fleming won his Ph.D. with honor, and was promptly offered a splendid position at Harvard. Moved by he knew not what drive, and following one or two other actions he had performed to his own surprise, Fleming went to Dr. Hillebrand's grave, for a gesture of respect and thanks.

It had seemed to him inappropriate to bring any flowers. Instead, as he sat by the grave, with small motions of his hands he sprinkled over it some bits of turquoise and shell he had held out from a necklace he had unearthed, and followed them with a pinch of pollen given him by a Navajo. Suddenly his face registered utter astonishment; then careful listening.

The following season, Fleming returned to Painted Mask Ruin by agreement with Dr. Klibben, who was delighted to get his Department entirely out of Southwestern archeology. There he ran a trench that led right into a magnificent polychrome pot containing a store of beans of high botanical interest.

Within a few years, he stopped visiting the grave, but he was sentimentalist enough to make a pilgrimage all alone to Tsekaiye Kin at the beginning of each field season. It was jokingly said among his confreres that there he communed with the spirit of old Hillebrand. Certainly he seemed to have inherited that legendary figure's gift for making spectacular finds.

PART FOUR

POLITICS, GOVERNMENT, AND LAW

An orderly social life is a rather astonishing achievement. It requires mechanisms that induce members of a society to keep their actions within well-defined limits. In contrast to other social animals, man has the potential for a wide range of behavior patterns. What each person *can* do is enormous when compared with what each *must* do as a member of a functioning society. Enculturation brings about some conformity; informal social pressures, rewards of recognition and praise, or sanctions of ridicule and criticism—these and other experiences remind us to behave in appropriate ways. Religious rituals and secular ceremonies of all kinds reinforce our common values and standards.

But the potential for disruptive behavior always lies just beneath the surface of every society. No culture satisfies the needs of all persons equally: cultural values are often contradictory, creating frustration and hostility; misunderstandings occur even when interacting parties believe they are living up to cultural expectations. People disagree on the allocation of scarce resources and the goals that should be jointly pursued. Disruptive behavior does occur in all societies, and conflict is a recurrent feature of social life. Resolving conflict and controlling disruptive behavior are the chief functions of politics, government, and law. These institutions have various forms in the world's many cultures; the purpose of each is to maintain order within the group.

Political systems allocate authority to make decisions and enforce laws. Legitimate authority may be based on age, inheritance, appointment, election, contest, charisma, religious sanction, or some other principle. The means of constituting legitimate authority in one society would often be considered illegitimate by members of another culture. Every political system is composed of various roles. Sometimes these are imbedded in the kinship system so that the father, eldest brother, or mother's brother is the political leader because of his kinship status. In some societies, political roles are closely linked to the religious system; in others, the roles may be specialized and distinct from other sectors of social life.

Law, in a cross-cultural sense, involves legitimate procedures for settling disputes and the allocation of power to enforce the settlement. Law means that individuals in a society can expect these procedures to take place when disputes occur. Many times they are informal, without written legal codes or courtrooms. In large pluralistic societies not all persons are treated in the same way under the law; the conflicts that arise from this situation are amply illustrated in the following selections. The ethnographer in the field must be alert to political and legal events because they are often enmeshed in other institutions such as religion or kinship.

THE SCAPEGOAT

The law is usually supposed to be a stern mistress, not to be lightly wooed, and yielding only to the most ardent pursuit. But even law, like love, sits more easily on some natures than on others.

This was the case with Mr. Robinson Asbury. Mr. Asbury had started life as a bootblack in the growing town of Cadgers. From this he had risen one step and become porter and messenger in a barbershop. This rise fired his ambition, and he was not content until he had learned to use the shears and the razor and had a chair of his own. From this, in a man of Robinson's temperament, it was only a step to a shop of his own, and he placed it where it would do the most good.

Fully one-half of the population of Cadgers was composed of Negroes, and with their usual tendency to colonize, a tendency encouraged, and in fact compelled, by circumstances, they had gathered into one part of the town. Here in alleys, and streets as dirty and hardly wider, they thronged like ants.

It was in this place that Mr. Asbury set up his shop, and he won the hearts of his prospective customers by putting up the significant sign, "Equal Rights Barbershop." This legend was quite unnecessary, because there was only one race about, to patronize the place. But it was a delicate sop to the people's vanity, and it served its purpose.

Asbury came to be known as a clever fellow, and his business grew. The shop really became a sort of club and, on Saturday nights especially, was the gathering-place of the men of the whole Negro quarter. He kept the illustrated and race journals there, and those who cared neither to talk nor listen to someone else might see pictured the doings of high society in very short skirts or read in the Negro papers how Miss Boston had entertained Miss Blueford to tea on such and such an afternoon. Also, he kept the policy returns, which was wise, if not moral.

It was his wisdom rather more than his morality that made the party managers after a while cast their glances towards him as a man who might be useful to their interests. It would be well to have a man—a shrewd, powerful man—down in that part of the town who could carry his people's vote in his vest pocket, and who at any time its delivery might be needed, could hand it

From *The Best Stories of Paul Laurence Dunbar*, edited by Benjamin Brawley. Reprinted by permission of Dodd, Mead & Company, Inc.

over without hesitation. Asbury seemed that man, and they settled upon him. They gave him money, and they gave him power and patronage. He took it all silently and he carried out his bargain faithfully. His hands and his lips alike closed tightly when there was anything within them. It was not long before he found himself the big Negro of the district and, of necessity, of the town. The time came when, at a critical moment, the managers saw that they had not reckoned without their host in choosing this barber of the black district as the leader of his people.

Now, so much success must have satisfied any other man. But in many ways Mr. Asbury was unique. For a long time he himself had done very little shaving—except of notes, to keep his hand in. His time had been otherwise employed. In the evening hours he had been wooing the coquettish Dame Law, and wonderful to say, she had yielded easily to his advances.

It was against the advice of his friends that he asked for admission to the bar. They felt that he could do more good in the place where he was.

"You see, Robinson," said old Judge Davis, "it's just like this: If you're not admitted, it'll hurt you with the people; if you are admitted, you'll move uptown to an office and get out of touch with them."

Asbury smiled an inscrutable smile. Then he whispered something into the judge's ear that made the old man wrinkle from his neck up with appreciative smiles.

"Asbury," he said, "you are—you are—well, you ought to be white, that's all. When we find a black man like you we send him to State's prison. If you were white, you'd go to the Senate."

The Negro laughed confidently.

He was admitted to the bar soon after, whether by merit or by connivance is not to be told.

"Now he will move uptown," said the black community. "Well, that's the way with a colored man when he gets a start."

But they did not know Robinson Asbury yet. He was a man of surprises, and they were destined to disappointment. He did not move uptown. He built an office in a small open space next to his shop, and there hung out his shingle.

"I will never desert the people who have done so much to elevate me," said Mr. Asbury. "I will live among them and I will die among them."

This was a strong card for the barber-lawyer. The people seized upon the statement as expressing a nobility of an altogether unique brand.

They held a mass meeting and endorsed him. They made resolutions that extolled him, and the Negro band came around and serenaded him, playing various things in varied time.

All this was very sweet to Mr. Asbury, and the party managers chuckled with satisfaction and said, "That Asbury, that Asbury!"

Now there is a fable extant of a man who tried to please everybody, and his failure is a matter of record. Robinson Asbury was not more successful. But be it said that his ill success was due to no fault or shortcoming of his.

Politics, Government, and Law

For a long time his growing power had been looked upon with disfavor by the colored law firm of Bingo & Latchett. Both Mr. Bingo and Mr. Latchett themselves aspired to be Negro leaders in Cadgers, and they were delivering Emancipation Day orations and riding at the head of processions when Mr. Asbury was blacking boots. Is it any wonder, then, that they viewed with alarm his sudden rise? They kept their counsel, however, and treated with him, for it was best. They allowed him his scope without open revolt until the day upon which he hung out his shingle. This was the last straw. They could stand no more. Asbury had stolen their other chances from them, and now he was poaching upon the last of their preserves. So Mr. Bingo and Mr. Latchett put their heads together to plan the downfall of their common enemy.

The plot was deep and embraced the formation of an opposing faction made up of the best Negroes of the town. It would have looked too much like what it was for the gentlemen to show themselves in the matter, and so they took into their confidence Mr. Isaac Morton, the principal of the colored school, and it was under his ostensible leadership that the new faction finally came into being.

Mr. Morton was really an innocent young man, and he had ideals which should never have been exposed to the air. When the wily confederates came to him with their plan he believed that his worth had been recognized, and at last he was to be what nature destined him for—a leader.

The better class of Negroes—by that is meant those who were particularly envious of Asbury's success—flocked to the new man's standard. But whether the race be white or black, political virtue is always in a minority, so Asbury could afford to smile at the force arrayed against him.

The new faction met together and resolved. They resolved, among other things, that Mr. Asbury was an enemy to his race and a menace to civilization. They decided that he should be abolished; but as they couldn't get out an injunction against him, and as he had the whole undignified but still voting black belt behind him, he went serenely on his way.

"They're after you hot and heavy, Asbury," said one of his friends to him.

"Oh, yes," was the reply, "they're after me, but after a while I'll get so far away that they'll be running in front."

"It's all the best people, they say."

"Yes. Well, it's good to be one of the best people, but your vote only counts one just the same."

The time came, however, when Mr. Asbury's theory was put to the test. The Cadgerites celebrated the first of January as Emancipation Day. On this day there was a large procession, with speechmaking in the afternoon and fireworks at night. It was the custom to concede the leadership of the colored people of the town to the man who managed to lead the procession. For two years past this honor had fallen, of course, to Robinson Asbury, and there had been no disposition on the part of anybody to try conclusions with him.

Mr. Morton's faction changed all this. When Asbury went to work to solicit contributions for the celebration, he suddenly became aware that he had a fight upon his hands. All the better-class Negroes were staying out of it. The next thing he knew was that plans were on foot for a rival demonstration.

"Oh," he said to himself, "that's it, is it? Well, if they want a fight they can have it."

He had a talk with the party managers, and he had another with Judge Davis.

"All I want is a little lift, Judge," he said, "and I'll make 'em think the sky has turned loose and is vomiting niggers."

The Judge believed that he could do it. So did the party managers. Asbury got his lift. Emancipation Day came.

There were two parades. At least, there was one parade and the shadow of another. Asbury's, however, was not the shadow. There was a great deal of substance about it—substance made up of many people, many banners, and numerous bands. He did not have the best people. Indeed among his cohorts there were a good many of the pronounced ragtag and bobtail. But he had noise and numbers. In such cases, nothing more is needed. The success of Asbury's side of the affair did everything to confirm his friends in their good opinion of him.

When he found himself defeated, Mr. Silas Bingo saw that it would be policy to placate his rival's just anger against him. He called upon him at his office the day after the celebration.

"Well, Asbury," he said, "you beat us, didn't you?"

"It wasn't a question of beating," said the other calmly. "It was only an inquiry as to who were the people—the few or the many."

"Well, it was well done, and you've shown that you are a manager. I confess that I haven't always thought that you were doing the wisest thing in living down here and catering to this class of people when you might, with your ability, be much more to the better class."

"What do they base their claims of being better on?"

"Oh, there ain't any use discussing that. We can't get along without you, we see that. So I, for one, have decided to work with you for harmony."

"Harmony. Yes, that's what we want."

"If I can do anything to help you at any time, why you have only to command me."

"I am glad to find such a friend in you. Be sure, if I ever need you, Bingo, I'll call on you."

"And I'll be ready to serve you."

Asbury smiled when his visitor was gone. He smiled, and knitted his brow. "I wonder what Bingo's got up his sleeve," he said. "He'll bear watching."

It may have been pride at his triumph, it may have been gratitude at his helpers, but Asbury went into the ensuing campaign with reckless enthusiasm. He did the most daring things for the party's sake. Bingo, true to his promise, was ever at his side ready to serve him. Finally, association and immunity made danger less fearsome; the rival no longer appeared a menace.

With the generosity born of obstacles overcome, Asbury determined to forgive Bingo and give him a chance. He let him in on a deal, and from that time they worked amicably together until the election came and passed.

It was a close election and many things had had to be done, but there were men there ready and waiting to do them. They were successful, and then the first cry of the defeated party was, as usual, "Fraud! Fraud!" The cry was taken up by the jealous, the disgruntled, and the virtuous.

Someone remembered how two years ago the registration books had been stolen. It was known upon good authority that money had been freely used. Men held up their hands in horror at the suggestion that the Negro vote had been juggled with, as if that were a new thing. From their pulpits ministers denounced the machine and bade their hearers rise and throw off the yoke of a corrupt municipal government. One of those sudden fevers of reform had taken possession of the town and threatened to destroy the successful party.

They began to look around them. They must purify themselves. They must give the people some tangible evidence of their own yearnings after purity. They looked around them for a sacrifice to lay upon the altar of municipal reform. Their eyes fell upon Mr. Bingo. No, he was not big enough. His blood was too scant to wash the political stains. Then they looked into each other's eyes and turned their gaze away to let it fall upon Mr. Asbury. They really hated to do it. But there must be a scapegoat. The god from the Machine commanded them to slay him.

Robinson Asbury was charged with many crimes—with all that he had committed and some that he had not. When Mr. Bingo saw what was afoot he threw himself heart and soul into the work of his old rival's enemies. He was of incalculable use to them.

Judge Davis refused to have anything to do with the matter. But in spite of his disapproval it went on. Asbury was indicted and tried. The evidence was all against him, and no one gave more damaging testimony than his friend Mr. Bingo. The judge's charge was favorable to the defendant, but the current of popular opinion could not be entirely stemmed. The jury brought in a verdict of guilty.

"Before I am sentenced, Judge, I have a statement to make to the court. It will take less than ten minutes."

"Go on, Robinson," said the judge kindly.

Asbury started, in a monotonous tone, a recital that brought the prosecuting attorney to his feet in a minute. The judge waved him down, and sat transfixed by a sort of fascinated horror as the convicted man went on. The before-mentioned attorney drew a knife and started for the prisoner's dock. With difficulty he was restrained. A dozen faces in the courtroom were red and pale by turns.

"He ought to be killed," whispered Mr. Bingo audibly.

Robinson Asbury looked at him and smiled, and then he told a few things of him. He gave the ins and outs of some of the misdemeanors of which he stood accused. He showed who were the men behind the throne. And still, pale and transfixed, Judge Davis waited for his own sentence.

Never were ten minutes so well taken up. It was a tale of rottenness and corruption in high places told simply and with the stamp of truth upon it.

He did not mention the judge's name. But he had torn the mask from the face of every other man who had been concerned in his downfall. They had shorn him of his strength, but they had forgotten that he was yet able to bring the roof and pillars tumbling about their heads.

The judge's voice shook as he pronounced sentence upon his old ally—a year in State's prison.

Some people said it was too light, but the judge knew what it was to wait for the sentence of doom, and he was grateful and sympathetic.

When the sheriff led Asbury away the judge hastened to have a short talk with him.

"I'm sorry, Robinson," he said, "and I want to tell you that you were no more guilty than the rest of us. But why did you spare me?"

"Because I knew you were my friend," answered the convict.

"I tried to be, but you were the first man that I've ever known since I've been in politics who ever gave me any decent return for friendship."

"I reckon you're about right, Judge."

In politics, party reform usually lies in making a scapegoat of someone who is only as criminal as the rest, but a little weaker. Asbury's friends and enemies had succeeded in making him bear the burden of all the party's crimes, but their reform was hardly a success, and their protestations of a change of heart were received with doubt. Already there were those who began to pity the victim and to say that he had been hardly dealt with.

Mr. Bingo was not of these; but he found, strange to say, that his opposition to the idea went but a little way, and that even with Asbury out of his path he was a smaller man than he was before. Fate was strong against him. His poor, prosperous humanity could not enter the lists against a martyr. Robinson Asbury was now a martyr.

II

A year is not a long time. It was short enough to prevent people from forgetting Robinson, and yet long enough for their pity to grow strong as they remembered. Indeed, he was not gone a year. Good behavior cut two months off the time of his sentence, and by the time people had come around to the notion that he was really the greatest and smartest man in Cadgers he was at home again.

He came back with no flourish of trumpets, but quietly, humbly. He went back again into the heart of the black district. His business had deteriorated during his absence, but he put new blood and new life into it. He did not go to work in the shop himself but, taking down the shingle that had swung idly before his office door during his imprisonment, he opened the little room as a news- and cigar-stand.

Here anxious, pitying customers came to him and he prospered again. He was very quiet. Uptown hardly knew that he was again in Cadgers, and it knew nothing whatever of his doings.

"I wonder why Asbury is so quiet," they said to one another. "It isn't like him to be quiet." And they felt vaguely uneasy about him.

So many people had begun to say, "Well, he was a mighty good fellow after all."

Mr. Bingo expressed the opinion that Asbury was quiet because he was crushed, but others expressed doubt as to this. There are calms and calms, some after and some before the storm. Which was this?

They waited a while, and, as no storm came, concluded that this must be the afterquiet. Bingo, reassured, volunteered to go and seek confirmation of this conclusion.

He went, and Asbury received him with an indifferent, not to say impolite, demeanor.

"Well, we're glad to see you back, Asbury," said Bingo patronizingly. He had variously demonstrated his inability to lead during his rival's absence and was proud of it. "What are you going to do?"

"I'm going to work."

"That's right. I reckon you'll stay out of politics."

"What could I do even if I went in?"

"Nothing now, of course; but I didn't know—"

He did not see the gleam in Asbury's half-shut eyes. He only marked his humility, and he went back swelling with the news.

"Completely crushed—all the run taken out of him," was his report.

The black district believed this, too, and a sullen, smouldering anger took possession of them. Here was a good man ruined. Some of the people whom he had helped in his former days—some of the rude, coarse people of the low quarter who were still sufficiently unenlightened to be grateful— talked among themselves and offered to get up a demonstration for him. But he denied them. No, he wanted nothing of the kind. It would only bring him into unfavorable notice. All he wanted was that they would always be his friends and would stick by him.

They would to the death.

There were again two factions in Cadgers. The schoolmaster could not forget how once on a time he had been made a tool of by Mr. Bingo. So he revolted against his rule and set himself up as the leader of an opposing clique. The fight had been long and strong, but had ended with odds slightly in Bingo's favor.

But Mr. Morton did not despair. As the first of January and Emancipation Day approached, he arrayed his hosts, and the fight for supremacy became fiercer than ever. The schoolteacher brought the schoolchildren in for chorus singing, secured an able orator, and the best essayist in town. With all this, he was formidable.

Mr. Bingo knew that he had the fight of his life on his hands, and he entered with fear as well as zest. He, too, found an orator, but he was not sure that he was good as Morton's. There was no doubt but that his essayist was not. He secured a band, but still he felt unsatisfied. He had hardly done enough, and for the schoolmaster to beat him now meant his political destruction.

It was in this state of mind that he was surprised to receive a visit from Mr. Asbury.

"I reckon you're surprised to see me here," said Asbury, smiling.

"I am pleased, I know." Bingo was astute.

"Well, I just dropped in on our business."

"To be sure, to be sure, Asbury. What can I do for you?"

"It's more what I can do for you that I came to talk about," was the reply.

"I don't believe I understand you."

"Well, it's plain enough. They say that the schoolteacher is giving you a pretty hard fight."

"Oh, not so hard."

"No man can be too sure of winning though. Mr. Morton once did me a mean turn when he started the faction against me."

Bingo's heart gave a great leap, and then stopped for the fraction of a second.

"You were in it, of course" pursued Asbury, "but I can look over your part in it in order to get even with the man who started it."

It was true, then, thought Bingo gladly. He did not know. He wanted revenge for his wrongs and upon the wrong man. How well the schemer had covered his tracks! Asbury should have his revenge and Morton would be the sufferer.

"Of course, Asbury, you know that I did what I did innocently."

"Oh, yes, in politics we are all lambs and the wolves are only to be found in the other party. We'll pass that, though. What I want to say is that I can help you to make your celebration an overwhelming success. I still have some influence down in my district."

"Certainly, and very justly, too. Why I should be delighted with your aid. I could give you a prominent position in the procession."

"I don't want it; I don't want to appear in this at all. All I want is revenge. You can have all the credit, but let me down my enemy."

Bingo was perfectly willing, and with their heads close together, they had a long and close consultation. When Asbury was gone, Mr. Bingo lay back in his chair and laughed. "I'm a slick duck," he said.

From that hour Mr. Bingo's cause began to take on the appearance of something very like a broom. More bands were hired. The interior of the

State was called upon and a more eloquent orator secured. The crowd hastened to array itself on the growing side.

With surprised eyes, the schoolmaster beheld the wonder of it, but he kept to his own purpose with dogged insistence, even when he saw that he could not turn aside the overwhelming defeat that threatened him. But in spite of his obstinacy, his hours were dark and bitter. Asbury worked like a mole, all underground, but he was indefatigable. Two days before the celebration time everything was perfected for the biggest demonstration that Cadgers had ever known. All the next day and night he was busy among his allies.

On the morning of the great day, Mr. Bingo, wonderfully caparisoned, rode down to the hall where the parade was to form. He was early. No one had yet come. In an hour a score of men all told had collected. Another hour passed, and no more had come. Then there smote upon his ear the sound of music. They were coming at last. Bringing his sword to his shoulder, he rode forward to the middle of the street. Ah, there they were. But—but—could he believe his eyes? They were going in another direction, and at their head rode—Morton! He gnashed his teeth in fury. He had been led into a trap and betrayed. The procession passing had been his—all his. He heard them cheering, and then, oh! climax of infidelity, he saw his own orator go past in a carriage, bowing and smiling to the crowd.

There was no doubting who had done this thing. The hand of Asbury was apparent in it. He must have known the truth all along, thought Bingo. His allies left him one by one for the other hall, and he rode home in a humiliation deeper than he had ever known before.

Asbury did not appear at the celebration. He was at his little newsstand all day.

In a day or two the defeated aspirant had further cause to curse his false friend. He found that not only had the people defected from him, but that the thing had been so adroitly managed that he appeared to be in fault, and three-fourths of those who knew him were angry at some supposed grievance. His cup of bitterness was full when his partner, a quietly ambitious man, suggested that they dissolve their relations.

His ruin was complete.

The lawyer was not alone in seeing Asbury's hand in his downfall. The party managers saw it too, and they met together to discuss the dangerous factor which, while it appeared to slumber, was so terribly awake. They decided that he must be appeased, and they visited him.

He was still busy at his newsstand. They talked to him adroitly, while he sorted papers and kept an impassive face. When they were all done, he looked up for a moment and replied, "You know, gentlemen, as an ex-convict I am not in politics."

Some of them had the grace to flush.

"But you can use your influence," they said.

"I am not in politics," was his only reply.

And the spring elections were coming on. Well, they worked hard, and he showed no sign. He treated with neither one party nor the other. "Perhaps," thought the managers, "he is out of politics," and they grew more confident.

It was nearing eleven o'clock on the morning of election when a cloud no bigger than a man's hand appeared upon the horizon. It came from the direction of the black district. It grew, and the managers of the party in power looked at it, fascinated by an ominous dread. Finally it began to rain Negro voters, and as one man they voted against their former candidates. Their organization was perfect. They simply came, voted, and left, but they overwhelmed everything. Not one of the party that had damned Robinson Asbury was left in power save old Judge Davis. His majority was overwhelming.

The generalship that had engineered the thing was perfect. There were loud threats against the newsdealer. But no one bothered him except a reporter. The reporter called to see just how it was done. He found Asbury very busy sorting papers. To the newspaperman's questions he had only this reply, "I am not in politics, sir."

But Cadgers had learned its lesson.

CHAPTER 21   CARTER WILSON

THE PRESIDENT

The President wandered onto the porch of the Cabildo. He was tempted to go down to the other end and have a look at the killer, but he put this off.

The office was empty, except for the red and green chairs, the oilcloth-covered tables, the paraphernalia of the village Secretary, Don Concepción—carbon paper, typewriter, reports. From their frames the great men of Mexico stared down at the President. Hidalgo, Juárez, Díaz, Cárdenas, López Mateos and the others. He went and looked again at the photograph of López Mateos, the only one of these men he knew.

They had met that great fiesta day the National President came to visit the village. López Mateos had given the President his big beefy hand and said, "So you are a President too. It's hard work, isn't it?" Everyone laughed. Then López Mateos had said, "I like your village." A polite thing to say, nothing more. But it had struck the President. For the moment he felt that this was his village, and whatever came of it was his work.

Don Concepción came in from his house next door, talking to himself. The Secretary was old, bald, squat and flabby, his face was a brown Saint Bernard's with four or five folds of chin, and he looked out at the world over rimless and useless spectacles. He wasn't an Indian but he could speak Tzotzil, the Indian language, in a graveled, halting voice. He typed the village's correspondence with painful slowness, and he was respectful to the President as he said good morning.

Don Concepción totally lacked ambition and had whiled away his eighteen years of servitude by planting eighteen babies, one a year, in the belly of his half-Indian wife. Many of the offspring still lived with their father in his house behind the government building.

The President told Don Concepción about the murder and the surprising fact that the murderer was the man's son. Then he took out a cigarette, and Don Concepción asked if he might borrow one. The President did not usually give away his cigarettes as other Indians did, but he sometimes lent them to Don Concepción.

The old clock on the wall with its weights and ornate face beat away the minutes. The President sucked the smoke of his cigarette. Outside he could hear the officials who had come for the morning's work. They talked among themselves, joking a little, but when he came outside they grew quiet.

He knew them, but still they fell silent before him. After a month they did not know what he thought. Just as well. These men were not his companions, they touched his life only at the edges. At the end of the year, in December, they would begin packing up their households in the village, their sons would come to help take their possessions home. Then at the New Year each of them would get drunk for a last time, and early some morning disappear, back to his hamlet. After the proper ceremonies a new sea of old faces would appear, and take on the names of the ones who disappeared. Gobernador, Alcalde, Síndico. There were sixty titles for the President to attach to new men. He found it more difficult to do each year.

Though it was early there were people waiting for him, so the President went to the cement bench in the courtyard. He sat in the middle and the officials shook his hand, one light pass, before each took his seat on the bench. Some tilted the brims of their hats down to keep out the sun.

An old woman sat waiting in the courtyard, pulling her shawl tight around her face. A young girl with a crying baby sat beside the woman. Near them, but separate, was a group of men and their own wives.

The old woman, unsure of herself, got up, came to the President and knelt before him. The girl with the baby followed. The President gave his hand for the woman to touch, and then rested his hand briefly on the girl's bowed head.

The old woman began, begging pardon for bothering the President, but her daughter (she barely indicated the girl with a turn of her head) had been wronged by her husband, after only a year of marriage.

The President sighed and threw his cigarette out on the grass. He knew all that would happen, but he had to ask where the husband was. The old woman nodded toward the group of men. The President called them and they came. The men touched the President's hand, touched the hands of the other officials, bowing to the oldest. They were as embarrassed and uncomfortable as the old woman. People from the hamlets were always uneasy when they brought cases to the President. These had been walking since daybreak, two silent groups, neither speaking to the other on the path. But now in the village, before the eminence of the President, they did not show their anger. They stared at the ground, the men standing, the women sitting.

The President asked again, and the old woman elaborated her story, weaving in the bright details as though she were making the fringe of a tunic. Her hands fumbled with stones on the ground.

Her husband is dead, she lives on little. When the boy came to ask for her daughter, she didn't want to, but she let them marry. Yes, the boy brought the wedding gifts. He brought liquor, bananas. He brought bread, meat, cigarettes which she gave away to her brother. Yes, the girl was happy to marry him, and they went away to live in the house of the boy's father. Within a few months the boy had a little piece of land and built a house of his own. The girl had a baby. Then for no reason the husband went home to his father's house, leaving the girl alone. She had no corn to make tortillas, she had no beans to eat, no vegetables, no greens. She came home to her mother's house. Now the boy was petitioning for another girl who lived nearby. He would not give his wife the things to eat, or for the baby. And the old woman herself is poor, she has only enough food for herself.

The President lit another cigarette, crossed his legs and spat on the ground. Other officials had come and crowded onto the cement bench. Some of the scribes, the young officials, arrived and leaned over the back of the bench, talking to each other. Like the buzz of flies.

"And why did the husband go home?" the President asked the old woman.

She shook her head, and dropped her shawl. She did not know. The boy just did it.

The husband began to laugh to himself, and then his own father laughed. When the old woman looked up at them, her eyes betrayed her bitterness.

Hearing laughter, the baby laughed, and its mother pulled her shawl over its face. She hoped it would go to sleep.

"President," the husband said, "that old woman knows why I went home. Everyone knows. I told them all. The girl does not know how to sleep with me. It's true, she doesn't."

The laughter began with the scribes. They punched one another and hooted. The officials chuckled, bobbing in their seats. The President himself enjoyed the joke and he looked at the husband to be sure it was a joke. But the boy's face was blank, his eyes were wide with his own excitement. His smile was deceptive, so the President found no clue to the truth.

"Let her watch sheep to learn," called one of the scribes to another.

"Let her come watch you and your wife," said the other, and the laughter came in new waves.

"All right." The President cleared his throat, and his leg bounced with impatience. The joke was not as good as that. "Then where does the baby come from? Isn't it yours?"

He pointed at the child, now almost asleep, just a bulge in his mother's shawl. The girl kept her eyes cast down, as though she were carefully examining the flies eating the President's spittle.

The father of the husband came forward. He pulled out a pack of cigarettes and offered one to the President. The President accepted, putting the cigarette in his own pack. "President," said the man, "it is not the boy's child. It was some stranger who came and stayed at her house. A man she knew, my son did not know him."

"How old is your son?"

"I don't know. Maybe sixteen, maybe seventeen."

"Maybe," said the President deliberately, "it is your son who does not know how to sleep with a woman." He himself began the laughter now, and he let it run up and down the bench.

The old woman was temporarily satisfied. She laughed and said "Huh!" Even the girl smiled, though she hid it behind her shawl.

"Here, take the boy to San Martín. Take him to the White Bridge," one of the scribes called out. The other scribes laughed again. The White Bridge in town was the place for prostitutes. Some of them, the old ones, would sleep with Indians.

"Let him spend the night in your house," said another scribe.

The boy in question came to the President and bowed. The President released him, and the boy said he *did* know how to sleep with women. But there was the stranger. His wife said the man was her brother, but the husband did not believe it.

"Then the child is not yours?" the President asked.

"Yes, it is my child."

The officials stirred and whispered to one another, their interest in the case renewed.

"My father doesn't know. It is my child. Not that my wife doesn't know how to sleep with a man, but she doesn't know how to make tortillas, she doesn't know how to make my food, how to make my clothes. I had to go home or I would have starved."

The old woman crept closer to the President. She said that none of the accusations was true. The daughter knew how to cook, and to spin. The daughter had made that very tunic for the boy.

"Let's see," the President said, beckoning the boy to him. The tunic was a thick one, good wool, with wide-spaced pink and green stripes and good long fringe at the bottom. He asked the daughter if she made this. He spoke kindly since tears were rolling down the girl's dirty cheeks. Muffling her voice with the shawl, the girl said she made the tunic.

"My mother made it. That girl does not even know how to weave!" said the boy, pulling away from the President. The President asked, and the boy's mother also claimed that she made the tunic.

They had reached an impasse, and the President was bored. Each side would now repeat its story over and over. Finally the President would make a decision which would satisfy no one, least of all himself, because he did not trust his own judgment. Whenever a case was brought to him he hoped there would be a single shaded path for him, one answer to each of his questions, and a single judgment so clear the others would see it coming before he even said the words.

The President only half listened. The boy's mother was telling how she took the wool from her own sheep to make him the tunic, because he came home from his married life almost in rags. And thin, for he had barely eaten.

The wife was crying, or perhaps it was the baby who cried. Yes, it was the baby, for the girl slipped her hand into the slit under the arm of her blouse and pushed the nipple into the baby's face. The baby refused and the girl squeezed a little until her nipple was softened and wet. Finally the crying stopped.

The other officials were quiet, staring at their feet, swatting flies, dozing off to sleep. Some of the scribes drifted away uninterested. Or they began to play, pushing into each other, joking.

All of the people from the hamlet talked at once. The President told them several times to shut up. The others did eventually, but the boy's mother continued her high singsong complaint.

"Shut up!" said the President vehemently. The old woman did. "Now then," he continued, "the boy is unsatisfied with his wife. She does not know how to cook his food, weave his clothes. So he goes home, and now is petitioning for a new wife. Well. He can do that."

The officials were awake and attentive. The President wondered why they cared. They had heard the same case, the same judgment many times.

The boy in question smiled at his father. The old woman had stopped fumbling with stones. She listened carefully.

The girl's shawl had fallen from her head. The baby lay exposed to the sun and untended. Soon, thought the President, it will begin squalling again. The girl was drawing breath heavily. Well, the President thought, looking at the two women, they probably tell the truth. They were dirty. No one had denied the old woman's husband was dead. The baby's hair was long and matted. Crusted with a scabby kind of dirt on his forehead, from sitting too close to the fire unwatched.

"But—but—" said the President loudly, waving his finger in the air, bobbing his foot, addressing the line of officials seated on either side of him, "but the girl has nothing to eat. Her mother cannot give her corn, or even beans. Someone must pay or she will starve."

Several officials nodded wisely in agreement.

"So the husband must provide for her. How much?" the President asked, turning to the officials beside him.

He did not know himself. He took out a notebook and a ballpoint pen, found a clean page, and played with figures for a moment. The figures were meaningless, but they gave him time enough to think. "A hundred and fifty pesos."

The old woman had hidden her despair, but now she could not hide her elation. She crawled to him and bowed her head for his touch. He released her. The girl did not seem affected, and she continued to breathe heavily. The son's smile was gone.

"But President, I'm a young man. I don't have that money. I don't have land, I don't grow much corn."

"Maybe you should not marry so soon again then," said the President. He had expected the storm from the boy's side, and waited for it to descend on him. When they began shouting he stared at his notebook and continued writing numbers. Sometimes his writing silenced people from the hamlets, and made them afraid.

Jacinto always brought his truck into the village slowly, almost grandly. Though the road was good, Jacinto took his time, riding the clutch in low gear.

The Maestro gave up his trip to the jail and went out into the sun to see who the magnificent new truck would deposit in front of Jacinto's store.

Jacinto had reached the bottom of the hill and now came up over a little rise into the plaza. He always put on speed to do this, and then had to slam on the brakes in front of his store. It was a flourish, a bit of bravura like a flashy signature.

The officials were standing to look out over the plaza from behind their cement bench, soldiers at a rampart. Even the President was interested. He saw Jacinto leap out of the cab and greet Eliseo, who always waited in front of the store. Then Jacinto strutted around to the red nose of his truck, threw open the hood and inspected his engine.

He was always cocky, thought the President, in his Mexican clothes with tennis shoes and a baseball cap, and always wearing the smile of a proud dishonest child on his round smiling face.

At the back end of the truck Jacinto's helper, Antun, jumped down and pulled out a ladder. Antun wore Mexican clothes also, but was not so proud. He didn't strut when he walked. An Indian came down the ladder first, carrying a white satchel. Then came three Mexican boys, who lit cigarettes as soon as they reached the ground, and who seemed from a distance to be reluctant to pay Antun the peso apiece they owed him for the ride. When they had finally handed over the money, they started walking toward the Cabildo, heads bent together in secret conversation.

The last passenger in the back of the truck was a young-looking Indian woman. Antun helped her down and then scrambled into the truck to bring out her belongings. She had a lot of them—a wooden box, two or three burlap bags, and finally a pure white lamb with its feet tied together. Antun carried each of these possessions to the door of the store beside Jacinto's.

Jacinto climbed down from the front end of the truck and went to open the cab door for his other rider. The man who got out was an Indian, but tall for an Indian. He wore Indian clothes, but the clothes, the hat, even the leather bag were all clean, new. He spoke briefly to Jacinto and to Antun, who did not try to collect his peso from the man. Then, going to the ramshackle store where the woman waited, the man unlocked the door and disappeared inside. The woman lugged the bundles inside and closed the door after her.

The officials buzzed, heads bent so that hats almost touched. The scribes, in their different, more confident way, made jokes. The Maestro was not quite sure why.

"Who's that?" he asked Mario.

"Juan Lopez Oso has come back," Mario said, and then laughed. "With his woman."

"What's funny about that?"

"Well, she's not the same woman Oso had before he went away."

The Maestro laughed too, and then Mario excused himself, and loped off across the plaza toward the church. The Maestro could hear a rising hubbub of young voices coming from his school and went to contend with disorder.

One of the scribes who spoke Spanish met the three Mexican boys when they came onto the porch.

"Where's the man in charge?" demanded one of the boys.

"The President is there," the scribe said, nodding toward the bench in the courtyard. All the officials and the President were watching.

"Not the fucking Indian, where's the Secretary?"

The President pretended he had not heard this, and the scribe, still smiling, went to bring Don Concepción, who led the boys into the cool office. There they lit new cigarettes and gave one to the Secretary, and then they explained how the blackhearted Indians had stolen a mule they brought to sell a week ago during the fiesta of San Sebastián.

When Don Concepción gave no promises to see that justice was done them, that their mule would be returned, they offered him twenty pesos in crumpled bills if he would retrieve their stolen property. Don Concepción eyed their money over his glasses, then looked at their flushed faces one by one to see how much they had had to drink in order to steel themselves before they came out from San Martín. They were a little drunk.

"Look here," said the oldest of the boys as he repocketed the bills, "I

Politics, Government, and Law

came all the way up from Flores to get either my money or the animal. My uncle is in the government there. My father is a well-known man. I'm not here to waste my time."

Don Concepción nodded, admitting the truth that no one ever wanted to waste time. He thought to himself that the son of an important legislator in the state capital doesn't waste his time coming up in the mountains to cheat a bunch of Indians out of a single mule. But Don Concepción pretended to believe the lie and took the Mexican boys out in the sun to talk to the President.

Don Concepción explained the situation to the President, and then withdrew to his own house to attend to his screaming grandson. The boys filled in the details for the President in hurried, nervous sentences, while the officials watched these strangers, unable to comprehend what they wanted.

The President beckoned one of the scribes and sent him off to fetch someone.

While they waited the Mexican boys sat on the cement bench, and watched the strange savages around them. The Mexicans had taken the President's seat, and he paced across the courtyard, thinking to himself, and muttering under his breath.

When the scribe returned, trotting, he was followed by an old woman with gray hair whose tattered skirt flapped behind her as she ran toward the Cabildo, already angry and shouting.

The President met her in the courtyard and, still standing, presented the Mexican boys' case to her. She was a mulekeeper and the boys claimed they had seen their mule grazing with her small herd as they rode into the village on the truck.

But how did they come to lose their precious mule? the President asked.

Well, they explained, some Indians had gotten them drunk in the fiesta, and when they got back to San Martín they discovered they had lost their mule. It must have been the old woman who stole it.

She denied all this, when the President translated for her. She lived here in the Center, she said. She was a widow and her whole life depended on her dozen mules.

She was angry and ready to argue. As she talked the Mexican boys stared at her with smirks on their faces. No longer afraid, they were impatient with these people. They told the President what the mule was like—it had a scar across its back, its tail was cut fancy to look like three tassels hanging below one another.

As they explained in Spanish, the old woman went on talking in Tzotzil. When she saw the President was not listening to her, she appealed to the mute officials.

On the other side of the plaza, Jacinto had climbed back into his red truck and had given a merry toot on the horn to announce his departure for San Martín. He started the motor and moved out to make a turn in the plaza.

One of the town boys saw him and ran to stop the truck, to persuade Jacinto to wait for them. The boy bribed Jacinto with cigarettes, and Jacinto cut his motor. The other two Mexicans went out into the valley with the old woman to retrieve the disputed mule, and many of the officials, having nothing to do, went with them.

When they returned with a handsome gray animal, the President inspected it closely. Bobbed, carefully cut tail, and the scar running from the neck down the left side. As the woman continued pleading, telling where she had bought the mule, how she walked it up from Esperanza herself, how she had cared for it, the President admitted in Spanish that the mule belonged to the Mexicans. The boys were jubilant and shouted the decision to their friend waiting beside Jacinto's truck.

"But," the President added, "the woman here has cared for your mule for two weeks, and you must pay her for that."

"How much?" Having won, the boys were anxious to leave.

"Forty pesos."

Both boys laughed, quick thin laughs which they barely forced out between their lips. "Thirty," said one, pulling the wadded bills from his pocket.

The President took these, carefully unfolding and smoothing each one before putting it away under his tunic. The old woman did not seem to understand what was going on, but she stopped talking when she saw the money disappear into the President's pocket.

The Mexicans escaped with their prize, leading the mule quickly out to Jacinto's waiting truck. Antun put down the ladder, but it proved almost too steep for the mule. Antun and the three Mexicans pushed the mule's rump again and again, as it resisted. Jacinto had started the motor again, and each time he roared the engine, the mule tried to back down. When it finally gave in, it went so quickly that two of the boys fell headlong onto the ground. The officials laughed, and even the President smiled. The old woman was talking fast now, but she was silenced when the President gave her the money.

Jacinto's truck pulled out with the thin faces of the three Chickens from town leering out the back.

The President calculated the woman's loss: the mule might be worth six hundred pesos; she had received thirty. He felt sorry for her, sorry that he couldn't take the chance of defying the Mexicans. But the woman had accepted the money he gave her so quickly. Maybe the lie was hers, not the Mexicans'. The President couldn't tell.

UZOWULU, THE NIGERIAN WIFEBEATER

Large crowds began to gather on the village *ilo* as soon as the edge had worn off the sun's heat and it was no longer painful on the body. Most communal ceremonies took place at that time of the day, so that even when it was said that a ceremony would begin "after the midday meal" everyone understood that it would begin a long time later, when the sun's heat had softened.

It was clear from the way the crowd stood or sat that the ceremony was for men. There were many women, but they looked on from the fringe like outsiders. The titled men and elders sat on their stools waiting for the trials to begin. In front of them was a row of stools on which nobody sat. There were nine of them. Two little groups of people stood at a respectable distance beyond the stools. They faced the elders. There were three men in one group and three men and one woman in the other. The woman was Mgbafo and the three men with her were her brothers. In the other group were her husband, Uzowulu, and his relatives. Mgbafo and her brothers were as still as statues into whose faces the artist has molded defiance. Uzowulu and his relatives, on the other hand, were whispering together. It looked like whispering, but they were really talking at the top of their voices. Everybody in the crowd was talking. It was like the market. From a distance the noise was a deep rumble carried by the wind.

An iron gong sounded, setting up a wave of expectation in the crowd. Everyone looked in the direction of the *egwugwu* house. *Gome, gome, gome, gome* went the gong, and a powerful flute blew a high-pitched blast. Then came the voices of the *egwugwu*, guttural and awesome. The wave struck the women and children and there was a backward stampede. But it was momentary. They were already far enough where they stood and there was room for running away if any of the *egwugwu* should go towards them.

The drum sounded again and the flute blew. The *egwugwu* house was now a pandemonium of quavering voices: *Aru oyim de de de dei!* filled the air as the spirits of the ancestors, just emerged from the earth, greeted themselves in their esoteric language. The *egwugwu* house into which they emerged faced the forest, away from the crowd, who saw only its back with the many-colored patterns and drawings done by specially chosen women at regular intervals. These women never saw the inside of the hut. No woman ever did. They scrubbed and painted the outside walls under the supervision of men. If they imagined what was inside, they kept their imagination to themselves. No woman ever asked questions about the most powerful and the most secret cult in the clan.

Aru oyim de de de dei! flew around the dark, closed hut like tongues of fire. The ancestral spirits of the clan were abroad. The metal gong beat continuously now and the flute, shrill and powerful, floated on the chaos.

And then the *egwugwu* appeared. The women and children sent up a great shout and took to their heels. It was instinctive. A woman fled as soon as an *egwugwu* came in sight. And when, as on that day, nine of the greatest masked spirits in the clan came out together it was a terrifying spectacle. Even Mgbafo took to her heels and had to be restrained by her brothers.

Each of the nine *egwugwu* represented a village of the clan. Their leader was called Evil Forest. Smoke poured out of his head.

The nine villages of Umuofia had grown out of the nine sons of the first father of the clan. Evil Forest represented the village of Umueru, or the children of Eru, who was the eldest of the nine sons.

"*Umuofia kwenu!*" shouted the leading *egwugwu,* pushing the air with his raffia arms. The elders of the clan replied, "*Yaa!*"

"*Umuofia kwenu!*"

"*Yaa!*"

"*Umuofia kwenu!*"

"*Yaa!*"

Evil Forest then thrust the pointed end of his rattling staff into the earth. And it began to shake and rattle, like something agitating with a metallic life. He took the first of the empty stools and the eight other *egwugwu* began to sit in order of seniority after him.

Okonkwo's wives, and perhaps other women as well, might have noticed that the second *egwugwu* had the springy walk of Okonkwo. And they might also have noticed that Okonkwo was not among the titled men and elders who sat behind the row of *egwugwu.* But if they thought these things they kept them within themselves. The *egwugwu* with the springy walk was one of the dead fathers of the clan. He looked terrible with the smoked raffia body, a huge wooden face painted white except for the round hollow eyes and the charred teeth that were as big as a man's fingers. On his head were two powerful horns.

When all the *egwugwu* had sat down and the sound of the many tiny bells and rattles on their bodies had subsided, Evil Forest addressed the two groups of people facing them.

"Uzowulu's body, I salute you," he said. Spirits always addressed humans as "bodies." Uzowulu bent down and touched the earth with his right hand as a sign of submission.

"Our father, my hand has touched the ground," he said.

"Uzowulu's body, do you know me?" asked the spirit.

"How can I know you, father? You are beyond our knowledge."

Evil Forest then turned to the other group and addressed the eldest of the three brothers.

"The body of Odukwe, I greet you," he said, and Odukwe bent down and touched the earth. The hearing then began.

Uzowulu stepped forward and presented his case.

"That woman standing there is my wife, Mgbafo. I married her with my money and my yams. I do not owe my in-laws anything. I owe them no yams. I owe them no coco-yams. One morning three of them came to my house, beat me up and took my wife and children away. This happened in the rainy season. I have waited in vain for my wife to return. At last I went to my in-laws and said to them, 'You have taken back your sister. I did not send her away. You yourselves took her. The law of the clan is that you should return her bride-price.' But my wife's brothers said they had nothing to tell me. So I have brought the matter to the fathers of the clan. My case is finished. I salute you."

"Your words are good," said the leader of the *egwugwu*. "Let us hear Odukwe. His words may also be good."

Odukwe was short and thickset. He stepped forward, saluted the spirits and began his story.

"My in-law has told you that we went to his house, beat him up and took our sister and her children away. All that is true. He told you that he came to take back her bride-price and we refused to give it him. That also is true. My in-law, Uzowulu, is a beast. My sister lived with him for nine years. During those years no single day passed in the sky without his beating the woman. We have tried to settle their quarrels time without number and on each occasion Uzowulu was guilty—"

"It is a lie!" Uzowulu shouted.

"Two years ago," continued Odukwe, "when she was pregnant, he beat her until she miscarried."

"It is a lie. She miscarried after she had gone to sleep with her lover."

"Uzowulu's body, I salute you," said Evil Forest, silencing him. "What kind of lover sleeps with a pregnant woman?" There was a loud murmur of approbation from the crowd. Odukwe continued:

"Last year when my sister was recovering from an illness, he beat her again so that if the neighbors had not gone in to save her she would have been killed. We heard of it, and did as you have been told. The law of Umuofia is that if a woman runs away from her husband her bride-price is returned. But in this case she ran away to save her life. Her two children belong to Uzowulu. We do not dispute it, but they are too young to leave their mother. If, on the other hand, Uzowulu should recover from his madness and come in the proper way to beg his wife to return she will do so on the understanding that if he ever beats her again we shall cut off his genitals for him."

The crowd roared with laughter. Evil Forest rose to his feet and order was immediately restored. A steady cloud of smoke rose from his head. He sat down again and called two witnesses. They were both Uzowulu's neighbors, and they agreed about the beating. Evil Forest then stood up, pulled out his staff and thrust it into the earth again. He ran a few steps in the direction of the women; they all fled in terror, only to return to their places almost immediately. The nine *egwugwu* then went away to consult together in their house. They were silent for a long time. Then the metal gong sounded and the flute was blown. The *egwugwu* had emerged once again from their underground home. They saluted one another and then reappeared on the *ilo*.

"*Umuofia kwenu!*" roared Evil Forest, facing the elders and grandees of the clan.

"*Yaa!*" replied the thunderous crowd; then silence descended from the sky and swallowed the noise.

Evil Forest began to speak and all the while he spoke everyone was silent. The eight other *egwugwu* were as still as statues.

"We have heard both sides of the case," said Evil Forest. "Our duty is not to blame this man or to praise that, but to settle the dispute." He turned to Uzowulu's group and allowed a short pause.

"Uzowulu's body, I salute you," he said.

"Our father, my hand has touched the ground," replied Uzowulu, touching the earth.

"Uzowulu's body, do you know me?"

"How can I know you, father? You are beyond our knowledge," Uzowulu replied.

"I am Evil Forest. I kill a man on the day that his life is sweetest to him."

"That is true," replied Uzowulu.

"Go to your in-laws with a pot of wine and beg your wife to return to you. It is not bravery when a man fights with a woman." He turned to Odukwe, and allowed a brief pause.

"Odukwe's body, I greet you," he said.

"My hand is on the ground," replied Odukwe.

"Do you know me?"

"No man can know you," replied Odukwe.

"I am Evil Forest, I am Dry-meat-that-fills-the-mouth, I am Fire-that-burns-without-faggots. If your in-law brings wine to you, let your sister go with him. I salute you." He pulled his staff from the hard earth and thrust it back.

"*Umuofia kwenu!*" he roared, and the crowd answered.

"I don't know why such a trifle should come before the *egwugwu*," said one elder to another.

"Don't you know what kind of man Uzowulu is? He will not listen to any other decision," replied the other.

As they spoke two other groups of people had replaced the first before the *egwugwu*, and a great land case began.

SIX FEET OF THE COUNTRY

My wife and I are not real farmers—not even Lerice, really. We bought our place, ten miles out of Johannesburg on one of the main roads, to change something in ourselves, I suppose; you seem to rattle about so much within a marriage like ours. You long to hear nothing but a deep satisfying silence when you sound a marriage. The farm hasn't managed that for us, of course, but it has done other things, unexpected, illogical. Lerice, who I thought would retire there in Chekhovian sadness for a month or two, and then leave the place to the servants while she tried yet again to get a part she wanted and become the actress she would like to be, has sunk into the business of running the farm with all the serious intensity with which she once imbued the shadows in a playwright's mind. I should have given it up long ago if it had not been for her. Her hands, once small and plain and well-kept—she was not the sort of actress who wears red paint and diamond rings—are hard as a dog's pads.

I, of course, am there only in the evenings and on weekends. I am a partner in a luxury-travel agency, which is flourishing—needs to be, as I tell Lerice, in order to carry the farm. Still, though I know we can't afford it, and though the sweetish smell of the fowls Lerice breeds sickens me, so that I avoid going past their runs, the farm is beautiful in a way I had almost forgotten—especially on a Sunday morning when I get up and go out into the paddock and see not the palm trees and fishpond and imitation-stone bird bath of the suburbs but white ducks on the dam, the lucerne field brilliant as window dresser's grass, and the little, stocky, mean-eyed bull, lustful but bored, having his face tenderly licked by one of his ladies. Lerice comes out with her hair uncombed, in her hand a stick dripping with cattle dip. She will stand and look dreamily for a moment, the way she would pretend to look sometimes in those plays. "They'll mate tomorrow," she will say. "This is their second day. Look how she loves him, my little Napoleon." So that when people come out to see us on Sunday afternoon, I am likely to hear myself saying as I pour out the drinks, "When I drive back home from the city everyday, past those rows of suburban houses, I wonder how the devil we ever did stand it. . . . Would you care to look around?" And there I am, taking some pretty girl and her young husband stumbling down to our riverbank, the girl catching her stockings on the mealie-stooks and stepping over cow-turds humming with jewel-green flies while she says, ". . . the *tensions* of the damned city. And you're near enough to get into town to a show, too! I think it's wonderful. Why, you've got it both ways!"

And for a moment I accept the triumph as if I *had* managed it—the impossibility that I've been trying for all my life—just as if the truth was that you could get it "both ways," instead of finding yourself with not even one way or the other but a third, one you had not provided for at all.

But even in our saner moments, when I find Lerice's earthy enthusiasms just as irritating as I once found her histrionical ones, and she finds what she calls my "jealousy" of her capacity for enthusiasm as big a proof of my inadequacy for her as a mate as ever it was, we do believe that we have at least honestly escaped those tensions peculiar to the city about which our visitors speak. When Johannesburg people speak of "tension," they don't mean hurrying people in crowded streets, the struggle for money, or the general competitive character of city life. They mean the guns under the white men's pillows and the burglar bars on the white men's windows. They mean those strange moments on city pavements when a black man won't stand aside for a white man.

Out in the country, even ten miles out, life is better than that. In the country, there is a lingering remnant of the pretransitional stage; our rela-tionship with the blacks is almost feudal. Wrong, I suppose, obsolete, but more comfortable all round. We have no burglar bars, no gun. Lerice's farm boys have their wives and their piccanins living with them on the land. They brew their sour beer without the fear of police raids. In fact, we've always rather prided ourselves that the poor devils have nothing much to fear, being with us; Lerice even keeps an eye on their children, with all the competence of a woman who has never had a child of her own, and she certainly doctors them all—children and adults—like babies whenever they happen to be sick.

It was because of this that we were not particularly startled one night last winter when the boy Albert came knocking at our window long after we had gone to bed. I wasn't in our bed but sleeping in the little dressing-room-*cum*-linen-room next door, because Lerice had annoyed me and I didn't want to find myself softening toward her simply because of the sweet smell of talcum powder on her flesh after her bath. She came and woke me up. "Albert says one of the boys is very sick," she said. "I think you'd better go down and see. He wouldn't get us up at this hour for nothing."

"What time is it?"

"What does it matter?" Lerice is maddeningly logical.

I got up awkwardly as she watched me—How is it I always feel a fool when I have deserted her bed? After all, I know from the way she never looks at me when she talks to me at breakfast the next day that she is hurt and humiliated at my not wanting her—and I went out, clumsy with sleep.

Politics, Government, and Law

"Which of the boys is it?" I asked Albert as we followed the dance of my torch.

"He's too sick. Very sick, *Baas,*" he said.

"But who? Franz?" I remembered Franz had had a bad cough for the past week.

Albert did not answer; he had given me the path, and was walking along beside me in the tall dead grass. When the light of the torch caught his face, I saw that he looked acutely embarrassed. "What's this all about?" I said.

He lowered his head under the glance of the light. "It's not me, *Baas.* I don't know. Petrus he send me."

Irritated, I hurried him along to the huts. And there, on Petrus's iron bedstead, with its brick stilts, was a young man, dead. On his forehead there was still a light, cold sweat; his body was warm. The boys stood around as they do in the kitchen when it is discovered that someone has broken a dish—uncoöperative, silent. Somebody's wife hung about in the shadows, her hands wrung together under her apron.

I had not seen a dead man since the war. This was very different. I felt like the others—extraneous, useless. "What was the matter?" I asked.

The woman patted at her chest and shook her head to indicate the painful impossibility of breathing.

He must have died of pneumonia.

I turned to Petrus. "Who was this boy? What was he doing here?" The light of a candle on the floor showed that Petrus was weeping. He followed me out the door.

When we were outside, in the dark, I waited for him to speak. But he didn't. "Now, come on, Petrus, you must tell me who this boy was. Was he a friend of yours?"

"He's my brother, *Baas.* He come from Rhodesia to look for work."

The story startled Lerice and me a little. The young boy had walked down from Rhodesia to look for work in Johannesburg, had caught a chill from sleeping out along the way, and had lain ill in his brother Petrus's hut since his arrival three days before. Our boys had been frightened to ask us for help for him because we had never been intended ever to know of his presence. Rhodesian natives are barred from entering the Union unless they have a permit; the young man was an illegal immigrant. No doubt our boys had managed the whole thing successfully several times before; a number of relatives must have walked the seven or eight hundred miles from poverty to the paradise of zoot suits, police raids, and black slum townships that is their *Egoli,* City of Gold—the Bantu name for Johannesburg. It was merely a matter of getting such a man to lie low on our farm until a job could be found with someone who would be glad to take the risk of prosecution for employing an illegal immigrant in exchange for the services of someone as yet untainted by the city.

Well, this was one who would never get up again.

"You would think they would have felt they could tell *us*," said Lerice next morning. "Once the man was ill. You would have thought at least—" When she is getting intense over something, she has a way of standing in the middle of a room as people do when they are shortly to leave on a journey, looking searchingly about her at the most familiar objects as if she had never seen them before. I had noticed that in Petrus's presence in the kitchen, earlier, she had had the air of being almost offended with him, almost hurt.

In any case, I really haven't the time or inclination any more to go into everything in our life that I know Lerice, from those alarmed and pressing eyes of hers, would like us to go into. She is the kind of woman who doesn't mind if she looks plain, or odd; I don't suppose she would even care if she knew how strange she looks when her whole face is out of proportion with urgent uncertainty. I said, "Now I'm the one who'll have to do all the dirty work, I suppose."

She was still staring at me, trying me out with those eyes—wasting her time, if she only knew.

"I'll have to notify the health authorities," I said calmly. "They can't just cart him off and bury him. After all, we don't really know what he died of."

She simply stood there, as if she had given up—simply ceased to see me at all.

I don't know when I've been so irritated. "It might have been something contagious," I said. "God knows?" There was no answer.

I am not enamored of holding conversations with myself. I went out to shout to one of the boys to open the garage and get the car ready for my morning drive to town.

As I had expected, it turned out to be quite a business. I had to notify the police as well as the health authorities, and answer a lot of tedious questions: How was it I was ignorant of the boy's presence? If I did not supervise my native quarters, how did I know that that sort of thing didn't go on all the time? Et cetera, et cetera. And when I flared up and told them that so long as my natives did their work, I didn't think it my right or concern to poke my nose into their private lives, I got from the coarse, dull-witted police sergeant one of those looks that come not from any thinking process going on in the brain but from that faculty common to all who are possessed by the master-race theory—a look of insanely inane certainty. He grinned at me with a mixture of scorn and delight at my stupidity.

Then I had to explain to Petrus why the health authorities had to take away the body for a post-mortem—and, in fact, what a post-mortem was. When I telephoned the health department some days later to find out the result, I was told that the cause of death was, as we had thought, pneumonia, and that the body had been suitably disposed of. I went out to where Petrus was mixing a mash for the fowls and told him that it was all right, there would be

Politics, Government, and Law

no trouble; his brother had died from that pain in his chest. Petrus put down the paraffin tin and said, "When can we go to fetch him, *Bass?*"

"To fetch him?"

"Will the *Baas* please ask them when we must come?"

I went back inside and called Lerice, all over the house. She came down the stairs from the spare bedrooms, and I said, "*Now* what am I going to do? When I told Petrus, he just asked calmly when they could go and fetch the body. They think they're going to bury him themselves."

"Well, go back and tell him," said Lerice. "You must tell him. Why didn't you tell him then?"

When I found Petrus again, he looked up politely. "Look, Petrus," I said. "You can't go to fetch your brother. They've done it already—they've *buried* him, you understand?"

"Where?" he said slowly, dully, as if he thought that perhaps he was getting this wrong.

"You see, he was a stranger. They knew he wasn't from here, and they didn't know he had some of his people here, so they thought they must bury him." It was difficult to make a pauper's grave sound like a privilege.

"Please, *Baas,* the *Baas* must ask them?" But he did not mean that he wanted to know the burial place. He simply ignored the incomprehensible machinery I told him had set to work on his dead brother; he wanted the brother back.

"But, Petrus," I said, "how can I? Your brother is buried already. I can't ask them now."

"Oh, *Baas!*" he said. He stood with his bran-smeared hands uncurled at his sides, one corner of his mouth twitching.

"Good God, Petrus, they won't listen to me! They can't, anyway. I'm sorry, but I can't do it. You understand?"

He just kept on looking at me, out of his knowledge that white men have everything, can do anything, if they don't, it is because they won't.

And then, at dinner, Lerice started. "You could at least phone," she said.

"Christ, what d'you think I am? Am I supposed to bring the dead back to life?"

But I could not exaggerate my way out of this ridiculous responsibility that had been thrust on me. "Phone them up," she went on. "And at least you'll be able to tell him you've done it and they've explained that it's impossible."

She disappeared somewhere into the kitchen quarters after coffee. A little later she came back to tell me, "The old father's coming down from Rhodesia to be at the funeral. He's got a permit and he's already on his way."

Unfortunately, it was not impossible to get the body back. The authorities said that it was somewhat irregular, but that since the hygiene conditions had been fulfilled, they could not refuse permission for exhumation. I found out that, with the undertaker's charges, it would cost twenty pounds. Ah, I thought, that settles it. On five pounds a month, Petrus won't have twenty pounds—and just as well, since it couldn't do the dead any good. Certainly I should not offer it to him myself. Twenty pounds—or anything else within reason, for that matter—I would have spent without grudging it on doctors or medicines that might have helped the boy when he was alive. Once he was dead, I had no intention of encouraging Petrus to throw away, on a gesture, more than he spent to clothe his whole family in a year.

When I told him, in the kitchen that night, he said, "Twenty pounds?"

I said, "Yes, that's right, twenty pounds."

For a moment, I had the feeling, from the look on his face, that he was calculating. But when he spoke again I thought I must have imagined it. "We must pay twenty pounds!" he said in the faraway voice in which a person speaks of something so unattainable that it does not bear thinking about.

"All right, Petrus," I said in dismissal, and went back to the living room.

The next morning before I went to town, Petrus asked to see me. "Please, *Baas,*" he said, awkwardly handing me a bundle of notes. They're so seldom on the giving rather than the receiving side, poor devils, that they don't really know how to hand money to a white man. There it was, the twenty pounds, in ones and halves, some creased and folded until they were soft as dirty rags, others smooth and fairly new—Franz's money, I suppose, and Albert's, and Dora the cook's, and Jacob the gardener's, and God knows who else's besides, from all the farms and small holdings round about. I took it in irritation more than in astonishment, really—irritation at the waste, the use-lessness of this sacrifice by people so poor. Just like the poor everywhere, I thought, who stint themselves the decencies of life in order to insure themselves the decencies of death. So incomprehensible to people like Lerice and me, who regard life as something to be spent extravagantly and, if we think about death at all, regard it as the final bankruptcy.

The servants don't work on Saturday afternoon anyway, so it was a good day for the funeral. Petrus and his father had borrowed our donkey cart to fetch the coffin from the city, where, Petrus told Lerice on their return, everything was "nice"—the coffin waiting for them, already sealed up to save them from what must have been a rather unpleasant sight after two weeks' interment. (It had taken all that time for the authorities and the undertaker to make the final arrangements for moving the body.) All morning, the coffin lay in Petrus's hut, awaiting the trip to the little old burial ground, just outside the eastern boundary of our farm, that was a relic of the days when this was a real farming district rather than a fashionable rural estate. It was pure chance that I happened to be down there near the fence when the procession came past; once again Lerice had forgotten her prom-ise to me and had made the house uninhabitable on a Saturday afternoon. I had come home and been infuriated to find her in a pair of filthy old slacks and with her hair uncombed since the night before, having all the varnish scraped off the living-room floor, if you please. So I had taken my No. 8 iron and gone off to practice my approach shots. In my annoyance, I had forgotten about the funeral, and was reminded only when I saw the procession coming up the path along the outside of the fence toward me; from where I was standing, you can see the graves quite clearly, and that day the sun glinted on bits of broken pottery, a lopsided homemade cross, and jam jars brown with rain water and dead flowers.

I felt a little awkward, and did not know whether to go on hitting my golf ball or stop at least until the whole gathering was decently past. The donkey cart creaks and screeches with every revolution of the wheels and it came along in a slow, halting fashion somehow peculiarly suited to the two donkeys who drew it, their little potbellies rubbed and rough, their heads sunk between the shafts, and their ears flattened back with an air submissive and downcast; peculiarly suited, too, to the group of men and women who came along slowly behind. The patient ass. Watching, I thought, You can see now why the creature became a Biblical symbol. Then the procession drew level with me and stopped, so I had to put down my club. The coffin was taken down off the cart—it was a shiny, yellow-varnished wood, like cheap furniture—and the donkeys twitched their ears against the flies. Petrus, Franz, Albert, and the old father from Rhodesia hoisted it on their shoulders and the procession moved on, on foot. It was really a very awkward moment. I stood there rather foolishly at the fence, quite still, and slowly they filed past, not looking up, the four men bent beneath the shiny wooden box, and the straggling troop of mourners. All of them were servants or neighbors' servants whom I knew as casual, easygoing gossipers about our lands or kitchen. I heard the old man's breathing.

I had just bent to pick up my club again when there was a sort of jar in the flowing solemnity of their processional mood; I felt it at once, like a wave of heat along the air, or one of those sudden currents of cold catching at your legs in a placid stream. The old man's voice was muttering something; the people had stopped, confused, and they bumped into one another, some pressing to go on, others hissing them to be still. I could see that they were embarrassed, but they could not ignore the voice; it was much the way that the mumblings of a prophet, though not clear at first, arrest the mind. The corner of the coffin the old man carried was sagging at an angle; he seemed to be trying to get out from under the weight of it. Now Petrus expostulated with him.

The little boy who had been left to watch the donkeys dropped the reins and ran to see. I don't know why—unless it was for the same reason people crowd round someone who has fainted in a cinema—but I parted the wires of the fence and went through, after him.

Petrus lifted his eyes to me—to anybody—with distress and horror. The old man from Rhodesia had let go of the coffin entirely, and the three others, unable to support it on their own, had laid it on the ground, in the pathway. Already there was a film of dust lightly wavering up its shiny sides. I did not understand what the old man was saying; I hesitated to interfere. But now the whole seething group turned on my silence. The old man himself came over to me, with his hands outspread and shaking, and spoke directly to me, saying something that I could tell from the tone, without understanding the words, was shocking and extraordinary.

"What is it, Petrus? What's wrong?" I appealed.

Petrus threw up his hands, bowed his head in a series of hysterical shakes, then thrust his face up at me suddenly. "He says, 'My son was not so heavy.' "

Silence. I could hear the old man breathing; he kept his mouth a little open, as old people do.

"My son was young and thin," he said at last, in English.

Again silence. Then babble broke out. The old man thundered against everybody; his teeth were yellowed and few, and he had one of those fine, grizzled, sweeping mustaches that one doesn't often see nowadays, which must have been grown in emulation of early Empire builders. It seemed to frame all his utterances with a special validity, perhaps merely because it was the symbol of the traditional wisdom of age—an idea so fearfully rooted that it carries still something awesome beyond reason. He shocked them; they thought he was mad, but they had to listen to him. With his own hands he began to prize the lid off the coffin and three of the men came forward to help him. Then he sat down on the ground; very old, very weak, and unable to speak, he merely lifted a trembling hand toward what was there. He abdicated, he handed it over to them; he was no good any more.

They crowded round to look (and so did I), and now they forgot the nature of this surprise and the occasion of grief to which it belonged, and for a few minutes were carried up in the delightful astonishment of the surprise itself. They gasped and flared noisily with excitement. I even noticed the little boy who had held the donkeys jumping up and down, almost weeping with rage because the back of the grownups crowded him out of his view.

In the coffin was someone no one had ever seen before: a heavily built, rather light-skinned native with a neatly stitched scar on his forehead—perhaps from a blow in a brawl that had also dealt him some other, slower-working injury, which had killed him.

I wrangled with the authorities for a week over that body. I had the feeling that they were shocked, in a laconic fashion, by their own mistake, but that in the confusion of their anonymous dead they were helpless to put it right. They said to me, "We are trying to find out," and "We are still making inquiries." It was as if at any moment they might conduct me into their mortuary and say, "There! Lift up the sheets; look for him—your poultry boy's brother. There are so many black faces—surely one will do?"

And every evening when I got home, Petrus was waiting in the kitchen. "Well, they're trying. They're still looking. The *Baas* is seeing to it for you, Petrus," I would tell him. "God, half the time I should be in the office I'm driving around the back end of the town chasing after this affair," I added aside, to Lerice, one night.

She and Petrus both kept their eyes turned on me as I spoke, and, oddly, for those moments they looked exactly alike, though it sounds impossible: my wife, with her high, white forehead and her attenuated Englishwoman's body, and the poultry boy, with his horny bare feet below khaki trousers tied at the knee with string and the peculiar rankness of his nervous sweat coming from his skin.

"What makes you so indignant, so determined about this now?" said Lerice suddenly.

I stared at her. "It's a matter of principle. Why should they get away with a swindle? It's time these officials had a jolt from someone who'll bother to take the trouble."

She said, "Oh." And as Petrus slowly opened the kitchen door to leave, sensing that the talk had gone beyond him, she turned away, too.

I continued to pass on assurances to Petrus every evening, but although what I said was the same and the voice in which I said it was the same, every evening it sounded weaker. At last, it became clear that we would never get Petrus's brother back, because nobody really knew where he was. Somewhere in a graveyard as uniform as a housing scheme, somewhere under a number that didn't belong to him, or in the medical school, perhaps, laboriously reduced to layers of muscle and strings of nerve? Goodness knows. He had no identity in this world anyway.

It was only then, and in a voice of shame, that Petrus asked me to try and get the money back.

"From the way he asks, you'd think he was robbing his dead brother," I said to Lerice later. But as I've said, Lerice had got so intense about this business that she couldn't even appreciate a little ironic smile.

I tried to get the money; Lerice tried. We both telephoned and wrote and argued, but nothing came of it. It appeared that the main expense had been the undertaker, and after all he had done his job. So the whole thing was a complete waste, even more of a waste for the poor devils than I had thought it would be.

The old man from Rhodesia was about Lerice's father's size, so she gave him one of her father's old suits, and he went back home rather better off, for the winter, than he had come.

A PUERTO RICAN IN CHICAGO

Carlos Alvarez, 33

He had come to the United States from a small Puerto Rican village sixteen years ago. He had worked in New York and Chicago as a hat blocker, assembler in a radio manufacturing plant, waiter at a fashionable Catskill resort, and clothing salesman. "When you first come to this country, you have to learn something from people all over. I have been among people of both states, they show they are very friendly."

For the last six years, he had been a night watchman at one of Chicago's smaller museums. "I enjoy work for them, otherwise I can find a job for more money any other place."

On a pleasant autumn morning, there was an unexpected encounter.

It was about six o'clock in the morning when I was getting ready to go home. I walk out about five feet away from the back door out there, at Academy. A police was approaching to our parking lot over there. The first question he asked me was what I was doing there? I told him I work here. He asked me if I have any identification. I said no, we don't have any right now. He asked me if I had the key. I said no, I just left it with the relief man. When he don't believe me, I ask him to come in and ask the relief man. He says in a kind of very rude manner, he pushed me against the car, he said he heard that before from other people, and he pushed me against the car again and called for help.

About six other cars answer his call. Another sergeant drop in, and this man grab me and put my hands in the back, cross my hands, throwed me into that holdup car. My cheek hit the glass, the hood. And my arm was hurt by the side of the car. And they were laughing about asking what my nationality I was. They were laughing, walking back and forth, back and forth, in a way that, like making fun of me. One particular fella was laughing and walking back and forth and he was trying to show off with the sergeant. He was talking to the other guys who come to help him, and he said, "Leave this one up to me, I'm gonna get him in jail, no matter what."

When I called the relief man and asked him to call Mr. Baird, who is the curator, Mr. Baird arrived about five minutes later. And he asked the police what happened. Nobody answered him any question. They asked him if he recognized me. He says, yeah, he worked for us for many years and we know him very good. What happened? Nobody happened to answer him. He went inside to call up the director.

When he went inside, there was about seven more cars, fourteen cars altogether, about fifteen policemen were surrounding me. I was innocent, I don't know what to do with myself. They were talking there for a good half an hour before they decided to take me to the station. I told the station, I think my arm is broken. And I need medical attention. One sergeant, he pushed me and told me, he said, if you need medical attention, we'll take you to the Cook County Hospital and lock you in there till tomorrow morning and you get your attention there, and you don't gonna be in court till tomorrow. Or you gotta wait over here till nine o'clock when the judge arrive. I say I rather stay over here in jail till nine o'clock and not wait till tomorrow.

They took my fingerprints, my name, my address, where I work, how long I been working here. They put me in a room, second floor in the back, where all the bums from Clark Street, there was about seventy-five or a hundred bums there. I was the only one in there clean and decent. Only one washroom, in the middle of the floor, for everyone to use there. I asked one of the bailiffs to please change me from this pigsty to another room, not to be between so many bums in there. I was sick in there. He said, no, here is where you belong. He pushed me against the wall and close the door.

About nine o'clock the judge arrive. Everybody in line, like a pig, went to the courtroom. The courtroom where nobody is admitted. The public is not allowed to there. Behind bars. The lawyer was not allowed to go there. My cousin was not allowed to go there, even Mr. Baird was not allowed to go in there. When I went there, they push me back into the room again because the police who was involved in my case was not there.

Once I wait there for ten minutes, they call me back again. The police was there, four policemen show up. They were the ones who talked. I wasn't allowed to say a word. When I tried to defend myself, they push me, they say, you have nothing to talk in here. When I wait for my turn to come, the judge said. They talk all they want, they said I tried to punch the sergeant in the mouth or in his face. When I was even handcuffed in the back. Which was not true, because I could do nothing myself when there is a man armed with guns, and so many men around me, for no reason at all. I was tired, nervous, exhausted, I didn't know what to do.

They talked so dirty in a way over there to the judge. And the judge, the only thing he asked me was if I have any family. And I say, yes, I have a family. He said, well, I'm gonna give you guilty with a suspended sentence. When I asked him guilty for what, he said, that's all, you're not allowed to talk any more. I say good-bye and I see you later.

My cousin drive me to the hospital and I stayed there from ten o'clock in the morning till three in the afternoon, waiting for the X rays. The doctor find out that I have a fracture in my arm, about two to three inches cracked. I came home, I don't know what to think, I don't know what to do, I don't know what to say.

Next day, what I did, I wrote to different personalities, who runs the city of Chicago. Also I wrote to Congress of the United States in Washington. I wrote the President and I wrote to the governor of Puerto Rico. I explain in three full pages what happened and how it happened. They all answered to me. It was kind of a glad lift that they answered to me and at least they did something. They wrote to Superintendent Wilson and they said that he said he will do everything in his power to be sure that something has to be done to the person who was involved in my case.

How long ago was this?

Four months already. Nothing has happened so far because I'm waiting for the doctor's discharge. I will know for sure what's wrong with the arm. There's 15 to 20 percent shorter, not only shorter, but curved. It still hurts when the weather is kind of damp and it's kinda cloudy, you know.

I took three weeks off. When I came back, the assistant director calls me and he says, I'm afraid we have to tell you right in your face that you have been fired. He said, I don't know if you receive a letter or not. A registered letter. The only reason that they said is that the insurance company complained that I cost the insurance company too much trouble. To my knowledge, this is the first time I ever had trouble with an insurance company.

The first time, the director, he was very shocked about what happened. He didn't believe it. He asked me how I feel and after a while he said, this happens to you for being against the police. And I told him I have nothing against the police. And I say, you talk this way because this doesn't happen to you. And the answer he gave me, he turned his back, he said, "They do this to me and nobody will have a job at that police station." That was his answer.

One day Mr. Baird, he was talking about me, about the same case, the director said, "Well, he cannot ever deny that he's a Puerto Rican." And also one day, when the director mentioned the case to the board of directors, one of the women's board said, I should go back to Puerto Rico, what was I waiting for here in Chicago that I didn't go back to Puerto Rico where I belong. They are the biggest society in Chicago.

This situation is the one that hurt me the most. I loved walking, and I enjoy walking in summertime and wintertime, I don't care. Sometimes police follow me in cars, asking me what I'm doing that time of night. But never have any trouble. They've always been very friendly to me and very nice to me, till now. But this change in the police station, to me they are nothing but like

Politics, Government, and Law

hungry dogs looking for a piece of fresh meat. Those two hours in the police station, that's the biggest experience in my life. I have been nervous ever since.

> *When this happened to you, were there other people around? Did they watch?*

No, they don't watch. They keep walking, because maybe they might be afraid that the police might grab them and say, well, you are involved, too. They walked by and they didn't pay much attention. Maybe they were afraid to stand by because the police might throw them in the can too.

If a person is wrongdoing, it's all right, the police should do what they're supposed to do and what the law tells them to do. But if a person is just coming out of work, minding his own business, now why do the police beat him up for no reason at all?

I think the way the police acts is a very very low way of doing. I was waiting for a bus about six weeks ago. Now a black car happened to drive north up the street. The police stopped the car. The man was well dressed, he come out of the car, he had a five-dollar bill in his hand. He just hand to the police. The police say no, I cannot do that. The guy put the money in his hand. The policeman's hand is against the handle of the motorcycle. Drove away about a half block south. He put his hand in his pocket, the money in his pocket, and the other guy drove north.

CHAPTER 25   MARGARET SANGER

HER DAY IN COURT

History is written in retrospect, but contemporary documents must be consulted; therefore I have gone to the official records for the facts. After all, one courtroom is much like another, and the attitude of one justice not so dissimilar from that of another. I was combating a mass ideology, and the judges who were its spokesmen merged into a single voice, all saying, "Be good and we'll let you off." This is what I heard:

You have been in court during the time that your counsel made the statement that pending the prosecution of appeal neither you nor those affiliated with you in this so called movement will violate the law; that is the promise your counsel makes for you. Now, the Court is considering extreme clemency in your case. Possibly you know what extreme clemency means. Now, do you personally make that promise?

THE DEFENDANT: Pending the appeal.

THE COURT: If Mrs. Sanger will state publicly and openly that she will be a law-abiding citizen without any qualifications whatsoever, this Court is prepared to exercise the highest degree of leniency.

THE DEFENDANT: I'd like to have it understood by the gentlemen of the Court that the offer of leniency is very kind and I appreciate it very much. It is with me not a question of personal imprisonment or personal disadvantage. I am today and always have been more concerned with changing the law regardless of what I have to undergo to have it done.

THE COURT: Then I take it that you are indifferent about this matter entirely.

THE DEFENDANT: No, I am not indifferent. I am indifferent as to the personal consequences to myself, but I am not indifferent to the cause and the influence which can be attained for the cause.

THE COURT: Since you are of that mind, am I to infer that you intend to go in this matter, violating the law, irrespective of the consequences?

THE DEFENDANT: I haven't said that. I said I am perfectly willing not to violate Section 1142—pending the appeal.

JUSTICE HERRMANN: The appeal has nothing to do with it. Either you do or you don't.

THE COURT: (to Mr. Goldstein) What is the use of beating around the bush? You have communicated to me in my chambers the physical condition of your client, and you told me that this woman would respect the law. This law was not made by us. We are simply here to judge the case. We harbor no feeling against Mrs. Sanger. We have nothing to do with her beliefs, except in so far as she carries those beliefs into practice and violates the law. But in view of your statement that you intend to prosecute this appeal and make a test case out of this and in view of the fact that we are to regard her as a first offender, surely we want to temper justice with mercy and that's all we are trying to do. And we ask her, openly and above board, "Will you publicly declare that you will respect the law and not violate it?" and then we get an answer with a qualification. Now, what can the prisoner at the bar for sentence expect? I don't know that a prisoner under such circumstances is entitled to very much consideration after all."

THE COURT: (to the Defendant) We don't want you to do impossible things, Mrs. Sanger, only the reasonable thing and that is to comply with this law as long as it remains the law. It is the law for you, it is the law for me, it is the law for all of us until it is changed; and you know what means and avenues are open to you to have it changed, and they are lawful ways. You may prosecute these methods, and no one can find fault with you. If you succeed in changing the law, well and good. If you fail, then you have to bow in submission to the majority rule.

THE DEFENDANT: It is just the chance, the opportunity to test it.

THE COURT: Very good. You have had your day in court; you advocated a cause, you were brought to the bar, you wanted to be tried here, you were judged, you didn't go on the stand and commit perjury in any sense, you took the facts and accepted them as true, and you are ready for judgment, even the worst. Now, we are prepared, however, under all the circumstances of this case, to be extremely lenient with you if you will tell us that you will respect this law and not violate it again.

THE DEFENDANT: I have given you my answer.

THE COURT: We don't want any qualifications. We are not concerned with the appeal.

MR. GOLDSTEIN: Just one other statement, your Honor, one final statement on my part. Your Honor did well say that you didn't want anything unreasonable. With all due deference to your Honor, to ask a person what her frame of mind will be with so many exigencies in future, that is, if the commission did nothing or the Legislature did nothing—

THE COURT: All we are concerned about is this statute, and as long as it remains the law will this woman promise here and now unqualifiedly to respect it and obey it? Now, it is yes or no. What is your answer, Mrs. Sanger? Is it yes or no?

THE DEFENDANT: I can't respect the law as it stands today.

THE COURT: Margaret Sanger, there is evidence that you established and maintained a birth control clinic where you kept for sale and exhibition to various women articles which purported to be for the prevention of conception, and that there you made a determined effort to disseminate birth control information and advice. You have challenged the constitutionality of the law under consideration and the jurisdiction of this Court. When this is done in an orderly way no one can find fault. It is your right as a citizen. . . . Refusal to obey the law becomes an open defiance of the rule of the majority. While the law is in its present form, defiance provokes anything but reasonable consideration. The judgment of the Court is that you be confined to the Workhouse for the period of thirty days.

A single cry, "Shame!" was followed by a sharp rap of the gavel, and silence fell.

PART FIVE

RELIGION AND WORLD VIEW

Early anthropologists speculated about the origin of religion; some even predicted its demise with the development of modern society. As they began to investigate the significance of the role of religion in social life, they recognized its permanency. Every religion fulfills numerous personal needs and serves to integrate communal experience.

All men are confronted with the frailties of human existence. Death, misfortune, and even life itself pose many ultimate questions. The question of inevitable death is not so difficult as "Why did my child die so young when other children are still living?" Misfortune and disaster strike in unpredictable ways. Sickness comes to some but not others. These things create anxiety for man, but the most difficult anxiety is to suffer such events with no explanation, with no way to account for what has occurred. Everywhere religion provides man with explanations and reasons. "It was God's will," "He offended the rock spirits," "She violated the taboo," "A bone has been sent by a sorcerer and entered your chest," "He has gone to heaven," "His soul will depart and be released if we burn his possessions." These kinds of religious beliefs reduce anxiety and uncertainty in a world that is never as secure as we would like to believe. And religion offers us a plan of action to cope with death and misfortune. Beliefs and rituals give us hope to brave the unknown, to alleviate anxiety, and to make our threatened existence more bearable.

Religion almost always involves belief in supernatural powers and beings beyond the human level. Animals, plants, and other objects may be inhabited by spirits; the ghosts of ancestors may continue to exist as part of the supernatural world; witches and sorcerers have special access to supernatural powers; magic can be used to manipulate these powers for good or evil. And in the beliefs and rituals of magic and religion we find an implicit view of the world. By this means, each human culture imposes a sense of order and meaning on the universe and from that constructs an enduring, legitimate reality.

But religion does more than reduce personal anxiety, account for suffering and unexpected misfortune, and give individuals hope and meaning. Rituals and beliefs are an important statement of a society's most fundamental values.

Rituals bring together the members of a society into an activity set apart from merely human activities—it is sacred. The performance of sacred rituals, the repetition of sacred myths, the awe one feels in the presence of sacred beings—all reinforce the social charter of values on which a society is built. The structure of group life is no longer merely human; it has the stamp of supernatural approval. Authority that may be questioned is no longer merely human authority, it is made legitimate by the gods. In these selections individuals are caught up in religious rituals, acting out their beliefs, and making contact with the supernatural. And, beyond immediate events, these selections portray the way in which different religions and world views satisfy both personal and social needs.

THE WOLF IS MY BROTHER

Buffalo Tongue

The boy was afraid.

Since there were none to see, he did not try to hide his fear. He twisted in his saddle from time to time, looking behind him. He spoke strong medicine words into the wind.

Four times that day he had stopped to offer smoke and prayer to the Spirit, and now the day was dying. The Sun, who was himself a great god, was sinking into the west, the land of the dead. Before him, the two hills lifted some three hundred feet into the air, their crests still touched with gold. Buffalo Tongue felt the tension of power in the shadowed air; it made it seem colder than it was.

Spirit Hill—he could not mistake it—loomed up ahead of him in silent challenge. It was a challenge to his faith as well as to his courage, a challenge only dimly grasped, half understood, felt with the senses rather than the mind. Ai-eee, was it not said that the Thunderbird lived in such a place, on such a hill? The Thunderbird that was immense and colored dark blue with the jagged red markings that were shaped like the lightning that ripped the sky? Had he not seen for himself that sacred spot, not far from here on the Red River, where the Thunderbird had touched the earth? There was a mark there—he remembered it vividly—a charred place where no grass ever grew. A mark in the shape of a giant bird with wings outstretched. Ah, with his own eyes he had seen this thing!

The gathering night seemed filled with the dark winds of invisible wings. Buffalo Tongue tried to be brave, but it was hard to be brave when you were alone. It was easier to be brave when others rode at your side. It was easier to be brave after you had the medicine that would protect you and shield you from harm.

He did not even consider turning back. There was only one way to go if he wanted to become a man, a man with horses of his own, and a wife, and the respect of The People.

He had to go up Spirit Hill.

He rode his pony between the two hills, into a small sheltered valley.

There was a small spring there, just as Fox Claw had said, and enough grass for many days. He unsaddled his horse and staked him out on a long rope. "I will be back for you, Ekaesi," he whispered into the ear of the red roan. "Wait here for me. Wait here for me and you will carry a warrior away from this place. We have hunted together many times, but this is a kind of hunting a man must do alone. Do you understand my words, Ekaesi?"

The roan nuzzled him affectionately. "I am glad that you are here," the boy said softly. "I will look down upon you and see you when I am too much alone, and my heart will be glad."

Reluctantly, he left the horse he had raised from a colt. He gathered up his buffalo robe, his tobacco and pipe, and his fire drill in its case of buffalo horn. He started up Spirit Hill.

It was not a hard climb, but he was not used to climbing on foot and his heart hammered in his chest. The wind stirred through the brush and the great rocks took on strange and fearful shapes. The Sun could not see him now and the air was filled with tiny cold teeth. Once, his foot dislodged a stone and it went bouncing down into the valley below; to the boy, it sounded like a landslide.

He reached the top. It was perfectly level, a flat cap rock some thirty yards across. Nothing grew there except four stunted, wind-sculptured cedars that had found purchase in a crevice on the south side. Four cedars! That was the medicine number.

Buffalo Tongue felt cold sweat on his hands. He could see for miles in every direction. Earth, the Mother, the guardian of the young, was below him: dark she was, and without color, but wrapped in a cloth of silver. Over him and around him was the night, filled now with the warm blaze of the stars. It came to him that this place stood outside of time, beyond time; it had waited here forever between the sky and the earth, waited here before The People had come out of the north, waited here before the buffalo were born. It had been the same when Fox Claw had come, and all the others who had come before Fox Claw. It would be the same for his sons, when he had sons. It would always be here, waiting, for those who could find it and use it. . . .

He did not know how long he stood there. But it seemed only a short time before the Moon rose above the rim of the world. It was big, bigger than he had ever seen it, fat and yellow and marked with strange dark lines. The Moon too was a Mother, the guardian of the warriors on a raid. He managed a smile. He told himself that he was not alone. He had Ekaesi below him and Mother Moon above him. And there were others, somewhere, watching.

He watched the Moon for a long time, watched it change into a small silver ball, watched it climb high into the night and float among the stars. The night was very clear, and very still. The only sound was the rustle of the wind.

Buffalo Tongue moved very carefully, making sure that he did all the right things. This time, there must be no mistake. He carried his buffalo robe to the south side of the cap rock, almost to the four cedar trees. He lay down on the stone, facing the east, and covered himself with the robe. He tried to sleep. That was the way.

He found that sleep was slow in coming. He could not forget where he was. The stories he had heard, the things that had happened in this place. . . .

How would his vision come to him? In the scream of an eagle, the cry of a wolf? Ah, the wolf medicine was good. No bullet could harm a man who was guarded by the wolf; only an arrow could be dangerous, and the soldiers had no arrows. Or it could be a Voice that spoke to him in the night—perhaps this very night—a Voice that gave him instructions and signs to watch for. Many of his friends had heard the Voice. Or it might be that the Thunderbird would roar over this place, and the heavens would light with fire—

He could not know. He would have to wait. But he could feel the forces around him in the night, hear them whispering in the black cedars. He would not fail again. He must not even think of failure.

He closed his eyes.

Somehow, sleep came to him—and then, suddenly, it was morning.

His eyes opened into the glare of the Sun. At once, he threw aside the robe that had covered him. He got to his feet. He stood facing the Sun, staring straight at it with narrowed eyes. He extended his hands, palms upward, reaching out for the sky. He felt the power of the Sun: the Sun was a god that warmed him and filled his body with strength and health. How strange it was—the warmth seemed to well up within him, moving out to the Sun, answering the Sun. It was good. He knew that it was a good sign.

He filled his bone pipe with tobacco that was as dry as dust. He took out his fire drill and tamped the tinder of dry Spanish moss into the hole in the wooden drill block. He inserted the hardwood drill into the hole and began to twirl it between the palms of his hands. It was a slow process and he sang to himself as he worked. Finally, a little smoke curled up from the edges of the hole, and then the tinder caught. Instantly, he removed the hardwood drill and scooped up the burning moss with his bare hand, putting it into the bowl of his pipe. He puffed carefully on the stem until the tobacco caught. He offered the pipe to the Sun and then to the Earth Mother and then to the four directions. He smoked and prayed until the tobacco in the bowl gave out. There were easier ways of making a fire, of course, but the old ways were best when a man was seeking power. The taste of the dry smoke was unpleasant, though; it made him thirsty.

There was nothing more he could do. He had to wait.

The Sun climbed high into the sky. He did not doubt that the Sun was a god and would help him, but just the same it got uncomfortably hot on top of Spirit Hill. The stunted cedars gave little shade. The winds swept across the great empty spaces and dried his skin, but the winds did not cool him. All that day he sat motionless on the cap rock. He ate no food and drank no water. The hours crawled by. That night he slept more easily, and in the morning he smoked and prayed again.

Nothing happened.

The hunger did not bother him much; he was used to hunger. But the heat and the dry wind sucked out his juices. His lips cracked and his throat turned raw. When he tried to swallow, there was nothing there. He thought less of visions and more of the little spring at the foot of Spirit Hill. He could not quite see the spring when he walked to the edge of the cap rock to look at his horse, but he could smell it. It had a green smell, the smell of fresh living grass, and it was moist and cool, cool. . . .

The day passed, and the night. On the afternoon of the third day, he had to move, had to do something. He would not have believed that time could pass so slowly. He climbed back down the slope of Spirit Hill; his legs were weak and twice he stumbled. He tried to talk to Ekaesi but no words would come from his cracked and bleeding lips. He went to the tiny spring and stared at it, drinking it with his eyes. He plunged his dusty head into the little pool. The shock of the water almost made him faint. He let it soak his hair and soothe the burning in the skin of his face. He opened his mouth and tasted the water with his parched tongue—sweet, cold water.

But he did not drink.

He turned away from the spring and made his way back up Spirit Hill. It was very hard going now; he was light-headed and dizzy and he seemed to have no control over his arms and legs. He fell before he reached the top. He pulled himself up on his hands and knees and crawled the last few feet to the cap rock. He dragged himself out into the white glare of the sunlight. The scorched rock scraped his chest and he left a slight, fast-drying trail of crimson behind him. The crimson quickly faded to brown in the sun.

He felt it when the Sun dropped down in the land of the dead; he could not watch it with his eyes. The evening breeze was cooler and revived him a little. He sat on the still hot stone. He was giddy and shook his head to clear it.

Listen!

He thought he could hear something.

He strained his ears, listening. Was that a Voice, whispering to him from the dead land beyond the grave of the Sun?

No. He could not fool himself. It was the wind, only the wind. . . .

He crawled under the buffalo robe, trembling. He was hot but he knew that he would be chilled when he slept. This was the fourth night, the last night. Tomorrow would be the final day. If he saw no sign—

Do not think of it. Do not think of it.

His thoughts raced on; he could not stop them. What if the old gods lost their power? What if the medicine could not come? So many things had changed. He was young; he had never seen the old days. Was it all a lie? Or was it only a dream, that time when the earth was free and The People rode with the wind? If he failed now, what could he do? What would happen to him?

He felt the stars burning into him, and then the Moon. Mother Moon, guardian of warriors. Ah, her light was soft and cool and silver this night. She eased his hurts.

Look down on me, Mother Moon. Help me, my heart is crying. . . .

He must have slept, for suddenly he was aware that he had awakened.

His first impression was one of light, light all around him. It was a strange light, it was a glow of silver-gold that seemed to fill the air and wash the rocks of Spirit Hill with radiance. He had never seen anything like it. He pushed aside the buffalo robe and struggled to his feet. Had the night ended? Was this the dawn? He did not know. Everything was different, changed, transformed. Every detail was vivid before his eyes: the twisted cedars, the sweep of the land below, the tiny cracks in the cap rock. The world was bathed in a magic light. It was a new world, a world he had never known.

An older world?

With shaking hands he twirled fire into being and lit his pipe. The smoke made his head swim. He offered the pipe to the silver-gold sky, to the Earth Mother below, to the north and the south and the west and—

And there it was.

Suddenly, quietly, it was there. He dropped his pipe; it clattered on the stone. A bull buffalo stood silently on the eastern edge of the cap rock, where no buffalo could ever be. It was a real buffalo, not a dream. He stared at it, transfixed. The long black-brown hair of the buffalo's head and neck was thick and luxuriant. The animal's weak red eyes looked straight at the boy in the strange light. His short white horns came to tiny sharp points that gleamed like stars. A curl of white spittle dripped down from the left side of his hard mouth into his dark beard. His shoulders and hump were enormous; they were like mountains. His little tufted tail twitched slightly. The boy could hear him breathing, distinctly. He could smell his sour breath and his warm, heavy animal scent.

He heard the Voice.

The Voice spoke in his head. It was not loud, but every word was clear.

> *Remember me. I am the Buffalo who gave to you your name. I am your power and your guardian spirit. I will be with you always. I will protect you and make you strong. You need have no fears. You will sing the Buffalo Song when you need me and I will hear. Listen to my words. You are to make a medicine bag. Into this bag you will place sweet grass and the claws of an eagle. Into this bag you will place also a buffalo stone for power, which you shall find where I have stood. You will carry this bag with you always. I am the Buffalo who gave to you your name. Remember me.*

The boy blinked his eyes and the buffalo was gone. Shaking with excitement, he ran across the cap rock to where the buffalo had been. He fell to his hands and knees, searching frantically. Ai-eee, there it was! A drop of spittle where the buffalo had stood; yes, he was certain of it, it was still wet to his touch. And there—a small smooth white stone. A buffalo stone from the stomach of the buffalo! He had seen many such in his lifetime—there was no mistaking it.

It was real. *It was real.* That stone could not possibly have been here before on top of Spirit Hill. He would have seen it, as would have the others before him. The stone was hard and warm and unyielding in his hand; he gripped it tightly. It was real!

The boy stood up, his heart hammering against his ribs. The strange silver-gold light was gone. A new light flooded the cap rock and the lands below, the pure soft light of dawn. The Father Sun lifted above the rim of the earth, framing the place where the buffalo had stood.

It was over. He had not failed.

He scooped up his robe and his pipe and his fire-drill case, still clutching the buffalo stone in his right hand. He scrambled down the side of Spirit Hill, almost running in his eagerness. He fell once, skinning his knee, but he hardly noticed it. His horse nickered when he saw him and the boy threw his arms around the roan's sleek neck, dropping everything to the ground except the hard white stone.

"Ekaesi, Ekaesi. You have a man to carry."

He fumbled out a strip of pemmican from the parfleche with his saddle. He carried it to the tiny spring. He fell down on his belly and dipped his head into the night-cold water. He opened his dry mouth and drank. The water poured into his parched body like a river of ice. It stabbed at his insides. No matter! He drank his fill. He rolled over, luxuriating in the sweet grass. He began to chew his pemmican. He ate as much as he could choke down, but he could not finish the dried meat. His stomach cramped in pain.

Buffalo Tongue lay there in the morning sun, completely exhausted. The roan walked up and nuzzled him. He closed his eyes. His stomach hurt him terribly but that was nothing. His happiness was too big for pain.

He would rest until he was stronger. Yes, that was the way. There was no need to hurry. He had a lifetime of years ahead of him. He could spend this day by the spring, drinking whenever he wished. He could finish the pemmican, in time. His strength would come back.

He would ride to the reservation with the news. He would tell Fox Claw and his father. He was a man!

He lay quite still, waiting for the cramping to stop. He held the buffalo stone tightly in his hand. The day was good, everything was good.

He slept, and in his sleep he smiled.

LORD, I AIN'T NO STRANGER NOW

> *Then I buckled up my shoes,*
> *And I started.*

He knew, without knowing how it had happened, that he lay on the floor, in the dusty space before the altar which he and Elisha had cleaned; and knew that above him burned the yellow light which he had himself switched on. Dust was in his nostrils, sharp and terrible, and the feet of the saints, shaking the floor beneath him, raised small clouds of dust that filmed his mouth. He heard their cries, so far, so high above him—he could never rise that far. He was like a rock, a dead man's body, a dying bird, fallen from an awful height; something that had no power of itself, any more, to turn.

And something moved in John's body which was not John. He was invaded, set at naught, possessed. This power had struck John, in the head or in the heart; and, in a moment, wholly, filling him with an anguish that he could never in his life have imagined, that he surely could not endure, that even now he could not believe, had opened him up; had cracked him open, as wood beneath the axe cracks down the middle, as rocks break up; had ripped him and felled him in a moment, so that John had not felt the wound, but only the agony, had not felt the fall, but only the fear; and lay here, now, helpless, screaming, at the very bottom of darkness.

He wanted to rise—a malicious, ironic voice insisted that he rise—and, at once, to leave this temple and go out into the world.

He wanted to obey the voice, which was the only voice that spoke to him; he tried to assure the voice that he would do his best to rise; he would only lie here a moment, after his dreadful fall, and catch his breath. It was at this moment, precisely, that he found he could not rise; something had happened to his arms, his legs, his feet—ah, something had happened to John! And he began to scream again in his great, bewildered terror, and felt himself, indeed, begin to move—not upward, toward the light, but down again, a sickness in his bowels, a tightening in his loin-strings; he felt himself turning, again and again, across the dusty floor, as though God's toe had touched him lightly. And the dust made him cough and retch; in his turning the center of the whole earth shifted, making of space a sheer void and a mockery of order, and balance, and time. Nothing remained: all was swallowed up in chaos. And: *Is this it?* John's terrified soul inquired—*What is it?*—to no purpose, receiving no answer. Only the ironic voice insisted yet once more that he rise from that filthy floor if he did not want to become like all the other niggers.

Then the anguish subsided for a moment, as water withdraws briefly to dash itself once more against the rocks: he knew that it subsided only to return. And he coughed and sobbed in the dusty space before the altar, lying on his face. And still he was going down, farther and farther from the joy, the singing, and the light above him.

He tried, but in such despair!—the utter darkness does not present any point of departure, contains no beginning, and no end—to rediscover, and, as it were, to trap and hold tightly in the palm of his hand, the moment preceding his fall, his change. But that moment was also locked in darkness, was wordless, and would not come forth. He remembered only the cross: he had turned again to kneel at the altar, and had faced the golden cross. And the Holy Ghost was speaking—seeming to say, as John spelled out the so abruptly present and gigantic legend adorning the cross: *Jesus Saves*. He had stared at this, an awful bitterness in his heart, wanting to curse—and the Spirit spoke, and spoke in him. Yes: there was Elisha, speaking from the floor, and his father, silent, at his back. In his heart there was a sudden yearning tenderness for holy Elisha; desire, sharp and awful as a reflecting knife, to usurp the body of Elisha, and lie where Elisha lay; to speak in tongues, as Elisha spoke, and, with that authority, to confound his father. Yet this had not been the moment; it was as far back as he could go, but the secret, the turning, the abysmal drop was farther back, in darkness. As he cursed his father, as he loved Elisha, he had, even then, been weeping; he had already passed his moment, was already under the power, had been struck, and was going down.

Ah, down!—and to what purpose, where? To the bottom of the sea, the bowels of the earth, to the heart of the fiery furnace? Into a dungeon deeper than Hell, into a madness louder than the grave? What trumpet sound would awaken him, what hand would lift him up? For he knew, as he was struck again, and screamed again, his throat like burning ashes, and as he turned again, his body hanging from him like a useless weight, a heavy, rotting carcass, that if he were not lifted he would never rise.

His father, his mother, his aunt, Elisha—all were far above him, waiting, watching his torment in the pit. They hung over the golden barrier, singing behind them, light around their heads, weeping, perhaps, for John, struck down so early. And, no, they could not help him any more—nothing could help him any more. He struggled, struggled to rise up, and meet them—he wanted wings to fly upward and meet them in that morning, that morning where they were. But his struggles only thrust him downward, his cries did not go upward, but rang in his own skull.

Yet, though he scarcely saw their faces, he knew that they were there.

He felt them move, every movement causing a trembling, an astonishment, a horror in the heart of darkness where he lay. He could not know if they wished him to come to them as passionately as he wished to rise. Perhaps they did not help him because they did not care—because they did not love him.

Then his father returned to him, in John's changed and low condition; and John thought, but for a moment only, that his father had come to help him. In the silence, then, that filled the void, John looked on his father. His father's face was black—like a sad, eternal night; yet in his father's face there burned a fire—a fire eternal in an eternal night. John trembled where he lay, feeling no warmth for him from this fire, trembled, and could not take his eyes away. A wind blew over him, saying: "Whosoever loveth and maketh a lie." And he knew that he had been thrust out of the holy, the joyful, the blood-washed community, that his father had thrust him out. His father's will was stronger than John's own. His power was greater because he belonged to God. Now, John felt no hatred, nothing, only a bitter, unbelieving despair: all prophecies were true, salvation was finished, damnation was real!

Then Death is real, John's soul said, and Death will have his moment.

"Set thine house in order," said his father, "for thou shalt die and not live."

And then the ironic voice spoke again, saying: "Get up, John. Get up, boy. Don't let him keep you here. You got everything your daddy got."

John tried to laugh—John thought that he was laughing—but found, instead, that his mouth was filled with salt, his ears were full of burning water. Whatever was happening in his distant body now, he could not change or stop; his chest heaved, his laughter rose and bubbled at his mouth, like blood.

And his father looked on him. His father's eyes looked down on him, and John began to scream. His father's eyes stripped him naked, and hated what they saw. And as he turned, screaming, in the dust again, trying to escape his father's eyes, those eyes, that face, and all their faces, and the far-off yellow light, all departed from his vision as though he had gone blind. He was going down again. There is, his soul cried out again, no bottom to the darkness!

He did not know where he was. There was silence everywhere—only a perpetual, distant, faint trembling far beneath him—the roaring, perhaps, of the fires of Hell, over which he was suspended, or the echo, persistent, invincible still, of the moving feet of the saints. He thought of the mountain-top, where he longed to be, where the sun would cover him like a cloth of gold, would cover his head like a crown of fire, and in his hands he would hold a living rod. But this was no mountain where John lay, here, no robe, no crown. And the living rod was uplifted in other hands.

"I'm going to beat sin out of him. I'm going to beat it out."

Yes, he had sinned, and his father was looking for him. Now, John did not make a sound, and did not move at all, hoping that his father would pass him by.

"Leave him be. Leave him alone. Let him pray to the Lord."

"Yes, Mama. I'm going to try to love the Lord."

"He done run off somewhere. I'm going to find him. I'm going to beat it out."

Yes, he had sinned: one morning, alone, in the dirty bathroom, in the square, dirt-gray cupboard room that was filled with the stink of his father. Sometimes, leaning over the cracked, "tattle-tale gray" bathtub, he scrubbed his father's back; and looked, as the accursed son of Noah had looked, on his father's hideous nakedness. It was secret, like sin, and slimy, like the serpent, and heavy, like the rod. Then he hated his father, and longed for the power to cut his father down.

Was this why he lay here, thrust out from all human or heavenly help tonight? This, and not that other, his deadly sin, having looked on his father's nakedness and mocked and cursed him in his heart? Ah, that son of Noah's had been cursed, down to the present groaning generation: *A servant of servants shall he be unto his brethren.*

Then the ironic voice, terrified, it seemed, of no depth, no darkness, demanded of John, scornfully, if he believed that he was cursed. All niggers had been cursed, the ironic voice reminded him, all niggers had come from this most undutiful of Noah's sons. How could John be cursed for having seen in a bathtub what another man—*if* that other man had ever lived—had seen ten thousand years ago, lying in an open tent? Could a curse come down so many ages? Did it live in time, or in the moment? But John found no answer for this voice, for he was in the moment, and out of time.

And his father approached. "I'm going to beat sin out of him. I'm going to beat it out." All the darkness rocked and wailed as his father's feet came closer; feet whose tread resounded like God's tread in the garden of Eden, searching the covered Adam and Eve. Then his father stood just above him, looking down. Then John knew that a curse was renewed from moment to moment, from father to son. Time was indifferent, like snow and ice; but the heart, crazed wanderer in the driving waste, carried the curse forever.

"John," said his father, "come with me."

Then they were in a straight street, a narrow, narrow way. They had been walking for many days. The street stretched before them, long, and silent, going down, and whiter than the snow. There was no one on the street, and John was frightened. The buildings on this street, so near that John could touch them on either side, were narrow, also, rising like spears into the sky, and they were made of beaten gold and silver. John knew that these buildings were not for him—not today—*no, nor tomorrow, either!* Then, coming up this straight and silent street, he saw a woman, very old and black, coming toward them, staggering on the crooked stones. She was drunk, and dirty, and very old, and her mouth was bigger than his mother's mouth, or his own; her mouth was loose and wet, and he had *never* seen anyone so black. His father was astonished to see her, and beside himself with anger; but John was glad. He clapped his hands and cried:

"See! She's uglier than Mama! She's uglier than me!"

"You mighty proud, ain't you," his father said, "to be the Devil's son?"

But John did not listen to his father. He turned to watch the woman pass. His father grabbed his arm.

"You see that? That's sin. That's what the Devil's son runs after."

"Whose son are you?" John asked.

His father slapped him. John laughed, and moved a little away.

"I seen it. I seen it. I ain't the Devil's son for nothing."

His father reached for him, but John was faster. He moved backward down the shining street, looking at his father—his father who moved toward him, one hand outstretched in fury.

"And I *heard* you—all the nighttime long. I know what you do in the dark, black man, when you think the Devil's son's asleep. I heard you, spitting, and groaning, and choking—and I *seen* you, riding up and down, and going in and out. I ain't the Devil's son for nothing."

The listening buildings, rising upward yet, leaned, closing out the sky. John's feet began to slip; tears and sweat were in his eyes; still moving backward before his father, he looked about him for deliverance; but there was no deliverance in this street for him.

"And I hate you. I hate you. I don't care about your golden crown. I don't care about your long white robe. I seen you under the robe, I seen you!"

Then his father was upon him; at his touch there was singing, and fire. John lay on his back in the narrow street, looking up at his father, that burning face beneath the burning towers.

"I'm going to beat it out of you. I'm going to beat it out."

His father raised his hand. The knife came down. John rolled away, down the white, descending street, screaming:

"Father! Father!"

These were the first words he uttered. In a moment there was silence, and his father was gone. Again, he felt the saints above him—and dust was in his mouth. There was singing somewhere; far away, above him; singing slow and mournful. He lay silent, racked beyond endurance, salt drying on his face, with nothing in him any more, no lust, no fear, no shame, no hope. And yet he knew that it would come again—the darkness was full of demons crouching, waiting to worry him with their teeth again.

Then I looked in the grave and I wondered.

Ah, down!—what was he searching here, all alone in darkness? But now he knew, for irony had left him, that he was searching something, hidden in the darkness, that must be found. He would die if it was not found; or, he was dead already, and would never again be joined to the living, if it was not found.

And the grave looked so sad and lonesome.

In the grave where he now wandered—he knew it was the grave, it was so cold and silent, and he moved in icy mist—he found his mother and his father, his mother dressed in scarlet, his father dressed in white. They did not see him: they looked backward, over their shoulders, at a cloud of witnesses. And there was his Aunt Florence, gold and silver flashing on her fingers, brazen earrings dangling from her ears; and there was another woman, whom he took to be that wife of his father's called Deborah—who had, as he had once believed, so much to tell him. But she, alone, of all that company, looked at him and signified that there was no speech in the grave. He was a stranger there—they did not see him pass, they did not know what he was looking for, they could not help him search. He wanted to find Elisha, who knew, perhaps, who would help him—but Elisha was not there. There was Roy: Roy also might have helped him, but he had been stabbed with a knife, and lay now, brown and silent, at his father's feet.

Then there began to flood John's soul the waters of despair. *Love is as strong as death, as deep as the grave.* But love, which had, perhaps, like a benevolent monarch, swelled the population of his neighboring kingdom, Death, had not himself descended: they owed him no allegiance here. Here there was no speech or language, and there was no love; no one to say: You are beautiful, John; no one to forgive him, no matter what his sin; no one to heal him, and lift him up. No one: father and mother looked backward, Roy was bloody, Elisha was not here.

Then the darkness began to murmur—a terrible sound—and John's ears trembled. In this murmur that filled the grave, like a thousand wings beating on the air, he recognized a sound that he had always heard. He began, for terror, to weep and moan—and this sound was swallowed up, and yet was magnified by the echoes that filled the darkness.

The sound had filled John's life, so it now seemed, from the moment he had first drawn breath. He had heard it everywhere, in prayer and in daily speech, and wherever the saints were gathered, and in the unbelieving streets. It was in his father's anger, and in his mother's calm insistence, and in the vehement mockery of his aunt; it had rung, so oddly, in Roy's voice this afternoon, and when Elisha played the piano it was there; it was in the beat and jangle of Sister McCandless's tambourine, it was in the very cadence of her testimony, and invested that testimony with a matchless, unimpeachable authority. Yes, he had heard it all his life, but it was only now that his ears were opened to this sound that came from darkness, that could only come from darkness, that yet bore such sure witness to the glory of the light. And now in his moaning, and so far from any help, he heard it in himself—it rose from his bleeding, his cracked-open heart. It was a sound of rage and weeping which filled the grave, rage and weeping from time set free, but bound now in eternity; rage that had no language, weeping with no voice—which yet spoke now, to John's startled soul, of boundless melancholy, of the bitterest patience, and the longest night; of the deepest water, the strongest chains, the most cruel lash; of humility most wretched, the dungeon most absolute, of love's bed defiled, and birth dishonored, and most bloody, unspeakable, sudden death. Yes, the darkness hummed with murder: the body in the water, the body in the fire, the body on the tree. John looked down

Religion and World View

the line of these armies of darkness, army upon army, and his soul whispered: *Who are these? Who are they?* And wondered: *Where shall I go?*

There was no answer. There was no help or healing in the grave, no answer in the darkness, no speech from all that company. They looked backward. And John looked back, seeing no deliverance.

I, John, saw the future, way up in the middle of the air.

Were the lash, the dungeon, and the night for him? And the sea for him? And the grave for him?

I, John, saw a number, way in the middle of the air.

And he struggled to flee—out of this darkness, out of this company— into the land of the living, so high, so far away. Fear was upon him, a more deadly fear than he had ever known, as he turned and turned in the darkness, as he moaned, and stumbled, and crawled through darkness, finding no hand, no voice, finding no door. *Who are these? Who are they?* They were the despised and rejected, the wretched and the spat upon, the earth's offscouring; and he was in their company, and they would swallow up his soul. The stripes they had endured would scar his back, their punishment would be his, their portion his, his their humiliation, anguish, chains, their dungeon his, their death his. *Thrice was I beaten with rods, once I was stoned, thrice I suffered shipwreck, a night and a day I have been in the deep.*

And their dread testimony would be his!

"In journeyings often, in perils of waters, in perils of robbers, in perils by mine own countrymen, in perils by the heathen, in perils in the city, in perils in the wilderness, in perils in the sea, in perils among false brethren.

And their desolation, his:

In weariness and painfulness in watchings often, in hunger and thirst, in fastings often, in cold and nakedness.

And he began to shout for help, seeing before him the lash, the fire, and the depthless water, seeing his head bowed down forever, he, John, the lowest among these lowly. And he looked for his mother, but her eyes were fixed on this dark army—she was claimed by this army. And his father would not help him, his father did not see him, and Roy lay dead.

Then he whispered, not knowing that he whispered: "Oh, Lord, have mercy on me. Have mercy on me."

And a voice, for the first time in all his terrible journey, spoke to John, through the rage and weeping, and fire, and darkness, and flood:

"Yes," said the voice, "go through. Go through."

"Lift me up," whispered John, "lift me up. I can't go through."

"Go through," said the voice, "go through."

Then there was silence. The murmuring ceased. There was only this trembling beneath him. And he knew there was a light somewhere.

"Go through."

"Ask Him to take you through."

But he could never go through this darkness, through this fire and this wrath. He could never go through. His strength was finished, and he could not move. He belonged to the darkness—the darkness from which he had thought to flee had claimed him. And he moaned again, weeping, and lifted up his hands.

"Call on Him. Call on Him."

"Ask Him to take you through."

Dust rose again in his nostrils, sharp as the fumes of Hell. And he turned again in the darkness, trying to remember something he had heard, something he had read.

Jesus saves.

And he saw before him the fire, red and gold, and waiting for him—yellow, and red, and gold, and burning in a night eternal, and waiting for him. He must go through this fire, and into this night.

Jesus saves.

Call on Him.

Ask Him to take you through.

He could not call, for his tongue would not unlock, and his heart was silent, and great with fear. In the darkness, how to move?—with death's ten thousand jaws agape, and waiting in the darkness. On any turning whatsoever the beast may spring—to move in the darkness is to move into the waiting jaws of death. And yet, it came to him that he must move; for there was a light somewhere, and life, and joy, and singing—somewhere, somewhere above him.

And he moaned again: "Oh, Lord, have mercy. Have mercy, Lord."

There came to him again the communion service at which Elisha had knelt at his father's feet. Now this service was in a great, high room, a room made golden by the light of the sun; and the room was filled with a multitude of people, all in long, white robes, the women with covered heads. They sat at a long, bare, wooden table. They broke at this table flat, unsalted bread, which was the body of the Lord, and drank from a heavy silver cup the scarlet wine of His blood. Then he saw that they were barefoot, and that their feet were stained with this same blood. And a sound of weeping filled the room as they broke the bread and drank the wine.

Then they rose, to come together over a great basin filled with water. And they divided into four groups, two of women and two of men; and they began, woman before woman, and man before man, to wash each other's feet. But the blood would not wash off; many washings only turned the crystal water red; and someone cried: *"Have you been to the river?"*

Then John saw the river, and the multitude was there. And now they had undergone a change; their robes were ragged, and stained with the road they had traveled, and stained with unholy blood; the robes of some barely covered their nakedness; and some indeed were naked. And some stumbled on the smooth stones at the river's edge, for they were blind; and some crawled with a terrible wailing, for they were lame; some did not cease to pluck at their flesh, which was rotten with running sores. All struggled to get to the river, in a dreadful hardness of heart: the strong struck down the weak, the ragged spat on the naked, the naked cursed the blind, the blind crawled over the lame. And someone cried: *"Sinner, do you love my Lord?"*

Then John saw the Lord—for a moment only; and the darkness, for a moment only, was filled with a light he could not bear. Then, in a moment, he was set free; his tears sprang as from a fountain; his heart, like a fountain of waters, burst. Then he cried: "Oh, blessed Jesus! Oh, Lord Jesus! Take me through!"

Of tears there was, yes, a very fountain—springing from a depth never sounded before, from depths John had not known were in him. And he wanted to rise up, singing, singing in that great morning, the morning of his new life. Ah, how his tears ran down, how they blessed his soul!—as he felt himself, out of the darkness, and the fire, and the terrors of death, rising upward to meet the saints.

"Oh, yes!" cried the voice of Elisha. "Bless our God forever!"

And a sweetness filled John as he heard this voice, and heard the sound of singing: the singing was for him. For his drifting soul was anchored in the love of God; in the rock that endured forever. The light and the darkness has kissed each other, and were married now, forever, in the life and the vision of John's soul.

> *I, John, saw a city, way in the middle of the air,*
> *Waiting, waiting, waiting up there.*

He opened his eyes on the morning, and found them, in the light of the morning, rejoicing for him. The trembling he had known in darkness had been the echo of their joyful feet—these feet, bloodstained forever, and washed in many rivers—they moved on the bloody road forever, with no continuing city, but seeking one to come: a city out of time, not made with hands, but eternal in the heavens. No power could hold this army back, no water disperse them, no fire consume them. One day they would compel the earth to heave upward, and surrender the waiting dead. They sang, where the darkness gathered, where the lion waited, where the fire cried, and where blood ran down:

My soul, don't you be uneasy!

They wandered in the valley forever; and they smote the rock, forever; and the waters sprang, perpetually, in the perpetual desert. They cried unto the Lord forever, and lifted up their eyes forever, they were cast down forever, and He lifted them up forever. No, the fire could not hurt them, and yes, the lion's jaws were stopped; the serpent was not their master, the grave was not their resting-place, the earth was not their home. Job bore them witness, and Abraham was their father, Moses had elected to suffer with them rather than glory in sin for a season. Shadrach, Meshach, and Abednego had gone before them into the fire, their grief had been sung by David, and Jeremiah had wept for them. Ezekiel had prophesied upon them, these scattered bones, these slain, and, in the fulness of time, the prophet, John, had come out of the wilderness, crying that the promise was for them. They were encompassed with a very cloud of witnesses: Judas, who had betrayed the Lord; Thomas, who had doubted Him; Peter, who had trembled at the crowing of a cock; Stephen, who had been stoned; Paul, who had been bound; the blind man crying in the dusty road, the dead man rising from the grave. And they looked unto Jesus, the author and the finisher of their faith, running with patience the race He had set before them; they endured the cross, and they despised the shame, and waited to join Him, one day, in glory, at the right hand of the Father.

My soul! don't you be uneasy!
Jesus going to make up my dying bed!

"Rise up, rise up, Brother Johnny, and talk about the Lord's deliverance."

It was Elisha who had spoken; he stood just above John, smiling; and behind him were the saints—Praying Mother Washington, and Sister McCandless, and Sister Price. Behind these, he saw his mother, and his aunt; his father, for the moment, was hidden from his view.

"Amen!" cried Sister McCandless, "rise up, and praise the Lord!"

He tried to speak, and could not, for the joy that rang in him this morning. He smiled up at Elisha, and his tears ran down; and Sister McCandless began to sing:

> *"Lord, I ain't*
> *No stranger now!"*

"Rise up, Johnny," said Elisha, again. "Are you saved, boy?"

"Yes," said John, "oh, yes!" And the words came upward, it seemed, of themselves, in the new voice God had given him. Elisha stretched out his hand, and John took the hand, and stood—so suddenly, and so strangely, and with such wonder!—once more on his feet.

> *"Lord, I ain't*
> *No stranger now!"*

Yes, the night had passed, the powers of darkness had been beaten back. He moved among the saints, he, John, who had come home, who was one of their company now; weeping, he yet could find no words to speak of his great gladness; and he scarcely knew how he moved, for his hands were new, and his feet were new, and he moved in a new and Heaven-bright air. Praying Mother Washington took him in her arms, and kissed him, and their tears, his tears and the tears of the old, black woman, mingled.

"God bless you, son. Run on, honey, and don't get weary!"

> *"Lord, I been introduced*
> *To the Father and the Son,*
> *And I ain't*
> *No stranger now!"*

Yet, as he moved among them, their hands touching, and tears falling, and the music rising—as though he moved down a great hall, full of a splendid company—something began to knock in that listening, astonished, newborn, and fragile heart of his; something recalling the terrors of the night, which were not finished, his heart seemed to say; which, in this company, were now to begin. And, while his heart was speaking, he found himself before his mother. Her face was full of tears, and for a long while they looked at each other, saying nothing. And once again, he tried to read the mystery of that face—which, as it has never before been so bright and pained with love, had never seemed before so far from him, so wholly in communion with a life beyond his life. He wanted to comfort her, but the night had given him no language, no second sight, no power to see into the heart of any other. He knew only—and now, looking at his mother, he knew that he could never tell it—that the heart was a fearful place. She kissed him, and she said: "I'm mighty proud, Johnny. You keep the faith, I'm going to be praying for you till the Lord puts me in my grave."

Then he stood before his father. In the moment that he forced himself to raise his eyes and look into his father's face, he felt in himself a stiffening, and a panic, and a blind rebellion, and a hope for peace. The tears still on his face, and smiling still, he said: "Praise the Lord."

"Praise the Lord," said his father. He did not move to touch him, did not kiss him, did not smile. They stood before each other in silence, while the saints rejoiced; and John struggled to speak the authoritative, the living word that would conquer the great division between his father and himself. But it did not come, the living word; in the silence something died in John, and something came alive. It came to him that he must testify: his tongue only could bear witness to the wonders he had seen. And he remembered, suddenly, the text of a sermon he had once heard his father preach. And he opened his mouth, feeling, as he watched his father, the darkness roar behind him, and the very earth beneath him seem to shake; yet he gave to his father their common testimony. "I'm saved," he said, "and I know I'm saved." And then, as his father did not speak, he repeated his father's text: "My witness is in Heaven and my record is on high."

"It come from your mouth," said his father then. "I want to see you live it. It's more than a notion."

"I'm going to pray God," said John—and his voice shook, whether with joy or grief he could not say—"to keep me, and make me strong . . . to stand . . . to stand against the enemy . . . and against everything and everybody . . . that wants to cut down my soul."

Then his tears came down again, like a wall between him and his father. His Aunt Florence came and took him in her arms. Her eyes were dry, and her face was old in the savage, morning light. But her voice, when she spoke, was gentler than he had ever known it to be before.

"You fight the good fight," she said, "you hear? Don't you get weary, and don't you get scared. Because I *know* the Lord's done laid His hands on you."

"Yes," he said, weeping, "yes. I'm going to serve the Lord."

"Amen!" cried Elisha. "Bless our God!"

CHAPTER 28   RICHARD T. GILL

HAVE YOU EVER FELT
THAT IT *WAS* TRUE?

I remember, almost to the hour, when I first began to question my religion. I don't mean that my ideas changed radically just at that time. I was only twelve, and I continued to go to church faithfully and to say something that could pass for prayers each night before I went to sleep. But I never again felt quite the same. For the first time in my life, it had occurred to me that when I grew up I might actually leave the Methodist faith.

It all happened just a few days after my brother died. He was five years old, and his illness was so brief and his death so unexpected that my whole family was almost crazed with grief. My three aunts, each of whom lived within a few blocks of our house, and my mother were all firm believers in religion, and they turned in unison, and without reservation, to this last support. For about a week, a kind of religious frenzy seized our household. We would all sit in the living room—my mother, my aunts, my two sisters, and I, and sometimes Mr. Dodds, the Methodist minister, too—saying prayers in low voices, comforting one another, staying together for hours at a time, until someone remembered that we had not had dinner or that it was time for my sisters and me to be in bed.

I was quite swept up by the mood that had come over the house. When I went to bed, I would say the most elaborate, intricate prayers. In the past, when I had finished my "Now I lay me down to sleep," I would bless individually all the members of my immediate family and then my aunts, and let it go at that. Now, however, I felt that I had to bless everyone in the world whose name I could remember. I would go through all my friends at school, includ-

From *The Code* by Richard T. Gill. Reprinted by permission; copyright © 1957 The New Yorker Magazine, Inc.

ing the teachers, the principal, and the janitor, and then through the names of people I had heard my mother and father mention, some of whom I had never even met. I did not quite know what to do about my brother, whom I wanted to pray for more than for anyone else. I hesitated to take his name out of its regular order, for fear I would be committed to believing that he had really died. But then I *knew* that he had died, so at the end of my prayers, having just barely mentioned his name as I went along, I would start blessing him over and over again, until I finally fell asleep.

The only one of us who was unmoved by this religious fervor was my father. Oddly enough, considering what a close family we were and how strongly my mother and aunts felt about religion, my father had never shown the least interest in it. In fact, I do not think that he had ever gone to church. Partly for this reason, partly because he was a rather brusque, impatient man, I always felt that he was something of a stranger in our home. He spent a great deal of time with us children, but through it all he seemed curiously unapproachable. I think we all felt constrained when he played with us and relieved when, at last, we were left to ourselves.

At the time of my brother's death, he was more of a stranger than ever. Except for one occasion, he took no part in the almost constant gatherings of the family in the living room. He was not going to his office that week—we lived in a small town outside Boston—and he was always around the house, but no one ever seemed to know exactly where. One of my aunts—Sarah, my mother's eldest sister—felt very definitely that my father should not be left to himself, and she was continually saying to me, "Jack, go upstairs and see if you can find him and talk to him." I remember going timidly along the hallway of the second floor and peeking into the bedrooms, not knowing what I should say if I found him and half afraid that he would scold me for going around looking into other people's rooms. One afternoon, not finding him in any of the bedrooms, I went up into the attic, where we had a sort of play-room. I remember discovering him there by the window. He was sitting absolutely motionless in an old wicker chair, an empty pipe in his hands, staring out fixedly over the treetops. I stood in the doorway for several minutes before he was aware of me. He turned as if to say something, but then, looking at me or just above my head—I was not sure which—he seemed to lose himself in his thoughts. Finally, he gave me a strangely awkward salute with his right hand and turned again to the window.

About the only times my father was with the rest of us were when we had meals or when, in the days immediately following the funeral, we all went out to the cemetery, taking fresh flowers or wreaths. But even at the cemetery he always stood slightly apart—a tall, lonely figure. Once, when we were at the grave and I was nearest him, he reached over and squeezed me around the shoulders. It made me feel almost embarrassed, as though he were breaking through some inviolable barrier between us. He must have felt as I did, because he at once removed his arm and looked away, as though he had never actually embraced me at all.

It was the one occasion when my father was sitting in the living room with us that started me to wondering about my religion. We had just returned from the cemetery—two carloads of us. It was three or four days after the funeral and just at the time when, the shock having worn off, we were all experiencing our first clear realization of what had happened. Even I, young as I was, sensed that there was a new air of desolation in our home.

For a long time, we all sat there in silence. Then my aunts, their eyes moist, began talking about my brother, and soon my mother joined in. They started off softly, telling of little things he had done in the days before his illness. Then they fell silent and dried their eyes, and then quickly remembered some other incident and began speaking again. Slowly the emotion mounted, and before long the words were flooding out. "God will take care of him!" my Aunt Sarah cried, almost ecstatically. "Oh, yes, He will! He will!" Presently, they were all talking in chorus—saying that my brother was happy at last and that they would all be with him again one day.

I believed what they were saying and I could barely hold back my tears. But swept up as I was, I had the feeling that they should not be talking that way while my father was there. The feeling was one that I did not understand at all at the moment. It was just that when I looked over to the corner where he was sitting and saw the deep, rigid lines of his face, saw him sitting there silently, all alone, I felt guilty. I wanted everyone to stop for a while—at least until he had gone upstairs. But there was no stopping the torrent once it had started.

"Oh, he was too perfect to live!" Aunt Agnes, my mother's youngest sister, cried. "He was never a bad boy. I've never seen a boy like that. I mean he was never even naughty. He was just too perfect."

"Oh, yes. Oh, yes," my mother sighed.

"It's true," Aunt Sarah said. "Even when he was a baby, he never really cried. There was never a baby like him. He was a saint."

"He *was* a saint!" Aunt Agnes cried. "That's why he was taken from us!"

"He was a perfect baby," my mother said.

"He was taken from us," Aunt Agnes went on, "because he was too perfect to live."

All through this conversation, my father's expression had been growing more and more tense. At last, while Aunt Agnes was speaking, he rose from his chair. His face was very pale, and his eyes flashed almost feverishly. "Don't talk like that, Agnes!" he exclaimed, with a strange violence that was not anger but something much deeper. "I won't have you talking like that any more. I don't want anybody talking like that!" His whole body seemed to tremble. I had never seen him so worked up before. "Of course he was a bad boy at times!" he cried. "Every boy's bad once in a while. What do you have to change him for? Why don't you leave him as he was?"

"But he was such a perfect baby," Aunt Sarah said.

"He *wasn't* perfect!" my father almost shouted, clenching his fist. "He was no more perfect than Jack here or Betty or Ellen. He was just an ordinary

Religion and World View

little boy. He wasn't perfect. And he wasn't a saint. He was just a little boy, and I won't have you making him over into something he wasn't!"

He looked as though he were going to go on talking like this, but just then he closed his eyes and ran his hand up over his forehead and through his hair. When he spoke again, his voice was subdued. "I just wish you wouldn't talk that way," he said. "That's all I mean." And then, after standing there silently for a minute, he left the living room and walked upstairs.

I sat watching the doorway through which he had gone. Suddenly, I had no feeling for what my mother and my aunts had been saying. It was all a mist, a dream. Out of the many words that had been spoken that day, it was those few sentences of my father's that explained to me how I felt about my brother. I wanted to be with my father to tell him so.

I went upstairs and found him once again in the playroom in the attic. As before, he was silent and staring out the window when I entered, and we sat without speaking for what seemed to me like half an hour or more. But I felt that he knew why I was there, and I was not uncomfortable with him.

Finally, he turned to me and shook his head. "I don't know what I can tell you, Jack," he said, raising his hands and letting them drop into his lap. "That's the worst part of it. There's just nothing I can say that will make it any better."

Though I only half understood him then, I see now that he was telling me of a drawback—that he had no refuge, no comfort, no support. He was telling me that you were all alone if you took the path that he had taken. Listening to him, I did not care about the drawback. I had begun to see what a noble thing it was for a man to bear the full loss of someone he had loved.

II

By the time I was thirteen or fourteen I was so thoroughly committed to my father's way of thinking that I considered it a great weakness in a man to believe in religion. I wanted to grow up to face life as he did—truthfully, without comfort, without support.

My attitude was never one of rebellion. Despite the early regimen of Sunday school and church that my mother had encouraged, she was wonderfully gentle with me, particularly when I began to express my doubts. She would come into my room each night after the light was out and ask me to say my prayers. Determined to be honest with her, I would explain that I could not say them sincerely, and therefore should not say them at all. "Now, Jack," she would reply, very quietly and calmly, "you mustn't talk like that. You'll really feel much better if you say them." I could tell from the tone of her voice that she was hurt, but she never tried to force me in any way. Indeed, it might have been easier for me if she *had* tried to oppose my decision strenuously. As it was, I felt so bad at having wounded her that I was continually trying to make things up—running errands, surprising her by doing the dishes when she went out shopping—behaving, in short, in the most conscientious, considerate fashion. But all this never brought me any closer to her religion. On the contrary, it only served to free me for my decision *not* to believe. And for that decision, as I say, my father was responsible.

Part of his influence, I suppose, was in his physical quality. Even at that time—when he was in his late forties and in only moderately good health—he was a most impressive figure. He was tall and heavy-chested, with leathery, rough-cast features and with an easy, relaxed rhythm in his walk. He had been an athlete in his youth, and, needless to say, I was enormously proud of his various feats and told about them, with due exaggeration, all over our neighborhood. Still, the physical thing had relatively little to do with the matter. My father, by that time, regarded athletes and athletics with contempt. Now and again, he would take me into the back yard to fool around with boxing gloves, but when it came to something serious, such as my going out for football in high school, he invariably put his foot down. "It takes too much time," he would tell me. "You ought to be thinking of college and your studies. It's nonsense what they make of sports nowadays!" I always wanted to remind him of *his* school days, but I knew it was no use. He had often told me what an unforgivable waste of time he considered his youth to have been.

Thus, although the physical thing was there, it was very much in the background—little more, really, than the simple assumption that a man ought to know how to take care of himself. The real bond between us was spiritual, in the sense that courage, as opposed to strength, is spiritual. It was this intangible quality of courage that I wanted desperately to possess and that, it seemed to me, captured everything that was essential about my father.

We never talked of this quality directly. The nearest we came to it was on certain occasions during the early part of the Second World War, just before I went off to college. We would sit in the living room listening to a speech by Winston Churchill, and my father would suddenly clap his fist against his palm. "My God!" he would exclaim, fairly beaming with admiration. "That man's got the heart of a tiger!" And I would listen to the rest of the speech, thrilling to every word, and then, thinking of my father, really, I would say aloud that, of all men in the world, the one I would most like to be was Churchill.

Nor did we often talk about religion. Yet our religion—our rejection of religion—was the deepest statement of the bond between us. My father, perhaps out of deference to my mother and my sisters and aunts, always put his own case very mildly. "It's certainly a great philosophy," he would say of Christianity. "No one could question that. But for the rest . . ." Here he would throw up his hands and cock his head to one side, as if to say that he had tried, but simply could not manage the hurdle of divinity. This view, however mildly it may have been expressed, became mine with absolute clarity and certainty. I concluded that religion was a refuge, without the least foundation in fact. More than that, I positively objected to those—I should say those *men*, for to me it was a peculiarly masculine matter—who turned to religion for support. As I saw it, a man ought to face life as it really is, on his own two feet, without a crutch, as my father did. That was the heart of the matter. By the time I left home for college, I was so deeply committed to this view that I would have considered it a disloyalty to him, to myself, to the code we had lived by, to alter my position in the least.

I did not see much of my father during the next four years or so. I was home during the summer vacation after my freshman year, but then, in the middle of the next year, I went into the Army. I was shipped to the Far East for the tail end of the war, and was in Japan at the start of the Occupation. I saw my father only once or twice during my entire training period, and, naturally, during the time I was overseas I did not see him at all.

While I was away, his health failed badly. In 1940, before I went off to college, he had taken a job at a defense plant. The plant was only forty miles from our home, but he was working on the night shift, and commuting was extremely complicated and tiresome. And, of course, he was always willing to overexert himself out of a sense of pride. The result was that late in 1942 he had a heart attack. He came through it quite well, but he made no effort to cut down on his work and, as a consequence, suffered a second, and more serious, attack, two years later. From that time on, he was almost completely bedridden.

I was on my way overseas at the time of the second attack, and I learned of it in a letter from my mother. I think she was trying to spare me, or perhaps it was simply that I could not imagine so robust a man as my father being seriously ill. In any event, I had only the haziest notion of what his real condition was, so when, many months later, I finally did realize what had been going on, I was terribly surprised and shaken. One day, some time after my arrival at an American Army post in Japan, I was called to the orderly room and told that my father was critically ill and that I was to be sent home immediately. Within forty-eight hours, I was standing in the early-morning light outside my father's bedroom, with my mother and sisters at my side. They had told me, as gently as they could, that he was not very well, that he had had another attack. But it was impossible to shield me then. I no sooner stepped into the room and saw him than I realized that he would not live more than a day or two longer.

From that moment on, I did not want to leave him for a second. Even that night, during the periods when he was sleeping and I was of no help being there, I could not get myself to go out of the room for more than a few minutes. A practical nurse had come to sit up with him, but since I was at the bedside, she finally spent the night in the hallway. I was really quite tired, and late that night my mother and my aunts begged me to go to my room and rest for a while, but I barely heard them. I was sure he would wake up soon, and when he did, I wanted to be there to talk to him.

We did talk a great deal that first day and night. It was difficult for both of us. Every once in a while, my father would shift position in the bed, and I would catch a glimpse of his wasted body. It was a knife in my heart. Even worse were the times when he would reach out for my hand, his eyes misted, and begin to tell me how he felt about me. I tried to look at him, but in the end I always looked down. And, knowing that he was dying, and feeling desperately guilty, I would keep repeating to myself that he knew how I felt, that he would understand why I looked away.

There was another thing, too. While we talked that day, I had a vague feeling that my father was on the verge of making some sort of confession to me. It was, as I say, only the vaguest impression, and I thought very little about it. The next morning, however, I began to sense what was in the air. Apparently, Mr. Dodds, the minister, whom I barely knew, had been coming to the house lately to talk to my father. My father had not said anything about this, and I learned it only indirectly, from something my mother said to my eldest sister at the breakfast table. At the moment, I brushed the matter aside. I told myself it was natural that Mother would want my father to see the minister at the last. Nevertheless, the very mention of the minister's name caused something to tighten inside me.

Later that day, the matter was further complicated. After lunch, I finally did go to my room for a nap, and when I returned to my father's room, I found him and my mother talking about Mr. Dodds. The conversation ended almost as soon as I entered, but I was left with the distinct impression that they were expecting the minister to pay a visit that day, whether very shortly or at suppertime or later in the evening, I could not tell. I did not ask. In fact, I made a great effort not to think of the matter at all.

Then, early that evening, my father spoke to me. I knew before he said a word that the minister *was* coming. My mother had straightened up the bedroom, and fluffed up my father's pillows so that he was half sitting in the bed. No one had told me anything, but I was sure what the preparations meant. "I guess you probably know," my father said to me when we were alone, "we're having a visitor tonight. It's—ah—Mr. Dodds. You know, the minister from your mother's church."

I nodded, half shrugging, as if I saw nothing the least unusual in the news.

"He's come here before once or twice," my father said. "Have I mentioned that? I can't remember if I've mentioned that."

"Yes, I know. I think Mother said something, or perhaps you did. I don't remember."

"I just thought I'd let you know. You see, your mother wanted me to talk to him. I— I've talked to him more for her sake than anything else."

"Sure. I can understand that."

"I think it makes her feel a little better. I think—" Here he broke off, seemingly dissatisfied with what he was saying. His eyes turned to the ceiling, and he shook his head slightly, as if to erase the memory of his words. He

Religion and World View

studied the ceiling for a long time before he spoke again. "I don't mean it was all your mother exactly," he said. "Well, what I mean is he's really quite an interesting man. I think you'd probably like him a good deal."

"I know Mother has always liked him," I replied. "From what I gather, most people seem to like him very much."

"Well, he's that sort," my father went on, with quickening interest. "I mean, he isn't what you'd imagine at all. To tell the truth, I wish you'd talk to him a little. I wish you'd talk things over with him right from scratch." My father was looking directly at me now, his eyes flashing.

"I'd be happy to talk with him sometime," I said. "As I say, everybody seems to think very well of him."

"Well, I wish you would. You see, when you're lying here day after day, you get to thinking about things. I mean, it's good to have someone to talk to." He paused for a moment. "Tell me," he said, "have you ever . . . have you ever wondered if there wasn't some truth in it? Have you ever thought about it that way at all?"

I made a faint gesture with my hand. "Of course, it's always possible to wonder," I replied. "I don't suppose you can ever be completely certain one way or the other."

"I know, I know," he said, almost impatiently. "But have you ever felt—well, all in a sort of flash—that it *was* true? I mean, have you ever had that feeling?"

He was half raised up from the pillow now, his eyes staring into me with a feverish concentration. Suddenly, I could not look at him any longer. I lowered my head.

"I don't mean permanently or anything like that," he went on. "But just for a few seconds. The feeling that you've been wrong all along. Have you had that feeling—ever?"

I could not look up. I could not move. I felt that every muscle in my body had suddenly frozen. Finally, after what seemed an eternity, I heard him sink back into the pillows. When I glanced up a moment later, he was lying there silent, his eyes closed, his lips parted, conveying somehow the image of the death that awaited him.

Presently, my mother came to the door. She called me into the hall to tell me that Mr. Dodds had arrived. I said that I thought my father had fallen asleep but that I would go back and see.

It was strangely disheartening to me to discover that he was awake. He was sitting there, his eyes open, staring grimly into the gathering shadows of the evening.

"Mr. Dodds is downstairs," I said matter-of-factly. "Mother wanted to know if you felt up to seeing him tonight."

For a moment, I thought he had not heard me; he gave no sign of recognition whatever. I went to the foot of the bed and repeated myself. He nodded, not answering the question but simply indicating that he had heard me. At length, he shook his head. "Tell your mother I'm a little tired tonight," he said. "Perhaps—well, perhaps some other time."

"I could ask him to come back later, if you'd like."

"No, no, don't bother. I—I could probably use the rest."

I waited a few seconds. "Are you sure?" I asked. "I'm certain he could come back in an hour or so."

Then, suddenly, my father was looking at me. I shall never forget his face at that moment and the expression burning in his eyes. He was pleading with me to speak. And all I could say was that I would be happy to ask Mr. Dodds to come back later, if he wanted it that way. It was not enough. I knew, instinctively, at that moment that it was not enough. But I could not say anything more.

As quickly as it had come, the burning flickered and went out. He sank back into the pillows again. "No, you can tell him I won't be needing him tonight," he said, without interest. "Tell him not to bother waiting around." Then he turned on his side, away from me, and said no more.

So my father did not see Mr. Dodds that night. Nor did he ever see him again. Shortly after midnight, just after my mother and sisters had gone to bed, he died. I was at his side then, but I could not have said exactly when it occurred. He must have gone off in his sleep, painlessly, while I sat there awake beside him.

In the days that followed, our family was together almost constantly. Curiously enough, I did not think much about my father just then. For some reason, I felt the strongest sense of responsibility toward the family. I found myself making the arrangements for the funeral, protecting Mother from the stream of people who came to the house, speaking words of consolation to my sisters and even to my aunts. I was never alone except at night, when a kind of oblivion seized me almost as soon as my head touched the pillow. My sleep was dreamless, numb.

Then, two weeks after the funeral, I left for Fort Devens, where I was to be discharged from the Army. I had been there three days when I was told that my terminal leave would begin immediately and that I was free to return home. I had half expected that when I was at the Fort, separated from the family, something would break inside me. But still no emotion came. I thought of my father often during that time, but, search as I would, I could find no sign of feeling.

Then, when I had boarded the train for home, it happened. Suddenly, for no reason whatever, I was thinking of the expression on my father's face that last night in the bedroom. I saw him as he lay there pleading with me to speak. And I knew then what he had wanted me to say to him—that it was really all right with me, that it wouldn't change anything between us if he gave way. And then I was thinking of myself and what I had said and what I had *not* said. Not a word to help! Not a word!

I wanted to beg his forgiveness. I wanted to cry out aloud to him. But I was in a crowded train, sitting with three elderly women just returning from a shopping tour. I turned my face to the window. There, silent, unnoticed, I thought of what I might have said.

CHAPTER 29   PETER MATTHIESSEN

THE DEATH OF WEAKE

For several days the Wittaia, unable to effect a death in battle or in their field raids from the Tokolik, had attempted a raid near the river, coming across early in the morning from the Turaba. The akuni were aware of this, and Weaklekek's kaio had been strengthened by Aloro, Husuk, and other warriors, who attempted to ambush the raiders; despite several alarms, no real battle had occurred.

This morning the men did not go to the kaio, for the feast of the Wilil was taking place. Aloro was an important Wilil, Weaklekek an important guest, and Husuk went off to war on the north frontier. No women were permitted in Weaklekek's fields, and the kaio was abandoned for the day. The Aike frontier, with the looming Turaba, had always been a dangerous place, and as Weaklekek's absence, like all other important matters, was common knowledge, no trouble was expected.

But the day was hot, and in the afternoon the solitary Woluklek went to the river to drink water. The people tire of the stale, silted waters of the ditches—they have no drink but water—and in dry weather will often go a long way to the river, where they squat on the bank and drink slowly and steadily for minutes. Woluklek took with him three little boys who were playing near Mapiatma.

One of the boys was Weake, whose father had been killed the year before on the Waraba. His mother had since run off to the Wittaia, and Weake was now the ward of his uncle, the warrior Huonke. He was a small yegerek, a friend of Tukum, with the large eyes and thick eyebrows which make many of the children beautiful. His name meant "Bad Path," and recently he had hurt his leg. For this reason, on this day, he was slower than his friends.

Near the Aike, on a little rise just short of the side path to Weaklekek's kaio, Woluklek and the three boys were ambushed by a party of Wittaia; the raiders sprang from the low reeds and bushes. Afterward Woluklek was not sure about their numbers, but a raiding party is usually comprised of about thirty men. There was nothing to be done. He dropped his spear and fled, the boys behind him.

All his life Weake had been taught to hate and fear the enemy, and when he saw the strange men with their spears he turned with the rest and ran. But he was not fast enough and was almost immediately run down. He screamed for help, but the others were running for their lives and did not turn. The face of a man, of several men, loomed above him on the bright blue sky, with harsh, loud breathing. The men rammed their spears through him over and over, pinning him to the ground, and then they were gone, and Weake was carried home.

The cry of *Kaio, kaio* carried swiftly past Homuak and to the pig feast: the hot stone fragment that had burned Huonke must have struck him close to the same instant that his nephew had been pierced by the long spears. While the rock fire was still steaming, word came from Abulopak about the boy. The two villages almost adjoin, and the pilai where Weake lived was scarcely a hundred yards across the fences from the Wilil fire. Huonke and Tamugi, his brother-in-law, ran toward Abulopak, where the women's wailing had already started.

In the long yard of the sili two women were kneeling, facing the mute pilai. The sili lies under the mountain, at the north end of the great grove of araucaria, and the pilai at its southern end is shaded by the tall pines against the hill. Inside the pilai were a few old men, and then Asikanalek arrived, and Tamugi and Huonke, and Siloba.

Weake lay on a banana frond beside the fire. He was still alive, and his clear childish voice seemed out of place in the brown solemnity of the men's round house: it cut through the decrepit snuffling of the old men as the shaft of daylight in the doorway cut through the motes of dust. Weake spoke of his own etai-eken, his seed-of-singing, the life he clung to with all his strength, as if the mourning he could hear must be some dark mistake. *An etai-eken werek!* But I'm alive! Though he not once screamed or whined, his voice was broken as he spoke by little calls of pain, and the blood flowed steadily onto the frond beneath him.

Huonke tried to quiet him, repeating the same terse phrase over and over, like a chant: *Hat nahalok loguluk! Hat nahalok loguluk!*—But you're not going to die! Huonke's voice was the only firm one in the pilai. Tamugi, a large-muscled man whose ready smile is bolder than his nature, sobbed as loudly as he could, while Asikanalek cried silently. The boy's voice answered Huonke obediently—*Oh, oh,* he repeated gently. Yes, yes. But now and then pain or terror overcame him, and he cried out and fought to escape the death that he felt in their hands. Huonke held his left arm and Siloba his right, while Tamugi and Asikanalek held down his legs. Siloba neither talked nor cried, but breathed earnestly and ceaselessly into the boy's ear, oo-Phuh, oo-Phuh: this ritual breathing, which brought health, would be used in the next hour on the wisa pig meat in the pilai of the Wilil.

Weake twisted in their grasp, his back arching; his legs were released and he drew his knees up to his chin, covering the gleam of the neat spear holes at his navel and lower belly. The old cut on the boy's leg still had its green patch of leaf dressing, but the spear holes, like small mouths in his chest and sides, his arm and leg and stomach, had not been tended. Some fresh leaf was brought at last, and the two stomach wounds were bound up hastily, almost carelessly, as if the true purpose of the leaf was to protect the pilai floor from blood; in their distress the men handled him ineptly, and he cried out. The figures hunched over him in the near-darkness, with the old men's snuffling and the steady oo-Phuh, oo-Phuh, and the harsh tearing of the leaf.

Behind Huonke, in the shadows, a woman sat as rigid as a stone. The custom excluding women from the pilai had been waived while the child lived, but nevertheless she maintained silence: when she spoke, but once, out of the darkness, her voice came clear and tragic, like a song. The woman was Huonke's sister, married to Tamugi; she has a wild sad quality in her face and is one of the handsomest women in the Kurelu. She counseled the men to take the boy down to the stream.

Weake clung to life and would not die. His writhings had covered him with blood, and he lay in a pool of darkness. When the woman finished speaking, the men agreed to take him to the water, which, entering his wounds, would leach out the dark blood of illness. He was picked up and carried outside, Siloba holding his head up by the hair. The women in the yard began an outcry, but the men did not pass through the yard. They took Weake through a hole in the back fencing, across a pig pasture, over a stile, down through a small garden to a ditch. There they laid him in the muddy water, so that it lapped up to his chest.

Tamugi did not come. After leaving the pilai with the other men, he kept on going, for the Wilil fire was now open, and he wished some pig. The others accompanied Huonke to the ditch. Soon they too left, for there was nothing to be done. Only Siloba remained, and his friend Yonokma. Yonokma sat in water up to his waist, holding the legs, while Huonke and Siloba, their own lower legs submerged, held the child's arms: Weake's head rested on Huonke's right thigh.

Fitfully Weake talked and now and then cried out: the voice rang through the silent garden, against the soft background of lament and the low hum of the men's voices at the pig feast. Once he cried, *Tege! Tege!* in terror of the spears, and Huonke shouted him down: *Hat ninom werek! Hat ninom werek!*—over and over and over: You are here with us, you are here with us! He said this dully every time Weake called out. You are here with us. Then

Weake would resume his own meek, rhythmic *Oh, oh, oh* of assent. *Hat ninom werek—oh. Hat ninom werek—oh.* His eyes closed, opened wide, and closed again; he seemed to doze. In the muddy ditch, with its water spiders, round black beetles, and detritus of old leaves, his blood drifted peacefully away. Against the firmament above soared the great arches of the banana trees, and the hill crest in a softening light, and the blue sky. Taro and hiperi grew about him, and the blue-flowered spiderwort lined the steep banks. Swiftlets coursed the garden, hunting insects, and the mosquitoes came; the men slapped one another.

Huonke sighed and leaned his head against the bank. In grief, Huonke's face had lost its hard, furtive quality and become handsome. Yonokma, sitting in the water, yawned with cold. Okal, who had gone with Weake to the river, came and stared down at his friend; he looked restless and unhappy and soon went away again.

In his last sleep Weake cried, a small, pure sound which came with every breath. When pain awakened him, he tried to talk, but his voice was faint and drowsy. Siloba breathed fitfully into his ear, but his efforts were disheartened: he only did it, guiltily, when the little boy called out. The small slim body had more than twenty wounds, and the wonder was that the boy had lived so long. But Weake would live until the twilight, asleep in the healing water, while the men attending him grew tired and cold. They coughed and slapped themselves and stared into the water, and the little boy's chest twitched up and down, up and down. Sometimes Siloba poured water on the wounds above the surface, and more blood was drawn forth, flowing down his side. Huonke said, You will stay with us, You will stay with us, and the child said Yes, yes yes, and did not speak again.

Siba came and stared at the little boy. He broke off the stem of a taro leaf and with it probed the wound on the left side. The belly leaf was floating, and the small horim: Siba attempted to push back a trace of white intestine which protruded near the navel as if, by concealing the evidence of hurt, he might somehow be of help. Weake was failing rapidly and did not cry out; his mouth was open, and his lips had puffed and dried. In the attack he had received a heavy blow, for the side of his face had grown swollen and distorted.

Yonokma leaned forward and removed a bit of straw from the dry lips.

Siba ran across the garden and sprang onto the roof of the pig shed by the fence. There, with a great cracking sound like anger, he broke off a banana frond and hurled it down into the sili yard: this leaf would be the little boy's last bed. Returning, he picked Weake up out of the water and carried him homeward through the garden. Huonke and the two elege trailed Siba through the dusk, shaking with cold.

The small body was limp, with one foot lying on the other, and arms hanging: the blood dripped very slowly on the weeds. His breathing had silenced, and his eyes, half closed, had glazed, like those of a fresh-killed animal. Nilik, Wereklowe, and Polik had come to look at him in his pilai, but it was evening now and he was dead.

The next morning, in the middle of the yard, Huonke and Tamgui built the chair. Four women emerged from the cooking shed and kneeled before it, and more women were already climbing the stile which separated the small sili from the main yard of Wereklowe. The wailing had commenced, and the Alua clan was coming through the fields from all across the southern Kurelu.

In the pilai crouched Asikanalek, twisted by grief. Against the wall, where sunlight filtered through the chinks, sat Weake's small silhouette, already arranged in the position he would be given in the chair. Asikanalek went to him and carried him outside into the day. Still holding the boy, he kneeled in the bright sun before the pilai and, staring upward at the sky, lamented. The men about him looked disheveled and distraught, and Asikanalek's shoulders were smeared with yellow clay. Weake's appearance in the yard had caused a stir among the women; the long day of fierce wailing had begun.

Weake was draped with two large shell bibs, which covered not only his mutilated chest but his torn stomach; the wife of Tamugi kneeled before him, binding up his legs. A man adjusted a new funeral horim to replace the one which had floated off in the brown ditch. Beside the chair Huonke and Tamugi cried out and rubbed their legs. Now and then Huonke would rub his hands together in a strange, stiff-fingered way, and glance about him, as if uneasy in the light of day.

Weake was carried to his chair. His bound legs were hung over the cross piece, and his head was held up by a strip of leaf passed by Tamugi beneath his chin. At the foot of the chair, wailing, Tamugi's wife crouched upon the ground and mopped at it with torn-up grass; she made a circular motion with her hand, scarring the earth. Other women, with girls and small children, filed steadily into the yard and arranged themselves upon the ground before lending their voices to the waves of sound.

A lizard darted from the fence to seize an insect. It gulped busily, its small head switching back and forth, and moved in quick fits and starts back to the shadows. Above, a honey eater bounded to the limb of an albizzia. It too cocked its head, unsettled by the wailing, but calmed before it fled, and sat there preening. In the blue sky over the hill the kites harassed one another, screeching.

The men draped shell belts on Weake, binding his brow with the bright colors and building the belts into a kind of crown. But his head was small, and most of the belts were lain along his sides and down the chair arms. While his attendants scratched and shuffled and thought thoughts, in the warm doldrums of their existence, the child sat alone in cold serenity. He seemed to grieve, nevertheless, as if oppressed by all his trappings; when the women came and draped their nets, they almost hid him in the shadows. Huonke came and smeared him with fresh pig grease, and his shins, still in the sun, took on a gleam: Tukum, himself gleaming from the pig grease of the day before, perched by the fence on a small stone and watched Weake. Tukum was one of the few children who seemed upset, though, like all his companions, he had seen many funerals and would see many more.

A group led by Polik sang wheezily and long the ancient chants of mourning, working the ground with gnarled old toes and rubbing spavined thighs. One of them, his wrinkled skin reptilian, felt peevishly for the tobacco roll buried in the pouch strung on his back. At the same time he contributed his mourning, a frail *woo, woo, woo,* and his long nose ran tumultuously with all the rest: the hole for boars' tusks in his septum had stretched wide with old age, so that the light shone through it.

Some of the men brought belts, and Huonke called out to them in greeting, a loud *wah-h, wah-h,* somehow impertinent, and at the same time self-ingratiating. He and his brother-in-law stood at the chair and haggled covertly about the placement of the belts. While haggling, Tamugi contrived to sob, rolling his eyes in the frank, open face of cant.

Four pigs came forth, and the pilai's owner destroyed them with a kind of sad authority. All four died speedily, snouting the ground, legs kicking, as if they were trying to bore into the earth. They were dressed swiftly, and the yegerek brought logs. Weake's friend Okal was among them: he wore the yellow clay of mourning and a pad of leaves to protect his shoulder from the wood. Like all the other boys, he played a large part in the funeral of his friend.

Nilik, with his affinity for pig, had come in time to finger the bloody pieces, which were hung on a rack behind the chair. Before the chair an old woman beat her breast with stumpy hands: *Aulk, aulk, aulk, aulk,* she cried—*Loo, loo, loo, loo.* The yellow clay was crusted in the skin folds of old breasts, of fallen hips. On the far side of the yard a giant butterfly, dead white and black, danced out of the shadows of the woods and, passing through the akuni, danced back again.

Huonke and Tamugi cried loud and long, mouths trembling and eyes alert. They watched the entrance of Weaklekek, his people behind him carrying three large flat *ye* stones decorated around the middle with fur and cowries. The ye stones are valuable but not sacred, though they may later become so; they are used, like cowrie belts, as a medium of exchange. *Wah! Wah!* cried Huonke. *Wah! Wah!* cried Tamugi. The party stopped before the chair to grieve, and then the men went onward toward the pilai, while the women and small children remained in the upper yard.

Weaklekek sat down quietly and stared into the earth. He was one of Weake's namis, and plainly he blamed himself for the boy's death, since it was his kaio that had been abandoned. But the raid and death were part of akuni existence, and neither Weaklekek nor Woluklek were blamed by any of the others. Even so, Woluklek, who had been unwise enough to lead the three boys to the river, did not come to the funeral at all.

U-mue's wives had come, and with them the children of his sili. Aku and Holake joined the little girls of the village, who were going about on small self-conscious errands; the girls smiled modestly at everyone, in the pretty illusion that all eyes were upon them. Nylare, who is very young, had a poor grasp of the situation, but she took up the wail of mourning, humming it contentedly to her own rhythms. Natorek, escaping his mother repeatedly, played in the narrow path through the massed women; like most akuni children, he accepted his mother's cuffs and cries in great good spirits and smiled expansively at all and everything even when latecomers stepped upon him. He was finally placed under the care of his brother Uwar, who took him to a corner of the yard and picked his lice.

While the food cooked, more men arrived; they overflowed into the woods behind the fencing. The mourning faltered in the midday pall, and nothing stirred. Only the stinging bees, black and yellow, toiled remorselessly on a small open hive, hanging upside down from a pandanus leaf beyond the fence; they hung in the air below the hive, their hair legs dangling, or clasped one another in dry, delicate embrace.

Near the main entrance of Abulopak the tips of the long grasses had been tied together in three places in the weeds: the tied grass forbids trespassing. The signs were a warning to the women, who were nearly two hundred strong, and whose use of the near weeds to urinate had become an offense to Wereklowe.

The rock fire was dismantled, and pig distributed among the men: a few bits were borne to certain women. Asikanalek's daughter Namilike walked around with her small net stuffed with hiperi, passing it out; Weake's little sister Iki Abusake was also there, as pretty in a baby way as Namilike herself. Iki Abusake's curious name means "Hand That Could Not Help Itself," the expression used by the akuni to account for the phenomenon of pig-stealing.

During the eating, soft waves of mourning rose and fell. The sun, sliding down into the west, burned hotly on Weake, and women tried to shield him with their nets. But now the men came forward and stripped him of his belts: the meal was over, and the day's business must begin. The belts were stretched on a frond before the pilai, with the kains seated in a line along each side. When the belts had been admired for a time, and their destiny decided, Wereklowe stood up to dispense them.

Until this time Wereklowe had remained out of the way, ceding the administration of the funeral to Asikanalek: Asikanalek was not only a sub-kain of the Alua but a fine warrior who had killed two, and a close relative of the dead boy. But the exchange of goods was an end purpose of the funeral, and the greatest leader of the clan usually directs it. With a weighty pause between the names, Wereklowe gave out the belts; he was attended by respectful silence. One belt was awarded to Weaklekek, but Weaklekek was still morose and waved it off; in his despair, and despite all his rich gifts, he felt he did not deserve it. Lakaloklek, more practical, came forth and took it in her husband's name.

Despite the great amount of grieving, there seemed small hint of outrage. Huonke complained that the *pavi* should not have done it, but then, Huonke has killed once himself, a harmless woman found near the frontier who had run away from the Siep-Elortak. Revenge there would be, inevitably, but without moral judgments. Nevertheless, for the funeral of a small boy, well over two hundred people had pushed into the small sili: more presents were brought, and more pigs killed, than for the funeral of Ekitama-lek, a kain's son and a warrior. Only a few could have come there in real sorrow, and only a few for the exchange of goods. The rest had come because the killing of a child, despite its ancient sanctions, had made them unhappy and uneasy.

His back to Wereklowe, the child sat naked in the chair. The women came to remove the nets, and Weake stirred; his head dropped slowly to his breast, for his chin strap had been loosened from behind. Then suddenly a man began to shout, and a complete silence fell. The speaker was Polik, and he was warning the people that they might be in danger.

In the fortnight previous Amoli, the violent kain of the Haiman, had killed the young brother of a man with whom he was having a dispute: taking the life of a relative of one's antagonist, or even that of his small child, is not unusual, being not only a more subtle punishment but a less dangerous one. The man had fled to the Siep-Kosi but had sworn revenge, and Polik, on behalf of Amoli, warned any of the latter's friends or kinsmen to be on guard. The fugitive's wife was ordered to come to him the next morning in Abulopak, so that he and Wereklowe might have a full explanation of the affair: it is one of the duties of the great kains to settle feuds within the tribe, not infre-quently at the expense of their own pigs. When Polik had finished speaking, the guests fidgeted uneasily, but after a while the voices mounted once again, and the women returned to remove Weake's nets.

People were already departing from the sili. The thongs were loosened, and Weake was carried back to the banana leaves where the shell belts had lain. The yegerek, grim, brought timber for the pyre: Tukum looked fright-ened and was openly upset. The mourning quickened. Huonke greased the body a last time and, when he was finished, took up the bow and arrow. Another man held up the great thatch bundle. The arrow was shot into it, releasing the spirit from the body, and the man ran with the bundle up the yard; he laid the bundle on the sili fence.

The fire had been assembled quickly, and a loud outcry erupted with the flames: the body was hurried to its pyre. Weake was laid upon his side, in the way that small boys sleep, with a rough timber pillowing his head. The flames came up beside him, and more wood was laid on top of him, and he disap-peared.

The mourning died after a time, and the sili emptied quickly. Huonke brought out a red parrot feather and performed the purification ceremony on the men who had handled the boy's body. The men, seated in a circle, held out both their hands, and Huonke passed the parrot feather through the air above the outstretched fingers. Afterward, as much was done for him.

The last of Weake was a sweet choking smell, carried upward by an acrid smoke from the crackling pyre, and diffusing itself at last against the pine trees, the high crest of the mountain wall, the sky. . . .

When the feast was over, Tukum ran straight around to Weake's sili in Abulopak. There, early that morning, a very different ceremony, *iki palin,* had taken place. Out of respect for the dead boy, the two outer joints had been removed from two fingers of Weake's sister, Iki Abusake, and three other little girls. In addition, the upper third of a young boy's left ear had been sliced off with a bamboo knife.

A half-hour before the ceremony the fingers of the little girls had been bound tight, to cut off circulation; just prior to the operation the children were struck forcibly on the upper arm, to render the hand numb. The fingers were placed on a piece of wood and severed with a blow of a stone adze. This latter task had been performed by Tamugi, who is considered skillful in such matters. The fingers are hung in the cooking shed to dry, and the next day burned, then buried in a special place behind the pilai.

The boy is a member of Wereklowe's sili, and his ear served as a token of that sili's grief. One little girl is Wereklowe's niece, another the daughter of a warrior who, having neither pig nor stone to bring to the funeral, offered the fingers of his child. A third is the daughter of Tamugi, and Iki Abusake is an orphan. One of these girls had taken the place of a fifth child, the one who had gotten hysterical and run off. Though this little girl had been beaten, she had not been forced back to the ceremony; as in the case of kepu men in time of war, her shame is thought to be sufficient punishment.

At three, Iki Abusake is the smallest of the girls, though the other children cannot be more than four. The children sat together in the cooking shed. Their hands had been bandaged heavily in leaves, bound round with grass, and to slow the bleeding each held the green mass upright, beside her face, like a toy or present to be shown to friends. The hands bled badly all that morning, and each little girl held a clump of grass under her elbow to absorb the blood. None of them gave evidence of more than slight discomfort, but all were silent in a way that children rarely are, and the eyes of Iki Abusake, whom the children call Kibusake, were round with shock.

Their relatives talked quietly to the little girls, and after a while the children were taken out into the yard. Many women had come, for this was their occasion, and they sat talking cheerfully by the funeral ashes. The women made a kind, mild fuss over the little girls, but otherwise no notice was taken of them. They were fed hiperi and ate it. Later the little boy with the sliced ear went to the men's feast of the Wilil and gnawed his rat meat with the rest; the side of his head had been smeared carelessly with clay.

Tamugi's wife sat by herself, picking the bones of Weake out of the ashes. She used small wooden tongs, and she laid the white scraps in a little pile on a banana leaf. The motion of her arm, though sure and graceful, was infinitely slow, as if she were entranced. Her eyes were wide and sad, and she looked peacefully at the others without really seeing them. When her task was finished, she folded the leaf over the bones and took it away into the cooking shed.

The few men in the sili kept out of the women's way. Weaklekek was silent still and spent most of the day weaving fiber, hunched in upon himself. But late in the afternoon the men asserted themselves once more. They raised a shout, and the yegerek came flying up the yard through the packed women, hurling stones at the fences and gateway of the sili and crying out: this was the banishment of Weake's ghost, reminding it of its journey to the Wittaia. The yegerek came back laughing, and all the women laughed as well, for the ghost-stoning is a constructive ceremony from which nothing but good can come. More hiperi were taken from the fires, and Tukum, still greasy with his pig, secured two round ones for himself and made off with them to the terrains of the men.

On the third day of the funeral another hiperi feast was given, this time in the sili of Wereklowe. Among matters discussed were steps to be taken in the future to safeguard the Aike Frontier, as well as the details of the retaliatory raid which was to come: the death of Weake, who had claimed Weaklekek as his nami and who had not only been a member of Wereklowe's village but related closely to Asikanalek and other important Alua, was not going to pass unavenged. Huwai had died for the death of Ekitamalek, and another enemy, and preferably more than one, would pay for the death of Weake: that Weake had died as a result of the death of Huwai, or of Torobia, or of Owak, Tegaolok, Wie, Haknisek, or Mali, all five of whom had died of wounds received in recent moons on the Tokolik and Waraba, was not the point: revenge was an ancient rhythm of akuni life, a cycle without end.

The feast was scarcely started when an alarm cry came, and this time the sili emptied of its warriors. The Wittaia were said to have struck again, on the mountain path to Lokoparek, killing both women and children.

The warriors ran through the araucarias in a swift, loping stride, past Wuperainma and up across the fields above Homaklep, into the trees. But the alarm was born of the high tensions of days past; if there had been Wittaia on the mountain, no trace of them was found. The men came down the hill, and most returned to Abulopak, where the feasting was resumed. Once again, to shouts and laughter, Weake's ghost was sent upon its way in a hail of stones. The ceremony was enacted a final time on the following afternoon, and on all these days the grass near the place of ambush was burned and burned again. Weake's ghost would linger near even a faint trace of his blood and would not, until all blood was gone, be free to cross into the country of the enemy.

The bones of Weake had already been placed in a fenced shelter behind the pilai. Until his death has been avenged, a kind of altar will be maintained in the cooking shed of his sili, where two of the funeral nets still hang upon the wall. The tails of the slaughtered pigs are fastened to the nets, and with them a stalk of toa, the heavy-bodied cultivated grass which tastes like a fine mixture of artichoke and celery; Weake had been very fond of toa, and its place on the nets is designed to please his ghost. In the rafters above hangs the grass bundle used as a sign to ghosts that all has been taken care of in the sili and that therefore they need not loiter but should get on about their business. When a Wittaia has been killed by Weake's people, the grass will be burned and the altar taken down.

The death of Weake was not called out to the Wittaia, for this was scarcely necessary; nonetheless, the enemy celebrated an etai. The boy's mother, who lives with the Wittaia, was certainly aware of Weake's identity, but what part she played in the celebration the akuni did not know.

CHAPTER 30   CHINUA ACHEBE

THINGS FALL APART:
AN IBO KILLS A CLANSMAN

Go-di-di-go-go-di-go. Di-go-go-di-go. It was the *ekwe* talking to the clan. One of the things every man learned was the language of the hollowed-out wooden instrument. Diim! Diim! Diim! boomed the cannon at intervals.

The first cock had not crowed, and Umuofia was still swallowed up in sleep and silence when the *ekwe* began to talk, and the cannon shattered the silence. Men stirred on their bamboo beds and listened anxiously. Somebody was dead. The cannon seemed to rend the sky. Di-go-go-di-go-di-di-go-go floated in the message-laden night air. The faint and distant wailing of women settled like a sediment of sorrow on the earth. Now and again a full-chested lamentation rose above the wailing whenever a man came into the place of death. He raised his voice once or twice in manly sorrow and then sat down with the other men listening to the endless wailing of the women and the esoteric language of the *ekwe*. Now and again the cannon boomed. The wailing of the women would not be heard beyond the village, but the *ekwe* carried the news to all the nine villages and even beyond. It began by naming the clan: *Umuofia obodo dike,* "the land of the brave." *Umuofia obodo dike! Umuofia obodo dike!* It said this over and over again, and as it dwelt on it, anxiety mounted in every heart that heaved on a bamboo bed that night. Then it went nearer and named the village: *Iguedo of the yellow grinding-stone!"* It was Okonkwo's village. Again and again Iguedo was called and men waited breathlessly in all the nine villages. At last the man was named and people sighed "E-u-u, Ezeudu is dead." A cold shiver ran down Okonkwo's back as he remembered the last time the old man had visited him. "That boy calls you father," he had said. "Bear no hand in his death."

Ezeudu was a great man, and so all the clan was at his funeral. The ancient drums of death beat, guns and cannon were fired, and men dashed about in frenzy, cutting down every tree or animal they saw, jumping over walls and dancing on the roof. It was a warrior's funeral, and from morning till night warriors came and went in their age groups. They all wore smoked raffia skirts and their bodies were painted with chalk and charcoal. Now and again an ancestral spirit or *egwugwu* appeared from the underworld, speaking in a tremulous, unearthly voice and completely covered in raffia. Some of them were very violent, and there had been a mad rush for shelter earlier in the day when one appeared with a sharp machete and was only prevented from doing serious harm by two men who restrained him with the help of a strong rope tied round his waist. Sometimes he turned round and chased those men, and they ran for their lives. But they always returned to the long rope he trailed behind. He sang, in a terrifying voice, that Ekwensu, or Evil Spirit, had entered his eye.

But the most dreaded of all was yet to come. He was always alone and was shaped like a coffin. A sickly odor hung in the air wherever he went, and flies went with him. Even the greatest medicine men took shelter when he was near. Many years ago another *egwugwu* had dared to stand his ground before him and had been transfixed to the spot for two days. This one had only one hand and it carried a basket full of water.

But some of the *egwugwu* were quite harmless. One of them was so old and infirm that he leaned heavily on a stick. He walked unsteadily to the place where the corpse was laid, gazed at it a while and went away again—to the underworld.

The land of the living was not far removed from the domain of the ancestors. There was coming and going between them, especially at festivals and also when an old man died, because an old man was very close to the ancestors. A man's life from birth to death was a series of transition rites which brought him nearer and nearer to his ancestors.

Ezeudu had been the oldest man in his village, and at his death there were only three men in the whole clan who were older, and four or five others in his own age group. Whenever one of these ancient men appeared in the crowd to dance unsteadily the funeral steps of the tribe, younger men gave way and the tumult subsided.

It was a great funeral, such as befitted a noble warrior. As the evening drew near, the shouting and the firing of guns, the beating of drums and the brandishing and clanging of machetes increased.

Ezeudu had taken three titles in his life. It was a rare achievement. There were only four titles in the clan, and only one or two men in any generation ever achieved the fourth and highest. When they did, they became the lords of the land. Because he had taken titles, Ezeudu was to be buried after dark with only a glowing brand to light the sacred ceremony.

But before this quiet and final rite, the tumult increased tenfold. Drums beat violently and men leaped up and down in frenzy. Guns were fired on all sides and sparks flew out as machetes clanged together in warriors' salutes. The air was full of dust and the smell of gunpowder. It was then that the one-handed spirit came, carrying a basket full of water. People made way for him on all sides and the noise subsided. Even the smell of gunpowder was swallowed in the sickly smell that now filled the air. He danced a few steps to the funeral drums and then went to see the corpse.

"Ezeudu!" he called in his guttural voice. "If you had been poor in your last life I would have asked you to be rich when you come again. But you were rich. If you had been a coward, I would have asked you to bring courage. But you were a fearless warrior. If you had died young, I would have asked you to get life. But you lived long. So I shall ask you to come again the way you came before. If your death was the death of nature, go in peace. But if a man caused it, do not allow him a moment's rest." He danced a few more steps and went away.

The drums and the dancing began again and reached fever-heat. Darkness was around the corner, and the burial was near. Guns fired the last salute and the cannon rent the sky. And then from the center of the delirious fury came a cry of agony and shouts of horror. It was as if a spell had been cast. All was silent. In the center of the crowd a boy lay in a pool of blood. It was the dead man's sixteen-year-old son, who with his brothers and half-brothers had been dancing the traditional farewell to their father. Okonkwo's gun had exploded and a piece of iron had pierced the boy's heart.

The confusion that followed was without parallel in the tradition of Umuofia. Violent deaths were frequent, but nothing like this had ever happened.

The only course open to Okonkwo was to flee from the clan. It was a crime against the earth goddess to kill a clansman, and a man who committed it must flee from the land. The crime was of two kinds, male and female. Okonkwo had committed the female, because it had been inadvertent. He could return to the clan after seven years.

That night he collected his most valuable belongings into head-loads. His wives wept bitterly and their children wept with them without knowing why. Obierika and half a dozen other friends came to help and to console him. They each made nine or ten trips carrying Okonkwo's yams to store in Obierika's barn. And before the cock crowed Okonkwo and his family were fleeing to his motherland. It was a little village called Mbanta, just beyond the borders of Mbaino.

As soon as the day broke, a large crowd of men from Ezeudu's quarter stormed Okonkwo's compound, dressed in garbs of war. They set fire to his houses, demolished his red walls, killed his animals and destroyed his barn. It was the justice of the earth goddess, and they were merely her messengers. They had no hatred in their hearts against Okonkwo. His greatest friend, Obierika, was among them. They were merely cleansing the land which Okonkwo had polluted with the blood of a clansman.

Obierika was a man who thought about things. When the will of the goddess had been done, he sat down in his *obi* and mourned his friend's calamity. Why should a man suffer so grievously for an offense he had committed inadvertently? But although he thought for a long time he found no answer. He was merely led into greater complexities. He remembered his wife's twin children, whom he had thrown away. What crime had they committed? The Earth had decreed that they were an offense on the land and must be destroyed. And if the clan did not exact punishment for an offense against the great goddess, her wrath was loosed on all the land and not just on the offender. As the elders said, if one finger brought oil it soiled the others.

• • •

Okonkwo was well received by his mother's kinsmen in Mbanta. The old man who received him was his mother's younger brother, who was now the eldest surviving member of that family. His name was Uchendu, and it was he who had received Okonkwo's mother twenty and ten years before when she had been brought home from Umuofia to be buried with her people. Okonkwo was only a boy then and Uchendu still remembered him crying the traditional farewell: "Mother, mother, mother is going."

That was many years ago. Today Okonkwo was not bringing his mother home to be buried with her people. He was taking his family of three wives and their children to seek refuge in his motherland. As soon as Uchendu saw him with his sad and weary company he guessed what had happened, and asked no questions. It was not until the following day that Okonkwo told him the full story. The old man listened silently to the end and then said with some relief: "It is a female *ochu*." And he arranged the requisite rites and sacrifices.

Okonkwo was given a plot of ground on which to build his compound, and two or three pieces of land on which to farm during the coming planting season. With the help of his mother's kinsmen he built himself an *obi* and three huts for his wives. He then installed his personal god and the symbols of his departed fathers. Each of Uchendu's five sons contributed three hundred seed-yams to enable their cousin to plant a farm, for as soon as the first rain came farming would begin.

At last the rain came. It was sudden and tremendous. For two or three moons the sun had been gathering strength till it seemed to breathe a breath of fire on the earth. All the grass had long been scorched brown, and the sands felt like live coals to the feet. Evergreen trees wore a dusty coat of brown. The birds were silenced in the forests, and the world lay panting

Religion and World View

under the live, vibrating heat. And then came the clap of thunder. It was an angry, metallic and thirsty clap, unlike the deep and liquid rumbling of the rainy season. A mighty wind arose and filled the air with dust. Palm trees swayed as the wind combed their leaves into flying crests like strange and fantastic coiffure.

When the rain finally came, it was in large, solid drops of frozen water which the people called "the nuts of the water of heaven." They were hard and painful on the body as they fell, yet young people ran about happily picking up the cold nuts and throwing them into their mouths to melt.

The earth quickly came to life and the birds in the forests fluttered around and chirped merrily. A vague scent of life and green vegetation was diffused in the air. As the rain began to fall more soberly and in smaller liquid drops, children sought for shelter, and all were happy, refreshed and thankful.

Okonkwo and his family worked very hard to plant a new farm. But it was like beginning life anew without the vigor and enthusiasm of youth, like learning to become left-handed in old age. Work no longer had for him the pleasure it used to have, and when there was no work to do he sat in a silent half-sleep.

His life had been ruled by a great passion—to become one of the lords of the clan. That had been his life-spring. And he had all but achieved it. Then everything had been broken. He had been cast out of his clan like a fish onto a dry, sandy beach, panting. Clearly his personal god or *chi* was not made for great things. A man could not rise beyond the destiny of his *chi*. The saying of the elders was not true—that if a man said yea his *chi* also affirmed. Here was a man whose *chi* said nay despite his own affirmation.

The old man, Uchendu, saw clearly that Okonkwo had yielded to despair and he was greatly troubled. He would speak to him after the *isa-ifi* ceremony.

The youngest of Uchendu's five sons, Amikwu, was marrying a new wife. The bride-price had been paid and all but the last ceremony had been performed. Amikwu and his people had taken palm-wine to the bride's kinsmen about two moons before Okonkwo's arrival in Mbanta. And so it was time for the final ceremony of confession.

The daughters of the family were all there, some of them having come a long way from their homes in distant villages. Uchendu's eldest daughter had come from Obodo, nearly half a day's journey away. The daughters of Uchendu's brothers were also there. It was a full gathering of *umuada*, in the same way as they would meet if a death occurred in the family. There were twenty-two of them.

They sat in a big circle on the ground and the bride sat in the center with a hen in her right hand. Uchendu sat by her, holding the ancestral staff of the family. All the other men stood outside the circle, watching. Their wives watched also. It was evening and the sun was setting.

Uchendu's eldest daughter, Njide, asked the questions.

"Remember that if you do not answer truthfully you will suffer or even die at childbirth," she began. "How many men have lain with you since my brother first expressed the desire to marry you?"

"None," she answered simply.

"Answer truthfully," urged the other women.

"None?" asked Njide.

"None," she answered.

"Swear on this staff of my fathers," said Uchendu.

"I swear," said the bride.

Uchendu took the hen from her, slit its throat with a sharp knife and allowed some of the blood to fall on his ancestral staff.

From that day Amikwu took the young bride to his hut and she became his wife. The daughters of the family did not return to their homes immediately but spent two or three days with their kinsmen.

On the second day Uchendu called together his sons and daughters and his nephew, Okonkwo. The men brought their goatskin mats, with which they sat on the floor, and the women sat on a sisal mat spread on a raised bank of earth. Uchendu pulled gently at his gray beard and gnashed his teeth. Then he began to speak, quietly and deliberately, picking his words with great care:

"It is Okonkwo that I primarily wish to speak to," he began. "But I want all of you to note what I am going to say. I am an old man and you are all children. I know more about the world than any of you. If there is any one among you who thinks he knows more let him speak up." He paused, but no one spoke.

"Why is Okonkwo with us today? This is not his clan. We are only his mother's kinsmen. He does not belong here. He is an exile, condemned for seven years to live in a strange land. And so he is bowed with grief. But there is just one question I would like to ask him. Can you tell me, Okonkwo, why it is that one of the commonest names we give our children is Nneka, or 'Mother is Supreme?' We all know that a man is the head of the family and his wives do his bidding. A child belongs to its father and his family and not to its mother and her family. A man belongs to his fatherland and not to his motherland. And yet we say Nneka—'Mother is Supreme.' Why is that?"

There was silence. "I want Okonkwo to answer me," said Uchendu.

"I do not know the answer," Okonkwo replied.

"You do not know the answer? So you see that you are a child. You have many wives and many children—more children than I have. You are a great man in your clan. But you are still a child, *my* child. Listen to me and I shall tell you. But there is one more question I shall ask you. Why is it that when a woman dies she is taken home to be buried with her own kinsmen? She is not buried with her husband's kinsmen. Why is that? Your mother was brought home to me and buried with my people. Why was that?"

Okonkwo shook his head.

"He does not know that either," said Uchendu, "and yet he is full of sorrow because he has come to live in his motherland for a few years." He laughed a mirthless laughter, and turned to his sons and daughters. "What about you? Can you answer my question?"

They all shook their heads.

"Then listen to me," he said and cleared his throat. "It's true that a child belongs to its father. But when a father beats his child, it seeks sympathy in its mother's hut. A man belongs to his fatherland when things are good and life is sweet. But when there is sorrow and bitterness he finds refuge in his motherland. Your mother is there to protect you. She is buried there. And that is why we say that mother is supreme. Is it right that you, Okonkwo, should bring to your mother a heavy face and refuse to be comforted? Be careful or you may displease the dead. Your duty is to comfort your wives and children and take them back to your fatherland after seven years. But if you allow sorrow to weigh you down and kill you, they will all die in exile." He paused for a long while. "These are now your kinsmen." He waved at his sons and daughters. "You think you are the greatest sufferer in the world? Do you know that men are sometimes banished for life? Do you know that men sometimes lose all their yams and even their children? I had six wives once. I have none now except that young girl who knows not her right from her left. Do you know how many children I have buried—children I begot in my youth and strength? Twenty-two. I did not hang myself, and I am still alive. If you think you are the greatest sufferer in the world ask my daughter, Akueni, how many twins she has borne and thrown away. Have you not heard the song they sing when a woman dies?

" *'For whom it is well, for whom is it well?*
There is no one for whom it is well.'

"I have no more to say to you."

PART SIX

LANGUAGE AND COMMUNICATION

Human social life would be impossible without some means of communication. It is necessary for cooperation and transmitting culture from one generation to the next. All animal species with any kind of orderly social life also have the ability to communicate.

Fundamental to all human communication is the *symbol*. To understand symbolic systems of communication we must first realize that we experience a vast physical world by many means. We hear sounds from the sky above, the earth below, animals, rivers, and other human beings. We see all around us with light that comes from the stars. We touch ourselves, objects, and other people. We feel inner states that are less well defined; we know about pain, comfort, frustration, elation, and satisfaction. Our capacity for experience and our ability to discriminate among experiences are both very great. Other animals know their worlds in similar ways, but they are more affected by the immediacy of experience and its inherent properties. Man has the capacity to take the sights, sounds, feelings, and other dimensions of daily life and transform them into things that by nature they are not. He does this by linking discrete experiences to other ones. In other words, man uses a *symbol* in relationship to a *referent*. In fact, without a referent, there can be no symbol.

A short, quick noise made in the throat can stand for any animal or plant we desire. A movement of the head can refer to past, present, or future. Inner states can be associated with other experiences and thus take on symbolic meaning. Thunder and lightning can be symbols of supernatural beings. The crucial characteristic of the symbol is that its connection to a referent is *arbitrary*. We might just as well call a heart a tongue—using a vocal symbol to stand for one part of our body rather than another. By *conditioning*, some animals can learn a few of the relationships that men have established between symbols and their referents; but animals cannot create such arbitrary relationships, learn to share their meaning, or pass them on from one generation to the next. No animal can ever comprehend the meaning of holy water or sacred days. Symbols not only refer to specific immediate experiences, they can refer to large classes of experiences, past, present, and future. Man learns that "fire" means specific instance of hot flames;

he also grasps that this symbol stands for all instances of this phenomenon that have ever occurred or will occur.

Language is a system of arbitrary vocal symbols. Three sets of rules underlie every language system: phonological rules for creating sounds; grammatical rules for arranging them meaningfully; and semantic rules for associating these sound symbols with their referents. Once a child has learned these rules for any language, he is considered a native speaker. But language is never an isolated cultural system; it is interwoven with every other aspect of culture and most human beings learn when and how to use their languages appropriately.

Vocal symbols are not the only ones man uses. Almost every physical event in our experience is used for communication. The way we dress, how we move our hands and arms, the manner in which we orient our bodies, the objects we see—these and many others become symbols that point to hidden referents. Nonverbal communication is required by some people without the capacity to hear, but it is also important in every human society.

The selections that follow show the importance of symbols in human life and raise important questions about the nature of human communication.

WORDS THAT WERE TO
MAKE THE WORLD BLOSSOM

The beginning of my life was simple and much like every other little life. I came, I saw, I conquered, as the first baby in the family always does. There was the usual amount of discussion as to a name for me. The first baby in the family was not to be lightly named, every one was emphatic about that. My father suggested the name of Mildred Campbell, an ancestor whom he highly esteemed, and he declined to take any further part in the discussion. My mother solved the problem by giving it as her wish that I should be called after her mother, whose maiden name was Helen Everett. But in the excitement of carrying me to church my father lost the name on the way, very naturally, since it was one in which he had declined to have a part. When the minister asked him for it, he just remembered that it had been decided to call me after my grandmother, and he gave her name as Helen Adams.

I am told that while I was still in long dresses I showed many signs of an eager, self-asserting disposition. Everything that I saw other people do I insisted upon imitating. At six months I could pipe out "How d'ye," and one day I attracted every one's attention by saying "Tea, tea, tea" quite plainly. Even after my illness I remembered one of the words I had learned in these early months. It was the word "water," and I continued to make some sound for that word after all other speech was lost. I ceased making the sound "wah-wah" only when I learned to spell the word.

They tell me I walked the day I was a year old. My mother had just taken me out of the bath-tub and was holding me in her lap, when I was suddenly attracted by the flickering shadows of leaves that danced in the sunlight on the smooth floor. I slipped from my mother's lap and almost ran toward them. The impulse gone, I fell down and cried for her to take me up in her arms.

These happy days did not last long. One brief spring, musical with the song of robin and mockingbird, one summer rich in fruit and roses, one autumn of gold and crimson sped by and left their gifts at the feet of an eager, delighted child. Then, in the dreary month of February, came the illness which closed my eyes and ears and plunged me into the unconsciousness of a new-born baby. They called it acute congestion of the stomach and brain. The doctor thought I could not live. Early one morning, however, the fever left me as suddenly and mysteriously as it had come. There was great rejoicing in the family that morning, but no one, not even the doctor, knew that I should never see or hear again.

I fancy I still have confused recollections of that illness. I especially remember the tenderness with which my mother tried to soothe me in my waking hours of fret and pain, and the agony and bewilderment with which I awoke after a tossing half sleep, and turned my eyes, so dry and hot, to the wall, away from the once-loved light, which came to me dim and yet more dim each day. But, except for these fleeting memories, if, indeed, they be memories, it all seems very unreal, like a nightmare. Gradually I got used to the silence and darkness that surrounded me and forgot that it had ever been different, until she came—my teacher—who was to set my spirit free. But during the first nineteen months of my life I had caught glimpses of broad, green fields, a luminous sky, trees and flowers which the darkness that followed could not wholly blot out. If we have once seen, "The day is ours, and what the day has shown."

I cannot recall what happened during the first months after my illness. I only know that I sat in my mother's lap or clung to her dress as she went about her household duties. My hands felt every object and observed every motion, and in this way I learned to know many things. Soon I felt the need of some communication with others and began to make crude signs. A shake of the head meant "No" and a nod, "Yes," a pull meant "Come" and a push, "Go." Was it bread that I wanted? Then I would imitate the acts of cutting the slices and buttering them. If I wanted my mother to make ice-cream for dinner I made the sign for working the freezer and shivered, indicating cold. My mother, moreover, succeeded in making me understand a good deal. I always knew when she wished me to bring her something, and I would run upstairs or anywhere else she indicated. Indeed, I owe to her loving wisdom all that was bright and good in my long night.

I understood a good deal of what was going on about me. At five I learned to fold and put away the clean clothes when they were brought in from the laundry, and I distinguished my own from the rest. I knew by the way my mother and aunt dressed when they were going out, and I invariably begged to go with them. I was always sent for when there was company, and when the guests took their leave, I waved my hand to them, I think with a vague remembrance of the meaning of the gesture. One day some gentlemen called on my mother, and I felt the shutting of the front door and other sounds that indicated their arrival. On a sudden thought I ran upstairs before any one could stop me, to put on my idea of a company dress. Standing before the mirror, as I had seen others do, I anointed mine head with oil and covered my face thickly with powder. Then I pinned a veil over my head so that it covered my face and fell in folds down to my shoulders, and tied an enormous bustle round my small waist, so that it dangled behind, almost meeting the hem of my skirt. Thus attired I went down to help entertain the company.

I do not remember when I first realized that I was different from other people; but I knew it before my teacher came to me. I had noticed that my mother and my friends did not use signs as I did when they wanted anything done, but talked with their mouths. Sometimes I stood between two persons who were conversing and touched their lips. I could not understand, and was vexed. I moved my lips and gesticulated frantically without result. This made me so angry at times that I kicked and screamed until I was exhausted.

I think I knew when I was naughty, for I knew that it hurt Ella, my nurse, to kick her, and when my fit of temper was over I had a feeling akin to regret. But I cannot remember any instance in which this feeling prevented me from repeating the naughtiness when I failed to get what I wanted.

In those days a little coloured girl, Martha Washington, the child of our cook, and Belle, an old setter, and a great hunter in her day, were my constant companions. Martha Washington understood my signs, and I seldom had any difficulty in making her do just as I wished. It pleased me to domineer over her, and she generally submitted to my tyranny rather than risk a hand-to-hand encounter. I was strong, active, indifferent to consequences. I knew my own mind well enough and always had my own way, even if I had to fight tooth and nail for it. We spent a greal deal of time in the kitchen, kneading dough balls, helping make ice-cream, grinding coffee, quarreling over the cake-bowl, and feeding the hens and turkeys that swarmed about the kitchen steps. Many of them were so tame that they would eat from my hand and let me feel them. One big gobbler snatched a tomato from me one day and ran away with it. Inspired, perhaps, by Master Gobbler's success, we carried off to the woodpile a cake which the cook had just frosted, and ate every bit of it. I was quite ill afterward, and I wonder if retribution also overtook the turkey.

The guinea-fowl likes to hide her nest in out-of-the-way places, and it was one of my greatest delights to hunt for the eggs in the long grass. I could not tell Martha Washington when I wanted to go egg-hunting, but I would double my hands and put them on the ground, which meant something round in the grass, and Martha always understood. When we were fortunate enough to find a nest I never allowed her to carry the eggs home, making her understand by emphatic signs that she might fall and break them.

The sheds where the corn was stored, the stable where the horses were kept, and the yard where the cows were milked morning and evening were unfailing sources of interest to Martha and me. The milkers would let me keep my hands on the cows while they milked, and I often got well switched by the cow for my curiosity.

The making ready for Christmas was always a delight to me. Of course I did not know what it was all about, but I enjoyed the pleasant odours that filled the house and the tidbits that were given to Martha Washington and me to keep us quiet. We were sadly in the way, but that did not interfere with our pleasure in the least. They allowed us to grind the spices, pick over the raisins and lick the stirring spoons. I hung my stocking because the others did; I cannot remember, however, that the ceremony interested me especially, nor did my curiosity cause me to wake before daylight to look for my gifts.

Martha Washington had as great a love of mischief as I. Two little children were seated on the veranda steps one hot July afternoon. One was black as ebony, with little bunches of fuzzy hair tied with shoestrings sticking out all over her head like corkscrews. The other was white, with long golden curls. One child was six years old, the other two or three years older. The younger child was blind—that was I—and the other was Martha Washington. We were busy cutting out paper dolls; but we soon wearied of this amusement, and after cutting up our shoestrings and clipping all the leaves off the honeysuckle that were within reach, I turned my attention to Martha's corkscrews. She objected at first, but finally submitted. Thinking that turn and turn about is fair play, she seized the scissors, and cut off one of my curls, and would have cut them all off but for my mother's timely interference.

Belle, our dog, my other companion, was old and lazy and liked to sleep by the open fire rather than to romp with me. I tried hard to teach her my sign language, but she was dull and inattentive. She sometimes started and quivered with excitement, then she became perfectly rigid, as dogs do when they point a bird. I did not then know why Belle acted in this way; but I knew she was not doing as I wished. This vexed me and the lesson always ended in a one-sided boxing match. Belle would get up, stretch herself lazily, give one or two contemptuous sniffs, go to the opposite side of the hearth and lie down again, and I, wearied and disappointed, went off in search of Martha.

Many incidents of those early years are fixed in my memory, isolated, but clear and distinct, making the sense of that silent, aimless, dayless life all the more intense.

One day I happened to spill water on my apron, and I spread it out to dry before the fire which was flickering on the sitting-room hearth. The apron did not dry quickly enough to suit me, so I drew nearer and threw it right over the hot ashes. The fire leaped into life; the flames encircling me so that in a moment my clothes were blazing. I made a terrified noise that brought Viny, my old nurse, to the rescue. Throwing a blanket over me, she almost suffocated me, but she put out the fire. Except for my hands and hair I was not badly burned.

About this time I found out the use of a key. One morning I locked my mother up in the pantry, where she was obliged to remain three hours, as the servants were in a detached part of the house. She kept pounding on the door, while I sat outside on the porch steps and laughed with glee as I felt the jar of the pounding. This most naughty prank of mine convinced my parents that I must be taught as soon as possible. After my teacher, Miss Sullivan, came to me, I sought an early opportunity to lock her in her room. I went upstairs with something which my mother made me understand I was to give to Miss Sullivan; but no sooner had I given it to her than I slammed the door to, locked it, and hid the key under the wardrobe in the hall. I could not be induced to tell where the key was. My father was obliged to get a ladder and

Language and Communication

take Miss Sullivan out through the window—much to my delight. Months after I produced the key.

When I was about five years old we moved from the little vine-covered house to a large new one. The family consisted of my father and mother, two older half-brothers, and, afterward, a little sister, Mildred. My earliest distinct recollection of my father is making my way through great drifts of newspapers to his side and finding him alone, holding a sheet of paper before his face. I was greatly puzzled to know what he was doing. I imitated this action, even wearing his spectacles, thinking they might help solve the mystery. But I did not find out the secret for several years. Then I learned what those papers were, and that my father edited one of them.

My father was most loving and indulgent, devoted to his home, seldom leaving us, except in the hunting season. He was a great hunter, I have been told, and a celebrated shot. Next to his family he loved his dogs and gun. His hospitality was great, almost to a fault, and he seldom came home without bringing a guest. His special pride was the big garden where, it was said, he raised the finest watermelons and strawberries in the county; and to me he brought the first ripe grapes and the choicest berries. I remember his caressing touch as he led me from tree to tree, from vine to vine, and his eager delight in whatever pleased me.

He was a famous story-teller; after I acquired language he used to spell clumsily into my hand his cleverest anecdotes, and nothing pleased him more than to have me repeat them at an opportune moment.

I was in the North, enjoying the last beautiful days of the summer of 1896, when I heard the news of my father's death. He had had a short illness, there had been a brief time of acute suffering, then all was over. This was my first great sorrow—my first personal experience with death.

How shall I write of my mother? She is so near to me that it almost seems indelicate to speak of her.

For a long time I regarded my little sister as an intruder. I knew that I had ceased to be my mother's only darling, and the thought filled me with jealousy. She sat in my mother's lap constantly, where I used to sit, and seemed to take up all her care and time. One day something happened which seemed to me to be adding insult to injury.

At that time I had a much-petted, much-abused doll, which I afterward named Nancy. She was, alas, the helpless victim of my outbursts of temper and of affection, so that she became much the worse for wear. I had dolls which talked, and cried, and opened and shut their eyes; yet I never loved one of them as I loved poor Nancy. She had a cradle, and I often spent an hour or more rocking her. I guarded both doll and cradle with the most jealous care; but once I discovered my little sister sleeping peacefully in the cradle. At this presumption on the part of one to whom as yet no tie of love bound me I grew angry. I rushed upon the cradle and overturned it, and the baby might have been killed had my mother not caught her as she fell. Thus it is that when we walk in the valley of twofold solitude we know little of the tender affections that grow out of endearing words and actions and companionship. But afterward, when I was restored to my human heritage, Mildred and I grew into each other's hearts, so that we were content to go hand-in-hand wherever caprice led us, although she could not understand my finger language, nor I her childish prattle.

Meanwhile the desire to express myself grew. The few signs I used became less and less adequate, and my failures to make myself understood were invariably followed by outbursts of passion. I felt as if invisible hands were holding me, and I made frantic efforts to free myself. I struggled—not that struggling helped matters, but the spirit of resistance was strong within me; I generally broke down in tears and physical exhaustion. If my mother happened to be near I crept into her arms, too miserable even to remember the cause of the tempest. After awhile the need of some means of communication became so urgent that these outbursts occurred daily, sometimes hourly.

My parents were deeply grieved and perplexed. We lived a long way from any school for the blind or the deaf, and it seemed unlikely that any one would come to such an out-of-the-way place as Tuscumbia to teach a child who was both deaf and blind. Indeed, my friends and relatives sometimes doubted whether I could be taught. My mother's only ray of hope came from Dickens's "American Notes." She had read his account of Laura Bridgman, and remembered vaguely that she was deaf and blind, yet had been educated. But she also remembered with a hopeless pang that Dr. Howe, who had discovered the way to teach the deaf and blind, had been dead many years. His methods had probably died with him; and if they had not, how was a little girl in a far-off town in Alabama to receive the benefit of them?

When I was about six years old, my father heard of an eminent oculist in Baltimore, who had been successful in many cases that had seemed hopeless. My parents at once determined to take me to Baltimore to see if anything could be done for my eyes.

The journey, which I remember well, was very pleasant. I made friends with many people on the train. One lady gave me a box of shells. My father made holes in these so that I could string them, and for a long time they kept me happy and contented. The conductor, too, was kind. Often when he went his rounds I clung to his coat tails while he collected and punched the tickets. His punch, with which he let me play, was a delightful toy. Curled up in a corner of the seat I amused myself for hours making funny little holes in bits of cardboard.

My aunt made me a big doll out of towels. It was the most comical, shapeless thing, this improvised doll, with no nose, mouth, ears or eyes—nothing that even the imagination of a child could convert into a face. Curiously enough, the absence of eyes struck me more than all the other defects put together. I pointed this out to everybody with provoking persistency, but no one seemed equal to the task of providing the doll with eyes. A bright idea, however, shot into my mind, and the problem was solved. I tumbled off the seat and searched under it until I found my aunt's cape, which was trimmed with large beads. I pulled two beads off and indicated to her that I wanted her to sew them on my doll. She raised my hand to her eyes in a questioning way, and I nodded energetically. The beads were sewed in the right place and I could not contain myself for joy; but immediately I lost all interest in the doll. During the whole trip I did not have one fit of temper, there were so many things to keep my mind and fingers busy.

When we arrived in Baltimore, Dr. Chisholm received us kindly: but he could do nothing. He said, however, that I could be educated, and advised my father to consult Dr. Alexander Graham Bell, of Washington, who would be able to give him information about schools and teachers of deaf or blind children. Acting on the doctor's advice, we went immediately to Washington to see Dr. Bell, my father with a sad heart and many misgivings, I wholly unconscious of his anguish finding pleasure in the excitement of moving from place to place. Child as I was, I at once felt the tenderness and sympathy which endeared Dr. Bell to so many hearts, as his wonderful achievements enlist their admiration. He held me on his knee while I examined his watch, and he made it strike for me. He understood my signs and I knew it and loved him at once. But I did not dream that that interview would be the door through which I should pass from darkness into light, from isolation to friendship, companionship, knowledge, love.

Dr. Bell advised my father to write to Mr. Anagnos, director of the Perkins Institution in Boston, the scene of Dr. Howe's great labours for the blind, and ask him if he had a teacher competent to begin my education. This my father did at once, and in a few weeks there came a kind letter from Mr. Anagnos with the comforting assurance that a teacher had been found. This was in the summer of 1886. But Miss Sullivan did not arrive until the following March.

Thus I came up out of Egypt and stood before Sinai, and a power divine touched my spirit and gave it sight, so that I beheld many wonders. And from the sacred mountain I heard a voice which said, "Knowledge is love and light and vision."

The most important day I remember in all my life is the one on which my teacher, Anne Mansfield Sullivan, came to me. I am filled with wonder when I consider the immeasurable contrasts between the two lives which it connects. It was the third of March, 1887, three months before I was seven years old.

On the afternoon of that eventful day, I stood on the porch, dumb, expectant. I guessed vaguely from my mother's signs and from the hurrying to and fro in the house that something unusual was about to happen, so I went to the door and waited on the steps. The afternoon sun penetrated the mass of honeysuckle that covered the porch, and fell on my upturned face. My fingers lingered almost unconsciously on the familiar leaves and blossoms which had just come forth to greet the sweet southern spring. I did not know what the future held of marvel or surprise for me. Anger and bitterness had preyed upon me continually for weeks and a deep languor had succeeded this passionate struggle.

Have you ever been at sea in a dense fog, when it seemed as if a tangible white darkness shut you in, and the great ship, tense and anxious, groped her way toward the shore with plummet and sounding-line, and you waited with beating heart for something to happen? I was like that ship before my education began, only I was without compass or sounding-line, and had no way of knowing how near the harbour was. "Light! give me light!" was the wordless cry of my soul, and the light of love shone on me in that very hour.

I felt approaching footsteps. I stretched out my hand as I supposed to my mother. Some one took it, and I was caught up and held close in the arms of her who had come to reveal all things to me, and, more than all things else, to love me.

The morning after my teacher came she led me into her room and gave me a doll. The little blind children at the Perkins Institution had sent it and Laura Bridgman had dressed it; but I did not know this until afterward. When I had played with it a little while, Miss Sullivan slowly spelled into my hand the word "d-o-l-l." I was at once interested in this finger play and tried to imitate it. When I finally succeeded in making the letters correctly I was flushed with childish pleasure and pride. Running downstairs to my mother I held up my hand and made the letters for doll. I did not know that I was spelling a word or even that words existed; I was simply making my fingers go in monkey-like imitation. In the days that followed I learned to spell in this uncomprehending way a great many words, among them *pin, hat, cup* and a few verbs like *sit, stand* and *walk*. But my teacher had been with me several weeks before I understood that everything has a name.

One day, while I was playing with my new doll, Miss Sullivan put my big rag doll into my lap also, spelled "d-o-l-l" and tried to make me understand that "d-o-l-l" applied to both. Earlier in the day we had had a tussle over the words "m-u-g" and "w-a-t-e-r." Miss Sullivan had tried to impress it upon me that "m-u-g" is *mug* and that "w-a-t-e-r" is *water*, but I persisted in confounding the two. In despair she had dropped the subject for the time, only to renew it at the first opportunity. I became impatient at her repeated attempts and, seizing the new doll, I dashed it upon the floor. I was keenly delighted when I felt the fragments of the broken doll at my feet. Neither sorrow nor regret followed my passionate outburst. I had not loved the doll. In the still, dark world in which I lived there was no strong sentiment or tenderness. I felt my teacher sweep the fragments to one side of the hearth, and I had a sense of satisfaction that the cause of my discomfort was removed. She brought me my hat, and I knew I was going out into the warm sunshine. This thought, if a wordless sensation may be called a thought, made me hop and skip with pleasure.

We walked down the path to the well-house, attracted by the fragrance of the honeysuckle with which it was covered. Some one was drawing water and my teacher placed my hand under the spout. As the cool stream gushed over one hand she spelled into the other the word *water,* first slowly, then rapidly. I stood still, my whole attention fixed upon the motions of her fingers. Suddenly I felt a misty consciousness as of something forgotten—a thrill of returning thought; and somehow the mystery of language was revealed to me. I knew then that "w-a-t-e-r" meant the wonderful cool something that was flowing over my hand. That living word awakened my soul, gave it light, hope, joy, set it free! There were barriers still, it is true, but barriers that could in time be swept away.

I left the well-house eager to learn. Everything had a name, and each name gave birth to a new thought. As we returned to the house every object which I touched seemed to quiver with life. That was because I saw everything with the strange, new sight that had come to me. On entering the door I remembered the doll I had broken. I felt my way to the hearth and picked up the pieces. I tried vainly to put them together. Then my eyes filled with tears; for I realized what I had done, and for the first time I felt repentance and sorrow.

I learned a great many new words that day. I do not remember what they all were; but I do know that *mother, father, sister, teacher* were among them—words that were to make the world blossom for me, "like Aaron's rod, with flowers." It would have been difficult to find a happier child than I was as I lay in my crib at the close of that eventful day and lived over the joys it had brought me, and for the first time longed for a new day to come.

I recall many incidents of the summer of 1887 that followed my soul's sudden awakening. I did nothing but explore with my hands and learn the name of every object that I touched; and the more I handled things and learned their names and uses, the more joyous and confident grew my sense of kinship with the rest of the world.

When the time of daisies and buttercups came Miss Sullivan took me by the hand across the fields, where men were preparing the earth for the seed, to the banks of the Tennessee River, and there, sitting on the warm grass, I had my first lessons in the beneficence of nature. I learned how the sun and the rain make to grow out of the ground every tree that is pleasant to the sight and good for food, how birds build their nests and live and thrive from land to land, how the squirrel, the deer, the lion and every other creature finds food and shelter. As my knowledge of things grew I felt more and more the delight of the world I was in. Long before I learned to do a sum in arithmetic or describe the shape of the earth, Miss Sullivan had taught me to find beauty in the fragrant woods, in every blade of grass, and in the curves and dimples of my baby sister's hand. She linked my earliest thoughts with nature, and made me feel that "birds and flowers and I were happy peers."

But about this time I had an experience which taught me that nature is not always kind. One day my teacher and I were returning from a long ramble. The morning had been fine, but it was growing warm and sultry when at last we turned our faces homeward. Two or three times we stopped to rest under a tree by the wayside. Our last halt was under a wild cherry tree a short distance from the house. The shade was grateful, and the tree was so easy to climb that with my teacher's assistance I was able to scramble to a seat in the branches. It was so cool up in the tree that Miss Sullivan proposed that we have our luncheon there. I promised to keep still while she went to the house to fetch it.

Suddenly a change passed over the tree. All the sun's warmth left the air. I knew the sky was black, because all the heat, which meant light to me, had died out of the atmosphere. A strange odour came up from the earth. I knew it, it was the odour that always precedes a thunderstorm, and a nameless fear clutched at my heart. I felt absolutely alone, cut off from my friends and the firm earth. The immense, the unknown, enfolded me. I remained still and expectant; a chilling terror crept over me. I longed for my teacher's return; but above all things I wanted to get down from that tree.

There was a moment of sinister silence, then a multitudinous stirring of the leaves. A shiver ran through the tree, and the wind sent forth a blast that would have knocked me off had I not clung to the branch with might and main. The tree swayed and strained. The small twigs snapped and fell about me in showers. A wild impulse to jump seized me, but terror held me fast. I crouched down in the fork of the tree. The branches lashed about me. I felt the intermittent jarring that came now and then, as if something heavy had fallen and the shock had traveled up till it reached the limb I sat on. It worked my suspense up to the highest point, and just as I was thinking the tree and I should fall together, my teacher seized my hand and helped me down. I clung to her, trembling with joy to feel the earth under my feet once more. I had learned a new lesson—that nature "wages open war against her children, and under softest touch hides treacherous claws."

After this experience it was a long time before I climbed another tree. The mere thought filled me with terror. It was the sweet allurement of the mimosa tree in full bloom that finally overcame my fears. One beautiful spring morning when I was alone in the summer-house, reading, I became aware of a wonderful subtle fragrance in the air. I started up and instinctively stretched out my hands. It seemed as if the spirit of spring had passed through the summer-house. "What is it?" I asked, and the next minute I recognized the odour of the mimosa blossoms. I felt my way to the end of the garden, knowing that the mimosa tree was near the fence, at the turn of the path. Yes, there it was, all quivering in the warm sunshine, its blossom-laden branches almost touching the long grass. Was there ever anything so exquisitely beautiful in the world before! Its delicate blossoms shrank from the slightest earthly touch; it seemed as if a tree of paradise had been transplanted to earth. I made my way through a shower of petals to the great trunk and for one minute stood irresolute; then, putting my foot in the broad space between the forked branches, I pulled myself up into the tree. I had some difficulty in holding on, for the branches were very large and the bark hurt my hands. But I had a delicious sense that I was doing something unusual and wonderful, so I kept on climbing higher and higher, until I reached a little seat which somebody had built there so long ago that it had grown part of the tree itself. I sat there for a long, long time, feeling like a fairy on a rosy cloud. After that I spent many happy hours in my tree of paradise, thinking fair thoughts and dreaming bright dreams.

I had now the key to all language, and I was eager to learn to use it. Children who hear acquire language without any particular effort; the words that fall from others' lips they catch on the wing, as it were, delightedly, while the little deaf child must trap them by a slow and often painful process. But whatever the process, the result is wonderful. Gradually from naming an object we advance step by step until we have traversed the vast distance between our first stammered syllable and the sweep of thought in a line of Shakespeare.

CHAPTER 32   JOANNE GREENBERG

THE SOUND BARRIER

They had to sell the ring that kept green sunlight. Abel had paid seventy dollars for it, and after Webendorf wrote about what interest was, he knew there was no choosing now between this hope and that. Janice cried and argued. She made him spend nights adding and adding again numbers that never changed. And in the end, he made her take the sunlight ring off her finger and they went back to the jeweler's with it.

Abel remembered the jeweler who was pleased with them, a happy and friendly man when they had come before. Now he looked at the ring with quick eyes and didn't hold it up to catch the light the same as before. He did not smile now, but was careful and kept his arms close to his body. "Twenty dollars," he said.

A fear came like something falling down inside of Abel. They tried to show the jeweler his mistake. They were careful, trying to make the man remember who they were, that they had bought his ring for seventy dollars. Janice spoke more clearly of the two—they knew this because people seemed less impatient with her than they were with Abel. Their faces did not always harden with dislike when she used her voice—and so she spoke, asking the jeweler if he remembered this ring, the same ring he sold them in the summer. She motioned to the box behind the shining glass. "I' wa' *ere, 'ere.*" She pointed again.

Abel remembered how carefully the ring was put in the fold that held it, in the box, how carefully the jeweler reached in and took it and lifted it to feed it with light and then held it out to them. Maybe he did not understand. He motioned to Janice with his eyes to write: "We are people we came in summer and buy this ring seventy dollar. Jewl is very good care. All ways take off before wash."

The jeweler read the note quickly and shook his head. Then he wrote *"Twenty Dollars"* and put a line under it. They didn't give up the ring and they didn't go, but stood stunned and pale in front of him. He took the paper again and wrote: "I am in business. I will give you twenty-five dollars and no more. The ring is used, not new any more. If you can't get a better price for it somewhere else, come back and I will still give you twenty-five."

Janice would never Sign in front of Hearing, but now she turned Abel away and began, in the smallest of Sign, to say what she had to: "I'm afraid. What is happening to them? Why are they doing this to us? What will we do?"

"I don't know. We can't go to the police."

"You are the husband. You must make him take the ring and give us our money."

"He won't do it."

"You must make him do it."

"Go on," he said, "and wait outside. I will talk to him—alone."

She looked away and made a small, quick sign of good-bye, leaving the store. Abel saw she felt better to go.

He picked up the ring from the glass where it was lying and with his left hand, motioned the jeweler to come with him toward the back of the store, darker, where Janice could not see them. Abel began to walk back, his loneliness pulled into a single place that reminded him of a time he could not name. The jeweler did not look at him. Then Abel took from his pocket the marvelous watch and the fob with the golden lion's head and red jewel eye that gleamed even in the dim place. "'ake it," he said. He could see the man's eyes narrowing with bad thoughts at the sound of his voice. The man turned to him and Abel said, "Uh ring an' wa' an' *ehv-ry'ting—*" and then wrote: "$70." Even then the jeweler didn't look at him; he only turned and struck his money-machine and the drawer ran open. He counted out money fast and put it on the counter and as Abel picked it up, the jeweler swept the wonderful things into his hand like crumbs from a table. How carefully they had come from the cases before—each thing was held like something alive and impor-tant. Now, their poorness—his and Janice's—spoiled the jewels; the green stone was unlucky, the watch had given bad hours to count. The jeweler took them to hide them away in shame. An assistant came from the back of the store and was standing too near for comfort. Abel walked with his head up, hoping he wouldn't bump into the door in his pain. He felt the shadows of the two men behind him. He wondered if they were laughing in The Hearing World behind him.

"Did you get the money?"

"Yes."

"All of it?"

"Yes."

They stood by a restaurant window and pretended to look in.

"When the owing is finished, we will buy it back."

"Never. I will never go there again."

"I want to hope for it."

"Never again. He made me ashamed."

There was someone on the other side of the window, watching them, so they turned and went on. As they came to the corner and started across the street, Abel took his hands out of his pockets and said fast into the cold, "This is Outside, Outside. This is where everyone wants to go, everyone runs!" Then he put back his hands and glared. Silence.

Outside was all everyone talked about at school. Their eyes shone when they spoke of it, and down the narrow halls, railed for the blind, they made their Signs sail over the teachers' heads, hide behind books, slip between the desks, and the Signs talked about Outside. For Abel there was never Sign before, on the farm, and no real words. He came to the school mute and deaf to everyone, even to all the others who were as deaf as he. He took the Boys' Program: lipreading, arithmetic, reading and writing and had a choice of three trades: kitchen helper, printer's helper, boilermaker's helper. The Girls' Programs taught lipreading and sewing. These things the school taught. The things the boys and girls learned from one another were the language of Signs, and the dream of Outside. Every day for two hours, candles were blown out to make the letter P and mouths moved to letters and pictures on the blackboard and the students stared at tongues and teeth and lips—dill, till, still, skill—but the words, the real words were behind the outhouse, waiting; the Language given and taken quickly at the fence; the forbidden Signs made their users rich.

After six months at the school, Abel had friends and enemies and Outside. Now he was Outside, and he had the words to lie awake in bed and think of the time in school. It was a bad-smelling place, without color or taste, a dark place (color and light are wasted on the blind; the school served blind as well as deaf and so denied both). It seemed strange to him that in the school's ugliness he had found Janice.

Janice had gold hair, a smile that made him burn and be cold at the same time, a quickness, a slowness, like water going over stones when the sun shines on it. He was pulled by her and changed by her the way the river changed him when he went under the water—it made him another creature in another world. He was shy about being overage in the school; he came for the trades training and after years of trying to understand lipreading and to talk, he had been amazed to find there were in the world, others of his kind. He was eighteen then, Janice was sixteen. She had grown up in the school and knew almost nothing about Outside. She did know Sign, the forbidden language. How confidently she joked and gossiped and talked behind the backs of the instructors. How busy she was and how wise, with plans and ideas, with friends, angers and the small wars of enemies. To Abel, hand-mute in the mind-silence of his farm and Hearing school, these plans and arguments were so wide a life, that they seemed magic, beyond belief. In three months he learned all the Signs that anyone knew; his finger-spelling was faith alone, but he dared it: listening, talking, telling, sharing, arguing, wondering. He was made free in a language learned in spite of watchful teachers. Until he began to go with Janice, this language took a part of the places where it was learned. It seemed to smell of standing water, bath-rooms, shame, hiddenness and lye-cleaner. Hands that masturbated in the storehouse doorway spoke about it before and after, and the boys Signed in their cold-sweat sleep. When the older ones had the twice-yearly lecture on the Dangers of Self-Abuse, Abel, sitting among them, wondered if the teacher who spoke of touching and rubbing, of fear and release, was refer-ring to speech.

The boys and the girls were seldom together, so he saw Janice many times before they met. After they spoke once or twice, he began to look for her and he found that she had her chore in the kitchen, washing the pots. His wanting to be with her made him learn more than ever. He had to watch the teachers and see what made them forget him so that he could get away. He had to learn the times when there were people busy around the kitchen so Janice could take the chance to be away from her work. There were not many times to slip away from training or meet her as she went to her own class. The need to see her made him watchful and keen and took away some of his innocence. He began to see how Mr. Conroy's habit of a smoke in the afternoon could be used, how his own regular habits, even faults like late-ness, began to have a kind of order about them until they were accepted as his way. He met Janice outdoors behind the kitchen, or when it was too cold, in the empty hall outside the dining room. He got cautious, so he stopped going with other boys to hide in the attic over the blind girls' dormitory; he stopped fighting with everyone who said things about his age; and he began, very slowly, to wonder about words and thoughts themselves. Perhaps there were words for things not seen or touched, and for thoughts not as simple as "go" or "stay." It was Janice who first asked him what he thought about the people and things they knew, and then about his wishes and his dreams. The idea came to him that there was a big open place inside him that felt and saw pictures of great meaning for which there were no words, and that someday he might be able to tell her some of the difference he felt between the world he saw and the world that saw him.

Of all the girls, Janice was the one most interested in Outside. When anyone spoke about it, she came alive. The more words Abel learned, the more things had meaning; the more meaning, the more memory. She began to ask him questions: What was his town like? Were there many cars? What kind of clothes did the rich people wear? What did their houses look like? Was it nice on the farm? Was the work hard? She asked more questions about town than about the farm, and even more about the city. City was Outside at its richest. City was everything that was new and joyful and always changing. Janice loved the idea of traveling; she loved all motion, all change, and Abel, who had spent his life in The World, who must have traveled easily from farm to town to city, seemed to her and the others a prince of promise. His smallest memory had the weight of great wisdom.

During his second year, he and Janice were together everywhere, and together they ruined all the attempts the school made to put them out of each other's way. They found forgotten windows and unused storage rooms. Most of all they used their deafness. They were all and completely mute; they understood nothing, they agreed to everything. They nodded and smiled and said yes to everyone, teacher, matron and master; they promised to reform and then went where they wished. In April they ran away together. Outside. They found a Church like one Abel knew at home. When the minister saw what they wanted and that they were deaf, he wrote another man's name on a paper for them and so they were directed finally to a Justice of the Peace, who married them without questions—for four times the usual fee. That Monday morning they presented themselves back at the school to start their week's work as though nothing had happened. The school was afraid of bad talk, so it pretended not to notice them and allowed Janice to graduate with her class. They told her to write to her parents immediately. She put off doing it and in the end, the superintendent wrote to both families and told them of the marriage. When school was over, Janice and Abel went to his parents' farm. Janice's parents had thirteen other children. They sent best wishes in a letter to Janice and no return address. Abel and Janice took the train. Outside, she opened her eyes wide to try to see all of it, touch all of it, taste, smell, feel all of Outside. She gleamed with life. . . .

Now Abel turned in the bed and watched her sleeping. Sometimes, brushing across his mind too quickly to make words, was a feeling. It was the beginning of an idea and it was about the courts and stores and people—that maybe they were not hating or angry at his deafness and Janice's, but that they did not care. Strangely, the not-caring was worse than hate. Always in school there was talk about hate, the laughter and cruelty of Hearing people. Some had things they told over and over again, their faces all stiff with anger, and they told these things to everyone many times, until everyone knew they had pleasure telling and a big pride in the pain and laughter that was put against them. Abel began to feel that Outside's real cruelness had to do not with hating but with not-caring. He did not have the words to tell this to Janice, and so the thought stayed haunting the rims of his mind, almost making itself plain. He was also sometimes close to another knowledge: that the world was working against them and that their ignorance of the world was against them more, much more. This too was only a sudden running of something across a place that was lit too late to see by; there were no words to hold it.

His trouble weighed all night in the close room. Every night for a week he tried to find a way to stop that money—six thousand dollars—and more because of what they called Interest. Interest meant liking something. It meant working well and staying awake. He knew the Sign for it; it was close, that Sign, to the one for *liking*. Now, by some strange Hearing law, this good thing was made into money, more money for Mr. Dengel. It was Mr. Dengel who was staying awake and interested enough. Janice and Abel could only live on Janice's fourteen dollars a week, and his own money this second half of second year of apprenticeship, $7.00 less seventy cents to pay the debt. If they were careful they could creep past the Court and the jail. If they were very careful and there was no more trouble. But there was no money left for hope. Each half-year there would be more money going to fill the debt. It was all to keep strangers calm; all to keep them from anger. The Hearing are always angry.

One thing they had always told him in school; Keep working. They had begun his trade, they said, because they wanted him kept safe; and working, they said, was safety. Beside him Janice Signed in a dream, vague, unreadable Signs, and she turned in her sleep. Just before The Summer ended, at the top of all the good things, they had met a Deaf man who had told them about a church for Deaf on the other side of the city. Once a week a minister came and had services in Sign. At school it was often said that one part of The Hearing World had time for them—churches. They had made a plan to go as soon as they could, with jobs and nice clothes, the ring, the watch. They wanted to make friends, to have habits, to invite and be invited. Now the world was cold; ring and watch and money and hope were gone. Even if they could pay the carfare to that church, they wouldn't go. The friends were too expensive now, and the hope too feared for. Abel stirred the bed again, trying to find the right position for sleep, and it came at last, heavy with scattering, gray dreams.

•   •   •

Summer came and Abel received his increase as a third-year apprentice. When the money came, Mr. Webendorf made him sit down and they figured that the debt was now $5,577.28. If things went all right this year, the debt would be $5,528. The boss had spent a long time telling Abel about Interest, and now the Interest seemed more important to him than the first money and he was careful to keep the Interest money added, dollar by dollar, in his mind. Mr. Webendorf wrote a note to him then, and told him that there were things the Court did not know. Wages had gone up in the printing trade and Abel, as a third-year apprentice, would be getting not only his eight dollars a week, but maybe extra money called Christmas Bonus. Mr. Webendorf told him to save out this money and not tell the Court. It was not going in his regular pay, and what the Court didn't know about, it could not claim. Abel had first thought to tell Janice, to make her happy with the thought of a dinner out or shoes or a dress, but he was afraid. If the Court found out, they would send him to jail. If Janice bought things with that money, maybe the store people would tell the Court. He could only go on, working his day, waiting. He tried to keep his thoughts away from the money.

That summer seemed good to Abel, a relief from the cold and the coal money. Janice complained of the heat as much as she did of the cold, but Abel liked the long evenings, the golden light that saw him home, the breeze lifting the heavy maple leaves. He remembered the old ladies fanning themselves in the church at home. He did not know what made him think of this. He liked the smell of sun burning the spring sap hard in new wood and the smell of the ground rich with the green leaves that fell and rotted there. After work on Saturday, and all day Sunday, they were able to go walking along the green-leaf streets of those nice sections of town. Large houses were there, sitting like comfortable old women, their cool lawns gathered around them. All day they walked and pretended, arm in arm, silent and wise and there was a new pleasure because of the map.

There had been an order one day for a printing of five thousand city maps to sell at the fairgrounds when the State Fair opened. Abel seldom looked at anything he printed except to check for errors in placement or the strength of the inking, but something about the maps interested him, so instead of throwing away the strikeoffs to litter the floor, he brought them home. In the last light he and Janice looked at them. They found their own street and it made Abel feel famous almost—that anyone could look and find where he lived. They found the mill, the printing plant and even the street of wonderful stores where the ring was and the lion with its unclosing eye. They found the court building, too; and then they began to see how much larger than these streets the city was.

"It doesn't matter," she said, "we are too poor."

"You are afraid of friends."

"I am not. I don't like people know we are poor."

"It makes me feel like a man in jail."

"You made me in jail too."

"I know," he said, "but see, it doesn't have to be a small jail—it's bigger than we thought, just work and nothing else. At least in summer, it can be a big and pretty jail."

"A jail, and poor—we are still poor!"

He didn't answer her, but took the map and with his pencil divided it into quarters. "This summer we will walk in this part," he told her, "only in this part."

They put the map on the wall and he had a feeling of pleasure and success; this surprised him because of the new freedom. A year ago, he knew, he could not have been so humble or so patient, putting his pleasure into parts to make it longer, and measuring so closely the movements of their day's freedom.

Each Sunday after that, rain or sunshine, they investigated their section of the summer. To the south they found only mills and factories; to the west the avenue of wonderful stores and busy streets in the newer part of the city; but north and spreading eastward, the workmen's streets, smelling of cabbage and backhouses, led on into a neighborhood of peaceful, treelined streets. The houses were solid and dignified, with large, deep porches and careful white-dress children sitting on slow porch swings, back and forth in the slow noon. No matter which part of the section they saw on their Sundays, they always came back to these streets and, dressed in the still bright clothes of last summer, they strolled up one side and down the other, nodding to the nursemaids and pretending that in just a few more steps they would turn in at their own house and go up on the wide porch where the rocking chairs were waiting and the cool drinks were set out. They walked silently, their arms linked, but their minds were storing the daydream, changing, improving it, choosing or rejecting parts of other houses on other blocks.

Back in their close, hot room before supper, they found themselves arguing, sometimes bitterly, over the new wishes or the old. Janice wanted a cat; Abel didn't. Janice wanted a nursemaid for the children, a uniformed, starched nurse; Abel didn't. Abel wanted two cars; Janice didn't. Sometimes these arguments took over their fingers and began of themselves to knit the strands of the car and the Court and the debt into these summer dreams. Then their eyes would narrow against each other and then they would pull away their hands, weak with fear, and they wouldn't argue again that day.

At the end of the summer they took down the map and put it away carefully. They planned to leave the far sections for summers when there was money for carfare and small lunches. The section of the Deaf church was the last one on the map. Both of them noticed where it was. Neither mentioned it.

On Thanksgiving, Mary at the mill gave Janice a pound of chestnuts. She took them home, trying not to seem too pleased, and said, " a girl at the mill," and nothing more. Abel was proud and impressed. She must have Hearing friends there. How wonderful she was still, even though the cold and poverty had faded her, and though she seldom smiled. How wonderful the magic that could go so easily into That Other World, gliding by its tricks and confusion, able to be given gifts.

At Christmas they had a letter from Abel's parents at the farm:

> *My dear son and daughter-in-law. I am taking pen in hand to write to you and tell you we are sorry not to send the things we had been hoping. Things is awful bad here this year all over the Valley and in town, too.*

The prices has fallen so bad there are people who didn't get nothing this year to get seed, and the ones that had hybrid crops in are just that worse out of luck. People blame the tractors, but I think it was mostly specalaters that done it. Eakers has lost their farm. Yosts, too. They are going out West. Mertens have lost their farm and hire theirselfs out to anyone who can pay them keep and the whole family is broke up. These are not Railroad-siding people, or shiftless people, but neighbors whose folks had land here since anyone can remember and it makes us sad to see such terrible things happen to them. Mr. Pearce down at the store says it isn't only the Valley, but the whole State, and maybe even the whole country, which he means farms. The prices have dropped to nothing. Your father and I don't mean to make you feel bad by this news, and where you are in the city, you don't get hurt by this none. We had a idea to send you some $ and things at Christmas, and with things like they are we will not be able to. We are both glad you got a trade and can make your way in the city and are not caught here like so many of the other boys. We miss you, your father and I both. We are glad you are not having any hard times. Best wishes for Christmas and we hope you have a good an easy winter.

> *Sincerely, your mother,*
> *Sarah, Windom Ryder.*

They read the letter twice and then Janice shrugged and got up. "Why write and say you can't do something?"

Abel put down the letter shaking his head: "I remember," he said, "something my father does in spring. We all go with him and he walks to the end where he owns. He walks around the whole farm and every field, to the edge. He goes by the creek to see where it changes its places and to the woods. . . ."

In his mind, he saw his father stopping to look at a fencepost eaten by some bugs. The picture he had was from the years before the school and the words; long before he had Janice and Words and brought them both back with him. Abel's father was a Deaf, too; a man without Words. He had no Sign. He could not show what he meant except by writing little notes sometimes. Only Abel's mother could understand his father's speaking. If anyone else understood him, even Abel, it was because of the straightness of his thinking. He could point to something or move his hand to show an action, and by that or by the reason and the need, people could sometimes see what he meant. Everyone, all the neighbors were always surprised at how much Matthew noticed on the land. Now, the letter said, things were bad. The letter worried Abel; it made him feel afraid.

The next day he went out during his lunch period and bought a Christmas card with a picture of a table full of good food and a big fire, and on the back of it he wrote his name and Janice's also. He did not write about the auto or the Court, but only Good Wishes, and his name, as he was taught to do at the school. Then he went to the post office to buy the stamp, feeling proud at having it to do. People were lined up to the window with letters and packages, stamping the cold out of their feet and moving as if to complain with their bodies, at the line and the waiting. Abel stamped also, and shook his head and shrugged every once in a while, so as to look impatient as Hearing did.

In the evening, he worked his talk around to say, "I had a long wait today. It was at the post office. I waited a long time because of the importance. I sent best wishes in the mail."

Janice's eyebrows went up and her mouth pulled up in the middle because she didn't want to commit herself by asking questions about it.

"It was to my parents," he said.

She moved her mouth again, in the way she did when she was first married when all her movements were faster and freer. It reminded him with pain of the summertime people they had been and were not any more.

"My parents must have an answer. They had the idea to send me to school to have a trade."

She was lying on the bed, looking at him.

"Did I ever tell you about my school before Deaf school?" he asked.

"No," she said, and picked at a hangnail. She put the side of the nail in her mouth to pull at it.

"Many things happened in those days," he said. "I had no Words in those days."

That day he was early to help his father get water. He worked the pump . . . much swinging. He tried to put his words into that single day, into a place where they had never been. He spoke of it until he was almost there himself, swinging on the pump handle until it came down, then pushing it up, trembling because of the cold of the metal. Down and up, until a cough began that he felt against his body through the handle. Then the water came. All around, the day was blue and bright-cold. It was a day for Woodlot. Soon, he thought, his father would point to the saw and ax and hatchet and then they would go up on the hill into the woods and cut the fallen trees for wood for the fire. There was fast wood and slow wood, big wood; and his work was fast wood, gathering it up, trimming branches, putting it on the sledge. His words made him smell the air, that air, that day. That blue-time day was like a wood day. He tried to tell Janice how the smell of sap is, and to show her the grainy and moist crumbs that dropped from the feeding of the saw. He told her about his father coming toward him, saying, "Oooo" which meant "go" and pointing with his head to the house.

His mother had taken his clothes and set them out by the stove. She motioned him to get dressed. Church clothes, but it isn't church-day. He began to show his mother it was a wood-day, sawing back and forth, the tree-fall. She laughed, but didn't look happy. She made her mouth into something he did not know, a mouth "Uuuuuu." Then Breakfast. Afterwards she kissed him, making with her hand: "Outside." And there was the wagon and his father sitting up on it, waiting and making "Uuuuu" with his mouth. Abel also tried "Uuuuu," and they looked at one another until his mother looked away. His mother was a Hearing. He only knew it later. Then he looked down at himself in his nice clothes. But Uuuuuuu is not a church-day.

Not church? They rode away from town, a way only gone when they went to visit the molasses-eating people. His mother was always trying to show or tell him something, but he could never find it. His mother's mouth was always trying to make him do and feel and the things were always mysteries that made him tired and angry. His father did not show with his mouth.

Children were on the road. His father stopped the cart and motioned them: Come up. They did and again and again until there were many. Then Abel had an idea. He was going where they were going. He got frightened. He did not want to keep moving toward that place. They went farther than he ever was, far past the house of the molasses-eating people. They turned in then and stopped at a building with a top made of stone.

A woman came out and there were children running and playing all around. Only children. There was a church bell hung on a slaughtering-frame-thing on the far side. The woman went over and pulled a rope and the bell-feeling went through Abel so that his teeth began to pull themselves inside his head and his face bones shook weak under his skin. The riding children opened their mouths and fell off the cart and everywhere they ran and ran, into the building.

His father leaned down and took up an egg box and showed it to him, opened it so that he could see the food inside and gave it to him. Then his father pushed him toward the edge of the seat and nodded and looked toward the building where all the children were swallowed. He made "Uuuuuu," and Abel knew that this was Uuuu. He got down, his face cold and his body feeling stiff and tired. He held the egg box tightly and went to the door. When he was almost there, he turned and looked back. The cart was pulled around and was moving away from him down the road.

Inside was large, and so much with things that for a long time he only stared. There was a sour-yellow smell of damp, cold, old, and bad-boy. The bad-boy reminded him that he needed to go to the backhouse. His stomach hurt with that. But the room held him, and only when he felt the first drops beginning did he turn and run. A girl was coming out of it and he almost ran into her at the door. She said something too fast and ugly-faced him, pointing to *another* backhouse all the way over on the other side of the schoolyard. Now the front of his pants were damp and his teeth were clenched with trying to hold. A long time to the other backhouse and unbutton the big bone buttons that wadded in the double thick of wet cloth. Too late. When he came out of the backhouse, he knew that he was only to be sad, very sad for the wood-day.

There was no one in the schoolyard now. He went back to the big building, opening the door that was closed, as he knew he must.

Everyone was sitting at the row of desks that filled the room, and at the front, facing the wrong way, was the desk at which the woman sat, against the children. Her mouth was speaking and there was something "Aaa." He quickly took off his hat, because he thought he understood "hat," but the whole room rose, big and small. Backs were to him, blocking him from the woman's mouth. Suddenly, they all sat down again. The woman came and took him to one of the desks, pointing into his chest with her finger and then at the seat. His eyes kept her face to make sure. A little nod, a lowering of eye. Yes. He sat.

Time-time. Years. The air got filled, got empty. Children were up and down, went and came back, some with books and some with papers, mouth-mouth, important-too-fast, nothing to follow, so he sat until the things were done for him, or until his seatmate, a tiny, whitehaired girl with no eyebrows, jabbed him in the ribs. Often he swept the room for signal. His row, he learned, was: Woman's teeth on lip, roll, teeth-smile-top and-bottom. When he saw that lip-thing beginning, he swept the room, hoping to see, to anticipate, to know, to do, quickly, before he should be punished or laughed at.

His seatmate showed him that he must copy from the book, lines, just as they were: A A A A. For a while he was happy at this, doing as the others did. Afterwards the woman spoke to them, but he caught no meaning, not even one word, as he sometimes could catch meaning with his mother. He wondered if he would ever see his mother again. He remembered her as very wonderful. She seemed so long a time dead, she and his father, and the farm. Then the desks yawned suddenly and went down by signals he could not see. Certain children were talking and some raised their arms up and then they got up and then they sat down, and then, without warning, his seatmate flung herself away from him, slamming her book away into her desk as she went, and all of them blew from the room like leaves, spinning from their seats and away out the door.

The woman came over then and sat with him and got him to say her name, or something like it. He remembered that look to the mouth between his mother and his father. She looked at a glass machine that was taken from her pocket. Such a glass machine, large, was on the wall. She waved him out to go with the children. He followed the movements of her eyes and the way her head turned a little toward the door, so he got up and went out slowly. He didn't want to go. He was afraid of the children.

Girls with a clothes rope, mouths gaping all together. His head began to ache with trying to understand. He walked away slowly, moving with great care around the outside of the schoolyard. He didn't want to alert the children to make them notice him.

The yard was a nice place. Children's feet had made its dust fine, fine, soft and smooth as flour. It was warm with sun. If no one was here, he would have made a mound of it, a big, warm pile and then taken off his shoes and walked around in it. There was a swing, too; and beyond that another big slaughtering-frame with the tying ropes hanging down, but the big boys were climbing up on them. Others were running after a boy. They turned and swooped past Abel, the last one pushing him away. Their mouths were busy, busy. How could he follow the mouths of the fast, wild, jumping, turning, over-the-shoulder players, the tar-chewers, the nail-biting head-bent ones? His head was pounding. If only he could stop them, freeze them in play, hold the jump in mid-air and face them front to make them form to his mother's round perfection, their casual, wild, fearful-friendly, sudden-gone.

He felt the bell again with the bones of his face. Everyone stopped then and they all went in. More hands up, hands down and getting up and down. Then they all took out lunches, so he did, too. The sun-square was gone from his desk. The afternoon passed. It went so slowly that by the end of it, he had long forgotten the beginning. The children wrote, the children spoke. He followed and did not follow, too tired and growing impatient at the mouths. They were only quick, passing, not real, the moving of them lost before they made meaning.

He copied a picture with no idea. He cut out a star from paper, eight arms, not six, but no better, and when the others left and the sun was making its window-squares far on the other side of the room, he found himself breathing the dust of it all alone with the woman who was not a mother and whose name he could not imitate.

When he was let go at last from the building, the light was long and golden and sad with its going. He was surprised and confused at the length of the light. Didn't he take all the day's pain with a strong face, never weeping once, never running away? Wasn't that enough, without the day being used away besides? In spite of all he could do, his eyes filled. He looked about, trying to find some secret place where he might creep away and cry. . . .

There was a cart coming toward the place from down the road. He watched the light catch its metal now and then, and once or twice it was overtaken by its own dust. A terrifying hope began. It came up and beat inside his body. His father, dead these long light-passing times, was coming back. His father-mother-farm-life was coming back to take him away, to take him home, to forgive him. He began to run in circles, unable to contain his joy and his gratitude. Then he stood humbly, as a person does at any miracle. Never had his father been so powerful or so straight, never so different and so much the same.

Abel was standing motionless as the cart came on. His father saw him and raised a hand and then smiled at him. They had forgiven him. He got up into the cart before it stopped and they burned and left the bad things behind him. The day of pain was over.

When they came back to the farm, his mother asked him about Uuuuuuu and he smiled and nodded because it was over and he had lived through it and came back into the season of living things, and into their forgiveness again. It was only when his mother set his clothes of that day carefully on the chair again did he realize what his punishment was to be. Tomorrow also. The day after that. He stopped breathing; there was a pushing in his throat.

That night, he lay staring out at the dark sky, unable to cry himself to sleep. In front of the window the maple tree moved. He felt angry that he had been in this bed this morning, knowing so little. Beside him lay his younger brother, sleeping. He began to shake the bed to wake up the little boy who was taking the days so easily. The boy turned and slept on. Once, Abel knew, he had trusted like that. Once, he, too, had been good. For a while he watched the night and the moon in balance on the slender tips of branches.

From that day on, the time, which before had been a long measure, was now hung for him in endless strings of five and two. His mother began to wait for him with pencil and paper, and sometimes he wrote words there, but only the ones he had learned in school. He did not understand what they meant to be, and he never understood her when she tried to make them important to him. She was eager, somehow, and then angry, and finally, only sad. It was his fault, for which he was being punished. Soon she got tired and stopped.

Janice lay sleeping, her head twisted around as she was when she had been awake, watching him. Her hands were loose and quiet on the cotton quilt she had pulled up to warm herself. He shook his head and began to undress. He was eager for the warm bed and no more thinking. All the years he had not thought about the way his father looked sitting up in that wagon on the first day of school. Suddenly, he saw his hands drop the stained shirt they were holding and begin to speak to him. *School.* Yes, it was *school* they were trying to say to him on that first day. *School* was the Uuuuuuu. Only now, years and years away, and with Words in his hands, was it plain to him. He smiled at himself in the weak light and made the Sign for it, shaking his head again. What was the use of it, now he no longer needed it, that knowledge? Still it came back to him again. All the mouths of his years, all the mouth-mouths of the city and the shop had meanings and reasons. Too many. Too many to know or to want to know. It was a strange thing, though, wanting to think backwards. It was too strange even to tell Janice, that his mind, here in another place, was still holding that cart and the school, holding them waiting.

He looked at Janice again and she moved her head away, putting her arm up over her head and then down again. She turned on her side and settled more, and slept. At the Deaf School she was held also, waiting. Then she was all alive, always moving, changing, laughing quickly, scowling and laughing again. She was like the light that changes but is always beautiful, always different, always to wonder at. It was different with her now. Now she was pinched-in and always tired. She would only eat and finish eating, wipe her mouth and crawl into bed and fall asleep with her clothes on.

He looked around the room. The dinner things were there, drying and crusting on the windowsill. He moved around the bed and picked up the coffee bowls. One of them stuck to the sill for a minute. Something on the bottom of it, something that was not washed and dried away. It put a greasy feeling in his mind, a greasy smell in his mind, like mice that died in the seed sacks of the barn. He had found a nest of them once, packed in tight among the sacks, in the close, hot corner where the outgrown, unmended things were put by against some unexpected need. The memory was in his body still. His hair rose along his neck and down under the collar of his underwear.

He took the bowls to the washstand and poured some cold water over them. For a minute he thought about washing the pots, but he was beginning to be too angry with Janice and he put the pots in with the bowls and turned away. It was her job to do that—the wife's job. She was getting away from him and from her jobs every night, going to sleep for the warm, secret dreams where he could not follow. Every night, as soon as she was home and warm with a little food. Tomorrow she would wake up and say she was still not rested, not ready, and she would drag off to work yawning, her face unwashed from the night and blurred with breakfast crumbs.

He muttered, making half-words, one-handed, and without waking her he got undressed, rinsed his mouth and spat the rinsings out the window. Then he pissed into the alley, which saved having to go all the way downstairs and out to the privy, losing all the warmth of his dinner. It was bitter cold. He shut the window fast and got into bed. It was good. She was sleeping still. Her turning had left him a warmed place and he went gratefully into it and took up his own secrets; one special one, to warm his own night. It was a little like making a magic toward sleep: The Christmas Bonus. The Christmas Bonus. . . .

A MAD TEA PARTY

There was a table set out under a tree in front of the house, and the March Hare and the Hatter were having tea at it: a Dormouse was sitting between them, fast asleep, and the other two were using it as a cushion, resting their elbows on it, and talking over its head. "Very uncomfortable for the Dormouse," thought Alice; "only as it's asleep, I suppose it doesn't mind."

The table was a large one, but the three were all crowded together at one corner of it. "No room! No room!" they cried out when they saw Alice coming. "There's *plenty* of room!" said Alice indignantly, and she sat down in a large arm-chair at one end of the table.

"Have some wine," the March Hare said in an encouraging tone.

Alice looked all round the table, but there was nothing on it but tea. "I don't see any wine," she remarked.

"There isn't any," said the March Hare.

"Then it wasn't very civil of you to offer it," said Alice angrily.

"It wasn't very civil of you to sit down without being invited," said the March Hare.

"I didn't know it was *your* table," said Alice: "it's laid for a great many more than three."

"Your hair wants cutting," said the Hatter. He had been looking at Alice for some time with great curiosity, and this was his first speech.

"You should learn not to make personal remarks," Alice said with some severity: "It's very rude."

The Hatter opened his eyes very wide on hearing this; but all he *said* was "Why is a raven like a writing-desk?"

"Come, we shall have some fun now!" thought Alice. "I'm glad they've begun asking riddles—I believe I can guess that," she added aloud.

"Do you mean that you think you can find out the answer to it?" said the March Hare.

"Exactly so," said Alice.

"Then you should say what you mean," the March Hare went on.

"I do," Alice hastily replied; "at least—at least I mean what I say—that's the same thing, you know."

"Not the same thing a bit!" said the Hatter. "Why, you might just as well say that 'I see what I eat' is the same thing as 'I eat what I see'!"

"You might just as well say," added the March Hare, "that 'I like what I get' is the same thing as 'I get what I like'!"

"You might just as well say," added the Dormouse, which seemed to be talking in its sleep, "that 'I breathe when I sleep' is the same thing as 'I sleep when I breathe'!"

"It *is* the same thing with you," said the Hatter, and here the conversation dropped, and the party sat silent for a minute, while Alice thought over all she could remember about ravens and writing-desks, which wasn't much.

The Hatter was the first to break the silence. "What day of the month is it?" he said, turning to Alice: he had taken his watch out of his pocket, and was looking at it uneasily, shaking it every now and then, and holding it to his ear.

Alice considered a little, and then said "The fourth."

"Two days wrong!" sighed the Hatter. "I told you butter wouldn't suit the works!" he added, looking angrily at the March Hare.

"It was the *best* butter," the March Hare meekly replied.

"Yes, but some crumbs must have got in as well," the Hatter grumbled: "you shouldn't have put it in with the bread-knife."

The March Hare took the watch and looked at it gloomily: then he dipped it into his cup of tea, and looked at it again: but he could think of nothing better to say than his first remark, "It was the *best* butter, you know."

Alice had been looking over his shoulder with some curiosity. "What a funny watch!" she remarked. "It tells the day of the month, and doesn't tell what o'clock it is!"

"Why should it?" muttered the Hatter. "Does *your* watch tell you what year it is?"

"Of course not," Alice replied very readily: "but that's because it stays the same year for such a long time together."

"Which is just the case with *mine,*" said the Hatter.

Alice felt dreadfully puzzled. The Hatter's remark seemed to her to have no sort of meaning in it, and yet it was certainly English. "I don't quite understand you," she said, as politely as she could.

"The Dormouse is asleep again," said the Hatter, and he poured a little hot tea upon its nose.

The Dormouse shook its head impatiently, and said, without opening its eyes, "Of course, of course: just what I was going to remark myself."

"Have you guessed the riddle yet?" the Hatter said, turning to Alice again.

"No, I give it up," Alice replied. "What's the answer?"

"I haven't the slightest idea," said the Hatter.

"Nor I," said the March Hare.

Alice sighed wearily. "I think you might do something better with the time," she said, "than wasting it in asking riddles that have no answers."

"If you knew Time as well as I do," said the Hatter, "you wouldn't talk about wasting *it*. It's *him*."

"I don't know what you mean," said Alice.

"Of course you don't!" the Hatter said, tossing his head contemptuously. "I dare say you never even spoke to Time!"

"Perhaps not," Alice cautiously replied; "but I know I have to beat time when I learn music."

"Ah! That accounts for it," said the Hatter. "He wo'n't stand beating. Now, if you only kept on good terms with him, he'd do almost anything you liked with the clock. For instance, suppose it were nine o'clock in the morning, just time to begin lessons; you'd only have to whisper a hint to Time, and round goes the clock in a twinkling! Half-past one, time for dinner!"

("I only wish it was," the March Hare said to itself in a whisper.)

"That would be grand, certainly," said Alice thoughtfully; "but then—I shouldn't be hungry for it, you know."

"Not at first, perhaps," said the Hatter: "but you could keep it to half-past one as long as you liked."

"Is that the way *you* manage?" Alice asked.

The Hatter shook his head mournfully. "Not I!" he replied. "We quarreled last March—— just before *he* went mad, you know——" (pointing with his teaspoon at the March Hare,) "——it was at the great concert given by the Queen of Hearts, and I had to sing

> *'Twinkle, twinkle, little bat!*
> *How I wonder what you're at!'*

You know the song, perhaps?"

"I've heard something like it," said Alice.

"It goes on, you know," the Hatter continued, "in this way:—

> *'Up above the world you fly,*
> *Like a tea-tray in the sky.*
> *Twinkle, twinkle——' "*

Here the Dormouse shook itself, and began singing in its sleep *"Twinkle, twinkle, twinkle, twinkle——"* and went on so long that they had to pinch it to make it stop.

"Well, I'd hardly finished the first verse," said the Hatter, "when the Queen bawled out 'He's murdering the time! Off with his head!' "

"How dreadfully savage!" exclaimed Alice.

"And ever since that," the Hatter went on in a mournful tone, "he wo'n't do a thing I ask! It's always six o'clock now."

A bright idea came into Alice's head. "Is that the reason so many tea-things are put out here?" she asked.

"Yes, that's it," said the Hatter with a sigh: "it's always tea-time, and we've no time to wash the things between whiles."

"Then you keep moving round, I suppose?" said Alice.

"Exactly so," said the Hatter: "as the things get used up."

"But what happens when you come to the beginning again?" Alice ventured to ask.

"Suppose we change the subject," the March Hare interrupted, yawning. "I'm getting tired of this. I vote the young lady tell us a story."

"I'm afraid I don't know one," said Alice, rather alarmed at the proposal.

"Then the Dormouse shall!" they both cried. "Wake up, Dormouse!" And they pinched it on both sides at once.

The Dormouse slowly opened its eyes. "I wasn't asleep," it said in a hoarse, feeble voice, "I heard every word you fellows were saying."

"Tell us a story!" said the March Hare.

"Yes, please do!" pleaded Alice.

"And be quick about it," added the Hatter, "or you'll be asleep again before it's done."

"Once upon a time there were three little sisters," the Dormouse began in a great hurry; "and their names were Elsie, Lacie, and Tillie; and they lived at the bottom of a well——"

"What did they live on?" said Alice, who always took a great interest in questions of eating and drinking.

"They lived on treacle," said the Dormouse, after thinking a minute or two.

"They couldn't have done that, you know," Alice gently remarked. "They'd have been ill."

"So they were," said the Dormouse; "*very* ill."

Alice tried a little to fancy to herself what such an extraordinary way of living would be like, but it puzzled her too much: so she went on: "But why did they live at the bottom of a well?"

"Take some more tea," the March Hare said to Alice, very earnestly.

"I've had nothing yet," Alice replied in an offended tone: "so I ca'n't take more."

"You mean you ca'n't take *less*," said the Hatter: "it's very easy to take *more* than nothing."

"Nobody asked *your* opinion," said Alice.

"Who's making personal remarks now?" the Hatter asked triumphantly.

Alice did not quite know what to say to this: so she helped herself to some tea and bread-and-butter, and then turned to the Dormouse, and repeated her question. "Why did they live at the bottom of a well?"

The Dormouse again took a minute or two to think about it, and then said "It was a treacle-well."

"There's no such thing!" Alice was beginning very angrily, but the Hatter and the March Hare went "Sh! Sh!" and the Dormouse sulkily remarked "If you ca'n't be civil, you'd better finish the story for yourself."

"No, please go on!" Alice said very humbly. "I wo'n't interrupt you again. I dare say there may be *one*."

"One, indeed!" said the Dormouse indignantly. However, he consented to go on. "And so these three little sisters—they were learning to draw, you know——"

"What did they draw?" said Alice, quite forgetting her promise.

"Treacle," said the Dormouse, without considering at all, this time.

"I want a clean cup," interrupted the Hatter: "let's all move one place on."

He moved on as he spoke, and the Dormouse followed him: the March Hare moved into the Dormouse's place, and Alice rather unwillingly took the place of the March Hare. The Hatter was the only one who got any advantage from the change; and Alice was a good deal worse off than before, as the March Hare had just upset the milk-jug into his plate.

Alice did not wish to offend the Dormouse again, so she began very cautiously: "But I don't understand. Where did they draw the treacle from?"

"You can draw water out of a water-well," said the Hatter; "so I should think you could draw treacle out of a treacle-well—eh, stupid?"

"But they were *in* the well," Alice said to the Dormouse, not choosing to notice this last remark.

"Of course they were," said the Dormouse: "well in."

This answer so confused poor Alice, that she let the Dormouse go on for some time without interrupting it.

"They were learning to draw," the Dormouse went on, yawning and rubbing its eyes, for it was getting very sleepy; "and they drew all manner of things—everything that begins with an M——"

"Why with an M?" said Alice.

"Why not?" said the March Hare.

Alice was silent.

The Dormouse had closed its eyes by this time, and was going off into a doze; but, on being pinched by the Hatter, it woke up again with a little shriek, and went on: "——that begins with an M, such as mouse-traps, and the moon, and memory, and muchness—you know you say things are 'much of a muchness'—did you ever see such a thing as a drawing of a muchness!"

"Really, now you ask me," said Alice, very much confused, "I don't think——"

"Then you shouldn't talk," said the Hatter.

This piece of rudeness was more than Alice could bear: she got up in great disgust, and walked off: the Dormouse fell asleep instantly, and neither of the others took the least notice of her going, though she looked back once or twice, half hoping that they would call after her: the last time she saw them, they were trying to put the Dormouse into the teapot.

"At any rate I'll never go *there* again!" said Alice, as she picked her way through the wood. "It's the stupidest tea-party I ever was at in all my life!"

Just as she said this, she noticed that one of the trees had a door leading right into it. "That's very curious!" she thought. "But everything's curious to-day. I think I may as well go in at once." And in she went.

Once more she found herself in the long hall, and close to the little glass table. "Now, I'll manage better this time," she said to herself, and began by taking the little golden key, and unlocking the door that led into the garden. Then she set to work nibbling at the mushroom (she had kept a piece of it in her pocket) till she was about a foot high: then she walked down the little passage: and *then*—she found herself at last in the beautiful garden, among the bright flower-beds and the cool fountains.

CHAPTER 34   ANHONY BURGESS

A CLOCKWORK ORANGE

"What's it going to be then, eh?"

There was me, that is Alex, and my three droogs, that is Pete, Georgie, and Dim, Dim being really dim, and we sat in the Korova Milkbar making up our rassoodocks what to do with the evening, a flip dark chill winter bastard though dry. The Korova Milkbar was a milk-plus mesto, and you may, O my brothers, have forgotten what these mestos were like, things changing so skorry these days and everybody very quick to forget, newspapers not being read much neither. Well, what they sold there was milk plus something else. They had no licence for selling liquor, but there was no law yet against prodding some of the new veshches which they used to put into the old moloko, so you could peet it with vellocet or synthemesc or drencrom or one or two other veshches which would give you a nice quiet horrorshow fifteen minutes admiring Bog And All His Holy Angels And Saints in your left shoe with lights bursting all over your mozg. Or you could peet milk with knives in it, as we used to say, and this would sharpen you up and make you ready for a bit of dirty twenty-to-one, and that was what we were peeting this evening I'm starting off the story with.

Our pockets were full of deng, so there was no real need from the point of view of crasting any more pretty polly to tolchock some old veck in an alley and viddy him swim in his blood while we counted the takings and divided by four, nor to do the ultra-violent on some shivering starry grey-haired ptitsa in a shop and go smecking off with the till's guts. But, as they say, money isn't everything.

The four of us were dressed in the heighth of fashion, which in those days was a pair of black very tight tights with the old jelly mould, as we called it, fitting on the crutch underneath the tights, this being to protect and also a sort of a design you could viddy clear enough in a certain light, so that I had one in the shape of a spider, Peter had a rooker (a hand, that is), Georgie had a very fancy one of a flower, and poor old Dim had a very hound-and-horny one of a clown's litso (face, that is), Dim not ever having much of an idea of things and being, beyond all shadow of a doubting thomas, the dimmest of we four. Then we wore waisty jackets without lapels but with these very big builtup shoulders ("pletchoes" we called them) which were a kind of a mockery of having real shoulders like that. Then, my brothers, we had these off-white cravats which looked like whipped-up kartoffel or spud with a sort of a design made on it with a fork. We wore our hair not too long and we had flip horrorshow boots for kicking.

"What's it going to be then, eh?"

There were three devotchkas sitting at the counter all together, but there were four of us malchicks and it was usually like one for all and all for one. These sharps were dressed in the heighth of fashion too, with purple and green and orange wigs on their gullivers, each one not costing less than three or four weeks of those sharps' wages, I should reckon, and make-up to match (rainbows round the glazzies, that is, and the rot painted very wide). Then they had long black very straight dresses, and on the groody part of them they had little badges of like silver with different malchicks' names on them—Joe and Mike and suchlike. These were supposed to be the names of the different malchicks they'd spatted with before they were fourteen. They kept looking our way and I nearly felt like saying the three of us (out of the corner of my rot, that is) should go off for a bit of pol and leave poor old Dim behind, because it would be just a matter of kupetting Dim a demi-litre of white but this time with a dollop of synthemesc in it, but that wouldn't really have been playing like the game. Dim was very very ugly and like his name, but he was a horrorshow filthy fighter and very handy with the boot.

"What's it going to be then, eh?"

The chelloveck sitting next to me, there being this long big plushy seat that ran round three walls, was well away with his glazzies glazed and sort of burbling slovos like "Aristotle wishy washy works outing cyclamen get forficulate smartish." He was in the land all right, well away, in orbit, and I knew what it was like, having tried it like everybody else had done, but at this time I'd got to thinking it was a cowardly sort of a veshch, O my brothers. You'd lay there after you'd drunk the old moloko and then you got the messel that everything all round you was sort of in the past. You could viddy it all right, all of it, very clear—tables, the stereo, the lights, the sharps and the malchicks—but it was like some veshch that used to be there but was not there not no more. And you were sort of hypnotized by your boot or shoe or a finger-nail as it might be, and at the same time you were sort of picked up by the old scruff and shook like it might be a cat. You got shook and shook till there was nothing left. You lost your name and your body and your self and you just didn't care, and you waited till your boot or your finger-nail got yellow, then yellower and yellower all the time. Then the lights started cracking like atomics and the boot or finger-nail or, as it might be, a bit of dirt on your trouser-bottom turned into a big big big mesto, bigger than the whole world, and you were just going to get introduced to old Bog or God when it was all over. You came back to here and now whimpering sort of, with your rot all squaring up for a boohoohoo. Now, that's very nice but very cowardly. You were not put on this earth just to get in touch with God. That sort of thing could sap all the strength and the goodness out of a chelloveck.

"What's it going to be then, eh?"

The stereo was on and you got the idea that the singer's goloss was moving from one part of the bar to another, flying up to the ceiling and then swooping down again and whizzing from wall to wall. It was Berti Laski rasping a real starry oldie called "You Blister My Paint." One of the three ptitsas at the counter, the one with the green wig, kept pushing her belly out and pulling it in in time to what they called the music. I could feel the knives in the old moloko starting to prick, and now I was ready for a bit of twenty-to-one. So I yelped: "Out out out out!" like a doggie, and then I cracked this veck who was sitting next to me and well away and burbling a horrorshow crack on the ooko or earhole, but he didn't feel it and went on with his "Telephonic hardware and when the farfarculule gets rubadubdub." He'd feel it all right when he came to, out of the land.

"Where out?" said Georgie.

"Oh, just to keep walking," I said, "and viddy what turns up, O my little brothers."

So we scatted out into the big winter nochy and walked down Margha-nita Boulevard and then turned into Boothby Avenue, and there we found what we were pretty well looking for, a malenky jest to start off the evening with. There was a doddery starry schoolmaster type veck, glasses on and his rot open to the cold nochy air. He had books under his arm and a crappy umbrella and was coming round the corner from the Public Biblio, which not many lewdies used those days. You never really saw many of the older bourgeois type out after nightfall those days, what with the shortage of police and we fine young malchickiwicks about, and this prof type chelloveck was the only one walking in the whole of the street. So we goolied up to him, very polite, and I said: "Pardon me, brother."

He looked a malenky bit poogly when he viddied the four of us like that, coming up so quiet and polite and smiling, but he said: "Yes? What is it?" in a very loud teacher-type goloss, as if he was trying to show us he wasn't poogly. I said:

"I see you have books under your arm, brother. It is indeed a rare pleasure these days to come across somebody that still reads, brother."

"Oh," he said, all shaky. "Is it? Oh, I see." And he kept looking from one to the other of we four, finding himself now like in the middle of a very smiling and polite square.

"Yes," I said. "It would interest me greatly, brother, if you would kindly allow me to see what books those are that you have under your arm. I like nothing better in this world than a good clean book, brother."

"Clean," he said. "Clean, eh?" And then Pete skvatted these three books from him and handed them round real skorry. Being three, we all had one each to viddy at except for Dim. The one I had was called *Elementary Crystallography,* so I opened it up and said: "Excellent, really first-class," keeping turning the pages. Then I said in a very shocked type goloss: "But what is this here? What is this filthy slovo? I blush to look at this word. You disappoint me, brother, you do really."

"But," he tried, "but, but."

"Now," said Georgie, "here is what I should call real dirt. There's one slovo beginning with an f and another with a c." He had a book called *The Miracle of the Snowflake.*

"Oh," said poor old Dim, smotting over Pete's shoulder and going too far, like he always did, "it says here what he done to her, and there's a picture and all. Why," he said, "you're nothing but a filthy-minded old skitebird."

"An old man of your age, brother," I said, and I started to rip up the book I'd got, and the others did the same with the ones they had, Dim and Peter doing a tug-of-war with *The Rhombohedral System.* The starry prof type began to creech: "But those are not mine, those are the property of the municipality, this is sheer wantonness and vandal work," or some such slovos. And he tried to sort of wrest the books back off of us, which was like pathetic. "You deserve to be taught a lesson, brother," I said, "that you do." This crystal book I had was very tough-bound and hard to razrez to bits, being real starry and made in days when things were made to last like, but I managed to rip the pages up and chuck them in handfuls of like snowflakes, though big, all over this creeching old veck, and then the others did the same with theirs, old Dim just dancing about like the clown he was. "There you are," said Peter. "There's the mackerel of the cornflake for you, you dirty reader of filth and nastiness."

"You naughty old veck, you," I said, and then we began to filly about with him. Pete held his rookers and Georgie sort of hooked his rot wide open for him and Dim yanked out his false zoobies, upper and lower. He threw these down on the pavement and then I treated them to the old bootcrush, though they were hard bastards like, being made of some new horrorshow plastic stuff. The old veck began to make sort of chumbling shooms—"wuf waf wof"—so Georgie let go of holding his goobers apart and just let him have one in the toothless rot with his ringy fist, and that made the old veck start moaning a lot then, then out comes the blood, my brothers, real beautiful. So all we did then was to pull his outer platties off, stripping him down to his vest and long underpants (very starry; Dim smecked his head off near), and then Pete kicks him lovely in his pot, and we let him go. He went sort of staggering off, it not having been too hard of a tolchock really, going "Oh oh oh," not knowing where or what was what really, and we had a snigger at him and then riffled through his pockets, Dim dancing round with his crappy umbrella meanwhile, but there wasn't much in them. There were a few starry letters, some of them dating right back to 1960, with "My dearest dearest" in them and all that chepooka, and a keyring and a starry leaky pen. Old Dim gave up his umbrella dance and of course had to start reading one of the letters out loud, like to show the empty street he could read. "My darling one," he recited, in this very high type goloss, "I shall be thinking of you while you are away and hope you will remember to wrap up warm when you go out at night." Then he let out a very shoomny smeck—"Ho ho ho"—pretending to start wiping his yahma with it. "All right," I said. "Let it go, O my brothers." In the trousers of this starry veck there was only a malenky bit of cutter (money, that is)—not more than three gollies—so we gave all his messy little coin the scatter treatment, it being hen-korm to the amount of pretty polly we had on us already. Then we smashed the umbrella and razrezzed his platties and gave them to the blowing winds, my brothers, and then we'd finished with the starry teacher type veck. We hadn't done much, I know, but that was only like the start of the evening and I make no appy polly loggies to thee or thine for that. The knives in the milk-plus were stabbing away nice and horrorshow now.

The next thing was to do the sammy act, which was one way to unload some of our cutter so we'd have more of an incentive like for some shop-crasting, as well as it being a way of buying an alibi in advance, so we went into the Duke of New York on Amis Avenue and sure enough in the snug there were three or four old baboochkas peeting their black and suds on SA (State Aid). Now we were the very good malchicks, smiling good evensong to one and all, though these wrinkled old lighters started to get all shook, their veiny old rookers all trembling round their glasses and making the suds spill on the table. "Leave us be, lads," said one of them, her face all mappy with being a thousand years old, "we're only poor old women." But we just made with the zoobies, flash flash flash, sat down, rang the bell, and waited for the boy to come. When he came, all nervous and rubbing his rookers on his grazzy apron, we ordered us four veterans—a veteran being rum and cherry brandy mixed, which was popular just then, some liking a dash of lime in it, that being the Canadian variation. Then I said to the boy:

"Give these poor old baboochkas over there a nourishing something. Large Scotchmen all round and something to take away." And I poured my pocket of deng all over the table, and the other three did likewise, O my brothers. So double firegolds were brought in for the scared starry lighters, and they knew not what to do or say. One of them got out "Thanks, lads," but you could see they thought there was something dirty like coming. Anyway, they were each given a bottle of Yank General, cognac that is, to take away, and I gave money for them to be delivered each a dozen of black and suds that following morning, they to leave their stinking old cheenas' addresses at the counter. Then with the cutter that was left over we did purchase, my brothers, all the meat pies, pretzels, cheese-snacks, crisps and chocbars in that mesto, and those too were for the old sharps. Then we said: "Back in a minoota," and the old ptitsas were still saying: "Thanks, lads," and "God bless you, boys," and we were going out without one cent of cutter in our carmans.

"Makes you feel real dobby, that does," said Pete. You could viddy that poor old Dim the dim didn't quite pony all that, but he said nothing for fear of being called gloopy and a domeless wonderboy. Well, we went off now round the corner to Attlee Avenue, and there was this sweets and cancers shop still open. We'd left them alone near three months now and the whole district had been very quiet on the whole, so the armed millicents or rozz patrols weren't round there much, being more north of the river these days. We put our maskies on—new jobs these were, real horrorshow, wonderfully done really; they were like faces of historical personalities (they gave you the name when you bought) and I had Disraeli, Pete had Elvis Presley, Georgie had Henry VIII and poor old Dim had a poet veck called Peebee Shelley; they were a real like disguise, hair and all, and they were some very special plastic veshch so you could roll up when you'd done with it and hide it in your boot—then three of us went in, Pete keeping chasso without, not that there was anything to worry about out there. As soon as we launched on the shop we went for Slouse who ran it, a big portwine jelly of a veck who viddied at once what was coming and made straight for the inside where the telephone was and perhaps his well-oiled pooshka, complete with six dirty rounds. Dim was round that counter skorry as a bird, sending packets of snoutie flying and cracking over a big cut-out showing a sharp with all her zoobies going flash at the customers and her groodies near hanging out to advertise some new brand of cancers. What you could viddy then was a sort of a big ball rolling into the inside of the shop behind the curtain, this being old Dim and Slouse sort of locked in a death struggle. Then you could slooshy panting and snoring and kicking behind the curtain and veshches falling over and swearing and then glass going smash smash smash. Mother Slouse, the wife, was sort of froze behind the counter. We could tell she would creech murder given one chance, so I was round that counter very skorry and had a hold of her, and a horrorshow big lump she was too, all nuking of scent and with flipflop big bobbing groodies on her. I'd got my rooker round her rot to stop her belting out death and destruction to the four winds of heaven, but this

Language and Communication

lady doggie gave me a large foul big bite on it and it was me that did the creeching, and then she opened up beautiful with a flip yell for the millicents. Well, then she had to be tolchocked proper with one of the weights for the scales, and then a fair tap with a crowbar they had for opening cases, and that brought the red out like an old friend. So we had her down on the floor and a rip of her platties for fun and a gentle bit of the boot to stop her moaning. And, viddying her lying there with her groodies on show, I wondered should I or not, but that was for later on in the evening. Then we cleaned the till, and there was flip horrorshow takings that nochy, and we had a few packs of the very best top cancers apiece, then off we went, my brothers.

"A real big heavy great bastard he was," Dim kept saying. I didn't like the look of Dim; he looked dirty and untidy, like a veck who'd been in a fight, which he had been, of course, but you should never *look* as though you have been. His cravat was like someone had trampled on it, his maskic had been pulled off and he had floor-dirt on his litso, so we got him in an alleyway and tidied him up a malenky bit, soaking our tashtooks in spit to cheest the dirt off. The things we did for old Dim. We were back in the Duke of New York very skorry, and I reckoned by my watch we hadn't been more than ten minutes away. The starry old baboochkas were still there on the black and suds and Scotchmen we'd bought them, and we said: "Hallo there, girlies, what's it going to be?" They started on the old "Very kind, lads, God bless you, boys," and so we rang the collocoll and brought a different waiter in this time and we ordered beers with rum in, being sore athirst, my brothers, and whatever the old ptitsas wanted. Then I said to the old baboochkas: "We haven't been out of here, have we? Been here all the time, haven't we?" They all caught on real skorry and said:

"That's right, lads. Not been out of our sight, you haven't. God bless you, boys," drinking.

Not that it mattered much, really. About half an hour went by before there was any sign of life among the millicents, and then it was only two very young rozzes that came in, very pink under their big copper's shlemmies. One said:

"You lot know anything about the happenings at Slouse's shop this night?"

"Us?" I said, innocent. "Why, what happened?"

"Stealing and roughing. Two hospitalizations. Where've you lot been this evening?"

"I don't go for that nasty tone," I said. "I don't care much for these nasty insinuations. A very suspicious nature all this betokeneth, my little brothers."

"They've been in here all night, lads," the old sharps started to creech out. "God bless them, there's no better lot of boys living for kindness and generosity. Been here all the time they have. Not seen them move we haven't."

"We're only asking," said the other young millicent. "We've got our job to do like anyone else." But they gave us the nasty warning look before they went out. As they were going out we handed them a bit of lip-music: brrrrzzzzrrrr. But, myself, I couldn't help a bit of disappointment at things as they were those days. Nothing to fight against really. Everything as easy as kiss-my-sharries. Still, the night was still very young.

PART SEVEN

CULTURE CONTACT AND CHANGE

Sociocultural change permeates the contemporary world. Many of the previous selections describe situations in which people of different cultures meet and the changes that result. Literature often reflects the empirical situation better than ethnographic studies, which sometimes convey the impression that human cultures are static. All cultures are constantly changing as people adapt to new social and physical conditions. The extent of change and the rate of change vary greatly but change itself occurs everywhere.

Cultures change whenever a new pattern of social behavior, which may involve discarding old patterns, is adopted by members of a society. When it becomes customary for people to organize themselves in new ways, to interpret things differently, to wear new items of clothing, or even to alter the customary length of their hair, culture change has taken place. The two primary sources of this change are *innovation* and *borrowing*. Innovation is a cognitive process whereby old elements of a culture are organized into new patterns or combined with new elements in a meaningful way. Some individuals in every society appear to be more innovative than the rest of their group. They seem able to tolerate ambiguity, to entertain deviations from the cultural norm without anxiety and guilt. But innovations can lead to culture change only if they are adopted by others. Acceptance often depends on how a new cultural element fits in with older patterns, what needs it will satisfy, and how it is perceived. Under conditions of culture contact, culture change often increases by means of borrowing.

When culture change becomes extensive and rapid, as it does in many contact situations, individuals develop different strategies for coping with it. Some will adopt the new ways of life and become assimilated, losing their previous cultural identity. Others may cling to the old ways even as they are disintegrating and losing their meaning for many; they respond by becoming more nativistic. Still others are caught between the two cultures, unable to find the goals of either tenable. They may attempt to create an altogether new way of life or remain suspended in a state of apathy. Recently, anthropologists have begun to turn more attention to those people who attempt to live up to the norms of more than one cultural tradition; that is, they respond to contact and change by becoming *bicultural*. These selections show the effect of culture change upon people, the conflicts it creates, and the coping responses that are developed to handle change.

INCENSE IN THE LAB

Every afternoon, the barefoot *chaprassi* brought tea into the lab. We used to keep milk in the refrigerator, along with the blood samples, and a sugar bowl stood on top of the centrifuge. Lab equipment has such a deadpan international character; among those bright, gleaming pipettes and burettes we might well have been anywhere—in New York, Switzerland, or Australia. But when the *chaprassi* showed up with tea, it was clear that we were in India. There had been a famine recently in parts of Bombay State. Narayan Ghodme and I were getting blood samples from people with advanced malnutrition, to determine serum-protein and cholesterol levels at three stages—before, during, and after treatment. I also planned to compare some of our data later on with those on well-fed Middle Westerners back home, people with lots of fat in their diet. So far, our project had been going well.

"I have an idea," said Narayan one afternoon, stirring his tea. "How about a study on cancer incidence among water-pipe smokers? Do people who use the hookah get lung cancer?"

"That's been done." I reached for the sugar.

Narayan sighed. "I *would* like to keep some sort of research going after our project ends."

I felt sure that Narayan would think of something. I had first met him in New York, where he had come on a medical-research fellowship, given him by the American foundation that was financing our present project. We were using the facilities of a lab attached to a government hospital.

Narayan always had ideas for a variety of projects. For example, he had rigged up a plethysmograph in a corner of the lab, and he fooled around with it in spare moments. He was a born scientist. This seemed strange to me, since he came from a fairly conservative Brahman family. I was staying with them as his guest (they weren't too conservative to take me in with the warmest hospitality), and I was amazed by all the religious rituals that went on in the household. Little statuettes of the gods—Shiva, Ganesha, Paryati—were always being set up, anointed, and strewn with flowers. The Ghodmes were wonderful people. They were all handsome, intelligent, and affectionate, but except for Narayan, they didn't have the scientific temper.

Sometimes, when he and I sat drinking tea in the lab, I tried to find out what his own religious views were. Once I asked him if he believed in reincarnation. For answer, he waved a thin brown hand toward the lab equipment and said, "I believe in *that*."

"The plethysmograph?"

"No. Science."

I liked to badger him. "But at home you take part in the family rituals," I said.

"Of course." Narayan shrugged. "Family is one thing, science another."

"But by taking part you give assent, don't you? Let's face it, Narayan—do you *want* people to go on worshipping elephant-headed gods?"

Narayan raised his eyebrows. "What's wrong with elephant-headed gods?"

I couldn't think of any very sensible answer, so I dropped this line of argument, and we went to work at the colorimeter.

At five o'clock each afternoon, the family chauffeur appeared at the door. He was barefooted, like the *chaprassi,* and looked rather seedy in his old turban. The Ghodmes weren't rich. They were middle-class people, and the automobile doubtless represented a big investment for them. I don't suppose barefoot chauffeurs cost much, since labor is cheap in India, but with the gas and everything else, the car must have been expensive to maintain. The family, however, were all behind Narayan. He was the eldest son, their chief hope, and he needed the car for collecting blood samples from patients outside the hospital. So they'd bought the automobile, an old English model, and we used to ride home in it from the lab. Narayan was terribly proud of this old car. He was even proud of the chauffeur, whose main skill, I should say, lay in his horn-honking. The horn was one of those rubber-balloon affairs that have to be sharply squeezed, and the chauffeur managed to blow it loudly all the way home—even when he didn't have to blow it to clear a pathway through the bullocks, cows, and human beings that choked up most of the streets.

The Ghodmes lived near the edge of town in a three-story house that barely contained them. Narayan's mother, father, and grandmother had rooms on the second floor, and Narayan, his wife, and their two children lived on the top floor, along with his two younger brothers and *their* wives and children. I had been given a room on the second floor, equipped with a bed, the only one in the house. (Everyone else slept on mattress rolls, which were put away during the day.) On the ground floor were Narayan's office, the kitchen, and the combination living room and dining room; they all opened onto a courtyard.

The women of the household, moving about in flowing saris, spent most of their time in the kitchen, preparing *chapatties,* stirring food in large brass bowls, grinding chick-pea flour at a circular stone hand mill, churning buttermilk, and performing a dozen other tasks, all of which looked picturesque, Biblical, and absorbing. On our return from work, Narayan and I sometimes found them sitting on the kitchen floor around a mound of grain and sifting through it with agile fingers. They would pick out pebbles and bits of chaff and toss them over their shoulders while the murmur of their conversation mingled with the twittering of sparrows attracted through the open windows by the free meal.

Usually, when Narayan and I entered the courtyard, some of the children would run up, and Narayan would exchange jokes with them—jokes that were generally incomprehensible to me. I'd studied Marathi a bit before leaving New York, but I couldn't follow their rapid conversation, so I just stood smiling vaguely, like a well-meaning deaf-and-dumb person. Then we'd go into the living room-dining room, where part of the family would frequently be gathered, sitting on square wooden boards or strips of carpet on the stone floor; there were no tables or chairs in the room. After saying hello all round, Narayan would go upstairs and change his clothes. He would take off the Western-style suit he wore to and from the lab and put on an Indian *dhoti,* a baggy white garment rather like an oversized diaper. Then he would rejoin the family. In changing his clothes, he seemed to put on a new personality. Instead of an earnest, ambitious scientist, he would be a genial, fatherly fellow; he would hand out jokes and advice and listen with interest to whatever complaints or bits of gossip there might be. Some of the Ghodmes could speak English well, especially Narayan's pretty wife, Sita, and his two younger brothers. Much of what they said was to tease Narayan and me—insinuations that we loafed at the lab. "Whenever anyone drops in, you are having tea," one of the brothers might say. "Always tea! The rest of the time you sleep. Isn't that true?" (Much laughter.) Then the other brother might baldly assert that all our mysterious glassware and fancy gadgets were just so much window dressing.

Sometimes, I must admit, I was afraid that they might be right, in a way, without knowing it. For science, like art, is built on uncertainty. It's hard to be sure that one is doing something worth while. I often thought of the skeleton-like patients we'd seen in the hospital, famine victims from outlying villages. It seemed a shame to draw blood samples from their queerly prominent veins. Would our research ultimately help these people? If not, what good could it be?

Before it got dark, Narayan, Sita, and I generally went for a walk. We would stroll along quiet dirt roads on the outskirts of town, while the sun hung low over the hills. The sky at this time was alive with little birds, who would swoop down, wriggle in the dust of the road, shake their feathers, and fly away. Sita always seemed to be wearing a fresh sari on these occasions, and she also wore little white flowers in her jet-black hair. She was most attractive when she was animated. Like many Indian women, she had a way of waggling her head when she wanted to emphasize something. A statement such as "It's very expensive!" might be accompanied by a head waggle full of elegance and verve.

Sita used to show the modesty of a good Hindu wife by walking a few yards behind her husband. The three of us would set out abreast of each other, but presently she would drop behind. On our first walk, when this happened, I suggested that we wait and let her catch up. Narayan assented. The three of us then went on together, but before long Sita dropped back once more, while Narayan and I walked ahead as if she weren't there. I regarded this system as unfriendly and unfair. Sometimes, after walking along with Narayan, I would turn round and join Sita. Narayan, meanwhile, kept going ahead. But after talking with Sita a few minutes I'd start to feel uneasy. Perhaps, after all, I shouldn't be gossiping with my friend's wife while he walked on alone, and no doubt the Hindus who passed us on the road would disapprove. So I'd quicken my step, hurrying Sita along to catch up with Narayan. Soon after we did so, however, she would fall back again.

Once, when Sita and I were walking along the road behind Narayan, she asked me with a mischievous waggle of the head, "Is it true that young men in your country kiss girls they are not married to?" She had seen it in the movies.

I said it was true.

With a giggle at her own boldness, Sita asked, "Have you done that?"
I nodded.

Then she shot me a glance and asked, "How *many* girls?"

"Around fifty," I said, without any attempt at accuracy of computation.

Her hands flew up to her face, and her large black eyes looked bigger than ever. "No! You have kissed *fifty* girls?"

"*Fifty!*" Sita waggled her head dazedly.

We had caught up with Narayan by this time. He frowned, as if he disapproved of the giggling he had heard. Sita, with downcast eyes, dropped behind us, and my friend and I walked along discussing our project. "We won't be able to work a full day tomorrow," Narayan said. "It's Dashahara, you know."

"What—another Hindu festival?"

"Yes, an important one."

I frowned. To tell the truth, each of us had some reservations about the other. I felt that Narayan gave in too much to tradition, while Narayan, for his part, felt that I was sometimes light-minded.

The next morning, Narayan and I didn't set off to work as early as usual. I stood in the doorway of his home and watched flocks of school children go by carrying books and slates heaped high with little flowers.

Narayan came up beside me. "Today, we worship tools," he said. "Before we go to the lab, I must offer *puja* to the automobile."

Then I noticed that there was an air of expectancy among the women and the children, who had gathered behind us. The women wore gaily colored saris. Narayan's mother was holding a large metal tray with garlands of flowers, some candy, coins, fruits, and various other articles on it. This, Narayan said, was for the *puja*, the ritual of worship. Almost every day is a day for honoring something or other in India. On one day, it's cows; on another, it's account books. Dashahara, Narayan said, had been set aside for the worship of tools, weapons, machines, bicycles, and automobiles.

Now a sound of honking was heard along the street, and the family car roared up in front of the house. It had been washed and polished, and shone brightly; the barefoot chauffeur had on a new turban. Behind the family car came a sleek taxi, whose hood had been draped with flower garlands. Led by Narayan, we all walked over to the cars. Narayan's bright-eyed little son Govind looked up at him proudly.

The *puja* began. First, Narayan's mother daubed some red turmeric powder on her son's forehead. Then Narayan applied some of the same stuff to the hood of his car. He promptly washed it off with milk and substituted a smear of sandalwood paste; then he laid a flower garland on the hood and scattered a handful of loose flowers over the fenders. After that, he stacked the coins neatly on the hood, between a betel nut and a banana. Narayan's mother offered candy to everyone present and placed a piece on the hood. Then Narayan handed a coconut to the chauffeur, who bashed it on a rock and splashed its milk liberally over the windshield.

While all this was going on, I watched Narayan's face to see how he was taking it. I wondered if he felt at all foolish, indulging in this abracadabra before his colleague. If he did, there was no sign of it. He performed his priestly role with the same grave earnestness he showed in carrying out some lab technique. The climax of the ceremony came when he joined his palms together and bowed low to the automobile. His family followed suit; even I couldn't resist nodding.

"Well done!" I said to him.

"We can go to the lab now," he said with composure.

The chauffeur, having appropriated the money, the betel nut, the piece of candy, and the banana, got behind the steering wheel, and Narayan and I crowded in beside him. To my surprise, Narayan's mother and Sita and several of the children squeezed into the back seat, while the rest of the family filled up the taxi behind us. Then the chauffeur blared his horn, and we were off.

"Now what?" I asked Narayan.

"Some more *pujas*—at the lab. It won't be long."

On the way, I noticed that most of the cars we passed were decorated like ours, with loops of flowers. It was all very festive, and the honking of horns had a holiday ring, like the sound of Christmas bells. When our car and the taxi reached the lab, everyone piled out and went inside. Narayan's mother still had her metal tray, which was only about half full now. The women in their bright saris stood in awe among the lab machines, the racks of test tubes, the bottles of reagents. Govind and the other children were hushed and solemn-looking. And now Narayan went through much the same ritual again. He respectfully daubed the refrigerator with turmeric powder, draped the centrifuge with a flower garland, and placed a betel nut on top of the colorimeter; his mother scattered flowers about the lab. Then he took the tray, which was now empty except for some candles and incense sticks. He lighted the incense and the candles and rotated the tray slowly, holding it aloft, while his mother rang a little silver bell; the other women and the children chanted in their sweet voices. I stood by in amazement. Presently, Narayan put down the tray, and, pressing his hands together, he bowed, in turn, to the refrigerator, the colorimeter, the centrifuge, and the plethysmograph.

It was all over. Narayan's mother gave him and me an approving look, like a blessing, and walked out of the lab. The others filed out after her, with Sita giving us a parting head waggle. We were alone. I looked down at the floor, all littered with flowers, and waited for Narayan to say something.

He found a broom and began to sweep the flowers into a corner. "It won't take long to clean up," he said.

I found a rag and got to work on the turmeric. Presently, I turned round, rag in hand, and said, "How can you do it?"

"Do what?" he asked.

"You said you believed in science. I didn't know you worshipped it this way."

Narayan shrugged. "Well, what do you want me to do?"

"You're a leader in the family. Can't you educate them?"

Narayan shook his head. "Never, as long as my parents are alive. I can't change their ways, or those of my sisters-in-law."

"But what about your son?" I asked. "Someday Govind will learn that you don't really believe in these things. Won't it come as a shock to him?"

Narayan walked to the window, where he looked out in silence for a while. Then he shook his head slowly. "It won't hurt him," he said.

I rubbed away at the turmeric spots. "It beats me what you'll do for the sake of family harmony!" I said.

Narayan turned; he looked upset, but stern, too. "Is anything more important than that?"

I tossed my cleaning rag into a waste basket. "Perhaps not. But the price you pay is pretty damned high, isn't it?"

"What price? Can any price be too high for family happiness? Do you know that my mother offers prayers for us every day at the temple? She gives shawls and money to the priests. She's vowed to make a pilgrimage to the Himalayas if our research project is a success. Could I tell her that she's simply wasting her time? Should I cause trouble between my wife and my mother by urging Sita to give up *pujas*? I could easily destroy our family that way. You haven't really thought about these questions."

I could see that we'd better not go on arguing. We were both becoming disturbed.

When the lab was ready to work in, I washed my hands at the sink and said, "We do know how to work together, anyway."

"That's right," said Narayan. He took down his white lab coat and gave me one of his warm smiles.

I opened the refrigerator door. There they were—racks of our neatly labelled test tubes full of the blood of men who had almost starved to death.

CHAPTER 36 WILLIAM EASTLAKE

A LONG DAY'S DYING

The summer solstice was another implacable, fierce, pure blue New Mexican day, another wide panorama of empty, impossible void without faint sign or distant signal for the very young man dying at the bottom of a vast and lonely canyon called the La Jara Arroyo. Quicksand. The young man tried to remove the word from his thoughts. Quicksand, a viscid, unsubstantial whorl—phantom. Neither is quicksand fluid nor solid; neither can you stand nor swim. Quicksand, the stuff a nightmare and the rest of my life is made of. But try to think of something else, try to think of something pleasant to pass this short time. Think of your Indian friend and the day you said to Rabbit Stockings: "How many chiefs are there in that summer wickiup?"

"It's not that wickiup, it's my home."

"How many chiefs are there?"

"Plenty. You know, Santo, you've got to stop thinking like a white person."

"That's going to be difficult."

"You've got to try. You know, the whites are going to be extincted."

"What's that?"

"Blown up. Isn't that what you're trying to do?"

"Are we?"

"Sure. And when you're all gone and then you try to come back again we Indians are not going to be so nice next time."

"You Indians are not going to let the next Columbus land?"

"That's right, Santo."

The boy Sant thought about this odd, unimportant conversation. He had a great deal of time to think now so he let his mind wander over all of his short, rich past, because he had tried everything to keep from sinking, but nothing worked. The thing that seemed to work best was to lie backward and try to float on the cool boiling sand. That seemed to work best, but each long alone hour that passed he was getting in deeper. It's a grave. That's it. It's as though the earth wanted you, decided to take you now, could not wait for you to become a man. So Sant did not whine or complain, he did not cry, because he wanted to behave now like a man. When you have tried absolutely everything else and there is no way out, then you try resignation and courage. Quicksand is heavy water in which swimming is impossible and it's as if the drain below were open and you were being sucked down into the earth. Sant had been struggling alone down at the bottom of the lonely arroyo for six hours now.

Six hours before he had begun to cross on his great black horse and the animal had refused. Sant got off and tried to pull the horse, but Luto stood rooted on the edge. Sant did not notice that he himself was going down, he did not realize it was impossible to move until the rein broke and the horse moved back to firmer ground. "All right," Sant called to the horse, "when I get out of here—!" But the young man was already descending like a slow elevator. It was not until the quicksand reached his chest that he realized the horse might go forever unpunished. What had the horse done? Behaved sensibly, that's all. But they had crossed at this point at the bottom of this arroyo many times. "Yes, but I know—" Sant tried to go more on his back. "I know," he said to the sky, "that quicksand moves. It needs water to percolate from below the sand like a spring, and at this exact spot of the percolation it will keep the sand in suspension and trap anything that enters. But this spot changes." Why had he entered? To get on the other side. That horse, Luto, continues to brood there in the shadow of the arroyo, continues to wait for me to finish whatever I am up to. I wonder if he knows I'm drowning. Maybe he suspects there's something wrong. Then why doesn't he go back to the corral with his empty saddle so they will know that something happened to me? Because I did not train him. That's the last time I'll neglect a horse. Yes, it's the last time you'll neglect anything. It's the last time you'll even think about it. Sant splashed the water with his arm as it flowed around him on its way to the Rio Grande.

If I was four hundred yards up the arroyo I would be on the other side of the Continental Divide and die into the Pacific. Now I am dying into the Rio Grande and the Atlantic. It's the last time you'll die into anything. It's the first and last time. Wait. They will find me. How? They will miss me and track me here. How are they going to track you over all those hard sand rock formations between here and the house? Well then, Rabbit Stockings will know where I am. How would any Indian know where you are? Particularly one as

brainless as Rabbit Stockings. Because Indians have got a lot of intuition.
The less brains the more intuition? Something like that.

Sant said abruptly, "Oh God!" aloud up into the sky and then resumed
his dialogue with himself. He was swimming gently and softly in fluid earth to
keep taking air and he was talking to himself to beat the death that tugged on
him from somewhere there below. What about the time you tamed the thunder? It will be the last time for that too. I don't think the thunder will be tamed
any more. The time all of the Indians convinced you—Afraid Of His Own
Horses, and Rabbit Stockings was in on it too—the time they convinced you
that if you could climb a high enough ridge and shoot enough arrows, throw
enough rocks into the air and shout horrible shouts, the thunder would go
away and never come back. It worked. That's right. As we flew along the high
pine-crested ridge hollering and shooting, the thunder paid us back. Remember it sent a bolt of lightning that nearly killed Rabbit Stockings when it
shattered a tree that Rabbit Stockings was shouting under. It all proves that
there is something in the Indian religion of worshipping things, and it proves
that things don't like us very much. I must ask Rabbit Stockings if they
worship quicksand. I will never get the chance.

The sun was fire-hot on the young man's face but he had to lie back in
this position to present as much body surface as he could to the fluid sand. At
times he could relieve his burning face with his wet hands but very quickly
because he had to use them as flippers, swinging them gently to stay alive.

On the great haunch of the Sangre de Cristo Mountains that rose like
another planet above the flat arroyo-cut land there were two riders appear-
ing like centaurs at a distance.

"Rabbit Stockings," Big Sant said, "it's a superstition or something you
dreamed up, I don't know which." The man called Big Sant, who didn't know
which, was the father of the boy at the bottom of the arroyo. He had a very
wide open face and a sharp, red, alive scar on his left jaw.

"I just have this feeling that Santo did not go to the mountains."

"But feeling is not enough, Rabbit Stockings."

"I have this feeling that he went the other way. Something happened to
him."

"What happened?"

"He drowned."

"In the small stream from the spring in the arroyo? It would be quite a
trick."

"Well, I've got this feeling." The young Indian who had this feeling was a
Navajo Indian, about the same age as his partner at the bottom of the arroyo.
He dressed like all the other Indians in this part of New Mexico, that is he
dressed like a cowboy except the way his bun of hair was tied in the back.
Cowboys didn't do that. It saves on barber's bills, Big Sant thought. But he
couldn't take this Indian seriously about his son at the bottom of the arroyo.
The Indian religion was part of their way of life that the white man had not

been able to make a dent in. The Indians still insisted on getting their inspiration from their guardian spirit. Sometimes it was a bear, an elk, or even a certain pine tree isolated and clinging to a ledge on the mesa which they would watch from below each day. Sometimes it was only a rock, a large yellow concretion about to tumble from a ledge, threatening and high.

"Where did you get your information, Rabbit Stockings?"

"From a snake."

"I thought so. We will continue up the mountain." And he touched his horse to increase their pace to a trot, the Indian keeping up on his matching Appaloosa that had to work hard to maintain the pace. They had been traveling for about an hour now, ever since Big Sant decided that Little Sant must have gotten into some kind of difficulty. Not serious. Probably a lame horse. Indians are alarmists. Little Sant was overdue about six hours on his trip up the mountain to gather the horses, and one hour ago the remuda had come in by themselves without the boy. A strange stallion had gathered up their mares and taken them to the mountain, but it must still be too cold on the Sangre de Cristos at ten thousand feet this time in June so their mares must have turned tail and fled back down to the ranch as soon as the stallion dropped his vigilance. The stallion was not bad, but the warm weather down here must be better. But what happened to the boy? What happened to Little Sant? Probably his horse went lame. Don't ask Rabbit Stockings; Indians are alarmists. "You are, you know, Rabbit Stockings."

"What's that?"

"You want to make a big thing out of nothing. Does the peace pipe go from right to left or from left to right?"

"What's a peace pipe?"

"You see, you have gotten over many of your superstitions. Why don't you get over the rest?"

"If an Indian believes something it's called superstition; when a white man believes something it's called progress."

"How did you figure that, Rabbit Stockings?"

"Why it's everywhere around you," Rabbit Stockings said carefully. "It's everywhere around you. Aren't they going to the moon now? Well, the white man doesn't even know the earth. What do they know about quicksand?"

"Little Sant didn't go that way, Rabbit Stockings." Big Sant was annoyed at this pecking away at the ridiculous. Indians will never let a thing go, particularly if it's a prejudice. This Indian has no evidence for his belief.

"You still didn't tell me what is quicksand," Rabbit Stockings queried.

"It's caused by water rising from below a table of sand. This causes a turbid—"

"What's that mean?"

"Something that is neither water nor sand, Rabbit Stockings. You can't swim in it, neither can you get any purchase on it to get out. You founder and die."

"There's nothing down there pulling you below? Nothing that wants you? Something that says, now is the time?"

"No, Rabbit Stockings. It's like your snake again. There is nothing to it."

"Nothing to it," Rabbit Stockings repeated, bouncing on his smaller horse. "Nothing to it. Another Indian superstition. Well, maybe you're right," Rabbit Stockings announced suddenly. "After all, we didn't chase away the thunder."

"Try to remember that, Rabbit Stockings," Big Sant said.

The young man sinking into eternity at the bottom of the arroyo was looking up at the soft gray-green slopes that led away to the world and thinking small thoughts to fight the insidious and larger thoughts as he lay dying.

Another thing about Indians, Little Sant thought, another thing about Indians is they don't plan for the future. Their future is now. Why plan for something that's happening? You notice this in the Navajo language, the past becomes the future and the present dissolves into their language mist of the day before yesterday. Navajos don't communicate, they confuse. No wonder they don't believe in progress. They couldn't tell you if they did, so it's more comfortable for the Navajos not to believe in the future. I bet they would pass a law against the future if they could—if they believed in laws. I remember Rabbit Stockings touching his head and saying, the future is here. In other words, the future isn't. It's another idea. That true? Yes, I guess it is. So why should we waste time with the future if it doesn't exist? Progress is part of the future, so that's a waste of time too. Right? Words, words, words. Now your snakes. Snakes exist, don't they? Bears, deer, elk, coyotes—they're real, really real. Right?

Really real. Right. Anything you say, Rabbit Stockings. And then the boy with the red hair, in the quicksand at the bottom of the long, deep, lonely arroyo cried suddenly up into the big, empty space. "But get me out! Find me, if your magic works." It was a quiet cry with no attempt to reach anyone, a cry to himself and the quiescent spirit of the rocks and sage, yucca and gray sad tamarisk that wept toward the Rio Grande. But there is no one, the young man thought. There is no spirit, no life, no death—no death outside this one right here. It's only a word until it happens to you. Where is the horse, Luto? I can see him there in the half shadows. Luto seems waiting for me to get it over with so he can carry me away. Was he in on this too? Was this exact time and place absolutely and perfectly arranged to the second? Luto is all black, a pure black horse. I never did like that horse waiting there in the checkered shade of the funeral tamarisk. But there was an understanding, there was always an understanding that he was the best horse in the country, the fastest, the quickest, and the best cow horse in the country. We were never friendly. We never spoke. I should have sold him, but when I had a customer Luto disappeared as though he knew. And I never bought him; that day he just showed up, unbranded, little more than a colt, but he knew everything, wasn't even green broke but he behaved like a ten-year-old. I wonder where he came from and where he will go back to now.

Little Sant felt himself sink a little more into the heavy fluid sand. He waved his slim arms, fluttered them like a wounded bird, but he could feel himself being pulled down deeper. No, no, no, he told himself. You are behaving like an Indian, thinking like a Navajo. You've been around them too long, like father, like Big Sant says, you should associate more with white boys. But where did the funeral-black horse come from? Why does Luto wait there in the solemn dappled shadows, and where is he going soon?

Sant ceased all movement and Luto emerged out of the shadow tentatively, the black horse bringing the shade, the darkness with him. Death is a cessation of movement, but more, the young man thought, life is the idea of movement. Death is a coffin-black horse, a shadow interlaced among the shadows in the tamarisk. And it wasn't my idea to cross this arroyo at this point, it was Luto who pushed down and across in that steady, stately stride, refusing only at the last second, and it was again Luto that flew, almost airborne, down Blind Wolf Canyon to bring us around in back of the ranch so that even Rabbit Stockings in his infinite stupidity would not select this arroyo as a place to search.

But it was Luto with a terrific, almost deathless delicacy, who had been able to cut out a calf from its mother, a colt from a stallion, and charge from cover, then whip a mule deer to the mesa and in the snow gambol like a hoyden with a jack until the rabbit, wraithlike in the matching frost, would founder in abject capitulation to the dark mountain that moved like a cougar. The sudden darkness of Luto ascending, then descending the pine-feathered slopes of the Sangre de Cristos like a writhing storm, somber and wild. Yes, the young man thought, Luto, yes, Luto is alive. Luto is the best horse, queer, yes, but Luto is the best damn horse.

Now watch. Luto, the shadow, has moved out of the tamarisk shadows, moving catlike, moving over here, the young man thought. Because I have been silent, ceased to struggle for seconds, now Luto is moving in. I will wait and when his tail passes by I will grab it and hold on. I will foil the horse. I will make it out of here. The young man did not believe this, he had been settling in the quicksand for too long now to have grand hope. Little Sant's helplessness had long since turned to hopelessness, but against utter despair he told to himself, I will make it out, I will make it out, as the horse nuzzled forward, fretting its monster nose towards the young man in long sweeping casts, but treading delicately in the beginning soft sand, trailing the broken reins like a shroud. Then Luto jerked up his head in discovery and wheeled to escape as Little Sant's arms rose to catch the flying, gossamer tail. He had it in his hands. It was like threads of ice, new-forming, fragile ice that exploded in his grip and Luto was gone. Now Luto came slowly back, then stopped ten feet away—Luto staring out of the beginning darkness, merging again into the shadows, spectral and huge.

"Luto!" Sant called weakly. "Luto!" Little Sant felt himself settling more into the quicksand. "Luto boy, what's happening?"

The pair of horsemen moving fast up the precipitous slope merged with mountain mahogany, then fled between brakes of aspen, trampling columbine, mariposa lilies, found a trail strewn red with gilias that led straight to the peaks, then entered a lowering and ominous cloud.

"Do you know what day it is, Rabbit Stockings?" Big Sant asked.

"Shrove Tuesday? The day after tomorrow? The day before yesterday? Ash Wednesday? What other days have you invented?"

"Invent one yourself."

"Can I?"

"It's may I, Rabbit Stockings."

"Sure you can," Rabbit Stockings said. "You whites are always doing it."

"Today is the day, three years to the day, we got Luto. I remember because it's the summer solstice."

"What's that?"

"The twenty-first of June."

"I mean, what's the summer solstice."

"It's the longest day and the shortest night of the year."

Rabbit Stockings thought about this as they cantered through bowers of ponderosa, then debouched into a quiet explosion of orange Cowboy's Delight on the old Circle B, ringed with high wavering Indian Paintbrush midst the gaunt and verdigrised collapse of a homestead, a monument to unhardihood and puerile myth; but some eastern hollyhocks rose in towering, weedlike formidability from out New England ruins in the yellow New Mexican sky. Rabbit Stockings plucked one as he passed and placed the garish Boston flower in his black Indian head knot.

"You see," Rabbit Stockings said, in sham Indian solemnity, "I've been thinking about your summer solstice. It could be the twenty-first but it could be the twenty-second because it seems to my thick Indian head that both days share that shortest night."

"Yes." Big Sant touched his head and blew out a forced breath, annoyed, and the Appaloosa horse started in sympathy. "Yes, but it was the twenty-first we got Luto." Then he said, flat and peremptory, "Rabbit Stockings, you should be a scientist."

"Yes," Rabbit Stockings said.

"They tell me, Rabbit Stockings," Big Sant said, "that an Indian can tell, that is, his religion gives him some secret insight into animals."

"That's not true," Rabbit Stockings said.

"That, for example, a horse like Luto, do you suppose—? What do you suppose? I've always felt that Luto was too damn cooperative, that it had some ulterior purpose."

"Ulterior?"

"That there is something wrong with Luto, I mean."

"What do you mean?" the Indian asked.

"If Indians believe that each person has a guardian spirit like a rock, a stone, a snake, could it be a horse?"

"I guess it could."

"Would the guardian spirit take care of everything?"

"Except dig the grave," the Indian said. "And sometimes that."

"What do you mean?"

"Well, if it were quicksand," Rabbit Stockings said.

"Why have you got this obsession with quicksand, Rabbit Stockings?"

"Because it's the only way a horse could kill Santo."

"Oh?"

"Yes. Santo is too smart for horses with the usual tricks."

"And why would Luto want to kill Sant?"

"I don't know. I'm only a poor Indian. I only work here."

"Do you have a guardian spirit, Rabbit Stockings?"

"No, I don't," Rabbit Stockings said. "Or maybe I do, but it doesn't count because I don't believe in it, not all the time. It's difficult to believe in anything all the time. You see, if you don't believe in your guardian spirit he can't help you."

"Or hurt you?"

"That's right. In other words, if Santo doesn't believe in the horse it can't hurt him or help him. In other words, if Santo's time had come and he didn't believe the horse was anything but a horse, then the horse would have no power."

"Well, I think there is something wrong with Luto. As I said, he's too perfect for a horse. What can we do?"

"It's probably too late now," Rabbit Stockings said. "All we can do is continue up the mountain. I guess your direction is as good as mine."

"I'm sure it is, Rabbit Stockings. A horse is a horse, no matter how perfect a horse."

"My guardian spirit is a snake."

"When we get back," Big Sant said, "we'll have a drink to the snakes."

"You don't believe it? The trouble with this country is—what is it? The trouble with this country is, we are overdeveloped."

"That's a profound thought, Rabbit Stockings, but we will leave all the profound Indian thoughts for later. Right now—"

"Look! Right now there's a snake!"

The horses plunged back, rising to enormous height on their hinder feet in blurred Appaloosa furious fright and comic dance, in high awkward prance before the dice, the hard clean rattle in the sage ahead.

"I don't see. I hear, but I don't see. Can you see the diamond-back?"

"There!" Rabbit Stockings hollered and the diamond-back rattler exploded toward the plunging and furious motions of the horses, some grenade, anti-personnel or anti-horse weapon planted in the innocent sage, lashing out with shrapnel speed and sidewind perfect accuracy to the falling mark and missing the falling-away Appaloosa, but recoiling, rearming itself in fluid automation before the rapt and cold stricken-eyed terror of the horse, as Big Sant slid off and seized himself a great, vari-colored trunk of petrified wood and hefted it in a vast surging motion above his head to crush the snake.

"Wait!"

"Why?"

"He's trying to tell us something."

"Yes, that's true, Rabbit Stockings. I got the message."

"You don't understand."

"Oh, I do. I understand rattlesnakes perfectly, and they understand me. Get out of the way before the snake kills you."

Rabbit Stockings stepped deftly and quickly in a timed ballet cadence as the snake exploded again and then quickly again and then again, the snake in surly, dusty diamonds, flinging itself at the mad Indian before the Indian gained a high boulder in an unfrantic, graceful leap, resting and looking down from there at the snake, his arms akimbo.

"Well done, Rabbit Stockings. Now can I kill the other half of the act?"

"Why do you, even in your overdeveloped country, why do you have to kill things?"

"Rattlesnakes."

"Still?"

"Rattlesnakes. Oh yes." From his safe distance Big Sant let down his trunk of petrified wood and sat on it. "Or is this one a friend of yours?"

"No."

"Your guardian spirit maybe, telling you to go back?"

"I don't know."

"Some Indian nonsense like that," Big Sant said. "Still, if you want to check the arroyo instead of the mountain we will check the arroyo instead of the mountain. Anything you say. Anything your snake says, any opinion a rattler holds. If you don't kill 'em, join 'em. What do you think?"

"We will check the arroyo," Rabbit Stockings said.

"Not that I hold with snakes," Big Sant said as they quickly mounted the trembling, subdued Appaloosas, "but in an overdeveloped country I'll always go along with a legend, a good Navajo myth. Look, Rabbit Stockings, your snake has called it quits."

They scattered down the mountain, their horses tumbling in mad pursuit of home, wild and uncontrolled, the riders allowing their horses to plunge downward in furious gyrations, careening and bouncing with awful abrupt speed like some kind of huge bright chunks of ore hurtling downward from a blast above on the high, still snow-coifed in June, scintillant, far peaks of the Sangre de Cristos, flashing down, down, down in twisting horse rapture to the sage avenues of the flat earth.

"The La Jara Arroyo," Rabbit Stockings hollered to Big Sant, and beginning now to direct the horse. "That's where Little Sant must be. That's where the quicksand is. The La Jara Arroyo."

"Yes," Big Sant said quietly to himself and the horse. "Yes. Yes, at my age I'm taking orders from a fool Navajo Indian and a snake, a guardian spirit Rabbit Stockings called it, but you and I," he told the still raging horse, "you and I saw a rattler. Wait! This way," and Big Sant went the way of Rabbit Stockings, both fleeing now between yellow plumes of yucca and among a bright festooned desert carpet of the twenty-first of June.

At the bottom of the arroyo nothing moved where the young man had been struggling. The water ran serene now, limpid and innocent. Where they watched from their horses atop the great canyon their searching eyes could see all the way to where the La Jara joined the Puerco but no sign, no clue of Little Sant, only the dusky, burnished copper fire sky above the arroyo heralding the slow end of a long day.

"The summer solstice you called it?"

"Yes, Rabbit Stockings."

"It was a long day all right."

"Rabbit Stockings, we should have continued to the mountain."

"No, I'm afraid we came in the right direction," Rabbit Stockings said. "But I don't understand. I don't understand why we weren't told sooner."

"We should have continued to the mountain," Big Sant insisted. "I don't know why I had to listen to a Navajo Indian and a rattlesnake."

Rabbit Stockings slid off down the sleek sweat of his speckled horse and stared from the ground with incredulous and uncomprehending disbelief at the vast empty cut one hundred feet deep, bottomed with a thin thread of water feeding the Rio Grande and becoming bronze now as it refracted in quick shimmers the maddening and molten sky. Rabbit Stockings crawled forward on the hard earth up to the sage-sprinkled lip of the arroyo, then he thumped the earth with the palm of his small rough red hand. "Yes."

"Yes, what?"

"Yes, they crossed here, Little Sant and Luto. Look, this is Luto's hoofprint. See how it goes like a heart in front?"

"Yes, almost cloven. Yes, that's Luto. But where did they go?"

"Down," Rabbit Stockings said, capping his vision and staring across. "But I don't see where they went up." Rabbit Stockings continued to search all along the arroyo while Big Sant sat frozen. "But there's something moving down there in the tamarisk," Rabbit Stockings said finally.

"Hello!" Big Sant shouted. "Who's there?"

"It's me!"

"It sounds like Little Sant," Rabbit Stockings said. "A little weak but what can you expect. That you, Santo? Okay?"

"Yes," the voice of Little Sant called up. "But don't come down. Please don't come down."

But Big Sant had already started his Appaloosa in a steep dive down the awful slope. Rabbit Stockings tried to arrest him with an upraised hand but Big Sant was already hurtling halfway to the bottom, horse and rider commingled in a vortex of riotous earth spinning down to the sliver of bronzed stream that lazied to the big river, guiltless.

"Me too," Rabbit Stockings shouted as he gained his horse and catapulted it in one great leap out and down, the horse sprawling as it hit and never quite recovering; foundering like a novice skier on busted skis it cavorted crazy to the bottom where it righted on all four scattered legs and stood amazed and triumphant.

"Don't come!" Little Sant shouted toward them both. "Don't come over here!"

"Why not?"

"Because I'm telling you why not."

"Go ahead."

There was a long silence from the tamarisks.

"Because there's a snake here, a dangerous rattler. He killed a horse. The snake killed Luto."

"Where's the snake?" Rabbit Stockings dropped off his horse and moved into the thick interlacing tamarisk. "Where's the snake, Santo?"

"He's gone. The snake was coiled there, where you're standing now. He's gone."

"What snake?" The heavy voice of Big Sant moved into the tamarisk. "What snake? Where's the horse? Where's Luto?"

"Luto's dead. Luto went down in the quicksand." Sant stood up, a small tower of mud. "I was stuck in the quicksand and Luto just stood here and watched. Then Luto was struck by this big snake. I could see the snake strike at Luto, then Luto panicked into the quicksand, got stuck, but I was able to get out using Luto to crawl up, but Luto got stuck worse and began to go under and there was nothing I could do. Luto's dead."

"No," Rabbit Stockings announced, "Luto's not dead."

"I saw Luto die."

"No, you saw Luto sink in the sand, that's all. Luto will be back."

"Oh, you bet I'll never buy a horse that looks like that again."

"Luto won't look like that again," Rabbit Stockings said. "The next time Luto could appear as a beautiful woman, for example."

"Well, I'll never buy a beautiful woman for example."

"Get up in back," Big Sant said down from his horse.

Little Sant squished up and clasped his mudded arms around Big Sant.

"And another thing," Rabbit Stockings advised in his advising tone, "Never do anything on Shrove Tuesday."

"It's not Shrove Tuesday, it's the summer solstice," Big Sant said.

"All right, be careful of that too," Rabbit Stockings advised. "Now that we don't have any medicine bundles—"

"What?"

"So now we've got to be careful all the time," Rabbit Stockings finished.

As they passed the stream in muddy file Little Sant pointed at the spot. "That's where it almost happened."

Rabbit Stockings turned in his saddle. "That's where it did happen."

"I mean to me."

"You're not the center of the world."

"I suppose the Indians are."

"That's nice of you, Santo. I've always supposed they were too."

The horses pounded now in wild scurry up out of the fast darkening arroyo and they gained the long flat country gilded in light, all of them in the gaudy sunset.

"Well, I'll tell you," Little Sant said, "it was terrible, my almost, then Luto's death down there, but outside of that—" He stared from behind his huge father with muddied eyes at the Indian. "Outside of that I don't believe any of it."

The Indian, Rabbit Stockings, trotted forward in a wild rhythm on his dazzling pony and pointed his luminous arm up at the faltering fire going out. "Don't you believe this was the day of the white man's summer solstice?"

"Yes," Little Sant said, grabbing his hard father with stiffening arms and looking towards the darkness back at the arroyo. "Yes, Rabbit Stockings, today was very long, today was the most long, the longest day there ever was." Now Little Sant looked straight ahead into the end of a Midsummer Day. "Yes, we've all got to pray we never have a summer solstice again."

CHAPTER 37   CHAIM POTOK

UNCLEAN

The twilight weeks came to an abrupt end in early December with a classroom conversation and a phone call.

December was cold, but without the snow and the sleet that often invade New York before the technical coming of winter. The leaves were gone from the sycamores but there was bright sunlight and clear skies, and I enjoyed the bus rides to school in the early mornings through the waking streets.

The school stood on Bedford Avenue a few blocks from Eastern Parkway. The rabbinical and college departments were housed in a whitestone building that fronted directly onto Bedford Avenue. Alongside were the half-dozen brownstones that comprised the various graduate departments. It was a busy, asphalt-paved street, noisy with traffic and crowded with shoppers who frequented the many stores directly across the street from the school. Even with the windows closed the sounds of the street came into the classrooms: the roar of accelerating buses, the loud hum of wheels, the blare of automobile horns, and occasionally a human voice or the barking of a dog.

The whitestone building had six stories. For four years I had climbed up and down the stairs of that building to get to my various college classes. Now almost everything I needed was on the street floor. To the left of the large marble lobby beyond the stone stairs and the metal double door of the school was a long, narrow, tiled corridor. Along the right side of this corridor were the doors that led to the school synagogue, which stood parallel to the corridor, with the Ark against the far right wall and fixed pews taking up half the length of the huge floor. The rest of the synagogue was filled with chairs and long tables. From nine to twelve every morning—except Friday and Shabbat when we had no classes, and Sunday when we had a different schedule—I sat at one of those tables with some of my classmates and prepared for my Talmud class, or shiur, as these classes are called. At noon I went down one flight of stairs and had lunch in the school cafeteria. Then, from one to three in the afternoon, I attended the shiur given by Rav Kalman—in the classroom directly across the corridor from the synagogue. On Tuesday and Thursday afternoons I left the shiur at three o'clock and took a Bedford Avenue bus to a nearby synagogue where I taught Hebrew school. On Monday and Wednesday I came out of the whitestone building and went into the adjoining three-story brownstone for my graduate philosophy classes. It was a fine arrangement.

During my last year in college I had attended the shiur given by Rav Gershenson. He was a kind, gentle person in his late sixties, with a long, pointed gray beard, brown eyes, and a soft, often barely audible voice. He was the greatest Orthodox scholar of Talmud in the United States. He was also a magnificent teacher, and often I would sit in awe, watching the thrusting gyrations of his hands as they danced through the air, thumbs extended and carving invisible circles of emphasis for the explanations with which he would untangle a difficult inyan, or Talmudic discussion. I did not know anyone who had ever been in his class who did not speak of him with respect and love.

Then Rav Jacob Kalman entered the school and was given the *Chullin* shiur. The Talmud tractate *Chullin* deals with the laws of ritual slaughter and with the dietary laws. A thorough knowledge of this tractate is one of the requirements for Orthodox ordination. I entered Rav Kalman's shiur.

Unclean   379

No one seemed to know anything about Rav Kalman beyond the facts that he had been a teacher in one of the great yeshivoth in Vilna before the Second World War and had spent two years in a German concentration camp in northern Poland. But during the first few months after his arrival at Hirsch the corridors and the cafeteria buzzed with all kinds of rumors about him: his wife and three daughters had been shot by Storm Troopers in front of his eyes in a wood outside of Warsaw; he had escaped from a concentration camp, been caught, and escaped again; he had crossed the Polish frontier into Russia and fought with Russian partisans for a year. One rumor had it that he had organized a group of Orthodox Jewish partisans that specialized in blowing up the tracks of German trains carrying Jews to the concentration camps. Another rumor had it that he had been concealed in a bunker for more than a year by a Polish farm family, had been discovered, had been forced to watch the execution of the family, and had somehow escaped again. He was said to have made his way across northern Russia into Siberia and from there to Shanghai, where he had waited out the war under the eyes of the Japanese, who were not possessed of Hitler's feelings toward Jews and who left the few Jews under their rule alone. According to this version of the life of Rav Kalman, he was brought to America by the administration of Hirsch University and was promptly invited to teach in the rabbinical department.

There were seventeen students in my class. The room in which we attended Rav Kalman's shiur was large, with light-green walls, a high white ceiling, and bright fluorescent lights. Almost the entire wall opposite the door was comprised of tall, wide windows that faced Bedford Avenue. On clear days the sun streamed through those windows—but it made little difference, for the room was always pervaded by the peculiar darkness that Rav Kalman brought with him whenever he came through the door. He seemed to radiate darkness. He was short but stockily built. He had a full black beard and dark eyes and thick black hair. His face was quite pale and contrasted sharply with the blackness of his beard. He wore a long black coatlike jacket that reached to just above the knees, a starched white shirt, a black tie, sharply pressed black trousers, black shoes, and a tall, shiny black skullcap.

He was an angry, impatient, sarcastic teacher. I had had angry teachers before, but their anger had always been accompanied by a redeeming humor. There was nothing humorous about Rav Kalman. He rarely sat still behind his desk. He paced. I would watch him pace back and forth along the narrow corridor of space between his desk and the blackboard, going to the windows, turning, going to the opposite wall near the door, turning, going back to the windows. Sometimes he would stop at the windows and incline his head and close his eyes for a moment, as if he were listening to an invisible voice—and I would see him nod his head. Then he would turn and continue his pacing. He smoked incessantly, waiting until the cigarettes were almost ashes in his fingers before dropping them into the ashtray on his desk. His voice was loud and high-pitched; often at the end of a shiur I had the feeling that a sudden silence had descended upon the school. His classes left me drained, nerveless, tense.

During our first week with him the year before, we had quickly realized that a student's request for further clarification of a passage, or the normal barrage of questions with which we had always confronted our Talmud teachers in the past, was now laden with danger. Two or three days after I had first entered his class, I asked him about a passage we were studying that seemed to me to be clearly contradicted by another passage I had suddenly remembered from a different tractate. He stopped pacing and fixed his dark eyes on me and tugged at his beard. He did not simply stroke his beard; he took strands of hair between the thumb and forefinger of his right hand, and tugged. "A contradiction," he muttered. "Malter has found a contradiction." I tensed in my seat. "Tell me, Malter, have you studied the"—he named an obscure late-medieval commentary no one in the class ever paid attention to—"on the inyan? You have not? If you would have studied that commentary, you would not find your contradiction. Come better prepared, Malter. You will find fewer contradictions." He did not answer my question. My father solved the problem for me that night by a simple emendation of the text in the other tractate. But I would not dare display that method to Rav Kalman. Textual emendation of Talmudic passages as practiced by those who studied Talmud in the modern, scientific manner was unheard of in my school.

We had no way of knowing how Rav Kalman might react to any of our questions, and I had no desire to become the target of his sarcasm. So I stopped asking questions. I read without errors whenever I was called on, answered all his questions correctly, and contributed nothing on my own to the class. A Talmud class in which a student is fearful of asking questions can become a suffocating experience. I suffocated.

His tirades were frightening. He talked about Hollywood as the symbol of American values; he ranted against a new instrument of horror called television; there was little about America he seemed to like. On occasion his tirades were based upon events occurring in the school. Students and teachers were attacked by name. A projected college course in Greek mythology was canceled because he labeled it paganism. A student was almost expelled because he caught him outside the school without a hat. The annual college senior show, to which girls had always been invited, was called off because he waged a vitriolic campaign against girls sitting together with boys in the yeshiva auditorium. The whole year was like that.

In somewhat cynical fashion we referred to those tirades as musar messages. "Musar" is the Hebrew term for ethics or a lecture exhorting one to ethical living. There had been a great musar movement among Jews in Eastern Europe, particularly in Lithuania, during the latter part of the last century and in the decades before the Second World War. Much about that movement had been quite ennobling. But there was nothing ennobling about Rav Kalman's musar messages. They were delivered with sarcasm and anger, and one is rarely ennobled by such exhortations.

It had taken a considerable effort on my part over the past months of autumn to grow accustomed to his tirades. But I had finally succeeded. At the onset of a tirade I would slump down in my seat. I sat in the last row of the class but I could not look away from him because he would notice that almost immediately. So I would look straight at him, moving my head to keep him in view as he paced back and forth—and not listen to his words. I would do a logic problem in my head; one part of me would be seeing to it that I kept looking directly at him; the other part would be doing a logic problem, or thinking of Michael and Danny and Rachel, or conjuring up images of the huge presses that were running off my father's book. There was a numbing sameness to those tirades, and by the end of November I discovered I could turn them off with ease and still convey the impression that I was listening. Then on the Monday morning of the first week of December he began to talk about something he had never mentioned before in class, and I found myself listening once again to his words.

We were studying the ninth chapter of *Chullin*, which deals with various kinds of uncleanness that can result from contact with reptiles and dead animals. One of the students was reading the text and explaining as he went along. The class was absolutely silent, except for the lone voice of the student. Rav Kalman paced back and forth behind his desk, smoking. He had called on the student to read at the beginning of the class, and then had not said a word. The student had been reading and explaining for almost a quarter of an hour. Rav Kalman remained silent. He stopped at the window for a while and peered out at the street. He closed his eyes and inclined his head and seemed to be listening to something. Then he resumed his pacing. I kept my eyes on the text—all of us kept our eyes on the text when someone was reading—but I could hear him pacing back and forth. Then the pacing suddenly stopped. I glanced up. He was standing behind his desk. Others were looking at him now too. I could feel the class go tense. The student who had been reading became silent. Another musar message, I told myself, and started to set up a logic problem in my head. I slumped down in my seat.

"Read," Rav Kalman said. "Who told you to stop? Continue reading. Explain again the words of Rabbi Yehuda . . . Yes. Go on. Go on. What does Tosefos say about the comment of Rashi? . . . Yes. Continue reading."

I sat up in my seat and looked down at the text. The student went on reading and explaining. Outside, Bedford Avenue was bathed in sunlight and thick with traffic. Inside, the room was filled with its normal atmosphere of oppressive tension.

Rav Kalman stood silently behind his desk, smoking a cigarette. Abruptly, without warning, he broke into the words of the student who was reading. The student stopped immediately.

"If the body is made unclean by contact with the smallest of things that

Culture Contact and Change

is unclean," Rav Kalman said in Yiddish, "how much more so is it made unclean by contact with bigger things which are unclean."

I started to work on my logic problem.

He did not pace. He stood stiffly behind his desk.

"In America, everything is called Yiddishkeit," Rav Kalman said. "A Jew travels to synagogue on Shabbos in his car, that is called Yiddishkeit. A Jew eats ham but gives money to philanthropy, that is called Yiddishkeit. A Jew prays three times a year but is a member of a synagogue, that is called Yiddishkeit. Judaism"—he pronounced the word in English, contemptuously: Joodaheeism—"everything in America calls itself Judaism."

He put his cigarette into the ashtray and looked at me across the room. "Are you listening, Malter?"

I nodded, without losing the thread of the logic problem. Outside, a car horn blared noisily, the sound strangely loud in the stillness of the room.

Rav Kalman took a pack of cigarettes from a pocket of his long jacket and put a cigarette between his lips. He lit it, placed the match carefully in the ashtray, and blew smoke from his nostrils. He took the cigarette from his lips and looked at me intently.

"In America there are schools that teach Judaism," he said, talking to the class and looking at me. "The students do not wear skullcaps and the teachers do not believe in Torah from heaven, and they teach Judaism." His voice was low but edged with contempt. "Judaism," he said. "Everything in America is Judaism."

I dropped the logic problem and sat up straight in my chair.

He was still looking at me. "What would you say of such a school, Malter?"

I stared at him and said nothing.

"How would you describe such a school, Malter? Is there a word for such a school?"

I saw some of my classmates glancing at me. This was the first time Rav Kalman had ever turned one of his tirades into a question-and-answer affair. I sat very rigidly in my seat, and said nothing.

"Unclean," he said, his voice suddenly angry. "Unclean. Such a school is unclean. And whoever has contact with it becomes unclean himself." Then he began pacing back and forth behind the desk and talking, not looking at us any more, but still talking. "Such a school is a falsehood. It is worse than a falsehood. It is a desecration of the Name of God. Do you hear? A desecration of the Name of God. It is a perversion. Where is the holiness in such a school? The Bible they change whenever they do not understand what they read. The Gemora"—he used the traditional synonym for the Talmud, though the Gemora, or Gemara, as I pronounced it, is actually only one part of the Talmud—"the Gemora they change. Whatever they do not like, they change. Where is the holiness in such a school?" He went on like that for a few more minutes. Then he carefully put out his cigarette in the ashtray and stood behind the desk. "Such a school is unclean. And whoever sets foot in it becomes unclean. Remember what I tell you. Now read further. Who was reading? Goldberg. Read. Read."

Two seats in front of me, the student who had been reading earlier began to read again. I looked at my hands on top of the open Talmud. They were trembling.

I did not hear a single word of what went on during the rest of that class session. I sat there in a frightened daze, wondering whether Rav Kalman's words had been deliberately directed at me or had simply been an accident of timing that had somehow managed to coincide closely with the weeks I had spent at the Zechariah Frankel Seminary working on my father's book. But the way he had looked at me . . . I did not think it was a coincidence.

I found out soon enough. Chairs scraped noisily and I came out of my daze. The room began to empty quickly. Hardly anyone ever stayed around to talk with Rav Kalman after a shiur. I started for the door. I wanted to get out of there. I heard someone call my name. I thought it was one of the students and I ignored him. I was almost at the door when someone tugged at the sleeve of my jacket. Rav Kalman wanted to talk to me, a classmate said, giving me a wide-eyed look. I turned and went back into the room.

Rav Kalman was standing behind his desk, smoking another cigarette and gazing at me. I came over to him. Standing close to him, I could see the dark circles beneath his eyes and the long diagonal line of a white scar on his right cheek. He smelled strongly of tobacco. He took the cigarette from his mouth, placed it in the ashtray, and gazed at me intently. He tugged at his beard.

"Malter, you understood what I said concerning schools for Judaism?" he asked in Yiddish.

I told him I had understood. I spoke in English. We were able to use either English or Yiddish in class. My Yiddish was very poor. I used English.

"You know which school I meant?"

"No," I said.

"You do not know?" He looked at me intently. His eyes narrowed. He swayed back and forth on his legs. "Malter, tell me. You know Gordon?"

"Which Gordon?" I heard myself ask.

"Which Gordon," he repeated with a faintly mocking smile. "Which Gordon."

"I know a lot of Gordons," I said.

"Yes? Very nice. I mean the Gordon of the Zechariah Frankel Seminary. You know that Gordon?"

"Abraham Gordon? Yes."

"You know him well?"

"I know him."

"How is it that you know him?"

"I know him," I said again.

"Yes. You know him. That much is now clear. Malter, tell me. You know

Gordon has been put into cherem?" "Cherem" is the Hebrew term for excommunication.

I felt my fingers tighten on the Talmud I held in my hand. Yes, I knew about that, I said.

"You know that. You tell me you know that. Now I must ask you, is it true that you were with Gordon in the Zechariah Frankel Library last month?"

I stared at him and heard myself tell him that I didn't know anyone who took that excommunication seriously.

"You do not know anyone who takes it seriously. You do not—" He broke off. "Tell me, Malter, you think placing someone in cherem is a light thing? Have you read the books of Gordon?"

I lied. I told him I had never read any of Abraham Gordon's books.

"Gordon destroys Yiddishkeit with his books. The cherem is not a light thing. Such a man is a danger." He paused for a moment. He had to tilt his head backward a little to look up at me. His eyes were dark. The collar of his shirt was white and starched. His tie was carefully knotted. He was still tugging at his beard, and I noticed for the first time that the third and fourth fingers of his right hand were faintly misshapen, as if they had been broken at one time and poorly reset.

"Tell me," he was saying. Danny's father talks that way, I thought. Rav Gershenson talks that way. They all talk that way. Tell me. Tell me. "Tell me, Malter. What were you doing all those weeks in the Zechariah Frankel Seminary?"

I wondered where he was getting all his information about me. But it did not really matter. Anyone could have seen me going in and out of there. The Zechariah Frankel Seminary was less than a half hour's walk from Hirsch. Rav Kalman might even have seen me himself. It made no difference *how* he knew. As far as I was concerned, it even made no difference *that* he knew. I had not intended to conceal my going to that library.

I told him I had been doing some work for my father.

"What work?" he asked.

I told him I had been checking the footnotes and the variant readings in the galleys to my father's book to save him time and spare him the physical effort of having to go back and forth to that library. He was very tired after more than a year of work on the book, I said. He was not a well man, I said.

I had used the term variant readings. I saw his eyes open wide at that. "Your father has written a book?" he asked.

"Yes."

"I know of your father. Tell me, the book, your father's book, what is it about? It is a book on the Gemora?"

I told him it contained many of the scholarly articles my father had published over the years, as well as a lengthy introduction on the nature of the Talmud. The introduction had been written especially for the book, I said, a little proudly. I omitted mentioning that the introduction also contained a long section on the methodology of Talmudic text criticism.

He was silent for a moment. He tugged at his beard. Then he lit another cigarette.

"It is forbidden to punish without first giving a warning," he said, his voice abruptly cold. "So I give you a warning. That school is unclean. You are not to set foot in that school."

I stared at him, not quite believing what I had heard. I told him I had seen dozens of Orthodox Jews in that library, studying, doing research, writing.

He became angry then. "Orthodox! Everything is Orthodox! What kind of Orthodox? There is one Yiddishkeit. I know nothing about Orthodox. The school is unclean and its books are unclean. My students will not go into their school."

I said nothing. My face was suddenly hot. I felt the slow mounting of anger.

"Malter, you understand that a student does not receive smicha from me simply because he knows Gemora. You understand that."

I did not say anything.

"You understand, Malter? I do not give smicha only for Gemora."

I nodded or did something to indicate acknowledgment of his words.

There was a brief silence.

"When does your father's book come out?" he asked quietly.

I told him.

He dismissed me with an abrupt wave of his hand and a curt nod of his head.

I went through the corridor and the marble lobby and out into the street. The afternoon air was cold and sharp. I stood there for a moment, breathing deeply. Then I realized I had forgotten my coat in the synagogue. I went back inside.

Irving Goldberg sat in a chair near the coat racks that stood against the wall opposite the Ark. He had obviously been waiting for me. He was short, round-faced, chubby, very solemn, and very good at Talmud. We studied together every morning to prepare for Rav Kalman's shiur. He had read for today's shiur.

He got to his feet. He was wearing his coat and hat. I put on my coat. He watched me solemnly. I told him he had done a good job in the shiur.

He shrugged. "What did he want?"

"A private musar message."

"How private?"

I did not respond.

"Are you in trouble, Reuven?"

"I don't know."

He looked uncomfortable. He stood there in his heavy coat, looking short and round and uncomfortable.

"Reuven," he said.

I looked at him.

He glanced around quickly. We were alone in our part of the synagogue. "Are you thinking of applying to the Frankel Seminary?"

That did it for me. "No, I'm not thinking of applying to the Frankel Seminary," I almost shouted. "What's going on around here? What've we got, our own version of the Spanish Inquisition?"

He stared, frightened. "For God's sake, not so loud. Are you crazy?"

"I'm going," I said.

"There are rumors that you're planning to apply to that seminary," he said somewhat plaintively. "Don't get angry at me, Reuven."

"What rumors? Where have there been rumors? I haven't heard any rumors."

"There have been rumors for the past three weeks."

"I haven't heard a thing."

"No one hears rumors about himself. People saw you going in and out of that place. They thought—"

"I was checking the galleys of my father's book," I said.

"Oh," he said. "Oh."

"Yes. Oh."

"God," he said. "You could kill a person with rumors."

"I'm going. I've got a logic class in fifteen minutes."

"I'll walk out with you." We went out of the synagogue. "You were only working on your father's book," he said, shaking his head.

We passed Rav Gershenson's classroom, which adjoined ours. It was a quarter after three, fifteen minutes past the end of the class hour. I peered through the small square window set in the door. Rav Gershenson was still there, standing behind his desk surrounded by more than half a dozen of his students.

We came outside. The metal door slammed shut behind me. I went quickly down the stone steps to the sidewalk. The street was crowded with people and traffic. But it felt good to be outside.

Irving Goldberg stuffed his hands into the pockets of his coat. The coat lay tight around his heavyset round frame. He smiled solemnly.

"You'd really stand this place on its head if you ever went to that seminary," he said.

"Very funny," I muttered. I was in no mood for his gloomy humor.

"Star Talmud student at Hirsch goes to Frankel," Irving Goldberg was saying. "That would be like what's his name—your friend—Danny Saunders—that would almost be like Danny Saunders going to that seminary." He looked at me. "Were you really there only for your father's book?" he asked seriously.

"No, I was there to take lessons in conversion to Catholicism. For God's sake. How can something as small as this get blown up that way?"

"Lashon hara," he said. "Gossip, gossip, gossip. Rumors. Tongues. 'Life and death are in the power of the tongue,' " he quoted in Hebrew.

"I'll see you tomorrow morning," I said. Then I said, "Why didn't you tell me earlier about the rumors?"

He smiled soberly. "I was afraid they might be true."

"I'll see you tomorrow," I said, and went off to my logic class.

Late that night I sat at my desk at home and worked automatically and without effort at a series of complicated problems in symbolic logic. I had turned down the covers of my bed and turned off the ceiling light. But I knew I would be unable to sleep, and so I sat at my desk in my pajamas with only the desk lamp on and filled pieces of paper with the conventional notations that form the language of logic. I must have sat there for hours; the top of the desk became heaped with paper. There was comfort and satisfaction in the effortless manipulation of neutral symbols, and I worked at it steadily. The only sound in the room was the faint scratching of my pencil on the sheets of paper.

It was after two in the morning when my father knocked quietly on my door.

He stood in the doorway, wearing his dark-blue robe over his pajamas, his gray hair uncombed. "I saw your light, Reuven," he said softly. "It is late."

I looked at him and did not say anything.

"You are doing assignments for class?"

I told him I wasn't doing assignments. I couldn't sleep, I said.

He came into the room and closed the door. "You were so quiet tonight," he said. "Even Manya commented to me on how quiet you were tonight."

I put down the pencil. He came over to the bed and sat down, drawing the robe over his thin knees. He looked tired and frail and I felt something turn over inside me as I gazed at him, and I looked away. Quantifiers stared up at me from the piece of paper on my desk.

I heard him sigh. "Little children little troubles, big children big troubles," he murmured in Yiddish. "When my big Reuven is so quiet, there are big troubles. Can I be of help to you, Reuven?"

I told him it wasn't anything I couldn't handle by myself.

He regarded me in silence for a moment through his steel-rimmed spectacles, his eyes heavy with fatigue. "I did not mean to pry, Reuven," he said quietly. "I want only to help if I can."

"You're not prying, abba. Since when do you pry?"

"With a grown son a father never knows when he is prying. Can I be of help to you, Reuven?" he asked again.

I had not wanted to tell him. I had not wanted him to know it had come about as a result of the weeks I had spent working on his book. Now I found I needed to tell him. I spoke with as much calm as I could bring to my words.

He blinked wearily. He sighed. He rubbed a hand over the gray stubble of beard on his cheeks and shook his head.

"I was right," he said quietly. "It is a big problem."

"He's a detestable human being."

"Detestable? From a single conversation you conclude that a person is detestable?"

"I'm in his class, abba."

"And you know enough about him to call him detestable? I am surprised at you, Reuven."

"I know enough about him to know that I can't stand him as a teacher. He's poisoned everything at Hirsch for me." They're poison, Michael had said. They'll poison all of us with their crazy ideas. I felt cold and stared down at the sheets of paper on my desk. The symbols stared back up at me, silent.

"I understand how you feel, Reuven. I understand what it means to have such a teacher." He spoke very quietly, his eyes narrow with sudden remembering. He was quiet a long time. Then he said, speaking more to himself than to me, "A teacher can change a person's life. A good teacher or a bad teacher. Each can change a person's life." He was silent again. Then he said, very softly, "But only if the person is ready to be changed. A teacher rarely causes such a change, Reuven. I am not saying it is impossible. Do not misunderstand me. I am saying it is rare. More often he can only occasion such a change. You understand what I am saying." He smiled faintly. "You are a student of philosophy and logic. I am certain you understand."

I was quiet.

"Yes," he said. "I am certain you understand." He paused. "Reuven, was Rav Kalman angry when he spoke to you?"

"He's always angry."

"I have been reading some of his articles. He also writes in anger. He attacked Abraham Gordon recently in an article. It was unpleasant to read. His choice of language was unpleasant. But he understands Abraham Gordon's thinking."

"He wants me to obey the cherem."

"What cherem?"

"Against Professor Gordon."

"You did not tell me you talked about Abraham Gordon."

"He said I was seen with Professor Gordon in the library. He wants me to obey the cherem."

"The cherem is nonsense."

"He wants me to obey it."

My father was quiet. "It is a bigger problem than I realized," he said after a moment. "What energies we waste fighting one another." He got slowly to his feet. "I am very tired, Reuven. I will not send you any more to the Frankel Library. The book is done. There is no need for you to go there any more. Unless you want to go for yourself. I do not know what to tell you about Abraham Gordon. I cannot think now. I am too tired." He looked at me wearily. "Reuven, you want smicha from the Hirsch Yeshiva?"

"Yes," I said.

"And Rav Kalman's approval is mandatory in order for you to obtain smicha?"

"Yes."

"You are no longer curious about the philosophy of Abraham Gordon?"

"I'm curious about Michael." Curious is not the word I wanted, I thought.

He sighed heavily. "I wish I knew what to tell you. I must go back to sleep. We will talk about it again another time. I do not know what to tell you now. Go to sleep yourself, Reuven. It is almost three o'clock. You will not be able to think in the morning."

He went slowly from the room. I heard the soft shuffling of his slippers as he moved through the hall. Then I heard nothing.

I sat at my desk and stared at the pieces of paper. I sat at my desk and the symbols stared back up at me, silent, inviting. I snapped off the lamp and went to bed and was awake a long time. The night wind blew against the window. In the apartment overhead a baby cried, then was silent. I fell asleep. There was the wind and the sun and the heaving waters of the lake and Michael and I on the Sailfish and Michael was shouting at me and I could not make out the words but I knew he was angry. I woke. I lay awake, thinking of Michael. Then I slid slowly into exhausted sleep.

The next day at the beginning of the shiur, Rav Kalman called on me to read. I was dull-headed with lack of sleep. Part of the time I did not even know what I was saying. Rav Kalman listened, asked questions, paced back and forth, smoked, tugged at his beard, asked more questions, and looked startled when I automatically and sleepily altered a word in the text that I instinctively sensed was wrong. He rushed to his desk, peered down at his Talmud, straightened, stared at me for a moment, then resumed his pacing. I realized then what I had done and glanced at the margin. The variant reading was listed; it had been inserted by a medieval scholar, which meant that it was an authorized reading. I took a deep breath. All of this had taken a second or two. But I was wide awake for the rest of the class session, reading slowly, explaining carefully. Rav Kalman paced and smoked. We had a brief skirmish over a passage in one of the major medieval commentaries. But I backed off quickly and went on reading. Rav Kalman said nothing to me when the class ended.

Two days later, he called on me again. I read. He paced and smoked and asked questions. Again, he said nothing to me when the class ended.

About half a dozen of my classmates followed me over to the coat racks inside the synagogue.

"He's picking on you," Irving Goldberg said mournfully. "Why is he picking on you?"

"Why don't you ask him?" I said.

"You're the best Gemora head in the class," another student said. "He always picks on those he loves."

"This isn't something to joke about," Irving Goldberg said.

I put on my coat. They crowded around me, waiting.

"All right," I said. "You want a public announcement. Here's a public announcement. I have not applied to the Frankel Seminary."

There were embarrassed smiles.

"They didn't believe me," Irving Goldberg said somberly.

"An unreliable witness," a student said in Hebrew, using the Talmudic term.

"You were really only working on your father's book?" another classmate said.

I looked at them. They stared back at me. The overhead fluorescents were reflected in their glasses; their faces seemed pale.

"You are all practicing to become future Rav Kalmans," I said.

There were more embarrassed smiles.

"He's got the whole school infected," I said.

"Not the whole school," someone said.

"Don't talk like that, Reuven," someone else said. "He's our Rav."

"I'm tired," I said. "I haven't slept much this week. And I've got to go teach. I'll see you all for the next musar message."

I left them there, bought an afternoon paper in a candy store across the street, and caught a bus. Inside the bus I read the paper, dozed for a few minutes, then woke and looked out the window at the streets. Dense clouds covered the sky. I sat there and stared out the window at the gray streets and did not look at the clouds.

I was tense and weary to the point of near exhaustion by the time Shabbat came that week. I almost fell asleep at the Shabbat meal on Friday night. I went to bed immediately after my father and I chanted the Grace and I tossed all night with ugly dreams but they slid steeply out of me and evaporated when I woke in the morning. I found myself heavy-lidded and nodding into sleep during the services, and later, after the meal, I went back to bed and slept and there were more dreams, and I woke late in the afternoon and felt my pillow cold with sweat, but I could remember nothing. My father and I said very little to one another all through that Shabbat.

Because Sunday Talmud classes at Hirsch ended at one in the afternoon, the period of preparation ran from nine to a few minutes before eleven, and the shiur ran from eleven to one. The next morning Rav Kalman called on me again. I saw my classmates exchange grim looks. I began to read. He let me read and explain for a long time. All the while he paced back and forth, smoking. Then he stopped me on a passage I had struggled with during the period of preparation and still did not clearly understand.

I started to give him one of the commentaries on the passage. He stopped me again.

"I did not ask you for the Maharsha, Malter. What do the words mean? Explain the words. Can you explain the words?"

I tried to put the words together as best I could; they did not hang together properly; there was clearly something wrong with the text.

"Explain it again, Malter," Rav Kalman said. "Make it clearer. It is not yet clear."

I explained it again. Then I was silent. He stood stiffly behind the desk.

"You cannot explain it better? No. I see you cannot. Can anyone explain it better?"

His question was answered with a stonelike silence.

He put his cigarette into the ashtray. "American students," I heard him mutter to himself. Then he launched into a loud and lengthy explanation of the passage. It was clever; it was very clever. But it took no account of some of the grammatical difficulties in the text.

"You understand now, Malter?"

I hesitated.

"You understand?"

I nodded.

"Yes? Good. Now tell us what the Maharsha says." And he paced back and forth as I went wearily through the explanation offered by the commentary.

At supper that night I mentioned the passage to my father.

"What do you think it means, Reuven?"

I told him I thought the text was wrong.

"And how would you correct it?"

I emended three of the words and rearranged a segment of the passage.

His eyes shone and he smiled proudly. "Very good, Reuven. Very good. The passage has been written on extensively." And he cited some articles in scholarly journals in which the passage had been discussed at great length. Two of the articles, he said, had emended the text in precisely the way I had suggested. And my father agreed that this probably had once been the correct text.

At that point Manya, who had been standing patiently by the stove listening to us talk, told us in her broken English to eat, the food was getting cold. We ate.

THE EDGE OF THE I.Q. STORM

A long-distance telephone call alerted me to the publication of Harvard Professor Richard Herrnstein's article "I.Q." in the September 1971 issue of *The Atlantic.* "You see it yet?" my friend inquired. "Here we go again," I replied.

The article, long and cogently written, turned out to be an eloquent restatement of a position Professor Arthur Jensen had taken months before in the *Harvard Educational Review.* Both men had drawn together an impressive collection of studies in which intelligence tests were administered to black and white school children and had come to the conclusion that a certain significant degree of intelligence, as measured by existing tests, could indeed be attributed to a heritability factor. More precisely, the distribution of intelligence scores that showed black children to have lower I.Q.s than white children seemed to indicate for Professors Jensen and Herrnstein that certain human differences are due not to environment but to native ability—native ability that contributes to a stratification of human groups that is predicated on intelligence.

To some people, the Jensen-Herrnstein argument, now legitimized in a new way by its publication in a popular rather than an academic journal, meant that blacks simply were born less intelligent than whites and would therefore have to acknowledge this newly discovered genetic basis for their inferior social standing. To others, Herrnstein was a despicable racist. Some people objected to the many critics of the article, claiming that Herrnstein's data and reasoning were sound, thoughtful, scholarly, and open to mature debate. Others, who had brought forth data and had written eloquent arguments against the genetic and statistical inadequacies in Jensen's notion of heritability, began to crank up for still another attack on an issue they hoped had been settled. Once again, the old war horse of nature versus nurture, biological versus sociological determinism, had come back to tantalize psychologists, and, as always, the political implications of the debate seemed unavoidable.

Cambridge dinner-party discussions inevitably turned to the Herrnstein article, its politics, its courage, its cruelty, its psychology. Some of the students attending Professor Herrnstein's lectures, claiming that he was openly teaching racist materials, protested to such an extent that a universitywide petition deploring the lack of academic freedom accorded him was passed around. Professors demanded that the students cease their harassment of Herrnstein. Signing the petition were many professors who, while they opposed the article and were in the process of writing rejoinders, felt, nonetheless, that academic freedom had to be preserved. Not signing the petition was a man who argued, interestingly, that controversial presentations in the popular press do not give a professor the right to claim academic freedom in his classroom. And, finally, there were the letters, the inevitable confetti that swirl about the parade of debate. One black approved of the Herrnstein article, and another mentioned Hitler and the gas chambers. Many whites were horrified. Some people offered qualifications; some produced substantiating evidence. Arthur Jensen himself, in a letter to *The Atlantic,* wrote: "The Herrnstein article is the most accurately informative psychological article I have ever read in the popular press."

Around Boston anyway, the academic community, which had for so long devised and sanctioned intelligence testing, was caught in the heat of debate about intelligence quotients and their implications. Herrnstein stood in the center of one camp; in the other were such men as Harvard psychologist Jerome Kagan. Writing in *Saturday Review,* Kagan stated, "The I.Q. test is a seriously biased instrument that almost guarantees middle-class white children higher I.Q. scores than any other group of children."

In the areas of poverty in and around Boston where I do my own research, however, I heard no debates. From black mothers and fathers I continued to hear requests to prepare their children for taking I.Q. tests. In these areas I.Q. scores are not the subject of scholarly argument; they are a currency—an element in the blood that a child better have a lot of if he or she is to survive beyond grade school and high school.

During this time I became acutely aware of the force of science. I could see, for example, how the periodic waves that emanate from the scientific community touch people in urban ghettos, sometimes threatening their sense of identity and possibility. I was somewhat surprised, however, that these waves had already reached the hollows of West Virginia. But a young woman whom I met quite accidentally, someone whose world and sense of history are very different from my own, reminded me of the enormous power of science and the universities and of how quickly the ideas and theories of one person can touch the soul of another, even though the two may never meet.

Hindi Buchanan was one of a small group of students from a college in eastern Kentucky who were traveling in New England at the time when the leaves begin to change. I never learned the exact details of their trip, but they visited several universities and, I must say, looked rather wide-eyed at the proportions of our city and our educational plants.

Hindi is tall, with smooth blue-black hair that falls freely about her face. Her skin is impure, and she uses her hair to hide her cheeks and forehead. Her eyes are a deep brown, her nose straight, her lips thin. She is embarrassed, it would seem, by her height, and so she slumps in a way that lifts her abdomen and brings her shoulders down and closer together. When she first visited my office, we talked about some of the small towns I knew around Morgantown and Wheeling, where she and the clusters of her family were born and still live.

At one point, after staring intently at me, Hindi said, "You think a lot, don't you?"

"Yes. So do you, I imagine."

"Not that much really. Visiting up here I seem to do a lot more. I think that it's a protection for me. It's like I'm standing guard when I'm thinking. No, maybe it's that when I'm aware I'm thinking I know that everybody around me isn't totally friendly."

Later, after talking about her schooling in West Virginia, I asked her, "Did some of the kids there make a distinction between, you know, city kids and rural kids?"

"You don't have to be so careful, Dr. Cottle," she said.

"Tom."

"Tom. Of course, they did. They still do distinguish between city people and the families from the creeks, hollows, mountains, and mining regions. You better believe they distinguish plenty. I learned the distinctions when I was a little girl. My pa told me never to mind them, just to live with dignity and believe in the Lord and all that stuff. But you don't forget what you learn from your peers."

"Like what?"

"Like the fact that Eastern or Northern or city people are smart, and that folks like us are, well, sorta dumb. From the Stone Age, museum examples—you know what I mean.

"But don't look so sad about it," she went on. "We're making it. Some of us, anyway. I'm in college along with a slew of other young people. It's not MIT, of course, but we're making it. People can think what they like. Strange, though, that I say that."

"What's that?" I asked.

"Oh, I guess I'm sounding a lot like my mother. I always remember her saying things like, 'Let people think what they like. You can't ever change people's minds. You can only improve yourself.' Stuff like that. I never thought I'd be quoting her."

"Is your mother alive?" I believed, for some reason, that she was not.

"No. My mother died when I was ten. She'd had tuberculosis for a long time. Her mother had it, too. Neither of them lived beyond thirty-five. I guess that's maybe another one of those distinctions, you know. We die sooner in the mountains than people in the city."

Hindi looked at her watch.

"Do you have to go?" I asked.

"You busy?"

"Nope."

"You're lying."

"No, I'm not. You late for your next appointment?"

"No. I was just thinking that I've known you less than ten minutes and already I've told you that my mother died. That's some kind of record for me, I think."

"Good. Or, well, I'm honored."

Hindi then turned away from me and began to investigate my bookshelf and small collection of magazines and journals. "What have you got that I should read?" she asked.

"Anything you like. Take your pick."

"What's this like?" The word "Politics" was printed in blue letters on a paperback. "Oh, Israel," she said, yanking the rest of the book from under a pile of papers. "I'm not ready for Israel yet."

She picked up another magazine and said, "*Journal of Experimental Social Psychology?* You actually read this?"

"Once upon a time," I said sheepishly.

"But no more?"

"Not too much."

"Good. That settles that. You don't mind me checking you out through your books, do you?" She didn't bother to look back at me.

"Nope. Check away."

"Now then, *The Foundation Directory.* Edition Three. Marianna O. Lewis, Editor. Analytical Introduction by F. Emerson Andrews. This must be exciting!"

"Don't laugh," I said. "That may be my most valuable book. In fact, now that you reminded me, I'm going to take that home with me tonight."

"Are you afraid someone might steal it?" she asked. She picked up another magazine and said, "Hey, look at this. I've heard about this. Let me . . . can I borrow this? I'll bring it back."

"What have you got?"

"This, here. *The Atlantic* with that I.Q. business article. Is it yours? Can I take it? I'll bring it back. Today, ah, day after tomorrow? Okay? We'll be here for a week or more."

"Of course. Take it. Keep it if you want," I said.

"No, I don't want to keep it. I just want to borrow it. Is it long?" She fingered through the pages of the issue until she reached the table of contents. Then she scanned page after page of Professor Richard Herrnstein's lengthy article.

"Take it, Hindi. Please."

"No." She was earnest about not taking the copy of the magazine. Disgust and pain showed on her face when she realized the article's length. "Ugh. Such small print, too." She shook her head from side to side. "I'm gonna do it. Everybody here's been talking about this. I guess I have to read it. Day after tomorrow, right?"

"Day after tomorrow. Hey, Hindi, let's make a date when you bring it back. Maybe we could talk about it then."

"Oh, that's cool. You read it?"

"Parts of it. But I'll prepare for you."

"But you won't have a copy if I take yours. Here, you keep this one. I'll get another." I threw her a don't-be-silly look.

"I've got another copy at home."

"You sure? Really?"

"Don't you trust me, West Virginia?" I grinned at her.

"You born in a city of over five hundred people?"

"Yeah. Chicago."

"Then I don't trust you, but I'll keep your crummy magazine." Like a schoolgirl, she held the copy of *The Atlantic* against her breasts with both hands. She looked down at the magazine. "I'll take good care of it," she promised.

"Wednesday," she said as she turned to leave. "Find me some other books, too. Okay? Or magazines. But not *The Foundation*...." We said "directory" in unison. In the outer office she stopped and called back to me, "What time on Wednesday?"

"Afternoon? Threeish? Okay?"

"Threeish? Boy, you *are* big-city."

"Three o'clock sharp, Miss Buchanan," I corrected myself. I heard her laugh and I smiled. As she went through the outer door to the main corridor, I heard her counting: "Threeish, fourish, fivish...."

Hindi returned two days later, wearing the same clothes and looking a bit more tired. She walked directly to the stool on which she had sat before and rolled it closer to the desk. The copy of *The Atlantic* lay in her lap, her hands, palms down, on top of it. "Well, what do you want to talk about?" she asked.

"What do *I* ...? Well, I thought we'd talk about the article, but we don't have to. I'd just as soon talk about you."

"Or *you*."

"Or me, though I think you're more...."

"Oh, God," she blurted out. "I didn't want to cry. Damn. Damn me. I'm a child."

"What's wrong, Hindi? Hey, you can cry in here." I rose to shut the door and cursed the thin walls that would not protect our voices.

"It's this." Moving her body forward, she bumped the magazine in her lap with her elbows. "This Mr.—Professor Herrnstein."

"What did he say?"

"Didn't you read it?" She was sniffling. "You said you'd read it, too."

"I did. I did. What is it?" My inquiry only made her weep more. I waited for her. When she spoke, her words were interrupted by her crying.

"He says so much. I know. I mean, he knows about black people and their intelligence, and it's horrible that they, that they are so, so . . . oh, help me."

"That blacks are supposedly born different?"

"Different? He says they're not intelligent or that they are inheriting, you know, different from the whites."

"I don't believe it for a minute."

"But it's true. He wouldn't lie. He's a Harvard professor. He wouldn't lie. He can't lie. He's studied this, and he knows. He knows. *You* must know that. He's at Harvard. That means everything, and he knows."

"But the data can be argued, and the notion of heritability is misinterpreted all over the place. What's more, it's not scientific."

"No! I don't believe it," she insisted.

"Hindi. You cannot read that article as being absolute truth. We went through this with another guy once, and hundreds of people wrote papers opposing his position and questioning the validity of intelligence tests in general. Good people. Just as good and informed. They fought it."

"*No!*" She screamed the word at me "It's true! It's all true! I *know* it! I know it just from talking with you. *You're* smarter. You *all* are smarter. I hear you. I see you. I've heard all these people since we've been here, and they're smarter. You know that! Professor Herrnstein is just not afraid to say it right out so that people will know. So that they'll have to face it. Once and for all."

"That's a lot of crap!"

"It's not!" She yelled back at me, at last looking up. "It's not crap. You don't have anything like this to face. You couldn't possibly know. He's a Harvard professor and an expert, so it's the truth. It's all the truth. You're denying it to make me feel good."

"Hindi. That's absurd. What do you want from me? I oppose that article with all my strength."

"I don't want anything from you but to admit that it's true. Pretty soon when everyone in this country can begin to admit just who's intelligent and just who isn't, some other Harvard professor, or MIT professor, like you, will come to West Virginia or Kentucky and Virginia and Pennsylvania and all over and start to give those tests to the school children back there. Then you'll see what they'll find."

"What? What will I see? What are they going to find that you're so sure about with tests that rich whites design and still don't understand." I tried to control my anger. "Really. I'm serious." She barely heard me. Momentarily, her voice had quieted.

"They'll find we're dumb, too. Dumber even than the black children in the schools."

"Hindi, c'mon." I reached for her hand, but she pulled away. The stool squeaked. Again her voice was loud and authoritative.

"No. They will! I went to school with black children, and we're dumber than they are. Much dumber. You don't know the children I do from the hills. They're part of my family. I grew up there with them. Not Chicago. They're my children. My children. I was once a child there. Don't you see that? Why do you keep forgetting that? I know exactly how smart they are. And when they have to take those tests, they'll find they can't even read the instructions. They can't read. They can't read. They're born dumb. They're born stupid and ugly and dumb, and they'll test them, and everyone will know it. Don't you see that?"

"No, I don't. That's preposterous. Literacy has nothing to do—"

"Yes. Yes. Yes. Yes. It does. It does."

"Hindi, please don't cry." My words sounded so pathetic. I looked at the walls, wondering whether anyone was listening to us.

"I can't help it. It's just that it's all so painful. They'll test us next. You read all that stuff." She motioned backward with her shoulder in the direction of the bookcase. *"The Journal of . . .* whatever that was, *Psychology. Social Psychology.* You read that stuff. Maybe it will be *you* they pick to come to Morgantown to go to the public schools and test the children. Us. Test us, I mean."

"Never! You're wrong."

"Maybe, though. Maybe. Maybe you will write in this magazine someday and tell everyone. Somebody has to. You can't keep hiding everything forever, you know. Somebody has to tell."

"They don't, Hindi. C'mon. Please."

"No. They do. Somebody has to tell. They'll test those dumb, dirty children from the hills, all the hillbillies, and they'll all score two and four and ten, and they'll never let us come out. They'll lock us in the hills, or in those rotten neighborhoods, just like they lock black people in the ghettos of every city. And they'll tell us we can't come out until we can read and do arithmetic and be intelligent like you. Just like you!"

"That's a ghastly thought."

"It's a ghastly truth, you mean. That's what you really mean. We're dumb. We're all dumb. I hear, I see, I talk with them. My father is so dumb you wouldn't believe it. He couldn't get past the first page of that intelligence test. My mother either. We're hillbillies! Born dumb hillbillies, and we're the next to be tested." She slammed her hands down on the magazine. "We're next!" We're next. Maybe they'll get the Indians first, but you can be plain sure that we'll be next. He wouldn't lie. So don't you lie, either."

"Hindi, please, we've got so much to talk about." I held my hands out to her.

"I'll talk," she began softly, "but you have to promise me you won't lie."

"I promise," I said as quickly as I could.

"And you must admit it's true."

"Never. Never ever," I responded quietly.

"Then I can never trust you. You patronize me. You do. I should kill myself for telling you about my mother. You didn't deserve it. You tricked me. Here. Take your damned magazine back. Maybe you better read it again, and maybe you better come to Appalachia and meet my folks and talk to those children, too. It might open your eyes and put an end to all your dreams and all your fuzzy, wishing ways of thinking about us. You may be a social scientist and all that, but in the end you'll see that I'm right. Like Professor Herrnstein is right, too. When they finish with all their testing, you will see how I was right and how we'll have to stay where we are, up in the hills and all, as bad as it is or as good as it is. It doesn't even matter at all anymore. Then you will feel shame. You'll see. Then you'll feel shame, too."

Suddenly, she sat up tall in the awkward chair, her posture showing pride and assuredness. "You may even cry then, Doctor."

CHAPTER 39   COLIN M. TURNBULL

THE LONELY AFRICAN

When Kasuku's younger wife gave birth to a girl the old man wept with joy. This wife was his favorite for she brought laughter and happiness into his old age at a time when he thought the world was full only of sorrow. It was so full of sorrow that he had taken just two wives when he decided that it was no good taking any more. His father had enjoyed some ten or eleven and Kasuku remembered with pleasure the fun it had been having so many mothers, and being able to run to them all and know that he would be fondled and fussed over. He had made up his mind that he would bring up a family to be equally happy, that he would take twenty or thirty wives, and that all his children would be proud of their father and everyone would point to him as a man of wealth and a model of contentment—a man to be envied—a man whose seed would grow and multiply and pass his name on for uncountable generations, a man who was favored by the ancestors.

But the white men who ruled the country from their brick houses at Mafia had said that it displeased them that one man should have so many wives, and they withdrew favors so that those who were wealthy with wives appeared poor in terms of favor, and lost the respect of their less fortunate brothers. And the white men of God taught all the children that to have more than one wife was evil, so that children came to have contempt for their fathers. And so those who had been blessed by the ancestors, and had brought them the blessings of many children in return, they became the unfortunate ones.

Kasuku had seen this happen, and after he had taken his second wife he was told that if he took another he would be put in prison on some pretext or other—and there were always plenty of pretexts because there were so many new laws that nobody could be expected to remember them all, and they made no sense, so one could not even reason them out. Just why, for instance should one not eat okapi flesh and wear its beautiful skin? The Pygmies were always killing them in the forest and bringing him the meat. Should he just let it rot? And the skins were better than any antelope skin. Yet he would be put in prison if he was seen with one over his shoulders. And why, on the other hand, did everyone have to plant that dreadful plant that grew up and gave the womenfolk so much trouble when it was time to pick the white fluffy balls the white man called cotton? Who could eat that? And everyone knew that it was bad for the ground, which became exhausted quickly enough anyway. When he had asked, once, that simple question, "Why?" he had been threatened with a stick and told, "Because I am the administrator, that's why!"

Kasuku had learned that it was better not to question and not to argue, so he had taken no more wives, and had grown old with only two. But as he grew old he began to care less and less about what the white man said. It still made no sense to him. And now he had children to look after the plantations and to provide him with food and clothing, so he consulted his two wives, who both agreed that it would be wonderful to have another co-wife, for they too were getting old, and they knew Kasuku had his eye on young Asofi. And even when Kasuku married Asofi and showed her so much favoritism they did not mind, because she did so much work, and took such good care of the old man, who really was getting very demanding. Only when Asofi became pregnant did they feel just a little jealous, and they put out the story that it had not been Kasuku, but one of Asofi's former lovers.

Kasuku was too delighted to care, however, and when the girl child was born he named her Safini, after his own sister. This was something of an innovation, as normally the girl child would have been named from her mother's family, and everyone shook their heads and said that if Kasuku did not uphold the traditions who would?

Safini grew up with her young mother and her old father in very happy circumstances and she grew to be beautiful.

It was just after she had been cursed with the first appearance of moon-blood that she set eyes on the man everyone called Bwana Banduki because he always carried so many guns. She had heard many strange tales about him, and she was surprised that he was not as white as the administrator, for everyone had said he was white. Perhaps it was because he was covered all over with so much hair. She really never got over her curiosity that his body should have been so completely covered, just like that of a chimpanzee. The other boys and men she knew only had hair on the top of their heads and between their legs.

But the strangest thing about Bwana Banduki was that he had been brought up among her own people, the Bafwamiti, and had even been through the initiation school with other boys of the same age. He spoke the language just like one of themselves. Only he had no home, and he owned no plantation. He traveled about a great deal, always taking one or two other white men with him. For weeks at a time they would remain in the forest, finally coming out with skins and antelope heads, and sometimes with elephant tusks. Occasionally the administrator went with him, and he was plainly considered an important person among his own people.

Bwana Banduki was, in fact, a white hunter. His real name was Jean-Paul, and his father had been one of the early survey team employed by the Congo government. Both his parents had thought it a good thing for their son to grow up with the people among whom they lived and worked, and were only mildly surprised when he said that his friends wanted him to join them in the initiation school. But for Jean-Paul it was more than a mere gesture; he knew that this was where he belonged, and he wanted to belong completely. When he was in his late teens he took to hunting as a career, feeling that this was the one way he could be sure of always making his living in the forest.

He had long thought of making Kasuku's village his headquarters, and he was pleased to find the old man agreeable. He was also pleased to find that young Safini was no longer the baby he remembered, but an exceptionally pretty and rapidly maturing young girl.

It was only three years after establishing himself in a neat little mud house, not far from Kasuku's, that he decided to ask the old man's permission to marry Safini. He knew that no white girl would want to live the way he did, and in any case he now felt almost more at home among the Bafwamiti than he did with his own people.

It seemed that Kasuku had been holding onto life for just this moment. He had been growing weaker for some years, and for a long time he had been unable to walk more than five paces without sitting down to rest. He was nearly blind, but he was more happy than ever because Asofi had given him new life . . . and a daughter. He told Jean-Paul that he could not wish for a finer son, and only asked that he look after Safini and give her lots of good clothes and beat her if she misbehaved. He asked Jean-Paul if he would take other wives, and when he was told no, that Safini would be his only wife, the old man sank back in his cushions with a slight sigh of disappointment. He called his daughter and told her that he wanted her to marry Bwana Banduki, to which Safini replied that she would do whatever her father said. This very meekness was as good as saying that she was delighted, and the old man gave his blessing. He died just before the wedding, but not before he had arranged for Jean-Paul to pay a handsome dowry of goats and cloth, a dowry that would do the girl justice and make everyone see how highly she was esteemed and respected.

For several years Safini and Jean-Paul lived in great happiness amongst the Bafwamiti. Every now and then he would go off to Stanleyville or to Bunia to meet wealthy white tourists, who paid him to take them through the forest and show them how to shoot the wild game, particularly the elephant and the *bongo*.* After a few weeks he was home again with his Safini, and together they worked to make their home even prettier than it was, planting all manner of flowers in the little border that ran right around, front and back. They also worked together in the plantation, where they grew all sorts of strange fruits and vegetables that Safini had never even seen before.

Sometimes Safini wondered why her husband never brought any of these white men home, but he explained that they were not really his friends, that they merely paid him and he was more of a servant; and in this way she understood it would have been improper to offer them hospitality. But she could not understand what kind of white men they were, because nobody else treated Jean-Paul as a servant—even the administrator, who was a frequent visitor to their home, seemed to look up to him. Safini began to resent these people who treated her husband as an inferior, because one day she saw three of them standing beside the government rest house. They were not smartly dressed, like Jean-Paul, and even worse, they were dirty. Even from the road her nostrils twitched at the smell of sweat. They were arguing among themselves as to how much they should pay a young boy who had brought them some eggs, and this was what really struck Safini, for she had been taught that important people never argue among themselves in front of inferiors, let alone quibble with them over money. She felt she knew now the real reason why her husband never brought such men home. He was ashamed that his own people could be like this.

The rest of the villagers had no such problems, and so it was difficult for Safini to talk to her friends about these matters. When she did they just laughed at her and said that anyone who had so much happiness as she did was bound to have some problems as well. And Safini was happy, very much so. Unlike other girls, she had not had to leave her home village when she married, so she was still among her own people; and she had a wonderful husband. She was proud to see him at the market, sitting down under the old Mbau tree to drink palm wine with the men as she went about her business. He was so very well liked by everyone, it seemed.

Safini's only unhappiness was that her husband did not want her to have any children. She tried every way she could to persuade him otherwise, but it was no good. When she asked him why, he merely told her that she would not understand, but that he just knew it to be right. And being what she was, Safini trusted her husband, and tried to make up for it by loving him all the more.

Then there came a time when the administrator and a number of other

*A forest antelope, not so much a rare animal as one that is seldom seen.

government people came to visit their home almost every week. Safini enjoyed cooking for them, and the administrator nearly always brought her some little present which he would slip into her hand as she shyly approached the table to serve the meal to the men. And afterwards, when the meal was over and the men were talking together in a language Safini did not understand, she used to sit in the shadows and watch, in case they had any needs. Then too the administrator or one of the others sometimes came and chatted with her, joking and teasing, and paying her compliments on her cooking. That made Safini very proud, because although she knew she was a good cook, it gave her great pleasure to be able to tell her friends all the nice things such great and important men as the administrator had said about her food.

Safini knew from the frequency of the visits that something was happening that her husband was not telling her, and she began to be afraid. She several times heard mention of places she knew to be many miles away, right by the Panga River. No Bafwamiti liked to even mention that country, because the people who lived there had been their hereditary enemies right up to the time the Belgians came and prevented them from fighting with weapons. The Belgians had not stopped the feeling of hostility, however, and the battle was still being waged, as strongly as ever. The BaSinga were much more powerful witches than the Bafwamiti, and they had many more sorcerers and a much greater knowledge of medicine that brought not only pain, but death. Even to mention the BaSinga, or their country, was to invite disaster, and Safini felt her home being slowly filled with evil.

One day Jean-Paul came back home from a week in Stanleyville. He told Safini that the government wanted him to take charge of a botanical research station that was being set up on the banks of the Panga River. The station would number about a hundred workers to start with, and there would be accommodation for half a dozen or more scientists. The research work would be directed by the resident scientist, a Belgian named Henri Dupont, who was already in Stanleyville with his wife; but Jean-Paul was to be in charge of the station as such, with full administrative powers. He was to leave as soon as possible to clear the ground and put up the necessary buildings . . . he wanted Safini to come with him.

Safini, like most of her people, had never traveled beyond the borders of the tribal territory, and it took Jean-Paul a long time to convince her that the countryside by the Panga River was just the same as it was right there. But Safini was not so worried about the countryside as she was about the people. Her husband assured her that the BaSinga were not nearly as bad as the Bafwamiti believed them to be, and he personally knew the chief and many of the people in Ndola, which would be the nearest village to the station. They were all his friends, and they would be her friends. Comforted to some extent by this, and by the assurance that she would be able to return to Mbau whenever she wanted for a visit, Safini subdued her fears. But when she was getting everything ready for the journey and she came across the small leather locket that had been tied around her neck as a child, to protect her from evil spirits, she carefully restrung it and fastened it in place. She was a little ashamed, because living with Jean-Paul she had grown away from such superstitions. But when he saw it, he did not make fun of her. He just smiled and put his arm around her and told her she was going to love her new home. He would build her a new house, whatever size she wanted, and she could have as many servants as she needed. He would not have to go away on hunting trips, they could be together all the time.

The clearing work went quickly enough, as the villagers of Ndola and from all around quickly learned that the new Bwana Mukubwa, The Great Master, paid well and did not use a whip. This was something new to those used only to working on the road gangs. Scaffolding was erected around the huge mahogany trees, and they came crashing down, one after another. The small sawmill brought in from Stanleyville cut the lumber into planks, and the rest was either stored as firewood, or just burned. Jean-Paul did not have all the trees cut down. He left them standing here and there, to cast their shade around the neat log cabins he built below. He had only three trained carpenters, two from the BaSinga tribe, and one, Lukamba, from a remote tribe on the far side of Bafwamiti country, the notorious BaKeti.* But Lukamba had been brought up in a mission school, where he had learned carpentry, and in many ways he seemed more European than he did African. It was largely with his help that Jean-Paul soon had half a dozen men capable of measuring and cutting wood for the others to assemble in the building of the house and the making of the necessary furniture.

At first Safini and her husband lived in a small hut built for them by the station workers in the manner of an ordinary village hut, with baked mud walls and a leaf roof. But theirs had a large veranda and a separate kitchen. It was close to Lukamba's hut, and Safini grew to know Lukamba and his wife well, and to like them. She had little to do with the other workers, because she had insisted on bringing three of her own villagers with her as servants, and they also acted as friends. In this way she had no need even to talk to the BaSingas. But Jean-Paul soon had their proper house built, not far from the banks of the Panga. He had it surrounded by a fence, which Safini thought was unfriendly, and when he explained that it was necessary to discourage the station workers and their wives from hanging around the kitchen she thought that odd too, but she did not mind as she did not particularly like any of the workers except Lukamba.

The house was made of rough-hewn logs, and it had large windows facing the river. There were four good-sized rooms in it; a large sitting room, an office, their bedroom and a guest room. The furniture was all made in traditional village style, but enlarged and adapted to their needs, with chairs made in the way that Lukamba had been taught at the Mission School. Safini

*The BaKeti have a widespread and evil reputation for sorcery.

was a little bewildered by the size and elegance of the new home, but it made her very proud. As soon as it was finished Jean-Paul set to work to build a house nearby for Henri Dupont. He made it in the same style, but took much more care with the finishing of the interior, to make it as much like a European home as possible. He designed the furniture himself, and had glass fitted to the windows. His own windows he left open, with wooden shutters that could be closed during a storm. The low overhanging eaves formed a wide veranda all around the house, protecting the rooms both from the heat of direct sunlight and from the rain that fell almost every afternoon throughout the year. When all was ready, and the workers' village was completed not far away, Jean-Paul sent word to Stanleyville for Monsieur Dupont to come and see that everything was to his liking.

Safini had found plenty to do at first, clearing a garden with the help of her friends from Bafwamiti so that in a few months they would have their own supply of bananas and manioc, peanuts and beans. She also helped with the furnishings, making drapes for the windows from trade cloths she bought at the little store at Ndola, and stuffing cushions and mattresses with locally grown cotton. But then she found time began to weigh heavily. It seemed to press down on her, making it more and more difficult to pass each hour, until the days seemed painfully long. She would walk to Ndola with her friends and pass time at the store there, and she would watch from a distance some of the dancing that was nearly always going on near the chief's house. But she and her friends from Bafwamiti were never invited to take part, and the chairs that were brought for them to sit on were always placed apart. Safini, with her natural kindness of heart, put it down to their respect for her husband, and in turn remained more aloof than she wanted to.

She waited to see Monsieur Dupont and his wife with eagerness, and spent many hours touching up their home. On the day they were to arrive she put flowers in each of the rooms, something that her husband had taught her that all Europeans liked. When they drove up and got out of their car at the entrance to the station, Safini was one of the first to see them. She had just returned from Ndola, and she ran to tell her husband. Jean-Paul told her to get the food ready, and went out to greet the newcomers. But the food had been ready for some time, so Safini just watched from the kitchen compound as the party walked toward the house. She heard Henri Dupont talking loudly in a high-pitched voice, and was surprised that he seemed to be arguing with her husband about something. Lukamba, who understood French, was also watching. He told her that the newcomer was complaining about not being able to drive right up to the door, and was saying that a proper road would have to be put through. It seemed a small matter to argue about. Safini set the food on the table.

The three sat down on the veranda for drinks, served by Jean-Paul, while Safini made sure everything was in order inside. Then they came in, strangely silent, and took their places at the table. As usual Safini came to serve them, it being her custom not to eat with her husband unless they were alone. She hesitated, waiting to be introduced, but Jean-Paul just motioned her to serve the meal. It was eaten in silence, and Safini noticed with pleasure that although they looked at the food with distaste, Monsieur Dupont and his wife ate heartily enough once they tasted it.

After dinner they went back to the veranda for coffee, and again Safini waited to be introduced, and again Jean-Paul motioned her away.

But Safini was not one to worry about such things. She had heard them arguing, and thought that must be the reason her husband was so forgetful. So she introduced herself. Shyly she came up with her own cup of coffee, and as there was no other chair on the veranda, she squatted down near Madame Dupont and asked her, in KiNgwana, if she liked the house her husband had built for her. Madame Dupont looked at her in embarrassment and said it was very quaint. She then looked at Henri Dupont and she said she would like to go and see their own house. She stood up, turned her back on Safini and walked down the veranda steps. Jean-Paul seemed about to say something, then he changed his mind and turned to Monsieur Dupont and said he would show them around at once. He took Safini's hand and, still talking to Monsieur Dupont, told him how his wife had helped to furnish the house. He spoke in KiNgwana, but Monsieur Dupont replied in French, and Safini could not understand.

It was only when they got to the new house that Safini began to comprehend. Madame Dupont walked from room to room, touching things gingerly, and then she spoke, loudly and clearly to her husband in KiNgwana. "But it is just like a native hut—we can't live here—we are not animals!" Safini was about to turn and run, but Jean-Paul held onto her tightly. "Madame," he said, "it is a great deal more comfortable than the house I built for my wife and myself; we could do no more in the time——" Madame Dupont interrupted, "That may be, but *I* am not a savage." She turned to her husband, and spoke again in French. They left shortly afterwards.

When her husband explained to her, later that day, that many Europeans felt as the Duponts did about white men having African wives, Safini found it difficult to understand. She could understand their not wanting to have to walk a hundred yards from the car to the house, she could understand their preferring a brick house to a wooden one, and she knew enough of Europeans to realize that they can get extraordinarily ill-tempered over such little things. But how could they be annoyed by Jean-Paul's having an African wife—didn't many of the men, even the administrators, have African wives? Jean-Paul explained that many of them had mistresses, but that was different, everyone could afford to ignore an association of that kind. But he and Safini were married, living openly as man and wife, and married according to tribal custom, not even according to the laws of the church.

All that Safini understood from this was that white men liked to do some things under cover of darkness of night, and pretend otherwise in the daytime. She saw quite clearly that she would have to keep herself in the background, even in her own house, when her husband's friends were visiting. This did not hurt her—they were, after all, no friends of hers—it just puzzled her. So Safini became a shadow in her own home, fading away at the sight of any European. Only in late evenings could she be a wife to her husband, and so precious was this time that she would lie awake most of the night looking at Jean-Paul as he slept. Even then there were often interruptions, as government agents came to regard the station as a convenient stopping place, and would turn up at any time of night and expect hospitality.

The Duponts came and settled down, but not in the house Jean-Paul had built for them. They imported bricks and had a fine brick house built. They cut down all the trees around it, so that it stood out in the open, catching the full glare and heat of the sun. The windows were small, like those of European houses, and the house was hot and stuffy at all times of the day and night. Jean-Paul gave the house he had built for them to Lukamba, a gesture which did not please the Duponts, but delighted Safini.

Several other Europeans came, but none of them stayed for long, and although some of them made a point of asking for Safini whenever they visited Jean-Paul's house, Safini was usually not to be found. Whenever she saw them coming she would run over to the kitchen and busy herself there. More and more she came to rely on her three friends and servants as the only people she could really talk to, apart from Lukamba and his wife. So it was a great shock to her when one day she found them all packing their bundles and preparing to leave on the weekly mail truck, back to Mbau. They were young, they said, and they wanted to dance and sleep with men, but these savages around them, the BaSinga, wanted nothing to do with them, and they wanted nothing to do with the BaSinga. It was all right for Safini, they said, she was happily married and had a husband and a fine house to live in. Safini was both too proud and too kind to argue. She prepared some food for them for the journey, and gave them presents, and told them to tell her mother that she would be back home to see her before long. But even as she spoke the words she regretted them—and for the first time fear came into her life. It was a momentary feeling, and it passed quickly. Safini stayed with her friends until the truck came, and then she stood and waved them goodbye. Long after the truck was out of sight, and only a cloud of dust remained, slowly swirling and settling down on the rough and twisting track, Safini stood there, looking with empty eyes in the direction of Mbau.

Jean-Paul told her to hire other servants, but Safini said no, she would like to do the work herself, as a wife should, and that Lukamba's wife would help her whenever needed. She would not admit that she did not want the BaSinga around her, in her home, handling her food. Knowing that they would be well paid, several of the wives of the workers came and asked Safini to hire them, and when she refused they went away and told their husbands that Safini was evil. She must be evil because she had refused to even let them into the kitchen, and it was well known that witches were afraid of others' even looking at the food they were preparing, because they were so evil themselves they thought that everyone else possessed the Evil Eye.

The extra work kept Safini busy, and Lukamba's wife was good to her, helping her whenever she needed help, and being a friend to her at all times. She and Lukamba, after all, were strangers among the BaSinga, just as was Safini herself. They went to the store at Ndola together, never alone, but they seldom went to the village market. The storekeeper wanted to make money, so he always served them—they had more money than any of the other villagers. But at the market, where women exchanged their goods rather than sell them, nobody seemed to want the fruits and vegetables that Safini brought, and when she tried to buy anything the BaSinga women just shook their heads as if they did not understand, and some of them drew cloths over their food lest it be cursed by a glance from the foreign witch.

Safini told her husband nothing of this. She only asked him once, timidly, if they could not go back to Mbau and live there as they had done once, so happily. Jean-Paul laughed at her, and said that he was making more money now than he had ever made before, and life was better for them than it could ever be at Mbau. So much so, he said, that he felt it time that they had children. The words that once would have filled Safini with joy now only made her more frightened than ever. And when her stomach began to swell, Safini fell ill.

She was up at the store at Ndola, buying some cloth; as usual there were a number of men sitting around outside, drinking palm wine. They looked pointedly at her belly as she passed by, and whispered among themselves. When she came out one of them said to the others, loud enough for her to hear: "The Bafwamiti circumcise foreigners and allow them to marry their daughters, but no child so conceived on our land will live—our laws forbid it. It is an offense to the ancestors and brings danger to us all."

It soon became the talk of the whole village, and of the station, that the witch doctor had cursed Safini's child to die, and that she would be barren the rest of her life for having desecrated BaSinga soil with her uncleanliness. People began not only to avoid her, but rather to pretend not to see her. As she passed by they would look right at her and through her, as though she were not there at all. And all the time she heard whispered remarks about the fact that her child was sure to die. And what scared her more than anything was that she too knew that it would die, because she wanted it to. Jean-Paul had said finally that he could never go back to Mbau, that his whole future was here now. One day the station would grow into a flourishing little town, right in the middle of the forest, where they could have the best of both worlds, he had said. But Safini only wanted one world, and that was the world she knew and could trust, the world of the Bafwamiti. If Ndola was no place for her, it was certainly no place for her child. So it had to die.

Jean-Paul saw so little of his wife these days that he was barely aware of her fears. She had told him once, and he had laughed and said she had left all that superstition behind. She had nodded, seeing another truth in what he had said. She had not spoken of it again. Jean-Paul was overjoyed at the thought of having a child, for he too had been the object of some talk among the Europeans at the station. There were some who still looked on his marriage as being nothing more than an eccentricity, and they pointed to the lack of children as evidence. He would not dare bring up children by an African wife in such a community. But Jean-Paul did dare, and it was almost as much to prove his loyalty to his wife as it was for the sake of having a child.

The Duponts had ordered the last of the trees near their house to be cut down. It was a huge old mahogany tree that stood near the entrance of their driveway, close to the main gate. They said it could block their road if it were to fall during a storm. Jean-Paul tried to dissuade them, assuring them there was no danger, but even he finally gave in just for the sake of maintaining peace.

The men were busy cutting the upper branches one day as Safini and Lukamba's wife set out for Ndola. As they were passing by the gate, Safini suddenly stopped, and her companion asked her what was wrong. Safini said someone had called her, and it sounded like her mother . . . calling her name . . . Safini, Safini, Safini. . . . Crying out her mother's name, Safini ran toward the tree just as the branch fell.

Jean-Paul could get nobody to look after Safini except Lukamba and his wife. The three of them took turns sitting by Safini's bedside as she fought for life. There was no good calling a doctor—she had not even been touched by the falling branch, but as it had fallen so had she, and she had lain on the ground, writhing as though the weight of the whole tree were on top of her. The workers had stood around in a cold and silent circle while Lukamba's wife ran for help. When she had been carried away, they went back to their work, and nobody even mentioned the incident again. Safini lost the baby that should have been born in a few weeks' time, and with it she lost all will to live.

In his bitterness Jean-Paul blamed the Duponts, and said it was all their fault, that they had never made the slightest move to be even courteous to his wife, and had made her sick and depressed, and finally they had insisted on having the tree cut down. The Duponts pointed out that there was not much logical connection between the two events, and that for one thing, Safini always disappeared any time they came near the house, and for another, Safini had merely fallen, the branch had not even touched her. But Jean-Paul's bitterness could not be diverted. He looked back over his time at the station, and saw in it nothing but a series of insults and slights to himself and his Safini, not only from the Duponts but from almost every other European who came by. The Duponts had even built a guest house so that passers-by would not be forced to accept hospitality in Jean-Paul's home. The spare room had remained empty then, except for one occasion on which his old friend the administrator had stayed overnight. And he remembered with increasing bitterness how his Safini had always kept fresh flowers in the spare room in case, some day, some other friend of her husband's might accept their hospitality.

Jean-Paul became more of a recluse. He ran the station as efficiently as ever, but he barely spoke a word to the Duponts or any of the other Europeans, and even the kindest of them found it best not to intrude. Safini slowly recovered, but her life had gone from her with her baby, and as soon as she was well enough she told Jean-Paul that she was going back to Mbau. She remembered how she had told her friends, when they left, that she would come back home to her mother one day. She had not meant to use the word *home,* because she had been taught that a woman's home is with her husband. But once she had spoken it she knew that it would not be so with her.

Jean-Paul had agreed readily, still not realizing what was the real nature of Safini's sickness. Shortly afterwards he resigned and accepted an offer of a post at Paulis, an important town many miles away from the station, in a completely different administrative district. He knew that several white men lived there with African wives, and formed a contented, if small, community of their own. He felt sure that Safini would be happy there.

He went to visit Safini at Mbau, and as she came out of their old house to greet him, a spark of life came to her sad eyes. It was a spark that held a question, but Jean-Paul did not understand it, and the light died as stillborn as their child. Safini simply said that she could no longer be his wife, she could no longer bear him children. The family offered him back the wealth that he had paid in expectancy of a wife that would raise his seed. Jean-Paul still did not understand, and said that he wanted Safini whether or not she could bear him children, he wanted her as a wife, as a companion, to live with him. "Where shall we live?" asked Safini, though the spark had long died. Jean-Paul began telling her all about Paulis, and how the Europeans were different there. Safini listened, and then told him to go to Paulis and settle there, if that was really what he was determined to do, and that he could write to her when he was ready. There was something in her voice that made Jean-Paul look, perhaps for the first time, beyond her words and into her heart.

She asked him if he would stay at Mbau for that night, and for that night Safini and Jean-Paul loved again as they had done years before, in the house where they had learned to love, far away from people, white and black, who did not understand the power of love, only the power of destruction. It was then that Safini told him that for the first few years she had taken medicine given to her by her mother to prevent her from conceiving. She had done it because she was afraid for the children, afraid for how her own people would accept them. "You were still called Bwana Banduki by my people," she said. "You did not carry the name of any of our families. What name would our children have carried? To what family would they have belonged? To whose ancestors would their spirits have gone?"

Jean-Paul left the next morning.

The Lonely African   411

Every week the mail truck brought a letter from him to Safini, telling her of his lovely home at Paulis, and asking her if she would not come to join him. And every week the mail truck brought a letter from Safini to the man she loved, saying that she was still his wife, and would be waiting for him when he grew tired of Paulis, and came back to live among their own people, at Mbau, where they *both* belonged.

DATE DUE

JUN 3 '74		
JUN 13 75 FAC		
JAN 2 2 1975		
OCT 23 '80 S		
APR 18 '84 S		
NOV 1 4 '85 P		
MAR 20 '87 X		
MAY 27 '90 S		
JAN 1 1 '99 X		
NOV 2 4 1998		

ntact and Change